# ELIZABETHAN
# TRAGEDIES

# ELIZABETHAN TRAGEDIES
## A Basic Anthology

DOVER THRIFT EDITIONS

DOVER PUBLICATIONS, INC.
MINEOLA, NEW YORK

# DOVER THRIFT EDITIONS

GENERAL EDITOR: SUSAN L. RATTINER
EDITOR OF THIS VOLUME: JANET B. KOPITO

*Bibliographical Note*

This Dover edition, first published in 2017, is a new compilation of plays reprinted from standard editions. A Note has been provided specially for this edition.

*International Standard Book Number*

ISBN-13: 978-0-486-81332-5
ISBN-10: 0-486-81332-0

Manufactured in the United States by LSC Communications
81332001    2017
www.doverpublications.com

# Contents

[The dates given for the plays are approximate, given the numerous versions published and performed at the time.]

# Note

The five plays selected for this collection represent a quarter century's worth of the great achievements of the Elizabethan era, and, as the successor to Queen Elizabeth's reign, the Jacobean period. Theaters were opening up in London, and poetry and music were flourishing. The well-educated queen brought her own curiosity and zest for learning to the general atmosphere of the time. It also is good to remember that some of Shakespeare's greatest tragedies—*Hamlet, Macbeth, Othello,* and *King Lear*—were contemporaneous with works in this anthology.

Thomas Kyd's *Spanish Tragedy* is typical of the "revenge play," a popular format of the time. The plot is replete with murder and madness. Some aspects of *The Spanish Tragedy* can be found in the work of the Roman dramatist Seneca, including the emphasis on violent outcomes and even the Ghost character, which may have been a source for *Hamlet*.

In *Doctor Faustus,* Christopher Marlowe invokes the nefarious character depicted in the German *Faustbuch* (1587), an astronomer and necromancer who was believed to have given up his soul to the Devil in order to receive supernatural powers. Faustus acknowledges the tragic consequences of his actions, however, and tells a group of scholarly gentlemen that his disease can't be cured by a physician, as "A surfeit of deadly sin [that] hath damn'd both body and soul."

*A Woman Killed with Kindness* by Thomas Heywood offers a domestic setting for its plot: a happy marriage that is damaged by a husband's fateful decision. John and Anne Frankford share a pleasant home life; the disruption occurs when John brings a young acquaintance, Wendoll, into the house as his companion.

The effect of this decision on Anne, and its impact on her well-being, spin the plot.

In addition to its literary merits, *The Tragedy of Mariam* is noteworthy as the first work written by a woman and published under her own name. Set in 29 BCE, the play concerns Mariam, the "faire queene of Jewry," and the violent events that take place at the court of the villainous King Herod, Mariam's husband. Drawing attention in the 1970s during the burgeoning growth of feminist studies and scholarship, *The Tragedy of Mariam* examines themes of morality in a patriarchal society, including the impact of marriage and divorce, while displaying the brutal acts typical of the genre.

The concluding work, John Webster's *The Duchess of Malfi*, shares the violent outcomes of the accompanying plays in this collection. Based on events in the life of Giovanna d'Aragone, Duchess of Amalfi (1478–1510) as depicted in Matteo Bandello's 1554 work *Novelle* (translated into English as *The Palace of Pleasure*, c. 1567), the play shows the lengths to which the Duchess's brothers will go to control her destiny. The manipulative Cardinal spies on the Duchess, and the Duchess's twin, Ferdinand, is obsessed with his sister's affairs as he descends into madness. Their cruel treatment of the Duchess for her decision to marry for love beneath her social class, prominent among other motives expressed by the brothers, moves the play's action to its inevitable, tragic conclusion.

# ELIZABETHAN
# TRAGEDIES

# THE SPANISH TRAGEDY

## Thomas Kyd

# DRAMATIS PERSONÆ

Ghost of Andrea, a Spanish nobleman, } Chorus
Revenge,
KING OF SPAIN
CYPRIAN DUKE OF CASTILE, his brother
LORENZO, the Duke's son
BELLIMPERIA, Lorenzo's sister
VICEROY OF PORTUGAL
BALTHAZAR, his son
DON PEDRO, the Viceroy's brother
HIERONIMO, Marshal of Spain
ISABELLA, his wife
HORATIO, their son
Spanish General
Deputy
DON BAZULTO, an old man
Three Citizens
Portuguese Ambassador
ALEXANDRO, } Portuguese Noblemen
VILLUPPO,
Two Portuguese
PEDRINCANO, Bellimperia's servant
CHRISTOPHIL, Bellimperia's custodian
Lorenzo's Page
CERBERINE, Balthazar's servant
Isabella's Maid
Messenger
Hangman
Three Kings and three Knights in the first Dumb-show
Hymen and two torch-bearers in the second
BAZARDO, a Painter
PEDRO and JACQUES, Hieronimo's servants
Army. Banquet. Royal suites. Noblemen. Halberdiers.
Officers. Three Watchmen. Trumpets. Servants, etc.

# ACT I

## SCENE I: *Induction*

*Enter the Ghost of Andrea, and with him Revenge.*

*Ghost.* When this eternal substance of my soul
    Did live imprison'd in my wanton flesh,
    Each in their function serving other's need,
    I was a courtier in the Spanish court:
    My name was Don Andrea; my descent,
    Though not ignoble, yet inferior far
    To gracious fortunes of my tender youth.
    For there in prime and pride of all my years,
    By duteous service and deserving love,
    In secret I possess'd a worthy dame,
    Which hight sweet Bellimperia by name.
    But, in the harvest of my summer joys,
    Death's winter nipp'd the blossoms of my bliss,
    Forcing divorce betwixt my love and me.
    For in the late conflict with Portingal
    My valour drew me into danger's mouth,
    Till life to death made passage through my wounds.
    When I was slain, my soul descended straight
    To pass the flowing stream of Acheron;
    But churlish Charon, only boatman there,
    Said that, my rites of burial not perform'd,
    I might not sit amongst his passengers.
    Ere Sol had slept three nights in Thetis' lap,
    And slak'd his smoking chariot in her flood,
    By Don Horatio, our knight marshal's son,
    My funerals and obsequies were done.

3

Then was the ferryman of hell content
To pass me over to the slimy strand,
That leads to fell Avernus' ugly waves.
There, pleasing Cerberus with honey'd speech,
I pass'd the perils of the foremost porch.
Not far from hence, amidst ten thousand souls,
Sat Minos, Aeacus, and Rhadamanth;
To whom no sooner 'gan I make approach,
To crave a passport for my wand'ring ghost,
But Minos, in graven leaves of lottery,
Drew forth the manner of my life and death.
"This knight," quoth he, 'both liv'd and died in love;
And for his love tried fortune of the wars;
And by war's fortune lost both love and life.'
"Why then," said Aeacus, 'convey him hence,
To walk with lovers in our fields of love,
And spend the course of everlasting time
Under green myrtle-trees and cypress shades.'
"No, no," said Rhadamanth, 'it were not well;
With loving souls to place a martialist:
He died in war, and must to martial fields,
Where wounded Hector lives in lasting pain,
And Achilles' Myrmidons do scour the plain.'
Then Minos, mildest censor of the three,
Made this device to end the difference:
"Send him," quoth he, 'to our infernal king,
To doom him as best seems his majesty.'
To this effect my passport straight was drawn.
In keeping on my way to Pluto's court,
Through dreadful shades of ever-glooming night,
I saw more sights than thousand tongues can tell,
Or pens can write, or mortal hearts can think.
Three ways there were: that on the right-hand side
Was ready way unto the 'foresaid fields,
Where lovers live and bloody martialists;
But either sort contain'd within his bounds.
The left-hand path, declining fearfully,
Was ready downfall to the deepest hell,
Where bloody Furies shakes their whips of steel,
And poor Ixion turns an endless wheel;
Where usurers are chok'd with melting gold,

And wantons are embrac'd with ugly snakes,
And murd'rers groan with never-killing wounds,
And perjur'd wights scalded in boiling lead,
And all foul sins with torments overwhelm'd.
'Twixt these two ways I trod the middle path,
Which brought me to the fair Elysian green,
In midst whereof there stands a stately tower,
The walls of brass, the gates of adamant:
Here finding Pluto with his Proserpine,
I show'd my passport, humbled on my knee;
Whereat fair Proserpine began to smile,
And begg'd that only she might give my doom:
Pluto was pleas'd, and seal'd it with a kiss.
Forthwith, Revenge, she rounded thee in th' ear,
And bad thee lead me through the gates of horn,
Where dreams have passage in the silent night.
No sooner had she spoke, but we were here—
I wot not how—in twinkling of an eye.

*Revenge*. Then know, Andrea, that thou art arriv'd
Where thou shalt see the author of thy death,
Don Balthazar, the prince of Portingal,
Depriv'd of life by Bellimperia.
Here sit we down to see the mystery,
And serve for Chorus in this tragedy.


# SCENE II

## *The Court of Spain.*

*Enter Spanish King, General, Castile, and Hieronimo.*

*King*. Now say, lord General, how fares our camp?
*Gen*. All well, my sovereign liege, except some few
    That are deceas'd by fortune of the war.
*King*. But what portends thy cheerful countenance,
    And posting to our presence thus in haste?
    Speak, man, hath fortune given us victory?
*Gen*. Victory, my liege, and that with little loss.
*King*. Our Portingals will pay us tribute then?
*Gen*. Tribute and wonted homage therewithal.

*King.* Then bless'd be heaven and guider of the heavens,
　　From whose fair influence such justice flows.
*Cast. O multum dilecte Deo, tibi militat aether,*
　　*Et conjuratae curvato poplite gentes*
　　*Succumbunt: recti soror est victoria juris.*
*King.* Thanks to my loving brother of Castile.
　　But, General, unfold in brief discourse
　　Your form of battle and your war's success,
　　That, adding all the pleasure of thy news
　　Unto the height of former happiness,
　　With deeper wage and greater dignity
　　We may reward thy blissful chivalry.
*Gen.* Where Spain and Portingal do jointly knit
　　Their frontiers, leaning on each other's bound,
　　There met our armies in their proud array:
　　Both furnish'd well, both full of hope and fear,
　　Both menacing alike with daring shows,
　　Both vaunting sundry colours of device,
　　Both cheerly sounding trumpets, drums, and fifes,
　　Both raising dreadful clamours to the sky,
　　That valleys, hills, and rivers made rebound,
　　And heav'n itself was frighted with the sound.
　　Our battles both were pitch'd in squadron form,
　　Each corner strongly fenc'd with wings of shot;
　　But ere we join'd and came to push of pike,
　　I brought a squadron of our readiest shot
　　From out our rearward, to begin the fight:
　　They brought another wing t' encounter us.
　　Meanwhile, our ordnance play'd on either side,
　　And captains strove to have their valours tried.
　　Don Pedro, their chief horsemen's colonel,
　　Did with his cornet bravely make attempt
　　To break the order of our battle ranks:
　　But Don Rogero, worthy man of war,
　　March'd forth against him with our musketeers,
　　And stopp'd the malice of his fell approach.
　　While they maintain hot skirmish to and fro,
　　Both battles join, and fall to handy-blows,
　　Their violent shot resembling th' ocean's rage,
　　When, roaring loud, and with a swelling tide,
　　It beats upon the rampiers of huge rocks,

And gapes to swallow neighbour-bounding lands.
Now while Bellona rageth here and there,
Thick storms of bullets ran like winter's hail,
And shiver'd lances dark the troubled air.

*Pede pes et cuspide cuspis;*
*Arma sonant armis, vir petiturque viro.*

On every side drop captains to the ground,
And soldiers, some ill-maim'd, some slain outright:
Here falls a body sunder'd from his head,
There legs and arms lie bleeding on the grass,
Mingled with weapons and unbowell'd steeds,
That scatt'ring overspread the purple plain.
In all this turmoil, three long hours and more,
The victory to neither part inclin'd;
Till Don Andrea, with his brave lanciers,
In their main battle made so great a breach,
That, half dismay'd, the multitude retir'd:
But Balthazar, the Portingals' young prince,
Brought rescue, and encourag'd them to stay.
Here-hence the fight was eagerly renew'd,
And in that conflict was Andrea slain:
Brave man at arms, but weak to Balthazar.
Yet while the prince, insulting over him,
Breath'd out proud vaunts, sounding to our reproach,
Friendship and hardy valour, join'd in one,
Prick'd forth Horatio, our knight marshal's son,
To challenge forth that prince in single fight.
Not long between these twain the fight endur'd,
But straight the prince was beaten from his horse,
And forc'd to yield him prisoner to his foe.
When he was taken, all the rest they fled,
And our carbines pursu'd them to the death,
Till, Phœbus waving to the western deep,
Our trumpeters were charg'd to sound retreat.

*King.* Thanks, good lord General, for these good news;
And for some argument of more to come,
Take this and wear it for thy sovereign's sake.

[*Gives him his chain.*

But tell me now, hast thou confirm'd a peace?
*Gen.* No peace, my liege, but peace conditional,
That if with homage tribute be well paid,

The fury of your forces will be stay'd:
And to this peace their viceroy hath subscrib'd,

[*Gives the King a paper.*

And made a solemn vow that, during life,
His tribute shall be truly paid to Spain.
*King.* These words, these deeds, become thy person well.
But now, knight marshal, frolic with thy king,
For 'tis thy son that wins this battle's prize.
*Hier.* Long may he live to serve my sovereign liege,
And soon decay, unless he serve my liege.
*King.* Nor thou, nor he, shall die without reward.

[*A tucket afar off.*

What means the warning of this trumpet's sound?
*Gen.* This tells me that your grace's men of war,
Such as war's fortune hath reserv'd from death,
Come marching on towards your royal seat,
To show themselves before your majesty:
For so I gave in charge at my depart.
Whereby by demonstration shall appear,
That all, except three hundred or few more,
Are safe return'd, and by their foes enrich'd.

*The Army enters; Balthazar, between Lorenzo and Horatio, captive.*

*King.* A gladsome sight! I long to see them here.

[*They enter and pass by.*

Was that the warlike prince of Portingal,
That by our nephew was in triumph led?
*Gen.* It was, my liege, the prince of Portingal.
*King.* But what was he that on the other side
Held him by th' arm, as partner of the prize?
*Hier.* That was my son, my gracious sovereign;
Of whom though from his tender infancy
My loving thoughts did never hope but well,
He never pleas'd his father's eyes till now,
Nor fill'd my heart with over-cloying joys.
*King.* Go, let them march once more about these walls,
That, staying them, we may confer and talk
With our brave prisoner and his double guard.
Hieronimo, it greatly pleaseth us
That in our victory thou have a share,
By virtue of thy worthy son's exploit    [*Enter again.*
Bring hither the young prince of Portingal:

The rest march on; but, ere they be dismiss'd,
We will bestow on every soldier
Two ducats and on every leader ten,
That they may know our largess welcomes them.

                    [*Exeunt all but Balthazar, Lorenzo, and Horatio.*

Welcome, Don Balthazar! welcome, nephew!
And thou, Horatio, thou art welcome too.
Young prince, although thy father's hard misdeeds,
In keeping back the tribute that he owes,
Deserve but evil measure at our hands,
Yet shalt thou know that Spain is honourable.

*Bal.* The trespass that my father made in peace
Is now controll'd by fortune of the wars;
And cards once dealt, it boots not ask why so.
His men are slain, a weak'ning to his realm;
His colours seiz'd, a blot unto his name;
His son distress'd, a cor'sive to his heart:
These punishments may clear his late offence.

*King.* Ay, Balthazar, if he observe this truce,
Our peace will grow the stronger for these wars.
Meanwhile live thou, though not in liberty,
Yet free from bearing any servile yoke;
For in our hearing thy deserts were great,
And in our sight thyself art gracious.

*Bal.* And I shall study to deserve this grace.

*King.* But tell me—for their holding makes me doubt—
To which of these twain art thou prisoner?

*Lor.* To me, my liege.

*Hor.*                         To me, my sovereign.

*Lor.* This hand first took his courser by the reins.

*Hor.* But first my lance did put him from his horse.

*Lor.* I seiz'd his weapon, and enjoy'd it first.

*Hor.* But first I forc'd him lay his weapons down.

*King.* Let go his arm, upon our privilege.

                                        [*They let him go.*

Say, worthy prince, to whether did'st thou yield?

*Bal.* To him in courtesy, to this perforce:
He spake me fair, this other gave me strokes;
He promis'd life, this other threaten'd death;
He won my love, this other conquer'd me,
And, truth to say, I yield myself to both.

*Hier.* But that I know your grace for just and wise,

And might seem partial in this difference,
Enforc'd by nature and by law of arms
My tongue should plead for young Horatio's right:
He hunted well that was a lion's death,
Not he that in a garment wore his skin;
So hares may pull dead lions by the beard.

*King.* Content thee, marshal, thou shalt have no wrong;
And, for thy sake, thy son shall want no right.
Will both abide the censure of my doom?

*Lor.* I crave no better than your grace awards.

*Hor.* Nor I, although I sit beside my right

*King.* Then, by my judgment, thus your strife shall end:
You both deserve, and both shall have reward.
Nephew, thou took'st his weapon and his horse:
His weapons and his horse are thy reward.
Horatio, thou did'st force him first to yield:
His ransom therefore is thy valour's fee;
Appoint the sum, as you shall both agree.
But, nephew, thou shalt have the prince in guard,
For thine estate best fitteth such a guest:
Horatio's house were small for all his train.
Yet, in regard thy substance passeth his,
And that just guerdon may befall desert,
To him we yield the armour of the prince.
How likes Don Balthazar of this device?

*Bal.* Right well, my liege, if this proviso were,
That Don Horatio bear us company,
Whom I admire and love for chivalry.

*King.* Horatio, leave him not that loves thee so.—
Now let us hence to see our soldiers paid,
And feast our prisoner as our friendly guest

                                                    [*Exeunt.*

# SCENE III

## *The Court of Portugal.*

### *Enter Viceroy, Alexandro, Villuppo.*

*Vic.* Is our ambassador despatch'd for Spain?

*Alex.* Two days, my liege, are past since his depart.

*Vic.* And tribute-payment gone along with him?
*Alex.* Ay, my good lord.
*Vic.* Then rest we here awhile in our unrest,
    And feed our sorrows with some inward sighs;
    For deepest cares break never into tears.
    But wherefore sit I in a regal throne?
    This better fits a wretch's endless moan.
                          *[Falls to the ground.*
    Yet this is higher than my fortunes reach,
    And therefore better than my state deserves.
    Ay, ay, this earth, image of melancholy,
    Seeks him whom fates adjudge to misery.
    Here let me lie; now am I at the lowest.
            *Qui jacet in terra, non habet unde cadat.*
            *In me consumpsit vires fortuna nocendo:*
            *Nil superest ut jam possit obesse magis.*
    Yes, Fortune may bereave me of my crown:
    Here, take it now;—let Fortune do her worst,
    She will not rob me of this sable weed:
    O no, she envies none but pleasant things.
    Such is the folly of despiteful chance!
    Fortune is blind, and sees not my deserts;
    So is she deaf, and hears not my laments;
    And could she hear, yet is she wilful-mad,
    And therefore will not pity my distress.
    Suppose that she could pity me, what then?
    What help can be expected at her hands
    Whose foot is standing on a rolling stone,
    And mind more mutable than fickle winds?
    Why wail I then, where's hope of no redress?
    O yes, complaining makes my grief seem less.
    My late ambition hath distain'd my faith;
    My breach of faith occasion'd bloody wars;
    Those bloody wars have spent my treasure;
    And with my treasure my people's blood;
    And with their blood, my joy and best belov'd,
    My best belov'd, my sweet and only son.
    O, wherefore went I not to war myself?
    The cause was mine; I might have died for both:
    My years were mellow, his but young and green;
    My death were natural, but his was forc'd.
*Alex.* No doubt, my liege, but still the prince survives.

*Vic.* Survives! ay, where?

*Alex.* In Spain—a prisoner by mischance of war.

*Vic.* Then they have slain him for his father's fault

*Alex.* That were a breach to common law of arms.

*Vic.* They reck no laws that meditate revenge.

*Alex.* His ransom's worth will stay from foul revenge.

*Vic.* No; if he liv'd, the news would soon be here.

*Alex.* Nay, evil news fly faster still than good.

*Vic.* Tell me no more of news; for he is dead.

*Vil.* My sovereign, pardon the author of ill news,
  And I'll bewray the fortune of thy son.

*Vic.* Speak on, I'll guerdon thee, whate'er it be:
  Mine ear is ready to receive ill news;
  My heart grown hard 'gainst mischief's battery.
  Stand up, I say, and tell thy tale at large.

*Vil.* Then hear that truth which these mine eyes have seen:
  When both the armies were in battle join'd,
  Don Balthazar, amidst the thickest troops,
  To win renown did wondrous feats of arms:
  Amongst the rest I saw him, hand to hand,
  In single fight with their lord-general;
  Till Alexandro, that here counterfeits,
  Under the colour of a duteous friend
  Discharg'd his pistol at the prince's back,
  As though he would have slain their general:
  But therewithal Don Balthazar fell down;
  And when he fell, then we began to fly:
  But, had he liv'd, the day had sure been ours.

*Alex.* O wicked forgery! O trait'rous miscreant!

*Vic.* Hold thou thy peace! But now, Villuppo, say,
  Where then became the carcase of my son?

*Vil.* I saw them drag it to the Spanish tents.

*Vic.* Ay, ay, my nightly dreams have told me this.—
  Thou false, unkind, unthankful, trait'rous beast,
  Wherein had Balthazar offended thee,
  That thou shouldst thus betray him to our foes?
  Was't Spanish gold that blearèd so thine eyes
  That thou couldst see no part of our deserts?
  Perchance, because thou art Terceira's lord,
  Thou hadst some hope to wear this diadem,
  If first my son and then myself were slain;

But thy ambitious thought shall break thy neck.
Ay, this was it that made thee spill his blood:
      [*Takes the crown and puts it on again.*
But I'll now wear it till thy blood be spilt.
*Alex.* Vouchsafe, dread sovereign, to hear me speak.
*Vic.* Away with him; his sight is second hell.
  Keep him till we determine of his death:
  If Balthazar be dead, he shall not live.
  Villuppo, follow us for thy reward.       [*Exit Viceroy.*
*Vil.* Thus have I with an envious, forged tale
  Deceiv'd the king, betray'd mine enemy,
  And hope for guerdon of my villany.       [*Exit.*

## SCENE IV

*Enter Horatio and Bellimperia.*

*Bel.* Signior Horatio, this is the place and hour,
  Wherein I must entreat thee to relate
  The circumstance of Don Andrea's death,
  Who, living, was my garland's sweetest flower,
  And in his death hath buried my delights.
*Hor.* For love of him and service to yourself,
  I nill refuse this heavy doleful charge;
  Yet tears and sighs, I fear, will hinder me.
  When both our armies were enjoin'd in fight,
  Your worthy chevalier amidst the thickest,
  For glorious cause still aiming at the fairest,
  Was at the last by young Don Balthazar
  Encounter'd hand to hand: their fight was long,
  Their hearts were great, their clamours menacing,
  Their strength alike, their strokes both dangerous.
  But wrathful Nemesis, that wicked power,
  Envying at Andrea's praise and worth,
  Cut short his life, to end his praise and worth.
  She, she herself, disguis'd in armour's mask—
  As Pallas was before proud Pergamus—
  Brought in a fresh supply of halberdiers,
  Which paunch'd his horse, and ding'd him to the ground.
  Then young Don Balthazar with ruthless rage,

Taking advantage of his foe's distress,
Did finish what his halberdiers begun,
And left not, till Andrea's life was done.
Then, though too late, incens'd with just remorse,
I with my band set forth against the prince,
And brought him prisoner from his halberdiers.
*Bel.* Would thou hadst slain him that so slew my love!
But then was Don Andrea's carcase lost?
*Hor.* No, that was it for which I chiefly strove,
Nor stepp'd I back till I recover'd him:
I took him up, and wound him in mine arms;
And wielding him unto my private tent,
There laid him down, and dew'd him with my tears,
And sigh'd and sorrow'd as became a friend.
But neither friendly sorrow, sighs, nor tears
Could win pale Death from his usurpèd right.
Yet this I did, and less I could not do:
I saw him honour'd with due funeral.
This scarf I pluck'd from off his lifeless arm,
And wear it in remembrance of my friend.
*Bel.* I know the scarf: would he had kept it still;
For had he liv'd, he would have kept it still,
And worn it for his Bellimperia's sake:
For 'twas my favour at his last depart.
But now wear thou it both for him and me;
For after him thou hast deserv'd it best
But for thy kindness in his life and death,
Be sure, while Bellimperia's life endures,
She will be Don Horatio's thankful friend.
*Hor.* And, madam, Don Horatio will not slack
Humbly to serve fair Bellimperia.
But now, if your good liking stand thereto,
I'll crave your pardon to go seek the prince;
For so the duke, your father, gave me charge.
*Bel.* Ay, go, Horatio, leave me here alone;
For solitude best fits my cheerless mood. [*Exit Hor.*
Yet what avails to wail Andrea's death,
From whence Horatio proves my second love?
Had he not lov'd Andrea as he did,
He could not sit in Bellimperia's thoughts.
But how can love find harbour in my breast,

Till I revenge the death of my belov'd?
Yes, second love shall further my revenge!
I'll love Horatio, my Andrea's friend,
The more to spite the prince that wrought his end,
And where Don Balthazar, that slew my love,
Himself now pleads for favour at my hands,
He shall, in rigour of my just disdain,
Reap long repentance for his murd'rous deed.
For what was 't else but murd'rous cowardice,
So many to oppress one valiant knight,
Without respect of honour in the fight?
And here he comes that murder'd my delight.

*Enter Lorenzo and Balthazar.*

*Lor.* Sister, what means this melancholy walk?
*Bel.* That for a while I wish no company.
*Lor.* But here the prince is come to visit you.
*Bel.* That argues that he lives in liberty.
*Bal.* No, madam, but in pleasing servitude.
*Bel.* Your prison then, belike, is your conceit.
*Bal.* Ay, by conceit my freedom is enthrall'd.
*Bel.* Then with conceit enlarge yourself again.
*Bal.* What, if conceit have laid my heart to gage?
*Bel.* Pay that you borrow'd, and recover it.
*Bal.* I die, if it return from whence it lies.
*Bel.* A heartless man, and live? A miracle!
*Bal.* Ay, lady, love can work such miracles.
*Lor.* Tush, tush, my lord! let go these ambages,
    And in plain terms acquaint her with your love.
*Bel.* What boots complaint, when there's no remedy?
*Bal.* Yes, to your gracious self must I complain,
    In whose fair answer lies my remedy;
    On whose perfection all my thoughts attend;
    On whose aspect mine eyes find beauty's bower;
    In whose translucent breast my heart is lodg'd.
*Bel.* Alas, my lord, these are but words of course,
    And but device to drive me from this place.
        [*She, in going in, lets fall her glove, which Horatio,*
            *coming out, takes up.*
*Hor.* Madam, your glove.
*Bel.* Thanks, good Horatio; take it for thy pains.

*Bal*. Signior Horatio stoop'd in happy time!

*Hor*. I reap'd more grace than I deserv'd or hop'd.

*Lor*. My lord, be not dismay'd for what is past:
  You know that women oft are humorous;
  These clouds will overblow with little wind:
  Let me alone, I'll scatter them myself.
  Meanwhile, let us devise to spend the time
  In some delightful sports and revelling.

*Hor*. The king, my lords, is coming hither straight,
  To feast the Portingal ambassador;
  Things were in readiness before I came.

*Bal*. Then here it fits us to attend the king,
  To welcome hither our ambassador,
  And learn my father and my country's health.

# SCENE V

*Enter the Banquet, Trumpets, the King, and Ambassador.*

*King*. See, lord Ambassador, how Spain entreats
  Their prisoner Balthazar, thy viceroy's son:
  We pleasure more in kindness than in wars.

*Amb*. Sad is our king, and Portingal laments,
  Supposing that Don Balthazar is slain.

*Bal*. So am I!—slain by beauty's tyranny.
  You see, my lord, how Balthazar is slain:
  I frolic with the Duke of Castile's son,
  Wrapp'd every hour in pleasures of the court,
  And grac'd with favours of his majesty.

*King*. Put off your greetings, till our feast be done;
  Now come and sit with us, and taste our cheer.
                                    [*Sit to the banquet*

  Sit down, young prince, you are our second guest;
  Brother, sit down; and, nephew, take your place.
  Signior Horatio, wait thou upon our cup;
  For well thou hast deservèd to be honour'd.
  Now, lordings, fall to; Spain is Portugal,
  And Portugal is Spain: we both are friends;
  Tribute is paid, and we enjoy our right.
  But where is old Hieronimo, our marshal?

He promis'd us, in honour of our guest,
To grace our banquet with some pompous jest

*Enter Hieronimo with a drum, three knights, each his scutcheon; then
he fetches three kings, they take their crowns and them captive.*

Hieronimo, this masque contents mine eye,
Although I sound not well the mystery.
*Hier.* The first arm'd knight, that hung his scutcheon up,
          [*He takes the scutcheon and gives it to the King.*
Was English Robert, Earl of Gloucester,
Who, when King Stephen bore sway in Albion,
Arriv'd with five and twenty thousand men
In Portingal, and by success of war
Enforc'd the king, then but a Saracen,
To bear the yoke of the English monarchy.
*King.* My lord of Portingal, by this you see
That which may comfort both your king and you,
And make your late discomfort seem the less.
But say, Hieronimo, what was the next?
*Hier.* The second knight, that hung his scutcheon up,
                              [*He doth as he did before.*
Was Edmond, Earl of Kent in Albion,
When English Richard wore the diadem.
He came likewise, and razèd Lisbon walls,
And took the King of Portingal in fight;
For which and other such-like service done
He after was created Duke of York.
*King.* This is another special argument,
That Portingal may deign to bear our yoke,
When it by little England hath been yok'd.
But now, Hieronimo, what were the last?
*Hier.* The third and last, not least, in our account,
                              [*Doing as before.*
Was, as the rest, a valiant Englishman,
Brave John of Gaunt, the Duke of Lancaster,
As by his scutcheon plainly may appear.
He with a puissant army came to Spain,
And took our King of Castile prisoner.
*Amb.* This is an argument for our viceroy
That Spain may not insult for her success,
Since English warriors likewise conquer'd Spain,

And made them bow their knees to Albion.
*King.* Hieronimo, I drink to thee for this device,
Which hath pleas'd both the ambassador and me:
Pledge me, Hieronimo, if thou love thy king.

                              [*Takes the cup of Horatio.*

My lord, I fear we sit but over-long,
Unless our dainties were more delicate;
But welcome are you to the best we have.
Now let us in, that you may be despatch'd:
I think our council is already set.         [*Exeunt omnes.*

# SCENE VI

## *Ghost of Andrea, Revenge.*

*Andrea.* Come we for this from depth of underground,
To see him feast that gave me my death's wound?
These pleasant sights are sorrow to my soul:
Nothing but league, and love, and banqueting?
*Revenge,* Be still, Andrea; ere we go from hence,
I'll turn their friendship into fell despite,
Their love to mortal hate, their day to night,
Their hope into despair, their peace to war,
Their joys to pain, their bliss to misery.

# ACT II

## SCENE I

*Enter Lorenzo and Balthazar.*

*Lor.* My lord, though Bellimperia seem thus coy,
    Let reason hold you in your wonted joy:
    In time the savage bull sustains the yoke,
    In time all haggard hawks will stoop to lure,
    In time small wedges cleave the hardest oak,
    In time the flint is pierc'd with softest shower,
    And she in time will fall from her disdain,
    And rue the suff'rance of your friendly pain.
*Bal.* No, she is wilder, and more hard withal,
    Than beast, or bird, or tree, or stony wall.
    But wherefore blot I Bellimperia's name?
    It is my fault, not she, that merits blame.
    My feature is not to content her sight,
    My words are rude, and work her no delight.
    The lines I send her are but harsh and ill,
    Such as do drop from Pan and Marsyas' quill.
    My presents are not of sufficient cost,
    And being worthless, all my labour's lost.
    Yet might she love me for my valiancy:
    Ay, but that's slander'd by captivity.
    Yet might she love me to content her sire:
    Ay, but her reason masters his desire.
    Yet might she love me as her brother's friend:
    Ay, but her hopes aim at some other end.
    Yet might she love me to uprear her state:

Ay, but perhaps she hopes some nobler mate.
Yet might she love me as her beauty's thrall:
Ay, but I fear she cannot love at all.
*Lor.* My lord, for my sake leave this ecstasy,
And doubt not but we'll find some remedy.
Some cause there is that lets you not be lov'd;
First that must needs be known, and then remov'd.
What, if my sister love some other knight?
*Bal.* My summer's day will turn to winter's night.
*Lor.* I have already found a stratagem,
To sound the bottom of this doubtful theme.
My lord, for once you shall be rul'd by me;
Hinder me not, whate'er you hear or see.
By force or fair means will I cast about
To find the truth of all this question out.
Ho, Pedringano!
*Ped. Signior!*
*Lor. Vien qui presto.*

*Enter Pedringano.*

*Ped.* Hath your lordship any service to command me?
*Lor.* Ay, Pedringano, service of import;
And—not to spend the time in trifling words—
Thus stands the case: It is not long, thou know'st,
Since I did shield thee from my father's wrath,
For thy conveyance in Andrea's love,
For which thou wert adjudg'd to punishment:
I stood betwixt thee and thy punishment,
And since, thou know'st how I have favour'd thee.
Now to these favours will I add reward,
Not with fair words, but store of golden coin,
And lands and living join'd with dignities,
If thou but satisfy my just demand:
Tell truth, and have me for thy lasting friend.
*Ped.* Whate'er it be your lordship shall demand,
My bounden duty bids me tell the truth,
If case it lie in me to tell the truth.
*Lor.* Then, Pedringano, this is my demand:
Whom loves my sister Bellimperia?
For she reposeth all her trust in thee.
Speak, man, and gain both friendship and reward:
I mean, whom loves she in Andrea's place?

*Ped.* Alas, my lord, since Don Andrea's death
  I have no credit with her as before;
  And therefore know not, if she love or no.
*Lor.* Nay, if thou dally, then I am thy foe,
                                    [*Draws his sword.*
  And fear shall force what friendship cannot win:
  Thy death shall bury what thy life conceals;
  Thou diest for more esteeming her than me.
*Ped.* O, stay, my lord.
*Lor.* Yet speak the truth, and I will guerdon thee,
  And shield thee from whatever can ensue,
  And will conceal whate'er proceeds from thee.
  But if thou dally once again, thou diest.
*Ped.* If madam Bellimperia be in love—
*Lor.* What, villain! ifs and ands?
*Ped.* O, stay, my lord, she loves Horatio.
                                    [*Balthazar starts back.*
*Lor.* What, Don Horatio, our knight marshal's son?
*Ped.* Even him, my lord.
*Lor.* Now say, but how know'st thou he is her love?
  And thou shalt find me kind and liberal:
  Stand up, I say, and fearless tell the truth.
*Ped.* She sent him letters, which myself perus'd,
  Full-fraught with lines and arguments of love,
  Preferring him before Prince Balthazar.
*Lor.* Swear on this cross that what thou say'st is true;
  And that thou wilt conceal what thou hast told.
*Ped.* I swear to both, by him that made us all.
*Lor.* In hope thine oath is true, here's thy reward:
  But if I prove thee perjur'd and unjust,
  This very sword, whereon thou took'st thine oath,
  Shall be the worker of thy tragedy.
*Ped.* What I have said is true, and shall—for me—
  Be still conceal'd from Bellimperia.
  Besides, your honour's liberality
  Deserves my duteous service, ev'n till death.
*Lor.* Let this be all that thou shalt do for me:
  Be watchful, when and where these lovers meet,
  And give me notice in some secret sort.
*Ped.* I will, my lord.
*Lor.* Then shalt thou find that I am liberal.
  Thou know'st that I can more advance thy state

Than she; be therefore wise, and fail me not.
Go and attend her, as thy custom is,
Lest absence make her think thou dost amiss.

　　　　　　　　　　　　　　　　[*Exit Pedringano.*

Why so: *tam armis quam ingenio:*
Where words prevail not, violence prevails;
But gold doth more than either of them both.
How likes Prince Balthazar this stratagem?

*Bal.* Both well and ill; it makes me glad and sad:
Glad, that I know the hind'rer of my love;
Sad, that I fear she hates me whom I love.
Glad, that I know on whom to be reveng'd;
Sad, that she'll fly me, if I take revenge.
Yet must I take revenge, or die myself,
For love resisted grows impatient.
I think Horatio be my destin'd plague:
First, in his hand he brandishèd a sword,
And with that sword he fiercely wagèd war,
And in that war he gave me dang'rous wounds,
And by those wounds he forcèd me to yield,
And by my yielding I became his slave.
Now in his mouth he carries pleasing words,
Which pleasing words do harbour sweet conceits,
Which sweet conceits are lim'd with sly deceits,
Which sly deceits smooth Bellimperia's ears,
And through her ears dive down into her heart,
And in her heart set him, where I should stand.
Thus hath he ta'en my body by his force,
And now by sleight would captivate my soul:
But in his fall I'll tempt the destinies,
And either lose my life, or win my love.

*Lor.* Let's go, my lord; your staying stays revenge.
Do you but follow me, and gain your love:
Her favour must be won by his remove.　　　[*Exeunt.*

## SCENE II

*Enter Horatio and Bellimperia.*

Hor. Now, madam, since by favour of your love
Our hidden smoke is turn'd to open flame,

And that with looks and words we feed our thought
(Two chief contents, where more cannot be had):
Thus, in the midst of love's fair blandishments,
Why show you sign of inward languishments?

> [*Pedringano showeth all to the Prince and*
> *Lorenzo, placing them in secret.*

*Bel.* My heart, sweet friend, is like a ship at sea:
    She wisheth port, where, riding all at ease,
    She may repair what stormy times have worn,
    And leaning on the shore, may sing with joy,
    That pleasure follows pain, and bliss annoy.
    Possession of thy love is th' only port,
    Wherein my heart, with fears and hopes long toss'd,
    Each hour doth wish and long to make resort,
    There to repair the joys that it hath lost,
    And, sitting safe, to sing in Cupid's quire
    That sweetest bliss is crown of love's desire.

> [*Balthazar and Lorenzo above.*

*Bal.* O sleep, mine eyes, see not my love profan'd;
    Be deaf, my ears, hear not my discontent;
    Die, heart: another joys what thou deserv'st.
*Lor.* Watch still, mine eyes, to see this love disjoin'd;
    Hear still, mine ears, to hear them both lament;
    Live, heart, to joy at fond Horatio's fall.
*Bel.* Why stands Horatio speechless all this while?
*Hor.* The less I speak, the more I meditate.
*Bel.* But whereon dost thou chiefly meditate?
*Hor.* On dangers past, and pleasures to ensue.
*Bal.* On pleasures past, and dangers to ensue.
*Bel.* What dangers and what pleasures dost thou mean?
*Hor.* Dangers of war, and pleasures of our love.
*Lor.* Dangers of death, but pleasures none at all.
*Bel.* Let dangers go, thy war shall be with me:
    But such a war, as breaks no bond of peace.
    Speak thou fair words, I'll cross them with fair words;
    Send thou sweet looks, I'll meet them with sweet looks;
    Write loving lines, I'll answer loving lines;
    Give me a kiss, I'll countercheck thy kiss:
    Be this our warring peace, or peaceful war.
*Hor.* But, gracious madam, then appoint the field,
    Where trial of this war shall first be made.
*Bal.* Ambitious villain, how his boldness grows!

*Bel.* Then be thy father's pleasant bow'r the field,
    Where first we vow'd a mutual amity;
    The court were dangerous, that place is safe.
    Our hour shall be, when Vesper 'gins to rise,
    That summons home distressful travellers:
    There none shall hear us but the harmless birds;
    Haply the gentle nightingale
    Shall carol us asleep, ere we be ware,
    And, singing with the prickle at her breast,
    Tell our delight and mirthful dalliance:
    Till then each hour will seem a year and more.
Hor. But, honey sweet and honourable love,
    Return we now into your father's sight:
    Dang'rous suspicion waits on our delight
*Lor.* Ay, danger mixed with jealous despite
    Shall send thy soul into eternal night.     [*Exeunt.*

# SCENE III

*Enter King of Spain, Portingal Ambassador, Don Cyprian, etc.*

*King.* Brother of Castile, to the prince's love
    What says your daughter Bellimperia?
*Cyp.* Although she coy it, as becomes her kind,
    And yet dissemble that she loves the prince,
    I doubt not, I, but she will stoop in time.
    And were she froward, which she will not be,
    Yet herein shall she follow my advice,
    Which is to love him, or forgo my love.
*King.* Then, lord Ambassador of Portingal,
    Advise thy king to make this marriage up,
    For strength'ning of our late-confirmèd league;
    I know no better means to make us friends.
    Her dowry shall be large and liberal:
    Besides that she is daughter and half-heir
    Unto our brother here, Don Cyprian,
    And shall enjoy the moiety of his land,
    I'll grace her marriage with an uncle's gift,
    And this it is—in case the match go forward—:
    The tribute which you pay, shall be releas'd;

And if by Balthazar she have a son,
    He shall enjoy the kingdom after us.
*Amb.* I'll make the motion to my sovereign liege,
    And work it, if my counsel may prevail.
*King.* Do so, my lord, and if he give consent,
    I hope his presence here will honour us,
    In celebration of the nuptial day;
    And let himself determine of the time.
*Amb.* Will't please your grace command me ought beside?
*King.* Commend me to the king, and so farewell.
    But where's Prince Balthazar to take his leave?
*Amb.* That is perform'd already, my good lord.
*King.* Amongst the rest of what you have in charge,
    The prince's ransom must not be forgot:
    That's none of mine, but his that took him prisoner;
    And well his forwardness deserves reward:
    It was Horatio, our knight marshal's son.
*Amb.* Between us there's a price already pitch'd,
    And shall be sent with all convenient speed.
*King.* Then once again farewell, my lord.
*Amb.* Farewell, my lord of Castile, and the rest.      [*Exit.*
*King.* Now, brother, you must take some little pains
    To win fair Bellimperia from her will:
    Young virgins must be rulèd by their friends.
    The prince is amiable, and loves her well;
    If she neglect him and forgo his love,
    She both will wrong her own estate and ours.
    Therefore, whiles I do entertain the prince
    With greatest pleasure that our court affords,
    Endeavour you to win your daughter's thought:
    If she give back, all this will come to naught.
                                                   [*Exeunt*


# SCENE IV


*Enter Horatio, Bellimperia, and Pedringano.*

*Hor.* Now that the night begins with sable wings
    To overcloud the brightness of the sun,
    And that in darkness pleasures may be done:

Come, Bellimperia, let us to the bow'r,
And there in safety pass a pleasant hour.
*Bel.* I follow thee, my love, and will not back,
Although my fainting heart controls my soul.
HOR. Why, make you doubt of Pedringano's faith?
*Bel.* No, he is as trusty as my second self.—
Go, Pedringano, watch without the gate,
And let us know if any make approach.
*Ped.* [*Aside*]. Instead of watching, I'll deserve more gold
By fetching Don Lorenzo to this match.

                                    [*Exit Pedringano.*

HOR. What means my love?
*Bel.*                          I know not what myself;
And yet my heart foretells me some mischance.
*Hor.* Sweet, say not so; fair fortune is our friend,
And heav'ns have shut up day to pleasure us.
The stars, thou see'st, hold back their twinkling shine,
And Luna hides herself to pleasure us.
*Bel.* Thou hast prevail'd; I'll conquer my misdoubt,
And in thy love and counsel drown my fear.
I fear no more; love now is all my thoughts.
Why sit we not? for pleasure asketh ease.
*Hor.* The more thou sitt'st within these leafy bowers,
The more will Flora deck it with her flowers.
*Bel.* Ay, but if Flora spy Horatio here,
Her jealous eye will think I sit too near,
*Hor.* Hark, madam, how the birds record by night,
For joy that Bellimperia sits in sight.
*Bel.* No, Cupid counterfeits the nightingale,
To frame sweet music to Horatio's tale.
*Hor.* If Cupid sing, then Venus is not far:
Ay, thou art Venus, or some fairer star.
*Bel.* If I be Venus, thou must needs be Mars;
And where Mars reigneth, there must needs be wars.
*Hor.* Then thus begin our wars: put forth thy hand,
That it may combat with my ruder hand.
*Bel.* Set forth thy foot to try the push of mine.
*Hor.* But first my looks shall combat against thine.
*Bel.* Then ward thyself: I dart this kiss at thee.
*Hor.* Thus I retort the dart thou threw'st at me.
*Bel.* Nay, then to gain the glory of the field,

My twining arms shall yoke and make thee yield.
*Hor.* Nay, then my arms are large and strong withal:
    Thus elms by vines are compass'd, till they fall.
*Bel.* O, let me go; for in my troubled eyes
    Now may'st thou read that life in passion dies.
*Hor.* O, stay a while, and I will die with thee;
    So shalt thou yield, and yet have conquer'd me.
*Bel.* Who's there?   Pedringano! we are betray'd!

   *Enter Lorenzo, Balthazar, Serberine, Pedringano, disguised.*

*Lor.* My lord, away with her, take her aside.—
    O, sir, forbear: your valour is already tried.
    Quickly despatch, my masters.
                                [*They hang him in the arbour.*
*Hor.*                         What, will you murder me?
*Lor.* Ay, thus, and thus: these are the fruits of love.
                                      [*They stab him.*
*Bel.* O, save his life, and let me die for him
    O, save him, brother; save him, Balthazar:
    I lov'd Horatio; but he lov'd not me.
*Bal.* But Balthazar loves Bellimperia.
*Lor.* Although his life were still ambitious-proud,
    Yet is he at the highest now he is dead.
*Bel.* Murder! murder!   Help, Hieronimo, help!
*Lor.* Come, stop her mouth; away with her.
                                    [*Exeunt.*


# SCENE V


       *Enter Hieronimo in his shirt, etc.*

*Bier.* What outcries pluck me from my naked bed,
    And chill my throbbing heart with trembling fear,
    Which never danger yet could daunt before?
    Who calls Hieronimo? speak, here I am.
    I did not slumber; therefore 'twas no dream.
    No, no, it was some woman cried for help;
    And here within this garden did she cry;
    And in this garden must I rescue her.—
    But stay, what murd'rous spectacle is this?

A man hang'd up and all the murd'rers gone!
And in my bower, to lay the guilt on me!
This place was made for pleasure, not for death.

*[He cuts him down.*

Those garments that he wears I oft have seen—:
Alas, it is Horatio, my sweet son!
O no, but he that whilom was my son!
O, was it thou that call'dst me from my bed?
O speak, if any spark of life remain:
I am thy father; who hath slain my son?
What savage monster, not of human kind,
Hath here been glutted with thy harmless blood,
And left thy bloody corpse dishonour'd here,
For me, amidst these dark and deathful shades,
To drown thee with an ocean of my tears?
O heav'ns, why made you night to cover sin?
By day this deed of darkness had not been.
O earth, why didst thou not in time devour
The vild profaner of this sacred bow'r?
O poor Horatio, what hadst thou misdone,
To leese thy life, ere life was new begun?
O wicked butcher, whatsoe'er thou wert,
How could thou strangle virtue and desert?
Ay me most wretched, that have lost my joy,
In leesing my Horatio, my sweet boy!

*Enter Isabella.*

*Isab.* My husband's absence makes my heart to throb:—
   Hieronimo!
*Hier.* Here, Isabella, help me to lament;
   For sighs are stopp'd, and all my tears are spent
*Isab.* What world of grief! my son Horatio!
   O, where's the author of this endless woe?
*Hier.* To know the author were some ease of grief;
   For in revenge my heart would find relief.
*Isab.* Then is he gone? and is my son gone too?
   O, gush out, tears, fountains and floods of tears;
   Blow, sighs, and raise an everlasting storm;
   For outrage fits our cursèd wretchedness.
   *[Ay me, Hieronimo, sweet husband, speak!*

Hier. *He supp'd with us to-night, frolic and merry,*
    *And said he would go visit Balthazar*
    *At the duke's palace: there the prince doth lodge.*
    *He had no custom to stay out so late:*
    *He may be in his chamber; some go see.*
    *Roderigo, ho!*

            Enter Pedro and Jaques.

Isab. *Ay me, he raves! sweet Hieronimo.*
Hier. *True, all Spain takes note of it.*
    *Besides, he is so generally belov'd;*
    *His majesty the other day did grace him*
    *With waiting on his cup: these be favours,*
    *Which do assure me he cannot be short-liv'd.*
Isab. *Sweet Hieronimo!*
Hier. *I wonder how this fellow got his clothes!—*
    *Sirrah, sirrah, I'll know the truth of all:*
    *Jaques, run to the Duke of Castile's presently,*
    *And bid my son Horatio to come home:*
    *I and his mother have had strange dreams to-night.*
    *Do ye hear me, sir?*
Jaques.            *Ay, sir.*
Hier.                    *Well, sir, be gone.*
    *Pedro, come hither; know'st thou who this is?*
Ped. *Too well, sir.*
Hier.        *Too well! who, who is it? Peace, Isabella!*
    *Nay, blush not, man.*
Ped.                *It is my lord Horatio.*
Hier. *Ha, ha, St. James! but this doth make me laugh,*
    *That there are more deluded than myself.*
Ped. *Deluded?*
Hier.       *Ay:*
    *I would have sworn myself, within this hour,*
    *That this had been my son Horatio:*
    *His garments are so like.*
    *Ha! are they not great persuasions?*
Isab. *O, would to God it were not so!*
Hier. *Were not, Isabella? dost thou dream it is?*
    *Can thy soft bosom entertain a thought,*
    *That such a black deed of mischief should be done*

*On one so pure and spotless as our son?*
*Away, I am ashamed.*
Isab.                          *Dear Hieronimo,*
  *Cast a more serious eye upon thy grief:*
  *Weak apprehension gives but weak belief*
Hier. *It was a man, sure, that was hang'd up here;*
  *A youth, as I remember: I cut him down.*
  *If it should prove my son now after all—*
  *Say you? say you?—Light! lend me a taper;*
  *Let me look again.—O God!*
  *Confusion, mischief, torment, death and hell,*
  *Drop all your stings at once in my cold bosom,*
  *That now is stiff with horror: kill me quickly!*
  *Be gracious to me, thou infective night,*
  *And drop this deed of murder down on me;*
  *Gird in my waste of grief with thy large darkness,*
  *And let me not survive to see the light*
  *May put me in the mind I had a son.*
Isab. *O sweet Horatio! O my dearest son!*
Hier. *How strangely had I lost my way to grief!*]
  Sweet, lovely rose, ill-pluck'd before thy time,
  Fair, worthy son, not conquer'd, but betray'd,
  I'll kiss thee now, for words with tears are stay'd.
*Isab.* And I'll close up the glasses of his sight,
  For once these eyes were only my delight
*Hier.* See'st thou this handkercher besmear'd with blood?
  It shall not from me, till I take revenge.
  See'st thou those wounds that yet are bleeding fresh?
  I'll not entomb them, till I have revenge.
  Then will I joy amidst my discontent;
  Till then my sorrow never shall be spent
*Isab.* The heav'ns are just; murder cannot be hid:
  Time is the author both of truth and right,
  And time will bring this treachery to light.
*Hier.* Meanwhile, good Isabella, cease thy plaints,
  Or, at the least, dissemble them awhile:
  So shall we sooner find the practice out,
  And learn by whom all this was brought about
  Come, Isabel, now let us take him up,
                                   [*They take him up.*
  And bear him in from out this cursèd place.

I'll say his dirge; singing fits not this case.

O aliquis mihi quas pulchrum ver educat herbas,
   [Hieronimo sets his breast unto his sword.
Misceat, & nostro detur medicina dolori;
Aut, si qui faciunt annorum oblivia, succos
Praebeat; ipse metam magnum quaecunque per orbem
Gramina Sol pulchras effert in luminis oras;
Ipse bibam quicquid meditatur saga veneni,
Quicquid & herbarum vi caeca nenia nectit:
Omnia perpetiar, lethum quoque, dum semel omnis
Nosier in extincto moriatur pectore sensus.—
Ergo tuos oculos nunquam, mea vita, videbo,
Et tua perpetuus sepelivit lumina somnus?
Emoriar tecum: sic, sic juvat ire sub umbras.—
Attamen absistam properato cedere letho,
Ne mortem vindicta tuam tam nulla sequatur.

        [Here he throws it from him and bears
             the body away.

## SCENE VI

*Ghost of Andrea, Revenge.*

*Andrea.* Brought'st thou me hither to increase my pain?
 I look'd that Balthazar should have been slain:
 But 'tis my friend Horatio that is slain,
 And they abuse fair Bellimperia,
 On whom I doted more than all the world,
 Because she lov'd me more than all the world.
*Revenge.* Thou talk'st of harvest, when the corn is green:
 The end is crown of every work well done;
 The sickle comes not, till the corn be ripe.
 Be still; and ere I lead thee from this place,
 I'll show thee Balthazar in heavy case.

# ACT III

## SCENE I

### *The Court of Portugal.*

*Enter Viceroy of Portingal, Nobles, Alexandro, Villuppo.*

*Vic.* Infortunate condition of kings,
    Seated amidst so many helpless doubts!
    First we are plac'd upon extremest height,
    And oft supplanted with exceeding hate,
    But ever subject to the wheel of chance;
    And at our highest never joy we so,
    As we both doubt and dread our overthrow.
    So striveth not the waves with sundry winds,
    As fortune toileth in the affairs of kings,
    That would be fear'd, yet fear to be belov'd,
    Sith fear or love to kings is flattery.
    For instance, lordings, look upon your king,
    By hate deprivèd of his dearest son,
    The only hope of our successive line.
*Nob.* I had not thought that Alexandro's heart
    Had been envenom'd with such extreme hate;
    But now I see that words have several works,
    And there's no credit in the countenance.
*Vil.* No; for, my lord, had you beheld the train,
    That feignèd love had colourèd in his looks,
    When he in camp consorted Balthazar,
    Far more inconstant had you thought the sun,
    That hourly coasts the centre of the earth,
    Than Alexandro's purpose to the prince.

*Vic.* No more, Villuppo, thou hast said enough,
   And with thy words thou slay'st our wounded thoughts.
   Nor shall I longer dally with the world,
   Procrastinating Alexandro's death:
   Go some of you, and fetch the traitor forth,
   That, as he is condemnèd, he may die.

*Enter Alexandro, with a Nobleman and halberts.*

*Nob.* In such extremes will nought but patience serve.
*Alex.* But in extremes what patience shall I use?
   Nor discontents it me to leave the world,
   With whom there nothing can prevail but wrong.
*Nob.* Yet hope the best.
*Alex.*                         'Tis heaven is my hope:
   As for the earth, it is too much infect
   To yield me hope of any of her mould.
*Vic.* Why linger ye? bring forth that daring fiend,
   And let him die for his accursèd deed.
*Alex.* Not that I fear the extremity of death
   (For nobles cannot stoop to servile fear)
   Do I, O king, thus discontented live.
   But this, O this, torments my labouring soul,
   That thus I die suspected of a sin,
   Whereof, as heav'ns have known my secret thoughts,
   So am I free from this suggestion.
*Vic.* No more, I say! to the tortures! when?
   Bind him, and burn his body in those flames,
                              [*They bind him to the stake.*
   That shall prefigure those unquenchèd fires
   Of Phlegethon, preparèd for his soul.
*Alex.* My guiltless death will be aveng'd on thee,
   On thee, Villuppo, that hath malic'd thus,
   Or for thy meed hast falsely me accus'd.
*Vil.* Nay, Alexandro, if thou menace me,
   I'll lend a hand to send thee to the lake,
   Where those thy words shall perish with thy works:
   Injurious traitor! monstrous homicide!

*Enter Ambassador.*

*Amb.* Stay, hold a while;
   And here—with pardon of his majesty—

Lay hands upon Villuppo.
*Vic.*                                      Ambassador,
    What news hath urg'd this sudden enterance?
*Amb.* Know, sovereign lord, that Balthazar doth live.
*Vic.* What say'st thou? liveth Balthazar our son?
*Amb.* Your highness' son, Lord Balthazar, doth live;
    And, well entreated in the court of Spain,
    Humbly commends him to your majesty.
    These eyes beheld—and these my followers—;
    With these, the letters of the king's commends
                                    [*Gives him letters.*
    Are happy witnesses of his highness' health.
            [*The King looks on the letters, and proceeds.*
*Vic.* 'Thy son doth live, your tribute is receiv'd;
    Thy peace is made, and we are satisfied.
    The rest resolve upon as things propos'd
    For both our honours and thy benefit.'
*Amb.* These are his highness' farther articles.
                              [*He gives him more letters.*
*Vic.* Accursèd wretch, to intimate these ills
    Against the life and reputation
    Of noble Alexandro! Come, my lord, unbind him:
    Let him unbind thee, that is bound to death,
    To make a quital for thy discontent.
                                    [*They unbind him.*
*Alex.* Dread lord, in kindness you could do no less,
    Upon report of such a damnèd fact;
    But thus we see our innocence hath sav'd
    The hopeless life which thou, Villuppo, sought
    By thy suggestions to have massacred.
*Vic.* Say, false Villuppo, wherefore didst thou thus
    Falsely betray Lord Alexandro's life?
    Him, whom thou know'st that no unkindness else,
    But ev'n the slaughter of our dearest son,
    Could once have mov'd us to have misconceiv'd.
*Alex.* Say, treacherous Villuppo, tell the king:
    Wherein hath Alexandro us'd thee ill?
*Vil.* Rent with remembrance of so foul a deed,
    My guilty soul submits me to thy doom:
    For not for Alexandro's injuries,

But for reward and hope to be preferr'd,
Thus have I shamelessly hazarded his life.

*Vic.* Which, villain, shall be ransom'd with thy death—:
  And not so mean a torment as we here
  Devis'd for him who, thou said'st, slew our son,
  But with the bitt'rest torments and extremes
  That may be yet invented for thine end.

                    [*Alexandro seems to entreat.*

  Entreat me not; go, take the traitor hence:

                              [*Exit Villuppo.*

  And, Alexandro, let us honour thee
  With public notice of thy loyalty.—
  To end those things articulated here
  By our great lord, the mighty King of Spain,
  We with our council will deliberate.
  Come, Alexandro, keep us company.        [*Exeunt.*

# SCENE II

*Enter Hieronimo.*

*Hier.* O eyes! no eyes, but fountains fraught with tears;
  O life! no life, but lively form of death;
  O world! no world, but mass of public wrongs,
  Confus'd and fill'd with murder and misdeeds!
  O sacred heav'ns! if this unhallow'd deed,
  If this inhuman and barbarous attempt,
  If this incomparable murder thus
  Of mine, but now no more my son,
  Shall unreveal'd and unrevengèd pass,
  How should we term your dealings to be just,
  If you unjustly deal with those that in your justice trust?
  The night, sad secretary to my moans,
  With direful visions wakes my vexèd soul,
  And with the wounds of my distressful son
  Solicits me for notice of his death.
  The ugly fiends do sally forth of hell,
  And frame my steps to unfrequented paths,
  And fear my heart with fierce inflamèd thoughts.

The cloudy day my discontents records,
Early begins to register my dreams,
And drive me forth to seek the murtherer.
Eyes, life, world, heav'ns, hell, night, and day,
See, search, shew, send some man, some mean, that may—

[*A letter falleth.*

What's here? a letter? tush! it is not so!—
A letter written to Hieronimo!        [*Red ink.*
"For want of ink, receive this bloody writ:
Me hath my hapless brother hid from thee;
Revenge thyself on Balthazar and him:
For these were they that murderèd thy son.
Hieronimo, revenge Horatio's death,
And better fare than Bellimperia doth.'
What means this unexpected miracle?
My son slain by Lorenzo and the prince!
What cause had they Horatio to malign?
Or what might move thee, Bellimperia,
To accuse thy brother, had he been the mean?
Hieronimo, beware!—thou art betray'd,
And to entrap thy life this train is laid.
Advise thee therefore, be not credulous:
This is devisèd to endanger thee,
That thou, by this, Lorenzo shouldst accuse;
And he, for thy dishonour done, should draw
Thy life in question and thy name in hate.
Dear was the life of my belovèd son,
And of his death behoves me be reveng'd:
Then hazard not thine own, Hieronimo,
But live t' effect thy resolution.
I therefore will by circumstances try,
What I can gather to confirm this writ;
And, heark'ning near the Duke of Castile's house,
Close, if I can, with Bellimperia,
To listen more, but nothing to bewray.

*Enter Pedringano.*

Now, Pedringano!
*Ped.*                    Now, Hieronimo!
*Hier.* Where's thy lady?
*Ped.*                    I know not; here's my ord.

*Enter Lorenzo.*

*Lor.* How now, who's this? Hieronimo?
*Hier.*                                                      My lord—
*Ped.* He asketh for my lady Bellimperia.
*Lor.* What to do, Hieronimo? The duke, my father, hath,
   Upon some disgrace, awhile remov'd her hence;
   But if it be ought I may inform her of,
   Tell me, Hieronimo, and I'll let her know it.
*Hier.* Nay, nay, my lord, I thank you; it shall not need.
   I had a suit unto her, but too late,
   And her disgrace makes me unfortunate.
*Lor.* Why so, Hieronimo? use me.
*Hier.* O no, my lord; I dare not; it must not be;
   I humbly thank your lordship.[1]
*Lor.*                                              Why then, farewell.
*Hier.* My grief no heart, my thoughts no tongue can tell.    [*Exit.*
*Lor.* Come hither, Pedringano, see'st thou this?
*Ped.* My lord, I see it, and suspect it too.
*Lor.* This is that damnèd villain Serberine,
   That hath, I fear, reveal'd Horatio's death.
*Ped.* My lord, he could not, 'twas so lately done;
   And since he hath not left my company.
*Lor.* Admit he have not, his condition's such,
   As fear or flatt'ring words may make him false.
   I know his humour, and therewith repent
   That e'er I us'd him in this enterprise.
   But, Pedringano, to prevent the worst,
   And 'cause I know thee secret as my soul,

---

[1] Line 65 and first part of 66 (O no . . . lordship) are replaced, in all the Qq.
   from 1602 onwards, by the following lines:
*Hier. Who? you, my lord?*
   *I reserve your favour for a greater honour;*
   *This is a very toy, my lord, a toy.*
*Lor. All's one, Hieronimo, acquaint me with it.*
*Hier. I'faith, my lord, it is an idle thing;*
   *I must confess I ha' been too slack, too tardy,*
   *Too remiss unto your honour.*
*Lor.*                                         *How now, Hieronimo?*
*Hier. In troth, my lord, it is a thing of nothing:*
   *The murder of a son, or so——*
   *A thing of nothing, my lord!*

Here, for thy further satisfaction, take thou this,
                             [*Gives him more gold.*
And hearken to me—thus it is devis'd:
This night thou must (and, prithee, so resolve)
Meet Serberíne at Saint Luigi's Park—
Thou know'st 'tis here hard by behind the house—
There take thy stand, and see thou strike him sure:
For die he must, if we do mean to live.
*Ped.* But how shall Serberine be there, my lord?
*Lor.* Let me alone; I'll send to him to meet
   The prince and me, where thou must do this deed.
*Ped.* It shall be done, my lord, it shall be done;
   And I'll go arm myself to meet him there.
*Lor.* When things shall alter, as I hope they will,
   Then shalt thou mount for this; thou know'st my mind.
                               [*Exit Pedríngano.*

   *Che le Ieron!*

### Enter Page.

*Page.*                My lord?
*Lor.*                         Go, sirrah,
   To Serberine, and bid him forthwith meet
   The prince and me at Saint Luigi's Park,
   Behind the house; this evening, boy!
*Page.*                       I go, my lord
*Lor.* But, sirrah, let the hour be eight o'clock:
   Bid him not fail.
*Page.*            I fly, my lord.         [*Exit.*
*Lor.* Now to confirm the complot thou hast cast
   Of all these practices, I'll spread the watch,
   Upon precise commandment from the king,
   Strongly to guard the place where Pedringano
   This night shall murder hapless Serberine.
   Thus must we work that will avoid distrust;
   Thus must we practise to prevent mishap,
   And thus one ill another must expulse.
   This sly enquiry of Hieronimo
   For Bellimperia breeds suspicion,
   And this suspicion bodes a further ill.
   As for myself, I know my secret fault,
   And so do they; but I have dealt for them:
   They that for coin their souls endangerèd,

To save my life, for coin shall venture theirs;
And better it's that base companions die,
Than by their life to hazard our good haps.
Nor shall they live, for me to fear their faith:
I'll trust myself, myself shall be my friend;
For die they shall, slaves are ordain'd to no other end.    [*Exit.*

## SCENE III

*Enter Pedringano, with a pistol.*

*Ped.* Now, Pedringano, bid thy pistol hold,
And hold on, Fortune! once more favour me;
Give but success to mine attempting spirit,
And let me shift for taking of mine aim.
Here is the gold: this is the gold propos'd;
It is no dream that I adventure for,
But Pedringano is possess'd thereof.
And he that would not strain his conscience
For him that thus his liberal purse hath stretch'd,
Unworthy such a favour, may he fail,
And, wishing, want, when such as I prevail.
As for the fear of apprehension,
I know, if need should be, my noble lord
Will stand between me and ensuing harms;
Besides, this place is free from all suspect:
Here therefore will I stay and take my stand.

*Enter the Watch.*

1. I wonder much to what intent it is
   That we are thus expressly charg'd to watch.
2. 'Tis by commandment in the king's own name.
3. But we were never wont to watch and ward
   So near the duke, his brother's, house before.
2. Content yourself, stand close, there's somewhat in't.

*Enter Serberine.*

Here, Serberine, attend and stay thy pace;
For here did Don Lorenzo's page appoint
That thou by his command shouldst meet with him.
How fit a place—if one were so dispos'd—

Methinks this corner is to close with one.
*Ped.* Here comes the bird that I must seize upon:
  Now, Pedringano, or never, play the man!
*Ser.* I wonder that his lordship stays so long,
  Or wherefore should he send for me so late?
*Ped.* For this, Serberine!—and thou shalt ha't.

                                    [*Shoots the dag.*
  So, there he lies; my promise is perform'd.

### The Watch.

  1. Hark, gentlemen, this is a pistol shot.
  2. And here's one slain;—stay the murderer.
*Ped.* Now by the sorrows of the souls in hell,
                              [*He strives with the watch.*
  Who first lays hand on me, I'll be his priest.
  3. Sirrah, confess, and therein play the priest,
      Why hast thou thus unkindly kill'd the man?
*Ped.* Why? because he walk'd abroad so late.
  3. Come, sir, you had been better kept your bed,
      Than have committed this misdeed so late.
  2. Come, to the marshal's with the murderer!
  1. On to Hieronimo's! help me here
      To bring the murder'd body with us too.
*Ped.* Hieronimo? carry me before whom you will:
  Whatever he be, I'll answer him and you;
  And do your worst, for I defy you all.      [*Exeunt.*


## SCENE IV

### *Enter Lorenzo and Balthazar.*

*Bal.* How now, my lord, what makes you rise so soon?
*Lor.* Fear of preventing our mishaps too late.
*Bal.* What mischief is it that we not mistrust?
*Lor.* Our greatest ills we least mistrust, my lord,
  And inexpected harms do hurt us most.
*Bal.* Why, tell me, Don Lorenzo, tell me, man,
  If ought concerns our honour and your own.
*Lor.* Nor you, nor me, my lord, but both in one:
  For I suspect—and the presumption's great—

That by those base confed'rates in our fault
Touching the death of Don Horatio,
We are betray'd to old Hieronimo.
*Bal.* Betray'd, Lorenzo? tush! it cannot be.
*Lor.* A guilty conscience, urgèd with the thought
Of former evils, easily cannot err:
I am persuaded—and dissuade me not—
That all's revealed to Hieronimo.
And therefore know that I have cast it thus:—

*Enter Page.*

But here's the page. How now? what news with thee?
*Page.* My lord, Serberine is slain.
*Bal.*                    Who? Serberine, my man?
*Page.* Your highness' man, my lord.
*Lor.*                    Speak, page, who murder'd him?
*Page.* He that is apprehended for the fact
*Lor.* Who?
*Page.*            Pedringano.
*Bal.* Is Serberine slain, that lov'd his lord so well?
Injurious villain, murd'rer of his friend!
*Lor.* Hath Pedringano murder'd Serberine?
My lord, let me entreat you to take the pains
To exasperate and hasten his revenge
With your complaints unto my lord the king.
This their dissension breeds a greater doubt
*Bal.* Assure thee, Don Lorenzo, he shall die,
Or else his highness hardly shall deny.
Meanwhile I'll haste the marshal-sessions:
For die he shall for this his damnèd deed.
                              [*Exit Balthazar.*
*Lor.* Why so, this fits our former policy,
And thus experience bids the wise to deal.
I lay the plot: he prosecutes the point;
I set the trap: he breaks the worthless twigs,
And sees not that wherewith the bird was lim'd.
Thus hopeful men, that mean to hold their own,
Must look like fowlers to their dearest friends.
He runs to kill whom I have holp to catch,
And no man knows it was my reaching fetch.
'Tis hard to trust unto a multitude,

Or any one, in mine opinion,
When men themselves their secrets will reveal.

*Enter a Messenger with a letter.*

Boy——
*Page.*                    My lord?
*Lor.* What's he?
*Mes.*                 I have a letter to your lordship.
*Lor.* From whence?
*Mes.*                    From Pedringano that's imprison'd.
*Lor.* So he is in prison then?
*Mes.* Ay, my good lord.
*Lor.* What would he with us?—He writes us here,
  To stand good lord, and help him in distress.—
  Tell him I have his letters, know his mind;
  And what we may, let him assure him of.
  Fellow, begone: my boy shall follow thee.
                            [*Exit Messenger.*
  This works like wax; yet once more try thy wits.
  Boy, go, convey this purse to Pedringano;
  Thou know'st the prison, closely give it him,
  And be advis'd that none be there about:
  Bid him be merry still, but secret;
  And though the marshal-sessions be to-day,
  Bid him not doubt of his delivery.
  Tell him his pardon is already sign'd,
  And thereon bid him boldly be resolv'd:
  For, were he ready to be turnèd off—
  As 'tis my will the uttermost be tried—
  Thou with his pardon shalt attend him still.
  Show him this box, tell him his pardon's in't;
  But open't not, and if thou lov'st thy life;
  But let him wisely keep his hopes unknown:
  He shall not want while Don Lorenzo lives.
  Away!
*Page.*              I go, my lord, I run.
*Lor.* But, sirrah, see that this be cleanly done.
                            [*Exit Page.*
  Now stands our fortune on a tickle point,
  And now or never ends Lorenzo's doubts.
  One only thing is uneffected yet,

And that's to see the executioner.
But to what end? I list not trust the air
With utterance of our pretence therein,
For fear the privy whisp'ring of the wind
Convey our words amongst unfriendly ears,
That lie too open to advantages.
*E quel che voglio io, nessun lo sa;*
*Intendo io: quel mi basterà.*                              [*Exit*

## SCENE V

*Enter Boy, with the box.*

*Boy.* My master hath forbidden me to look in this box; and, by
my troth, 'tis likely, if he had not warned me, I should not
have had so much idle time; for we men's-kind, in our minor-
ity, are like women in their uncertainty: that they are most
forbidden, they will soonest attempt: so I now.——By my
bare honesty, here's nothing but the bare empty box: were it
not sin against secrecy, I would say it were a piece of gentle-
manlike knavery. I must go to Pedringano, and tell him his
pardon is in this box; nay, I would have sworn it, had I not
seen the contrary.—I cannot choose but smile to think how
the villain will flout the gallows, scorn the audience, and des-
cant on the hangman, and all presuming of his pardon from
hence. Will't not be an odd jest for me to stand and grace every
jest he makes, pointing my finger at this box, as who would
say: "Mock on, here's thy warrant.' Is't not a scurvy jest that
a man should jest himself to death? Alas! poor Pedringano, I
am in a sort sorry for thee; but if I should be hanged with thee,
I cannot weep.                                              [*Exit.*

## SCENE VI

*Enter Hieronimo and the Deputy.*

*Hier.* Thus must we toil in other men's extremes,
    That know not how to remedy our own;
    And do them justice, when unjustly we,

For all our wrongs, can compass no redress.
But shall I never live to see the day,
That I may come, by justice of the heavens,
To know the cause that may my cares allay?
This toils my body, this consumeth age,
That only I to all men just must be,
And neither gods nor men be just to me.

*Dep.* Worthy Hieronimo, your office asks
A care to punish such as do transgress.

*Hier.* So is't my duty to regard his death
Who, when he liv'd, deserv'd my dearest blood.
But come, for that we came for: let's begin;
For here lies that which bids me to be gone.

*Enter Officers, Boy, and Pedringano, with a letter
in his hand, bound.*

*Dep.* Bring forth the prisoner, for the court is set
*Ped.* Gramercy, boy, but it was time to come;
For I had written to my lord anew
A nearer matter that concerneth him,
For fear his lordship had forgotten me.
But sith he hath remember'd me so well—
Come, come, come on, when shall we to this gear?

*Hier.* Stand forth, thou monster, murderer of men,
And here, for satisfaction of the world,
Confess thy folly, and repent thy fault;
For there's thy place of execution.

*Ped.* This is short work: well, to your marshalship
First I confess—nor fear I death therefore—:
I am the man, 'twas I slew Serberine.
But, sir, then you think this shall be the place,
Where we shall satisfy you for this gear?

*Dep.* Ay, Pedringano.
*Ped.*                                 Now I think not so.

*Hier.* Peace, impudent; for thou shalt find it so:
For blood with blood shall, while I sit as judge,
Be satisfièd, and the law discharg'd.
And though myself cannot receive the like,
Yet will I see that others have their right.
Despatch: the fault's approvèd and confess'd,
And by our law he is condemn'd to die.

*Hangm.* Come on, sir, are you ready?

*Ped.* To do what, my fine, officious knave?

*Hangm.* To go to this gear.

*Ped.* O sir, you are too forward: thou wouldst fain furnish me with a halter, to disfurnish me of my habit. So I should go out of this gear, my raiment, into that gear, the rope. But, hangman, now I spy your knavery, I'll not change without boot, that's flat.

*Hangm.* Come, sir.

*Ped.* So, then, I must up?

*Hangm.* No remedy.

*Ped.* Yes, but there shall be for my coming down.

*Hangm.* Indeed, here's a remedy for that.

*Ped.* How? be turned off?

*Hangm.* Ay, truly; come, are you ready? I pray, sir, despatch; the day goes away.

*Ped.* What, do you hang by the hour? if you do, I may chance to break your old custom.

*Hangm.* Faith, you have reason; for I am like to break your young neck.

*Ped.* Dost thou mock me, hangman? pray God, I be not preserved to break your knave's pate for this.

*Hangm.* Alas, sir! you are a foot too low to reach it, and I hope you will never grow so high while I am in the office.

*Ped.* Sirrah, dost see yonder boy with the box in his hand?

*Hangm.* What, he that points to it with his finger?

*Ped.* Ay, that companion.

*Hangm.* I know him not; but what of him?

*Ped.* Dost thou think to live till his old doublet will make thee a new truss?

*Hangm.* Ay, and many a fair year after, to truss up many an honester man than either thou or he.

*Ped.* What hath he in his box, as thou thinkest?

*Hangm.* Faith, I cannot tell, nor I care not greatly; methinks you should rather hearken to your soul's health.

*Ped.* Why, sirrah hangman, I take it that that is good for the body is likewise good for the soul: and it may be, in that box is balm for both.

*Hangm.* Well, thou art even the merriest piece of man's flesh that e'er groaned at my office door!

*Ped.* Is your roguery become an office with a knave's name?

*Hangm.* Ay, and that shall all they witness that see you seal it with
a thief's name.

*Ped.* I prithee, request this good company to pray with me.

*Hangm.* Ay, marry, sir, this is a good motion: my masters, you
see here's a good fellow.

*Ped.* Nay, nay, now I remember me, let them alone till some
other time; for now I have no great need.

*Hier.* I have not seen a wretch so impudent
  O monstrous times, where murder's set so light,
  And where the soul, that should be shrin'd in heaven,
  Solely delights in interdicted things,
  Still wand'ring in the thorny passages,
  That intercepts itself of happiness.
  Murder! O bloody monster! God forbid
  A fault so foul should 'scape unpunishèd.
  Despatch, and see this execution done!—
  This makes me to remember thee, my son.
                                        [*Exit Hieronimo.*

*Ped.* Nay, soft, no haste.

*Dep.* Why, wherefore stay you? Have you hope of life?

*Ped.* Why, ay!

*Hangm.*            As how?

*Ped.* Why, rascal, by my pardon from the king.

*Hangm.* Stand you on that? then you shall off with this.
                                        [*He turns him off.*

*Dep.* So, executioner;—convey him hence;
  But let his body be unburièd:
  Let not the earth be chokèd or infect
  With that which heav'n contemns, and men neglect.
                                        [*Exeunt.*


# SCENE VII

*Enter Hieronimo.*

*Hier.* Where shall I run to breathe abroad my woes,
  My woes, whose weight hath wearièd the earth?
  Or mine exclaims, that have surcharg'd the air
  With ceaseless plaints for my deceasèd son?
  The blust'ring winds, conspiring with my words,

At my lament have mov'd the leafless trees,
Disrob'd the meadows of their flower'd green,
Made mountains marsh with spring-tides of my tears,
And broken through the brazen gates of hell.
Yet still tormented is my tortur'd soul
With broken sighs and restless passions,
That wingèd mount; and, hov'ring in the air,
Beat at the windows of the brightest heavens,
Soliciting for justice and revenge:
But they are plac'd in those empyreal heights,
Where, countermur'd with walls of diamond,
I find the place impregnable; and they
Resist my woes, and give my words no way.

*Enter Hangman with a letter.*

*Hangm.* O lord, sir! God bless you, sir! the man, sir, Petergade,
  sir, he that was so full of merry conceits——
*Hier.* Well, what of him?
*Hangm.* O lord, sir, he went the wrong way; the fellow had a fair
  commission to the contrary. Sir, here is his passport; I pray
  you, sir, we have done him wrong.
*Hier.* I warrant thee, give it me.
*Hangm.* You will stand between the gallows and me?
*Hier.* Ay, ay.
*Hangm.* I thank your lord worship.          [*Exit Hangman.*
*Hier.* And yet, though somewhat nearer me concerns,
  I will, to ease the grief that I sustain,
  Take truce with sorrow while I read on this.
  "My lord, I write, as mine extremes requir'd,
  That you would labour my delivery:
  If you neglect, my life is desperate,
  And in my death I shall reveal the troth.
  You know, my lord, I slew him for your sake,
  And was confed'rate with the prince and you;
  Won by rewards and hopeful promises,
  I holp to murder Don Horatio too.'——
  Holp he to murder mine Horatio?
  And actors in th' accursèd tragedy
  Wast thou, Lorenzo, Balthazar and thou,
  Of whom my son, my son deserv'd so well?
  What have I heard, what have mine eyes beheld?

O sacred heavens, may it come to pass
That such a monstrous and detested deed,
So closely smother'd, and so long conceal'd,
Shall thus by this be vengèd or reveal'd?
Now see I what I durst not then suspect,
That Bellimperia's letter was not feign'd.
Nor feignèd she, though falsely they have wrong'd
Both her, myself, Horatio, and themselves.
Now may I make compare 'twixt hers and this,
Of every accident I ne'er could find
Till now, and now I feelingly perceive
They did what heav'n unpunish'd would not leave.
O false Lorenzo! are these thy flatt'ring looks?
Is this the honour that thou didst my son?
And Balthazar—bane to thy soul and me!—
Was this the ransom he reserv'd thee for?
Woe to the cause of these constrainèd wars!
Woe to thy baseness and captivity,
Woe to thy birth, thy body and thy soul,
Thy cursèd father, and thy conquer'd self!
And bann'd with bitter execrations be
The day and place where he did pity thee!
But wherefore waste I mine unfruitful words,
When naught but blood will satisfy my woes?
I will go plain me to my lord the king,
And cry aloud for justice through the court,
Wearing the flints with these my wither'd feet;
And either purchase justice by entreats,
Or tire them all with my revenging threats.           [*Exit.*

## SCENE VIII

*Enter Isabella and her Maid.*

*Isab.* So that, you say, this herb, will purge the eye,
     And this, the head?—
     Ah!—but none of them will purge the heart!
     No, there's no medicine left for my disease,
     Nor any physic to recure the dead.

                                        [*She runs lunatic.*

Horatio! O, where's Horatio?

*Maid.* Good madam, affright not thus yourself
    With outrage for your son Horatio:
    He sleeps in quiet in the Elysian fields.

*Isab.* Why, did I not give you gowns and goodly things,
    Bought you a whistle and a whipstalk too,
    To be revengèd on their villanies?

*Maid.* Madam, these humours do torment my soul.

*Isab.* My soul—poor soul! thou talk'st of things—
    Thou know'st not what: my soul hath silver wings,
    That mounts me up unto the highest heavens;
    To heav'n: ay, there sits my Horatio,
    Back'd with a troop of fiery Cherubins,
    Dancing about his newly healèd wounds,
    Singing sweet hymns and chanting heav'nly notes:
    Rare harmony to greet his innocence,
    That died, ay died, a mirror in our days.
    But say, where shall I find the men, the murderers,
    That slew Horatio? Whither shall I run
    To find them out that murderèd my son?          [*Exeunt.*

# SCENE IX

*Bellimperia at a window.*

*Bel.* What means this outrage that is offer'd me?
    Why am I thus sequester'd from the court?
    No notice! Shall I not know the cause
    Of these my secret and suspicious ills?
    Accursèd brother, unkind murderer,
    Why bend'st thou thus thy mind to martyr me?
    Hieronimo, why writ I of thy wrongs,
    Or why art thou so slack in thy revenge?
    Andrea, O Andrea! that thou saw'st
    Me for thy friend Horatio handled thus,
    And him for me thus causeless murderèd!—
    Well, force perforce, I must constrain myself
    To patience, and apply me to the time,

Till heav'n, as I have hop'd, shall set me free.

*Enter Christophil.*

*Chris.* Come, madam Bellimperia, this may not be.

[*Exeunt.*

## SCENE X

*Enter Lorenzo, Balthazar, and the Page.*

*Lor.* Boy, talk no further; thus far things go well.
    Thou art assurèd that thou saw'st him dead?
*Page.* Or else, my lord, I live not.
*Lor.*                         That's enough.
    As for his resolution in his end,
    Leave that to him with whom he sojourns now.—
    Here, take my ring and give it Christophil,
    And bid him let my sister be enlarg'd,
    And bring her hither straight—        [*Exit Page.*
    This that I did was for a policy,
    To smooth and keep the murder secret,
    Which, as a nine-days' wonder, being o'erblown,
    My gentle sister will I now enlarge.
*Bal.* And time, Lorenzo: for my lord the duke,
    You heard enquirèd for her yester-night.
*Lor.* Why, and my lord, I hope you heard me say
    Sufficient reason why she kept away;
    But that's all one. My lord, you love her?
*Bal.*                            Ay.
*Lor.* Then in your love beware; deal cunningly:
    Salve all suspicions, only soothe me up;
    And if she hap to stand on terms with us—
    As for her sweetheart and concealment so—
    Jest with her gently: under feignèd jest
    Are things conceal'd that else would breed unrest.—
    But here she comes.

*Enter Bellimperia.*

              Now, sister?
*Bel.*                      Sister?—No!

Thou art no brother, but an enemy;
Else wouldst thou not have us'd thy sister so:
First, to affright me with thy weapons drawn,
And with extremes abuse my company;
And then to hurry me, like whirlwind's rage,
Amidst a crew of thy confederates,
And clap me up, where none might come at me,
Nor I at any, to reveal my wrongs.
What madding fury did possess thy wits?
Or wherein is 't that I offended thee?

*Lor.* Advise you better, Bellimperia,
For I have done you no disparagement;
Unless, by more discretion than deserv'd,
I sought to save your honour and mine own.

*Bel.* Mine honour? why, Lorenzo, wherein is't
That I neglect my reputation so,
As you, or any, need to rescue it?

*Lor.* His highness and my father were resolv'd
To come confer with old Hieronimo,
Concerning certain matters of estate,
That by the viceroy was determinèd.

*Bel.* And wherein was mine honour touch'd in that?

*Bal.* Have patience, Bellimperia; hear the rest.

*Lor.* Me (next in sight) as messenger they sent,
To give him notice that they were so nigh:
Now when I came, consorted with the prince,
And unexpected, in an arbour there,
Found Bellimperia with Horatio—

*Bel.* How then?

*Lor.* Why, then, remembering that old disgrace,
Which you for Don Andrea had endur'd,
And now were likely longer to sustain,
By being found so meanly accompanied,
Thought rather—for I knew no readier mean—
To thrust Horatio forth my father's way.

*Bal.* And carry you obscurely somewhere else,
Lest that his highness should have found you there.

*Bel.* Ev'n so, my lord? And you are witness
That this is true which he entreateth of?
You, gentle brother, forg'd this for my sake,
And you, my lord, were made his instrument?

    A work of worth, worthy the noting too!
    But what's the cause that you conceal'd me since?
*Lor.* Your melancholy, sister, since the news
    Of your first favourite Don Andrea's death,
    My father's old wrath hath exasperate.
*Bal.* And better was't for you, being in disgrace,
    To absent yourself, and give his fury place.
*Bel.* But why had I no notice of his ire?
*Lor.* That were to add more fuel to your fire,
    Who burnt like Ætna. for Andrea's loss.
*Bel.* Hath not my father then enquir'd for me?
*Lor.* Sister, he hath, and thus excus'd I thee.
                              [*He whispereth in her ear.*
    But, Bellimperia, see the gentle prince;
    Look on thy love, behold young Balthazar,
    Whose passions by thy presence are increas'd;
    And in whose melancholy thou may'st see
    Thy hate, his love; thy flight, his following thee.
*Bel.* Brother, you are become an orator—
    I know not, I, by what experience—
    Too politic for me, past all compare,
    Since last I saw you; but content yourself:
    The prince is meditating higher things.
*Bal.* 'Tis of thy beauty then that conquers kings;
    Of those thy tresses, Ariadne's twines,
    Wherewith my liberty thou hast surpris'd;
    Of that thine ivory front, my sorrow's map,
    Wherein I see no hav'n to rest my hope.
*Bel.* To love and fear, and both at once, my lord,
    In my conceit, are things of more import
    Than women's wits are to be busied with.
*Bal.* 'Tis I that love.
*Bel.*                    Whom?
*Bal.*                                    Bellimperia.
*Bel.* But I that fear.
*Bal.*                    Whom?
*Bel.*                                    Bellimperia.
*Lor.* Fear yourself?
*Bel.*                    Ay, brother.
*Lor.*                                        How?
*Bel.*                                                    As those

That, what they love, are loath and fear to lose.
*Bal.* Then, fair, let Balthazar your keeper be.
*Bel.* No, Balthazar doth fear as well as we:
   *Et tremulo metui pavidum junxere timorem—*
   *Est vanum stolidae proditionis opus.*
*Lor.* Nay, and you argue things so cunningly,
   We'll go continue this discourse at court
*Bal.* Led by the loadstar of her heav'nly looks,
   Wends poor, oppressèd Balthazar,
   As o'er the mountains walks the wanderer,
   Incertain to effect his pilgrimage.                    [*Exeunt.*


# SCENE XI

*Enter two Portingals, and Hieronimo meets them.*


1. By your leave, sir.
*Hier.* ['*Tis neither as you think, nor as you think,*
   *Nor as you think; you're wide all:*
   *These slippers are not mine, they were my son Horatio's.*
   *My son! and what's a son? A thing begot*
   *Within a pair of minutes—thereabout;*
   *A lump bred up in darkness, and doth serve*
   *To ballace these light creatures we call women;*
   *And, at nine months' end, creeps forth to light.*
   *What is there yet in a son,*
   *To make a father dote, rave, or run mad?*
   *Being born, it pouts, cries, and breeds teeth.*
   *What is there yet in a son? He must be fed,*
   *Be taught to go, and speak. Ay, or yet*
   *Why might not a man love a calf as well?*
   *Or melt in passion o'er a frisking kid,*
   *As for a son? Methinks, a young bacon,*
   *Or a fine little smooth horse colt,*
   *Should move a man as much as doth a son:*
   *For one of these, in very little time,*
   *Will grow to some good use; whereas a son,*
   *The more he grows in stature and in years,*
   *The more unsquar'd, unbevell'd, he appears,*
   *Reckons his parents among the rank of fools,*

*Strikes care upon their heads with his mad riots;*
*Makes them look old, before they meet with age.*
*This is a son!—And what a loss were this,*
*Consider'd truly?———O, but my Horatio*
*Grew out of reach of these insatiate humours:*
*He lov'd his loving parents;*
*He was my comfort, and his mother's joy,*
*The very arm that did hold up our house:*
*Our hopes were storèd up in him,*
*Hone but a damnèd murderer could hate him.*
*He had not seen the back of nineteen year,*
*When his strong arm unhors'd*
*The proud Prince Balthazar, and his great mind,*
*Too full of honour, took him to his mercy—*
*That valiant, but ignoble Portingal!*
*Well, heaven is heaven still!*
*And there is Nemesis, and Furies,*
*And things call'd whips,*
*And they sometimes do meet with murderers:*
*They do not always 'scape, that is some comfort.*
*Ay, ay, ay; and then time steals on,*
*And Steals, and steals, till violence leaps forth*
*Like thunder wrappèd in a ball of fire,*
*And so doth bring confusion to them all.*]
Good leave have you: nay, I pray you go,
For I'll leave you, if you can leave me so.
2. Pray you, which is the next way to my lord the duke's?
*Hier.* The next way from me.
1.                                    To his house, we mean.
*Hier.* O, hard by: 'tis yon house that you see.
2. You could not tell us if his son were there?
*Hier.* Who, my Lord Lorenzo?
1.                                    Ay, sir.
[*He goeth in at one door and comes out at another.*
*Hier.*                                    O, forbear!
For other talk for us far fitter were.
But if you be importunate to know
The way to him, and where to find him out,
Then list to me, and I'll resolve your doubt.
There is a path upon your left-hand side,
That leadeth from a guilty conscience

Unto a forest of distrust and fear—
A darksome place, and dangerous to pass:
There shall you meet with melancholy thoughts,
Whose baleful humours if you but uphold,
It will conduct you to Despair and Death—
Whose rocky cliffs when you have once beheld,
Within a hugy dale of lasting night,
That, kindled with the world's iniquities,
Doth cast up filthy and detested fumes—:
Not far from thence, where murderers have built
A habitation for their cursèd souls,
There, in a brazen cauldron, fix'd by Jove,
In his fell wrath, upon a sulphur flame,
Yourselves shall find Lorenzo bathing him
In boiling lead and blood of innocents.
1. Ha, ha, ha!
*Hier.* Ha, ha, ha! Why, ha, ha, ha! Farewell, good ha, ha, ha!

[*Exit.*

2. Doubtless this man is passing lunatic,
Or imperfection of his age doth make him dote.
Come, let's away to seek my lord the duke.

[*Exeunt.*

# SCENE XII

*Enter Hieronimo, with a poniard in one hand and a rope in the other.*

*Hier.* Now, sir, perhaps I come and see the king;
The king sees me, and fain would hear my suit:
Why, is not this a strange and seld-seen thing,
That standers-by with toys should strike me mute?—
Go to, I see their shifts, and say no more.—
Hieronimo, 'tis time for thee to trudge:
Down by the dale that flows with purple gore,
Standeth a fiery tower; there sits a judge
Upon a seat of steel and molten brass,
And 'twixt his teeth he holds a fire-brand,
That leads unto the lake where hell doth stand
Away, Hieronimo! to him be gone:
He'll do thee justice for Horatio's death.

Turn down this path: thou shalt be with him straight;
Or this, and then thou need'st not take thy breath:
This way or that way!——Soft and fair, not so:
For if I hang or kill myself, let's know
Who will revenge Horatio's murther then?
No, no! fie, no! pardon me, I'll none of that.
                    [*He flings away the dagger and halter.*
This way I'll take, and this way comes the king:
                    [*He takes them up again.*
And here I'll have a fling at him, that's flat;
And, Balthazar, I'll be with thee to bring,
And thee, Lorenzo! Here's the king—nay, stay;
And here, ay here—there goes the hare away.

          *Enter King, Ambassador, Castile, and Lorenzo.*

*King.* Now show, ambassador, what our viceroy saith:
    Hath he receiv'd the articles we sent?
*Hier.* Justice, O, justice to Hieronimo.
*Lor.* Back! see'st thou not the king is busy?
*Hier.*                                        O, is he so?
*King.* Who is he that interrupts our business?
*Hier.* Not I. Hieronimo, beware! go by, go by!
*Amb.* Renownèd King, he hath receiv'd and read
    Thy kingly proffers, and thy promis'd league;
    And, as a man extremely over-joy'd
    To hear his son so princely entertain'd,
    Whose death he had so solemnly bewail'd,
    This for thy further satisfaction,
    And kingly love, he kindly lets thee know:
    First, for the marriage of his princely son
    With Bellimperia, thy belovèd niece,
    The news are more delightful to his soul,
    Than myrrh or incense to the offended heavens.
    In person, therefore, will he come himself,
    To see the marriage rites solemnizèd,
    And, in the presence of the court of Spain,
    To knit a sure inextricable band
    Of kingly love and everlasting league
    Betwixt the crowns of Spain and Portingal.
    There will he give his crown to Balthazar,
    And make a queen of Bellimperia.

*King.* Brother, how like you this our viceroy's love?
*Cast.* No doubt, my lord, it is an argument
   Of honourable care to keep his friend,
   And wondrous zeal to Balthazar his son;
   Nor am I least indebted to his grace,
   That bends his liking to my daughter thus.
*Amb.* Now last, dread lord, here hath his highness sent
   (Although he send not that his son return)
   His ransom due to Don Horatio.
*Hier.* Horatio! who calls Horatio?
*King.* And well remember'd: thank his majesty.
   Here, see it given to Horatio.
*Hier.* Justice, O, justice, justice, gentle king!
*King.* Who is that? Hieronimo?
*Hier.* Justice, O, justice! O my son, my son!
   My son, whom naught can ransom or redeem!
*Lor.* Hieronimo, you are not well-advis'd.
*Hier.* Away, Lorenzo, hinder me no more;
   For thou hast made me bankrupt of my bliss.
   Give me my son! you shall not ransom him!
   Away! I'll rip the bowels of the earth,
                              [*He diggeth with his dagger.*
   And ferry over to th' Elysian plains,
   And bring my son to show his deadly wounds.
   Stand from about me!
   I'll make a pickaxe of my poniard,
   And here surrender up my marshalship;
   For I'll go marshal up the fiends in hell,
   To be avengèd on you all for this.
*King.* What means this outrage?
   Will none of you restrain his fury?
*Hier.* Nay, soft and fair! you shall not need to strive:
   For needs must he go that the devils drive.
                              [*Exit.*
*King.* What accident hath happ'd Hieronimo?
   I have not seen him to demean him so.
*Lor.* My gracious lord, he is with extreme pride,
   Conceiv'd of young Horatio his son—
   And covetous of having to himself
   The ransom of the young prince Balthazar—
   Distract, and in a manner lunatic.

*King.* Believe me, nephew, we are sorry for't:
　　This is the love that fathers bear their sons.
　　But, gentle brother, go give to him this gold,
　　The prince's ransom; let him have his due.
　　For what he hath, Horatio shall not want;
　　Haply Hieronimo hath need thereof.
*Lor.* But if he be thus helplessly distract,
　　'Tis requisite his office be resign'd,
　　And giv'n to one of more discretion.
*King.* We shall increase his melancholy so.
　　'Tis best that we see further in it first,
　　Till when ourself will hold exempt the place.
　　And, brother, now bring in the ambassador,
　　That he may be a witness of the match
　　'Twixt Balthazar and Bellimperia,
　　And that we may prefix a certain time,
　　Wherein the marriage shall be solemniz'd,
　　That we may have thy lord, the viceroy, here.
*Amb.* Therein your highness highly shall content
　　His majesty, that longs to hear from hence.
*King.* On, then, and hear you, lord ambassador—

　　　　　　　　　　　　　　　　　　　　[*Exeunt.*

# SCENE XIIA.

## Enter Jaques and Pedro.

*Jaq. I wonder, Pedro, why our master thus
　　At midnight sends us with our torches light,
　　When man, and bird, and beast, are all at rest,
　　Save those that watch for rape and bloody murder.*
*Ped. O Jaques, know thou that our master's mind
　　Is much distraught, since his Horatio died,
　　And—now his agèd years should sleep in rest,
　　His heart in quiet—like a desp'rate man,
　　Crows lunatic and childish for his son.
　　Sometimes, as he doth at his table sit,
　　He speaks as if Horatio stood by him;
　　Then starting in a rage, falls on the earth,*

*Cries out "Horatio, where is my Horatio?"*
*So that with extreme grief and cutting sorrow*
*There is not left in him one inch of man:*
*See, where he comes.*

Enter Hieronimo.

Hier. *I pry through every crevice of each wall,*
   *Look on each tree, and search through every brake,*
   *Beat at the bushes, stamp our grandam earth,*
   *Dive in the water, and stare up to heaven:*
   *Yet cannot I behold my son Horatio.—*
   *How now, who's there? spirits, spirits?*
Ped. *We are your servants that attend you, sir.*
Hier. *What make you with your torches in the dark?*
Ped. *You bid us light them, and attend you here.*
Hier. *No, no, you are deceiv'd! not I;—you are deceiv'd!*
   *Was I so mad to bid you light your torches now?*
   *Light me your torches at the mid of noon,*
   *When-as the sun-god rides in all his glory;*
   *Light me your torches then.*
Ped.                                    *Then we burn daylight.*
Hier. *Let it be burnt; Night is a murd'rous slut,*
   *That would not have her treasons to be seen;*
   *And yonder pale-fac'd Hecate there, the moon,*
   *Doth give consent to that is done in darkness;*
   *And all those stars that gaze upon her face,*
   *Are aglets on her sleeve, pins on her train;*
   *And those that should be powerful and divine,*
   *Do sleep in darkness, when they most should shine.*
Ped. *Provoke them not, fair sir, with tempting words:*
   *The heav'ns are gracious, and your miseries*
   *And sorrow makes you speak, you know not what.*
Hier. *Villain, thou liest! and thou dost nought*
   *But tell me I am mad: thou liest, I am not mad!*
   *I'll know thee to be Pedro, and he Jaques.*
   *I'll prove it to thee; and were I mad, how could I?*
   *Where was she that same night,*
   *When my Horatio was murder'd?*
   *She should have shone: search thou the book.—Had the moon shone,*
   *In my boy's face there was a kind of grace,*

That I know—nay, I do know—had the murd'rer seen him,
His weapon would have fall'n and cut the earth,
Had he been fram'd of naught but blood and death.
Alack! when mischief doth it knows not what,
What shall we say to mischief?

                    Enter Isabella.

Isab. *Dear Hieronimo, come in a-doors;*
   *O, seek not means so to increase thy sorrow.*
Hier. *Indeed, Isabella, we do nothing here;*
   *I do not cry: ask Pedro, and ask Jaques;*
   *Not I indeed; we are very merry, very merry.*
Isab. *How? be merry here, be merry here?*
   *Is not this the place, and this the very tree,*
   *Where my Horatio died, where he was murder'd?*
Hier. *Was—do not say what: let her weep it out.*
   *This was the tree; I set it of a kernel:*
   *And when our hot Spain could not let it grow,*
   *But that the infant and the human sap*
   *Began to wither, duly twice a morning*
   *Would I be sprinkling it with fountain-water.*
   *At last it grew and grew, and bore and bore,*
   *Till at the length*
   *It grew a gallows, and did bear our son:*
   *It bore thy fruit and mine—O wicked, wicked plant!*
                              [One knocks within at the door.
   *See, who knock there.*
Ped.                    *It is a painter, sir.*
Hier. *Bid him come in, and paint some comfort,*
   *For surely there's none lives but painted comfort.*
   *Let him come in!—One knows not what may chance:*
   *God's will that I should set this tree!—but even so*
   *Masters ungrateful servants rear from nought,*
   *And then they hate them that did bring them up.*

                  Enter the Painter.

Paint. *God bless you, sir.*
Hier. *Wherefore? why, thou scornful villain?*
   *How, where, or by what means should I be bless'd?*
Isab. *What wouldst thou have, good fellow?*

Paint.                                   *Justice, madam.*

Hier. *O ambitious beggar!*
  *Wouldst thou have that that lives not in the world?*
  *Why, all the undelved mines cannot buy*
  *An ounce of justice!*
  *'Tis a jewel so inestimable. I tell thee,*
  *God hath engross'd all justice in his hands,*
  *And there is none but what comes from him.*

Paint.                          *O, then I see*
  *That God must right me for my murder'd son.*

Hier. *How, was thy son murder'd?*

Paint *Ay, sir; no man did hold a son so dear.*

Hier. *What, not as thine? that's a lie,*
  *As massy as the earth: I had a son,*
  *Whose least unvalu'd hair did weigh*
  *A thousand of thy sons: and he was murder'd.*

  Paint *Alas, sir, I had no more but he.*

Hier. *Nor I, nor I: but this same one of mine*
  *Was worth a legion. But all is one.*
  *Pedro, Jaques, go in a-doors; Isabella, go,*
  *And this good fellow here and I*
  *Will range this hideous orchard up and down,*
  *Like to two lions reavèd of their young.*
  *Go in a-doors, I say.*

            [Exeunt. The painter and he sits down.
                    *Come, let's talk wisely now.*

  *Was thy son murder'd?*

Paint.                     *Ay, sir.*

Hier.                              *So was mine.*
  *How dost take it? art thou not sometimes mad?*
  *Is there no tricks that comes before thine eyes?*

Paint. *O Lord, yes, sir.*

Hier. *Art a painter? canst paint me a tear, or a wound, a groan, or a*
  *sigh? canst paint me such a tree as this?*

Paint. *Sir, I am sure you have heard of my painting: my name's Bazardo.*

Hier. *Bazardo! afore God, an excellent fellow. Look you, sir, do you*
  *see, I'd have you paint me for my gallery, in your oil-colours matted,*
  *and draw me five years younger than I am—do ye see, sir, let five*
  *years go; let them go like the marshal of Spain—my wife Isabella*
  *standing by me, with a speaking look to my son Horatio, which should*

intend to this or some such-like purpose: "God bless thee, my sweet
son"; and my hand leaning upon his head, thus, sir; do you see?—
may it be done?

Paint. _Very welly sir._

Hier. _Nay, I pray, mark me, sir: then, sir, would I have you paint me
this tree, this very tree. Canst paint a doleful cry?_

Paint. _Seemingly, sir._

Hier. _Nay, it should cry; but all is one. Well, sir, paint me a youth
run through and through with villain's swords, hanging upon this tree.
Canst thou draw a murderer?_

Paint. _I'll warrant you, sir; I have the pattern of the most notorious
villains that ever lived in all Spain._

Hier. _Oy let them be worse, worse: stretch thine art, and let their beards
be of Judas his own colour; and let their eye-brows jutty over; in any
case observe that. Then, sir, after some violent noise, bring me forth
in my shirt, and my gown under mine arm, with my torch in my
hand, and my sword reared up thus:—and with these words:_

"What noise is this? who calls Hitronimo?"

_May it be done?_

Paint. _Yea, sir._

Hier. _Well, sir; then bring me forth, bring me through alley and alley,
still with a distracted countenance going along, and let my hair heave
up my nightcap. Let the clouds scowl, make the moon dark, the stars
extinct, the winds blowing, the bells tolling, the owls shrieking, the
toads croaking, the minutes jarring, and the clock striking twelve. And
then at last, sir, starting, behold a man hanging, and tottering and
tottering, as you know the wind will wave a man, and I with a trice
to cut him down. And looking upon him by the advantage of my
torch, find it to be my son Horatio. There you may show a passion,
there you may show a passion! Draw me like old Priam of Troy,
crying: "The house is a-fire, the house is a-fire, as the torch over my
head!' Make me curse, make me rave, make me cry, make me mad,
make me well again, make me curse hell, invocate heaven, and in the
end leave me in a trance—and so forth._

Paint. _And is this the end?_

Hier. _O no, there is no end: the end is death and madness! As I am
never better than when I am mad: then methinks I am a brave fellow;
then I do wonders: but reason abuseth me, and, there's the torment,
there's the hell. At the last, sir, bring me to one of the murderers; were
he as strong as Hector, thus would I tear and drag him up and down._

[*He beats the painter in, then comes out again,
with a book in his hand.*

# SCENE XIII

*Enter Hieronimo, with a book in his hand.*

*Vindicta mihi!*
Ay, heav'n will be reveng'd of every ill;
Nor will they suffer murder unrepaid.
Then stay, Hieronimo, attend their will:
For mortal men may not appoint their time!—
*"Per scelus semper tutum est sceleribus iter."*
Strike, and strike home, where wrong is offer'd thee;
For evils unto ills conductors be,
And death's the worst of resolution.
For he that thinks with patience to contend
To quiet life, his life shall easily end.—
*"Fata si miseros juvant, habes salutem;
Fata si vitam negant, habes sepulchrum"*:
If destiny thy miseries do ease,
Then hast thou health, and happy shalt thou be;
If destiny deny thee life, Hieronimo,
Yet shalt thou be assurèd of a tomb——:
If neither, yet let this thy comfort be:
Heav'n cov'reth him that hath no burial.
And to conclude, I will revenge his death!
But how? not as the vulgar wits of men,
With open, but inevitable ills,
As by a secret, yet a certain mean,
Which under kindship will be cloakèd best.
Wise men will take their opportunity
Closely and safely, fitting things to time.—
But in extremes advantage hath no time;
And therefore all times fit not for revenge.
Thus therefore will I rest me in unrest,
Dissembling quiet in unquietness,
Not seeming that I know their villanies,
That my simplicity may make them think.
That ignorantly I will let all slip;

For ignorance, I wot, and well they know,
*Remedium malorum iners est.*
Nor ought avails it me to menace them
Who, as a wintry storm upon a plain,
Will bear me down with their nobility.
No, no, Hieronimo, thou must enjoin
Thine eyes to observation, and thy tongue
To milder speeches than thy spirit affords,
Thy heart to patience, and thy hands to rest.
Thy cap to courtesy, and thy knee to bow,
Till to revenge thou know, when, where and how.

            [*A noise within.*

How now, what noise? what coil is that you keep?

*Enter a Servant.*

*Serv.* Here are a sort of poor petitioners,
 That are importunate, and it shall please you, sir,
 That you should plead their cases to the king.
*Hier.* That I should plead their several actions?
 Why, let them enter, and let me see them.

*Enter three Citizens and an Old Man.*

1.              So,
I tell you this: for learning and for law,
There is not any advocate in Spain
That can prevail, or will take half the pain
That he will, in pursuit of equity.
*Hier.* Come near, you men, that thus importune me.—
 [*Aside.*] Now must I bear a face of gravity;
 For thus I us'd, before my marshalship,
 To plead in causes as corregidor.—
 Come on, sirs, what's the matter?
2.           Sir, an action,
*Hier.* Of battery?
1.      Mine of debt
*Hier.*          Give place.
 2. No, sir, mine is an action of the case.
 3. Mine an *ejectione firmae* by a lease.
*Hier.* Content you, sirs; are you determinèd
 That I should plead your several actions?
 1. Ay, sir, and here's my declaration.

2. And here's my band.

3.                              And here's my lease.

[*They give him papers.*

*Hier.* But wherefore stands yon silly man so mute,
   With mournful eyes and hands to heav'n uprear'd?
   Come hither, father, let me know thy cause.

*Senex.* O worthy sir, my cause, but slightly known,
   May move the hearts of warlike Myrmidons,
   And melt the Corsic rocks with ruthful tears.

*Hier.* Say, father, tell me what's thy suit?

*Senex.*                           No, sir, could my woes
   Give way unto my most distressful words,
   Then should I not in paper, as you see,
   With ink bewray what blood began in me.

*Hier.* What's here? 'The humble supplication
   Of Don Bazulto for his murder'd son.'

*Senex.* Ay, sir.

*Hier.*            No, sir, it was my murder'd son:
   O my son, my son, O my son Horatio!
   But mine, or thine, Bazulto, be content.
   Here, take my handkercher, and wipe thine eyes,
   Whiles wretched I in thy mishaps may see
   The lively portrait of my dying self.

[*He draweth out a bloody napkin.*

   O no, not this; Horatio, this was thine;
   And when I dy'd it in thy dearest blood,
   This was a token 'twixt thy soul and me,
   That of thy death revengèd I should be.
   But here, take this, and this—what, my purse?—
   Ay, this, and that, and all of them are thine;
   For all as one are our extremities.

1. O, see the kindness of Hieronimo!

2. This gentleness shows him a gentleman.

*Hier.* See, see, O see thy shame, Hieronimo;
   See here a loving father to his son!
   Behold the sorrows and the sad laments,
   That he deliv'reth for his son's decease!
   If love's effects so strive in lesser things,
   If love enforce such moods in meaner wits,
   If love express such power in poor estates:
   Hieronimo, when as a raging sea,

Toss'd with the wind and tide, o'erturnest then
The upper billows course of waves to keep,
Whilst lesser waters labour in the deep:
Then sham'st thou not, Hieronimo, to neglect
The sweet revenge of thy Horatio?
Though on this earth justice will not be found,
I'll down to hell, and in this passion
Knock at the dismal gates of Pluto's court,
Getting by force, as once Alcides did,
A troop of Furies and tormenting hags
To torture Don Lorenzo and the rest.
Yet lest the triple-headed porter should
Deny my passage to the slimy strand,
The Thracian poet thou shalt counterfeit:
Come on, old father, be my Orpheus,
And if thou canst no notes upon the harp,
Then sound the burden of thy sore heart's-grief,
Till we do gain that Proserpine may grant
Revenge on them that murderèd my son.
Then will I rent and tear them, thus and thus,
Shiv'ring their limbs in pieces with my teeth.

                                *[Tears the papers.*

1. O sir, my declaration!

                         *[Exit Hieronimo, and they after.*
2.                                Save my bond!

               *Enter Hieronimo.*

2. Save my bond!
3. Alas, my lease! it cost me ten pound,
And you my lord, have torn the same.
*Hier.* That cannot be, I gave it never a wound;
Show me one drop of blood fall from the same:
How is it possible I should slay it then?
Tush, no; run after, catch me if you can.

          *[Exeunt all but the Old Man. Bazulto remains till*
               *Hieronimo enters again, who, staring him in*
               *the face, speaks.*
*Hier.* And art thou come, Horatio, from the depth,
   To ask for justice in this upper earth,
   To tell thy father thou art unreveng'd,

To wring more tears from Isabella's eyes,
Whose lights are dimm'd with over-long laments?
Go back, my son, complain to Aeacus,
For here's no justice; gentle boy, be gone,
For justice is exilèd from the earth:
Hieronimo will bear thee company.
Thy mother cries on righteous Rhadamanth
For just revenge against the murderers.

*Senex.* Alas, my lord, whence springs this troubled speech?

*Hier.* But let me look on my Horatio.
Sweet boy, how art thou chang'd in death's black shade!
Had Proserpine no pity on thy youth,
But suffer'd thy fair crimson-colour'd spring
With wither'd winter to be blasted thus?
Horatio, thou art older than thy father:
Ah, ruthless fate, that favour thus transforms!

*Baz.* Ah, my good lord, I am not your young son.

*Hier.* What, not my son? thou then a Fury art,
Sent from the empty kingdom of black night
To summon me to make appearance
Before grim Minos and just Rhadamanth,
To plague Hieronimo that is remiss,
And seeks not vengeance for Horatio's death.

*Baz.* I am a grievèd man, and not a ghost,
That came for justice for my murder'd son.

*Hier.* Ay, now I know thee, now thou nam'st thy son:
Thou art the lively image of my grief;
Within thy face, my sorrows I may see.
Thy eyes are gumm'd with tears, thy cheeks are wan,
Thy forehead troubled, and thy mutt'ring lips
Murmur sad words abruptly broken off;
By force of windy sighs thy spirit breathes,
And all this sorrow riseth for thy son:
And selfsame sorrow feel I for my son.
Come in, old man, thou shalt to Isabel;
Lean on my arm: I thee, thou me, shalt stay,
And thou, and I, and she will sing a song,
Three parts in one, but all of discords fram'd—:
Talk not of chords, but let us now be gone,
For with a cord Horatio was slain.                    [*Exeunt.*

## SCENE XIV

*Enter King of Spain, the Duke, Viceroy, and Lorenzo, Balthazar,*
*Don Pedro, and Bellimperia.*

*King.* Go, brother, 'tis the Duke of Castile's cause;
    Salute the Viceroy in our name.
*Cast.*                               I go.
*Vic.* Go forth, Don Pedro, for thy nephew's sake,
    And greet the Duke of Castile.
*Ped.*                      It shall be so.
*King.* And now to meet these Portuguese:
    For as we now are, so sometimes were these,
    Kings and commanders of the western Indies.
    Welcome, brave Viceroy, to the court of Spain,
    And welcome all his honourable train!
    'Tis not unknown to us for why you come,
    Or have so kingly cross'd the seas:
    Sufficeth it, in this we note the troth
    And more than common love you lend to us.
    So is it that mine honourable niece
    (For it beseems us now that it be known)
    Already is betroth'd to Balthazar:
    And by appointment and our condescent
    To-morrow are they to be marrièd.
    To this intent we entertain thyself,
    Thy followers, their pleasure, and our peace.
    Speak, men of Portingal, shall it be so?
    If ay, say so; if not, say flatly no.
*Vic.* Renowmèd King, I come not, as thou think'st,
    With doubtful followers, unresolvèd men,
    But such as have upon thine articles
    Confirm'd thy motion, and contented me.
    Know, sovereign, I come to solemnize
    The marriàge of thy belovèd niece,
    Fair Bellimperia, with my Balthazar,
    With thee, my son; whom sith I live to see,
    Here take my crown, I give it her and thee;
    And let me live a solitary life,
    In ceaseless prayers,
    To think how strangely heav'n hath thee preserv'd.
*King.* See, brother, see, how nature strives in him!

Come, worthy Viceroy, and accompany
Thy friend with thine extremities:
A place more private fits this princely mood.
*Vic.* Or here, or where your highness thinks it good.
                    [*Exeunt all but Castile and Lorenzo.*

# SCENE XV

*Castile, Lorenzo.*

*Cast.* Nay, stay, Lorenzo, let me talk with you.
    See'st thou this entertainment of these kings?
*Lor.* I do, my lord, and joy to see the same.
*Cast.* And know'st thou why this meeting is?
*Lor.* For her, my lord, whom Balthazar doth love,
    And to confirm their promis'd marriàge.
*Cast.* She is thy sister?
*Lor.*                          Who, Bellimperia? ay,
    My gracious lord, and this is the day,
    That I have long'd so happily to see.
*Cast* Thou wouldst be loath that any fault of thine
    Should intercept her in her happiness?
*Lor.* Heav'ns will not let Lorenzo err so much.
*Cast.* Why then, Lorenzo, listen to my words:
    It is suspected, and reported too,
    That thou, Lorenzo, wrong'st Hieronimo,
    And in his suits towards his majesty
    Still keep'st him back, and seek'st to cross his suit.
*Lor.* That I, my lord——?
*Cast.* I tell thee, son, myself have heard it said,
    When (to my sorrow) I have been asham'd
    To answer for thee, though thou art my son.
    Lorenzo, know'st thou hot the common love
    And kindness that Hieronimo hath won
    By his deserts within the court of Spain?
    Or see'st thou not the king my brother's care
    In his behalf, and to procure his health?
    Lorenzo, shouldst thou thwart his passions,
    And he exclaim against thee to the king,
    What honour were 't in this assembly,
    Or what a scandal were 't among the kings

To hear Hieronimo exclaim on thee?
Tell me—and look thou tell me truly too—
Whence grows the ground of this report in court?

*Lor.* My lord, it lies not in Lorenzo's power
To stop the vulgar, liberal of their tongues:
A small advantage makes a water-breach,
And no man lives that long contenteth all.

*Cast.* Myself have seen thee busy to keep back
Him and his supplications from the king.

*Lor.* Yourself, my lord, hath seen his passions,
That ill beseem'd the presence of a king;
And for I pitied him in his distress,
I held him thence with kind and courteous words,
As free from malice to Hieronimo
As to my soul, my lord.

*Cast.* Hieronimo, my son, mistakes thee then.

*Lor.* My gracious father, believe me, so he doth.
But what's a silly man, distract in mind
To think upon the murder of his son?
Alas! how easy is it for him to err!
But for his satisfaction and the world's,
'Twere good, my lord, that Hieronimo and I
Were reconcil'd, if he misconster me.

*Cast.* Lorenzo, thou hast said; it shall be so.
Go one of you, and call Hieronimo.

*Enter Balthazar and Bellimperia.*

*Bal.* Come, Bellimperia, Balthazar's content,
My sorrow's ease and sovereign of my bliss,
Sith heaven hath ordain'd thee to be mine:
Disperse those clouds and melancholy looks,
And clear them up with those thy sun-bright eyes,
Wherein my hope and heaven's fair beauty lies.

*Bel.* My looks, my lord, are fitting for my love,
Which, new-begun, can show no brighter yet

*Bal.* New-kindled flames should burn as morning sun.

*Bel.* But not too fast, lest heat and all be done.
I see my lord my father.

*Bal.*                Truce, my love;
I'll go salute him.

*Cast.*                    Welcome, Balthazar,
  Welcome, brave prince, the pledge of Castile's peace!
  And welcome, Bellimperia!—How now, girl?
  Why com'st thou sadly to salute us thus?
  Content thyself, for I am satisfied:
  It is not now as when Andrea liv'd;
  We have forgotten and forgiven that,
  And thou art gracèd with a happier love.—
  But, Balthazar, here comes Hieronimo;
  I'll have a word with him.

                *Enter Hieronimo and a Servant.*

*Hier.* And where's the duke?
*Serv.*                    Yonder.
*Hier.*                    Ev'n so.—
  What new device have they devisèd, trow?
  *Pocas palabras!* mild as the lamb!
  Is't I will be reveng'd? No, I am not the man.—
*Cast.* Welcome, Hieronimo.
*Lor.* Welcome, Hieronimo.
*Bal.* Welcome, Hieronimo.
*Hier.* My lords, I thank you for Horatio.
*Cast.* Hieronimo, the reason that I sent
  To speak with you, is this.
*Hier.*                    What, so short?
  Then I'll be gone, I thank you for 't.
*Cast.* Nay, stay, Hieronimo!—go call him, son.
*Lor.* Hieronimo, my father craves a word with you.
*Hier.* With me, sir? why, my lord, I thought you had done.
*Lor.* No; [*Aside*] would he had!
*Cast.*                    Hieronimo, I hear
  You find yourself aggrievèd at my son,
  Because you have not access unto the king;
  And say 'tis he that intercepts your suits.
*Hier.* Why, is not this a miserable thing, my lord?
*Cast.* Hieronimo, I hope you have no cause,
  And would be loath that one of your deserts
  Should once have reason to suspect my son,
  Consid'ring how I think of you myself.
*Hier.* Your son Lorenzo! whom, my noble lord?

The hope of Spain, mine honourable friend?
Grant me the combat of them, if they dare:
                              [*Draws out his sword.*
I'll meet him face to face, to tell me so!
These be the scandalous reports of such
As love not me, and hate my lord too much:
Should I suspect Lorenzo would prevent
Or cross my suit, that lov'd my son so well?
My lord, I am asham'd it should be said.
*Lor.* Hieronimo, I never gave you cause.
*Hier.* My good lord, I know you did not.
*Cast.*                              There then pause;
And for the satisfaction of the world,
Hieronimo, frequent my homely house,
The Duke of Castile, Cyprian's ancient seat;
And when thou wilt, use me, my son, and it:
But here, before Prince Balthazar and me,
Embrace each other, and be perfect friends.
*Hier.* Ay, marry, my lord, and shall.
Friends, quoth he? see, I'll be friends with you all:
Especially with you, my lovely lord;
For divers causes it is fit for us
That we be friends: the world's suspicious,
And men may think what we imagine not
*Bal.* Why, this is friendly done, Hieronimo.
*Lor.* And that I hope: old grudges are forgot?
*Hier.* What else? it were a shame it should not be so.
*Cast.* Come on, Hieronimo, at my request;
Let us entreat your company to-day.          [*Exeunt.*
*Hier.* Your lordship's to command.—Pah! keep your way:
  *Chi mi fa più carezze che non suole,*
  *Tradito mi ha, o tradir mi vuole.*          [*Exit.*


# SCENE XVI

*Enter Ghost and Revenge.*


*Ghost.* Awake, Erichtho! Cerberus, awake!
  Solicit Pluto, gentle Proserpine!
  To combat, Acheron and Erebus!

For ne'er, by Styx and Phlegethon in hell,
O'er-ferried Charon to the fiery lakes
Such fearful sights, as poor Andrea sees.
Revenge, awake!

*Revenge.*               Awake? for why?
*Ghost.* Awake, Revenge; for thou art ill-advis'd
To sleep—awake! what, thou art warn'd to watch!
*Revenge.* Content thyself, and do not trouble me.
*Ghost.* Awake, Revenge, if love—as love hath had—
Have yet the power or prevalence in hell!
Hieronimo with Lorenzo is join'd in league,
And intercepts our passage to revenge:
Awake, Revenge, or we are woe-begone!
*Revenge.* Thus worldlings ground, what they have dream'd, upon.
Content thyself, Andrea: though I sleep,
Yet is my mood soliciting their souls.
Sufficeth thee that poor Hieronimo
Cannot forget his son Horatio.
Nor dies Revenge, although he sleep awhile;
For in unquiet quietness is feign'd,
And slumb'ring is a common worldly wile.—
Behold, Andrea, for an instance, how
Revenge hath slept, and then imagine thou,
What 'tis to be subject to destiny.

*Enter a Dumb-Show.*

*Ghost.* Awake, Revenge; reveal this mystery.
*Revenge.* Lo! the two first the nuptial torches bore
As brightly burning as the mid-day's sun;
But after them doth Hymen hie as fast,
Clothèd in sable and a saffron robe,
And blows them out, and quencheth them with blood,
As discontent that things continue so.
*Ghost.* Sufficeth me; thy meaning's understood,
And thanks to thee and those infernal powers,
That will not tolerate a lover's woe.—
Rest thee, for I will sit to see the rest.
*Revenge.* Then argue not, for thou hast thy request
                                        [*Exeunt.*

# ACT IV

## SCENE I

*Enter Bellimperia and Hieronimo.*

*Bel.* Is this the love thou bear'st Horatio?
    Is this the kindness that thou counterfeit'st?
    Are these the fruits of thine incessant tears?
    Hieronimo, are these thy passions,
    Thy protestations and thy deep laments,
    That thou wert wont to weary men withal?
    O unkind father! O deceitful world!
    With what excuses canst thou show thyself
    From this dishonour and the hate of men?
    Thus to neglect the loss and life of him
    Whom both my letters and thine own belief
    Assures thee to be causeless slaughterèd!
    Hieronimo, for shame, Hieronimo,
    Be not a history to after-times
    Of such ingratitude unto thy son:
    Unhappy mothers of such children then,
    But monstrous fathers to forget so soon
    The death of those, whom they with care and cost
    Have tender'd so, thus careless should be lost.
    Myself, a stranger in respect of thee,
    So lov'd his life, as still I wish their deaths.
    Nor shall his death be unreveng'd by me,
    Although I bear it out for fashion's sake:
    For here I swear, in sight of heav'n and earth,
    Shouldst thou neglect the love thou shouldst retain,

74

And give it over, and devise no more,
Myself should send their hateful souls to hell,
That wrought his downfall with extremest death.

*Hier.* But may it be that Bellimperia
Vows such revenge as she hath deign'd to say?
Why, then I see that heav'n applies our drift,
And all the saints do sit soliciting
For vengeance on those cursèd murtherers.
Madam, 'tis true, and now I find it so:
I found a letter, written in your name,
And in that letter, how Horatio died.
Pardon, O pardon, Bellimperia,
My fear and care in not believing it;
Nor think I thoughtless think upon a mean
To let his death be unreveng'd at full.
And here I vow—so you but give consent,
And will conceal my resolution—:
I will ere long determine of their deaths
That causeless thus have murderèd my son.

*Bel.* Hieronimo, I will consent, conceal,
And ought that may effect for thine avail,
Join with thee to revenge Horatio's death.

*Hier.* On, then; and whatsoever I devise,
Let me entreat you, grace my practices,
For why the plot's already in mine head.
Here they are.

*Enter Balthazar and Lorenzo.*

*Bal.*                    How now, Hieronimo?
What, courting Bellimperia?

*Hier.*                    Ay, my lord;
Such courting as (I promise you):
She hath my heart, but you, my lord, have hers.

*Lor.* But now, Hieronimo, or never,
We are to entreat your help.

*Hier.*                    My help?
Why, my good lords, assure yourselves of me;
For you have giv'n me cause—:
Ay, by my faith have you!

*Bal.*                    It pleased you,

At the entertainment of the ambassador,
To grace the king so much as with a show.
Now, were your study so well furnishèd,
As for the passing of the first night's sport
To entertain my father with the like,
Or any such-like pleasing motion,
Assure yourself, it would content them well.

*Hier.* Is this all?

*Bal.*                    Ay, this is all.

*Hier.* Why then, I'll fit you; say no more.
When I was young, I gave my mind
And plied myself to fruitless poetry;
Which though it profit the professor naught,
Yet is it passing pleasing to the world

*Lor.* And how for that?

*Hier.*                    Marry, my good lord, thus:
(And yet, methinks, you are too quick with us)—:
When in Toledo there I studièd,
It was my chance to write a tragedy:
See here, my lords—                    [*He shows them a book.*
Which, long forgot, I found this other day.
Now would your lordships favour me so much
As but to grace me with your acting it—
I mean each one of you to play a part—
Assure you it will prove most passing strange,
And wondrous plausible to that assembly.

*Bal.* What, would you have us play a tragedy?

*Hier.* Why, Nero thought it no disparagement,
And kings and emperors have ta'en delight
To make experience of their wits in plays.

*Lor.* Nay, be not angry, good Hieronimo;
The prince but ask'd a question.

*Bal.* In faith, Hieronimo, and you be in earnest,
I'll make one.

*Lor.*            And I another.

*Hier.* Now, my good lord, could you entreat
Your sister Bellimperia to make one?
For what's a play without a woman in

*Bel.* Little entreaty shall serve me, Hieronimo;
For I must needs be employèd in your play.

*Hier.* Why, this is well: I tell you, lordings,

It was determinèd to have been acted,
By gentlemen and scholars too,
Such as could tell what to speak.
*Bal.*                                    And now
It shall be play'd by princes and courtiers,
Such as can tell how to speak:
If, as it is our country manner,
You will but let us know the argument.
*Hier.* That shall I roundly.    The chronicles of Spain
Record this written of a knight of Rhodes:
He was betroth'd, and wedded at the length,
To one Perseda, an Italian dame,
Whose beauty ravish'd all that her beheld,
Especially the soul of Soliman,
Who at the marriage was the chiefest guest.
By sundry means sought Soliman to win
Perseda's love, and could not gain the same.
Then 'gan he break his passions to a friend,
One of his bashaws, whom he held full dear;
Her had this bashaw long solicited,
And saw she was not otherwise to be won,
But by her husband's death, this knight of Rhodes,
Whom presently by treachery he slew.
She, stirr'd with an exceeding hate therefore,
As cause of this slew Soliman,
And, to escape the bashaw's tyranny,
Did stab herself: and this the tragedy.
*Lor.* O excellent!
*Bel.* But say, Hieronimo, what then became
Of him that was the bashaw?
*Hier.*                                    Marry, thus:
Mov'd with remorse of his misdeeds,
Ran to a mountain-top, and hung himself.
*Bal.* But which of us is to perform that part?
*Hier.* O, that will I, my lords; make no doubt of it:
I'll play the murderer, I warrant you;
For I already have conceited that
*Bal.* And what shall I?
*Hier.* Great Soliman, the Turkish emperor.
*Lor.* And I?
*Hier.*          Erastus, the knight of Rhodes.

*Bel.* And I?

*Hier.*       Perseda, chaste and resolute.—
  And here, my lords, are several abstracts drawn,
  For each of you to note your parts,
  And act it, as occasion's offer'd you.
  You must provide a Turkish cap,
  A black mustachio and a falchion;

                    [*Gives a paper to Balthazar.*

  You with a cross, like to a knight of Rhodes;

                    [*Gives another to Lorenzo.*

  And, madam, you must attire yourself

                    [*He giveth Bellimperia another.*

  Like Phœbe, Flora, or the hunteress,
  Which to your discretion shall seem best.
  And as for me, my lords, I'll look to one,
  And, with the ransom that the viceroy sent,
  So furnish and perform this tragedy,
  As all the world shall say, Hieronimo
  Was liberal in gracing of it so.

*Bal.* Hieronimo, methinks a comedy were better.

*Hier.* A comedy?
  Fie! comedies are fit for common wits:
  But to present a kingly troop withal,
  Give me a stately-written tragedy;
  *Tragœdia cothurnata,* fitting kings,
  Containing matter, and not common things.
  My lords, all this must be perform'd,
  As fitting for the first night's revelling.
  The Italian tragedians were so sharp of wit,
  That in one hour's meditation
  They would perform anything in action.

*Lor.* And well it may; for I have seen the like
  In Paris 'mongst the French tragedians.

*Hier.* In Paris? mass! and well rememberèd!
  There's one thing more that rests for us to do.

*Bal.* What's that, Hieronimo? forget not anything.

*Hier.* Each one of us
  Must act his part in unknown languages,
  That it may breed the more variety:
  As you, my lord, in Latin, I in Greek,
  You in Italian, and for because I know

That Bellimperia hath practised the French,
In courtly French shall all her phrases be.
*Bel.* You mean to try my cunning then, Hieronimo?
*Bal.* But this will be a mere confusion,
And hardly shall we all be understood.
*Hier.* It must be so; for the conclusion
Shall prove the invention and all was good:
And I myself in an oration,
And with a strange and wondrous show besides,
That I will have there behind a curtain,
Assure yourself, shall make the matter known:
And all shall be concluded in one scene,
For there's no pleasure ta'en in tediousness.
*Bal.* How like you this?
*Lor.*                              Why, thus my lord:
We must resolve to soothe his humours up.
*Bal.* On then, Hieronimo; farewell till soon.
*Hier.* You'll ply this gear?
*Lor.*                              I warrant you.

                                        [*Exeunt all but Hieronimo.*

*Hier.*                                    Why so:
Now shall I see the fall of Babylon,
Wrought by the heav'ns in this confusion.
And if the world like not this tragedy,
Hard is the hap of old Hieronimo.          [*Exit.*

# SCENE II

*Enter Isabella with a weapon.*

*Isab.* Tell me no more!—O monstrous homicides!
Since neither piety nor pity moves
The king to justice or compassion,
I will revenge myself upon this place,
Where thus they murder'd my belovèd son.

                                        [*She cuts down the arbour.*

Down with these branches and these loathsome boughs
Of this unfortunate and fatal pine:
Down with them, Isabella; rent them up,
And burn the roots from whence the rest is sprung.

I will not leave a root, a stalk, a tree,
A bough, a branch, a blossom, nor a leaf,
No, not an herb within this garden-plot—:
Accursèd complot of my misery!
Fruitless for ever may this garden be,
Barren the earth, and blissless whosoe'er
Imagines not to keep it unmanur'd!
An eastern wind, commix'd with noisome airs,
Shall blast the plants and the young saplings;
The earth with serpents shall be pesterèd,
And passengers, for fear to be infect,
Shall stand aloof, and, looking at it, tell:
"There, murder'd, died the son of Isabel."
Ay, here he died, and here I him embrace:
See, where his ghost solicits, with his wounds,
Revenge on her that should revenge his death.
Hieronimo, make haste to see thy son;
For sorrow and despair hath cited me
To hear Horatio plead with Rhadamanth:
Make haste, Hieronimo, to hold excus'd
Thy negligence in pursuit of their deaths
Whose hateful wrath bereav'd him of his breath.—
Ah, nay, thou dost delay their deaths,
Forgiv'st the murd'rers of thy noble son,
And none but I bestir me—to no end!
And as I curse this tree from further fruit,
So shall my womb be cursèd for his sake;
And with this weapon will I wound the breast,
The hapless breast, that gave Horatio suck.

                                              [*She stabs herself.*

# SCENE III

*Enter Hieronimo; he knocks up the curtain.*
*Enter the Duke of Castile.*

*Cast.* How now, Hieronimo, where 's your fellows,
    That you take all this pain?
*Hier.* O sir, it is for the author's credit,

To look that all things may go well.
But, good my lord, let me entreat your grace,
To give the king the copy of the play:
This is the argument of what we show.

*Cast.* I will, Hieronimo.

*Hier.* One thing more, my good lord.

*Cast.* What's that?

*Hier.* Let me entreat your grace
That, when the train are pass'd into the gallery,
You would vouchsafe to throw me down the key.

*Cast.* I will, Hieronimo.                    [*Exit Castile.*

*Hier.*                    What, are you ready, Balthazar?
Bring a chair and a cushion for the king.

*Enter Balthazar, with a chair.*

Well done, Balthazar! hang up the title:
Our scene is Rhodes;—what, is your beard on?

*Bal.* Half on; the other is in my hand.

*Hier.* Despatch for shame; are you so long?

[*Exit Balthazar.*

Bethink thyself, Hieronimo,
Recall thy wits, recount thy former wrongs
Thou hast receiv'd by murder of thy son,
And lastly—not least!—how Isabel,
Once his mother and thy dearest wife,
All woe-begone for him, hath slain herself.
Behoves thee then, Hieronimo, to be reveng'd!
The plot is laid of dire revenge:
On, then, Hieronimo, pursue revenge;
For nothing wants but acting of revenge!

[*Exit Hieronimo.*

## SCENE IV

*Enter Spanish King, Viceroy, the Duke of Castile,
and their train.*

*King.* Now, Viceroy, shall we see the tragedy
Of Soliman, the Turkish emperor,

Perform'd—of pleasure—by your son the prince,
My nephew Don Lorenzo, and my niece.
*Vic.* Who? Bellimperia?
*King.*                              Ay, and Hieronimo, our marshal,
At whose request they deign to do 't themselves:
These be our pastimes in the court of Spain.
Here, brother, you shall be the bookkeeper:
This is the argument of that they show.

                                        [*He giveth him a book.*
*Gentlemen, this play of Hieronimo, in sundry languages, was thought
good to be set down in English more largely, for the easier understanding to every public reader.*

            Enter Balthazar, Bellimperia, and Hieronimo.

*Bal. Bashaw, that Rhodes is ours, yield heav'ns the honour,
    And holy Mahomet, our sacred prophet!
    And be thou grac'd with every excellence
    That Soliman can give, or thou desire.
    But thy desert in conquering Rhodes is less
    Than in reserving this fair Christian nymph,
    Perseda, blissful lamp of excellence,
    Whose eyes compel, like powerful adamant,
    The warlike heart of Soliman to wait,*
*King.* See, Viceroy, that is Balthazar, your son,
    That represents the emperor Soliman:
    How well he acts his amorous passion!
*Vic.* Ay, Bellimperia hath taught him that
*Cast.* That's because his mind runs all on Bellimperia.
*Hier. Whatever joy earth yields, betide your majesty.*
*Bal. Earth yields no joy without Perseda's love.*
*Hier. Let then Perseda on your grace attend.*
*Bal. She shall not wait on me, but I on her:
    Drawn by the influence of her lights, I yield.
    But let my friend, the Rhodian knight, come forth,
    Erasto, dearer than my life to me,
    That he may see Perseda, my belov'd.*

                            *Enter Erasto.*

*King.* Here comes Lorenzo: look upon the plot,
    And tell me, brother, what part plays he?

Bel. *Ah, my Erasto, welcome to Perseda.*
Lor. *Thrice happy is Erasto that thou liv'st;*
  *Rhodes' loss is nothing to Erasto's joy:*
  *Sith his Perseda lives, his life survives.*
Bal. *Ah, bashaw, here is love between Erasto*
  *And fair Perseda, sovereign of my soul.*
Hier. *Remove Erasto, mighty Soliman,*
  *And then Perseda will be quickly won.*
Bal. *Erasto is my friend; and while he lives,*
  *Perseda never will remove her love.*
Hier. *Let not Erasto live to grieve great Soliman.*
Bal. *Dear is Erasto in our princely eye.*
Hier. *But if he be your rival, let him die.*
Bal. *Why, let him die!—so love commandeth me.*
  *Yet grieve I that Erasto should so die.*
Hier. *Erasto, Soliman saluteth thee,*
  *And lets thee wit by me his highness' will,*
  *Which is, thou shouldst be thus employ'd.*

[Stabs him.

Bel.                    *Ay me!*
  *Erasto! see, Soliman, Erasto's slain!*
Bal. *Yet liveth Soliman to comfort thee.*
  *Fair queen of beauty, let not favour die,*
  *But with a gracious eye behold his grief,*
  *That with Perseda's beauty is increas'd,*
  *If by Perseda his grief be not releas'd.*
Bel. *Tyrant, desist soliciting vain suits;*
  *Relentless are mine ears to thy laments,*
  *As thy butcher is pitiless and base,*
  *Which seiz'd on my Erasto, harmless knight.*
  *Yet by thy power thou thinkest to command,*
  *And to thy power Perseda doth obey:*
  *But, were she able, thus she would revenge*
  *Thy treacheries on thee, ignoble prince:*       [Stabs him.
  *And on herself she would be thus reveng'd.*

[Stabs herself.

*King.* Well said!—Old marshal, this was bravely done!
*Hier.* But Bellimperia plays Perseda well!
*Vic.* Were this in earnest, Bellimperia,
  You would be better to my son than so.

*King.* But now what follows for Hieronimo?
*Hier.* Marry, this follows for Hieronimo:
  Here break we off our sundry languages,
  And thus conclude I in our vulgar tongue.
  Haply you think—but bootless are your thoughts—
  That this is fabulously counterfeit,
  And that we do as all tragedians do:
  To die to-day (for fashioning our scene)
  The death of Ajax or some Roman peer,
  And in a minute starting up again,
  Revive to please to-morrow's audience.
  No, princes; know I am Hieronimo,
  The hopeless father of a hapless son,
  Whose tongue is tun'd to tell his latest tale,
  Not to excuse gross errors in the play.
  I see, your looks urge instance of these words;
  Behold the reason urging me to this:
                        [*Shows his dead son.*
  See here my show, look on this spectacle:
  Here lay my hope, and here my hope hath end;
  Here lay my heart, and here my heart was slain;
  Here lay my treasure, here my treasure lost;
  Here lay my bliss, and here my bliss bereft:
  But hope, heart, treasure, joy, and bliss,
  All fled, fail'd, died, yea, all decay'd with this.
  From forth these wounds came breath that gave me life;
  They murder'd me that made these fatal marks.
  The cause was love, whence grew this mortal hate;
  The hate: Lorenzo and young Balthazar;
  The love: my son to Bellimperia.
  But night, the cov'rer of accursèd crimes,
  With pitchy silence hush'd these traitors' harms,
  And lent them leave, for they had sorted leisure
  To take advantage in my garden-plot
  Upon my son, my dear Horatio:
  There merciless they butcher'd up my boy,
  In black, dark night, to pale, dim, cruel death.
  He shrieks: I heard (and yet, methinks, I hear)
  His dismal outcry echo in the air.
  With soonest speed I hasted to the noise,

Where hanging on a tree I found my son,
Through-girt with wounds, and slaughter'd as you see.
And griev'd I, think you, at this spectacle?
Speak, Portuguese, whose loss resembles mine:
If thou canst weep upon thy Balthazar,
'Tis like I wail'd for my Horatio.
And you, my lord, whose reconcilèd son
March'd in a net, and thought himself unseen,
And rated me for brainsick lunacy,
With "God amend that mad Hieronimo!"—
How can you brook our play's catastrophe?
And here behold this bloody hand-kercher,
Which at Horatio's death I weeping dipp'd
Within the river of his bleeding wounds:
It as propitious, see, I have reserv'd,
And never hath it left my bloody heart,
Soliciting remembrance of my vow
With these, O, these accursèd murderers:
Which now perform'd my heart is satisfied.
And to this end the bashaw I became
That might revenge me on Lorenzo's life,
Who therefore was appointed to the part,
And was to represent the knight of Rhodes,
That I might kill him more conveniently.
So, Viceroy, was this Balthazar, thy son,
That Soliman which Bellimperia,
In person of Perseda, murderèd:
Solely appointed to that tragic part
That she might slay him that offended her.
Poor Bellimperia miss'd her part in this:
For though the story saith she should have died,
Yet I of kindness, and of care to her,
Did otherwise determine of her end;
But love of him whom they did hate too much
Did urge her resolution to be such.—
And, princes, now behold Hieronimo,
Author and actor in this tragedy,
Bearing his latest fortune in his fist;
And will as resolute conclude his part,
As any of the actors gone before.

And, gentles, thus I end my play;
Urge no more words: I have no more to say.
                              [*He runs to hang himself.*
*King.* O hearken, Viceroy! Hold, Hieronimo!
Brother, my nephew and thy son are slain!
*Vic.* We are betray'd; my Balthazar is slain!
Break ope the doors; run, save Hieronimo.
                    [*They break in and hold Hieronimo.*
                              Hieronimo,
Do but inform the king of these events;
Upon mine honour, thou shalt have no harm.
*Hier.* Viceroy, I will not trust thee with my life,
Which I this day have offer'd to my son.
Accursèd wretch!
Why stay'st thou him that was resolv'd to die?
*King.* Speak, traitor! damnèd, bloody murd'rer, speak!
For now I have thee, I will make thee speak.
Why hast thou done this undeserving deed?
*Vic.* Why hast thou murderèd my Balthazar?
*Cast.* Why hast thou butcher'd both my children thus?
Hier. [*But are you sure they are dead?*
Cast.                          *Ay, slave, too sure.*
Hier. *What, and yours too?*
*Vic.* Ay, all are dead; not one of them survive.
Hier. *Nay, then I care not; come, and we shall be friends;*
   *Let us lay our heads together:*
   *See, here's a goodly noose will hold them all.*
*Vic.* O damnèd devil, how secure he is!
Hier. *Secure? why, dost thou wonder at it?*
   *I tell thee, Viceroy, this day I have seen revenge,*
   *And in that sight am grown a prouder monarch,*
   *Than ever sat under the crown of Spain.*
   *Had I as many lives as there be stars,*
   *As many heav'ns to go to, as those lives,*
   *I'd give them all, ay, and my soul to boot,*
   *But I would see thee ride in this red pool.*]
   O, good words!
As dear to me was my Horatio,
As yours, or yours, or yours, my lord, to you.
My guiltless son was by Lorenzo slain,

And by Lorenzo and that Balthazar
Am I at last revengèd thoroughly,
Upon whose souls may heav'ns be yet aveng'd
With greater far than these afflictions.

*Cast.* But who were thy confederates in this?

*Vic.* That was thy daughter Bellimperia;
For by her hand my Balthazar was slain:
I saw her stab him.

*King.*                    Why speak'st thou not?[1]

*Hier.* What lesser liberty can kings afford
Than harmless silence? then afford it me.
Sufficeth, I may not, nor I will not tell thee.

*King.* Fetch forth the tortures: traitor as thou art,
I'll make thee tell.

[*Hier.*] *Methinks, since I grew inward with revenge,*
*I cannot look with scorn enough on death.*

King. *What, dost thou mock us, slave? bring tortures forth.*

Hier. *Do, do, do: and meantime I'll torture you.*
*You had a son, as I take it; and your son*
*Should ha' been married to your daughter:*
*Ha, was it not so?—You had a son too,*
*He was my liege's nephew; he was proud*
*And politic; had he liv'd, he might have come*
*To wear the crown of Spain (I think 'twas so)—:*
*'Twas I that kill'd him; look you, this same hand,*
*'Twas it that stabb'd his heart—do ye see this hand?*
*For one Horatio, if you ever knew him: a youth,*
*One that they hang'd up in his father's garden;*
*One that did force your valiant son to yield,*
*While your more valiant son did take him prisoner,*

Vic. *Be deaf, my senses; I can hear no more.*

King. *Fall, heav'n, and cover us with thy sad ruins.*

Cast. *Roll all the world within thy pitchy cloud.*

Hier. *Now do I applaud what I have acted.*
*Nunc iners cadat manus!*
*Now to express the rupture of my part—*

---

[1] Instead of ll. 193 (second half: 'Why speak'st thou not') to 204, the Qq. from 1602 onwards have the following passage (they have also put ll. 190-193, first half, before l. 182):

*Hier.*                              Indeed,
   Thou may'st torment me, as his wretched son
   Hath done in murd'ring my Horatio:
   But never shalt thou force me to reveal
   The thing which I have vow'd inviolate.
   And therefore, in despite of all thy threats,
   Pleas'd with their deaths, and eas'd with their revenge,
   First take my tongue, and afterwards my heart.
                              [*He bites out his tongue.*
*King.* O monstrous resolution of a wretch!
   See, Viceroy, he hath bitten forth his tongue,
   Rather than to reveal what we requir'd.
*Cast.* Yet can he write.
*King.* And if in this he satisfy us not,
   We will devise th' extremest kind of death
   That ever was invented for a wretch.
                 [*Then he makes signs for a knife to mend his pen.*
*Cast.* O, he would have a knife to mend his pen.
*Vic.* Here, and advise thee that thou write the troth.—
   Look to my brother! save Hieronimo!
                    [*He with a knife stabs the duke and himself.*
*King.* What age hath ever heard such monstrous deeds?
   My brother, and the whole succeeding hope
   That Spain expected after my decease!—
   Go, bear his body hence, that we may mourn
   The loss of our belovèd brother's death—:
   That he may be entomb'd!—Whate'er befall,
   I am the next, the nearest, last of all.
*Vic.* And thou, Don Pedro, do the like for us:
   Take up our hapless son, untimely slain;
   Set me with him, and he with woeful me,
   Upon the main-mast of a ship unmann'd,
   And let the wind and tide haul me along
   To Scylla's barking and untamèd gulf,
   Or to the loathsome pool of Acheron,
   To weep my want for my sweet Balthazar:
   Spain hath no refuge for a Portingal.
              [*The trumpets sound a dead march; the King of Spain
                 mourning after his brothers body, and the King of
                 Portingal bearing the body of his son.*

# SCENE V

*Enter Ghost and Revenge.*

*Ghost.* Ay, now my hopes have end in their effects,
　　When blood and sorrow finish my desires:
　　Horatio murder'd in his father's bower;
　　Vild Serberine by Pedringano slain;
　　False Pedringano hang'd by quaint device;
　　Fair Isabella by herself misdone;
　　Prince Balthazar by Bellimperia stabb'd;
　　The Duke of Castile and his wicked son
　　Both done to death by old Hieronimo;
　　My Bellimperia fall'n, as Dido fell,
　　And good Hieronimo slain by himself:
　　Ay, these were spectacles to please my soul!—
　　Now will I beg at lovely Proserpine
　　That, by the virtue of her princely doom,
　　I may consort my friends in pleasing sort,
　　And on my foes work just and sharp revenge.
　　I'll lead my friend Horatio through those fields,
　　Where never-dying wars are still inur'd;
　　I'll lead fair Isabella to that train,
　　Where pity weeps, but never feeleth pain;
　　I'll lead my Bellimperia to those joys,
　　That vestal virgins and fair queens possess;
　　I'll lead Hieronimo where Orpheus plays,
　　Adding sweet pleasure to eternal days.
　　But say, Revenge—for thou must help, or none—
　　Against the rest how shall my hate be shown?
*Rev.* This hand shall hale them down to deepest hell,
　　Where none but Furies, bugs and tortures dwell.
*Ghost.* Then, sweet Revenge, do this at my request:
　　Let me be judge, and doom them to unrest
　　Let loose poor Tityus from the vulture's gripe,
　　And let Don Cyprian supply his room;
　　Place Don Lorenzo on Ixion's wheel,
　　And let the lover's endless pains surcease
　　(Juno forgets old wrath, and grants him ease);
　　Hang Balthazar about Chimæra's neck,

And let him there bewail his bloody love,
Repining at our joys that are above;
Let Serberine go roll the fatal stone,
And take from Sisyphus his endless moan;
False Pedringano, for his treachery,
Let him be dragg'd through boiling Acheron,
And there live, dying still in endless flames,
Blaspheming gods and all their holy names.

*Rev.* Then haste we down to meet thy friends and foes:
To place thy friends in ease, the rest in woes;
For here though death hath end their misery,
I'll there begin their endless tragedy.                    [*Exeunt.*

## FINIS

# DR. FAUSTUS

## Christopher Marlowe

# DRAMATIS PERSONÆ

THE POPE.
CARDINAL OF LORRAIN.
EMPEROR OF GERMANY.
DUKE OF VANHOLT.
FAUSTUS.
VALDES and CORNELIUS, Friends to FAUSTUS.
WAGNER, Servant to FAUSTUS.
Clown.
ROBIN.
RALPH.
Vintner.
Horse-Courser.
Knight.
Old Man.
Scholars, Friars, and Attendants.
DUCHESS OF VANHOLT.
LUCIFER.
BELZEBUB.
MEPHISTOPHILIS.
Good Angel.
Evil Angel.
The Seven Deadly Sins.
Devils.
Spirits in the shape of ALEXANDER THE GREAT, of his Paramour,
and of HELEN OF TROY.
CHORUS.

*Enter* CHORUS

CHORUS. Not marching now in fields of Thrasimene,
  Where Mars did mate[1] the Carthaginians;
  Nor sporting in the dalliance of love,
  In courts of kings where state is overturn'd;
  Nor in the pomp of proud audacious deeds,
  Intends our Muse to vaunt his heavenly verse:
  Only this, gentlemen,—we must perform
  The form of Faustus' fortunes, good or bad.
  To patient judgments we appeal our plaud,[2]
  And speak for Faustus in his infancy.
  Now is he born, his parents base of stock,
  In Germany, within a town call'd Rhodes;[3]
  Of riper years to Wittenberg he went,
  Whereas his kinsmen chiefly brought him up.
  So soon he profits in divinity,
  The fruitful plot of scholarism grac'd,[4]
  That shortly he was grac'd with doctor's name,
  Excelling all whose sweet delight disputes
  In heavenly matters of theology;
  Till swollen with cunning,[5] of a self-conceit,
  His waxen wings[6] did mount above his reach,
  And, melting, Heavens conspir'd his overthrow;
  For, falling to a devilish exercise,

---

[1] Confound. But Hannibal was victorious at Lake Trasumennus, B.C. 217.
[2] For applause.
[3] Roda, in the Duchy of Saxe-Altenburg, near Jena.
[4] The garden of scholarship being adorned by him.
[5] Knowledge.
[6] An allusion to the myth of Icarus, who flew too near the sun.

And glutted [now] with learning's golden gifts,
He surfeits upon cursed necromancy.
Nothing so sweet as magic is to him,
Which he prefers before his chiefest bliss.
And this the man that in his study sits!                    *Exit.*

# SCENE I.

*Enter* FAUSTUS *in his Study.*

FAUSTUS. Settle my studies, Faustus, and begin
    To sound the depth of that thou wilt profess;[1]
    Having commenc'd, be a divine in show.
    Yet level[2] at the end of every art,
    And live and die in Aristotle's works.
    Sweet Analytics,[3] 'tis thou hast ravish'd me,
    *Bene disserere est finis logices.*
    Is to dispute well logic's chiefest end?
    Affords this art no greater miracle?
    Then read no more, thou hast attain'd the end;
    A greater subject fitteth Faustus' wit.
    Bid ὂν καὶ μὴ 'όν[4] farewell; Galen[5] come,
    Seeing *Ubi desinit Philosophus, ibi incipit Medicus;*[6]
    Be a physician, Faustus, heap up gold,
    And be eternis'd for some wondrous cure.
    *Summum bonum medicinæ sanitas,*[7]
    "The end of physic is our body's health."
    Why, Faustus, hast thou not attain'd that end?
    Is not thy common talk sound Aphorisms?[8]
    Are not thy bills[9] hung up as monuments,
    Whereby whole cities have escap'd the plague,

---

[1] Teach publicly.
[2] Aim.
[3] Logic.
[4] The Aristotelian phrase for "being and not being."
[5] Greek physician whose theories were highly regarded in the Middle Ages.
[6] "Where the philosopher leaves off, there the physician begins."
[7] This and the previous quotation are from Aristotle.
[8] Medical maxims.
[9] Announcements.

And thousand desperate maladies been eas'd?
Yet art thou still but Faustus and a man.
Wouldst thou make men to live eternally,
Or, being dead, raise them to life again?
Then this profession were to be esteem'd.
Physic, farewell. —Where is Justinian?                [*Reads.*]
*Si una eademque res legatur duobus, alter rem, alter valorem rei, & c.*[10]
A pretty case of paltry legacies!                     [*Reads.*]
*Exhœreditare filium non potest pater nisi, &c.*[11]
Such is the subject of the Institute[12]
And universal Body of the Law.
His[13] study fits a mercenary drudge,
Who aims at nothing but external trash;
Too servile and illiberal for me.
When all is done, divinity is best;
Jerome's Bible,[14] Faustus, view it well.            [*Reads.*]
*Stipendium peccati mors est.* Ha! *Stipendium, &c.*
"The reward of sin is death." That's hard.            [*Reads.*]
*Si peccasse negamus, fallimur, et nulla est in nobis veritas.*
"If we say that we have no sin we deceive ourselves, and there's
   no truth in us." Why then, belike we must sin and so con-
   sequently die.
Ay, we must die an everlasting death.
What doctrine call you this, *Che sera sera,*
"What will be shall be?" Divinity, adieu!
These metaphysics of magicians
And necromantic books are heavenly;
Lines, circles, scenes, letters, and characters,
Ay, these are those that Faustus most desires.
O what a world of profit and delight,
Of power, of honour, of omnipotence
Is promis'd to the studious artisan!
All things that move between the quiet poles
Shall be at my command. Emperors and kings

---

[10] "If one and the same thing is bequeathed to two persons, one gets the thing
    and the other the value of the thing."
[11] "A father cannot disinherit the son except," etc.
[12] Of Justinian, under whom the Roman law was codified.
[13] Its.
[14] The Vulgate.

Are but obeyed in their several provinces,
Nor can they raise the wind or rend the clouds;
But his dominion that exceeds[15] in this
Stretcheth as far as doth the mind of man.
A sound magician is a mighty god:
Here, Faustus, try thy brains to gain a deity.
Wagner!

*Enter* WAGNER.

                 Commend me to my dearest friends,
The German Valdes and Cornelius;
Request them earnestly to visit me.
WAG. I will, sir. *Exit.*
FAUSTUS. Their conference will be a greater help to me
    Than all my labours, plod I ne'er so fast.

*Enter* GOOD ANGEL *and* EVIL ANGEL.

G. ANG.  O Faustus! lay that damned book aside,
    And gaze not upon it lest it tempt thy soul,
    And heap God's heavy wrath upon thy head.
    Read, read the Scriptures: that is blasphemy.
E. ANG.  Go forward, Faustus, in that famous art,
    Wherein all Nature's treasure is contain'd:
    Be thou on earth as Jove is in the sky,
    Lord and commander of these elements.   *Exeunt* [ANGELS.]
FAUSTUS.  How am I glutted with conceit[16] of this!
    Shall I make spirits fetch me what I please,
    Resolve me of all ambiguities,
    Perform what desperate enterprise I will?
    I'll have them fly to India for gold,
    Ransack the ocean for orient pearl,
    And search all corners of the new-found world
    For pleasant fruits and princely delicates;
    I'll have them read me strange philosophy
    And tell the secrets of all foreign kings;
    I'll have them wall all Germany with brass,
    And make swift Rhine circle fair Wittenberg;
    I'll have them fill the public schools with silk,

---

[15] Excels.
[16] Idea.

Wherewith the students shall be bravely clad;
I'll levy soldiers with the coin they bring,
And chase the Prince of Parma from our land,[17]
And reign sole king of all the provinces;
Yea, stranger engines for the brunt of war
Than was the fiery keel[18] at Antwerp's bridge,
I'll make my servile spirits to invent.
Come, German Valdes and Cornelius,
And make me blest with your sage conference.

*Enter* VALDES *and* CORNELIUS.[19]

Valdes, sweet Valdes, and Cornelius,
Know that your words have won me at the last
To practise magic and concealed arts:
Yet not your words only, but mine own fantasy,
That will receive no object, for my head
But ruminates on necromantic skill.
Philosophy is odious and obscure,
Both law and physic are for petty wits;
Divinity is basest of the three,
Unpleasant, harsh, contemptible, and vile:
'Tis magic, magic, that hath ravish'd me.
Then, gentle friends, aid me in this attempt;
And I that have with concise syllogisms
Gravell'd the pastors of the German church,
And made the flow'ring pride of Wittenberg
Swarm to my problems, as the infernal spirits
On sweet Musæus,[20] when he came to hell,
Will be as cunning as Agrippa was,
Whose shadows made all Europe honour him.
VALD. Faustus, these books, thy wit, and our experience
Shall make all nations to canónise us.
As Indian Moors[21] obey their Spanish lords,
So shall the subjects of every element
Be always serviceable to us three;

---

[17] The Netherlands, over which Parma re-established the Spanish dominion.
[18] A ship filled with explosives used to blow up a bridge built by Parma in 1585 at the siege of Antwerp.
[19] The famous Cornelius Agrippa. German Valdes is not known.
[20] Cf. Virgil, *Aeneid,* vi. 667.
[21] Americans Indians.

Like lions shall they guard us when we please;
Like Almain rutters[22] with their horsemen's staves,
Or Lapland giants, trotting by our sides;
Sometimes like women or unwedded maids,
Shadowing more beauty in their airy brows
Than have the white breasts of the queen of love:
From Venice shall they drag huge argosies,
And from America the golden fleece
That yearly stuffs old Philip's treasury;
If learned Faustus will be resolute.

FAUSTUS. Valdes, as resolute am I in this
As thou to live; therefore object it not.

CORN. The miracles that magic will perform
Will make thee vow to study nothing else.
He that is grounded in astrology,
Enrich'd with tongues, well seen[23] in minerals,
Hath all the principles magic doth require.
Then doubt not, Faustus, but to be renown'd,
And more frequented for this mystery
Than heretofore the Delphian Oracle.
The spirits tell me they can dry the sea,
And fetch the treasure of all foreign wracks,
Ay, all the wealth that our forefathers hid
Within the massy entrails of the earth;
Then tell me, Faustus, what shall we three want?

FAUSTUS. Nothing, Cornelius! O this cheers my soul!
Come show me some demonstrations magical,
That I may conjure in some lusty grove,
And have these joys in full possession.

VALD. Then haste thee to some solitary grove
And bear wise Bacon's[24] and Albanus'[25] works,
The Hebrew Psalter and New Testament;
And whatsoever else is requisite
We will inform thee ere our conference cease.

CORN. Valdes, first let him know the words of art;
And then, all other ceremonies learn'd,

---

[22] Troopers. Germ. *Reiters*.
[23] Versed.
[24] Roger Bacon.
[25] Perhaps Pietro d'Abano, a medieval alchemist; perhaps a misprint for Albertus (Magnus), the great schoolman.

Faustus may try his cunning by himself.

VALD. First I'll instruct thee in the rudiments.

And then wilt thou be perfecter than I.

FAUSTUS. Then come and dine with me, and after meat,

We'll canvass every quiddity[26] thereof;

For ere I sleep I'll try what I can do:

This night I'll conjure though I die therefore.          *Exeunt.*

# SCENE II.

## *Before Faustus' House.*

*Enter two* SCHOLARS.

1 SCHOL.     I wonder what's become of Faustus that was wont
to make our schools ring with *sic probo*?[1]

2 SCHOL. That shall we know, for see here comes his boy.

*Enter* WAGNER.

1 SCHOL. How now, sirrah! Where's thy master?

WAG. God in heaven knows!

2 SCHOL. Why, dost not thou know?

WAG. Yes, I know. But that follows not.

1 SCHOL. Go to, sirrah! Leave your jesting, and tell us where
he is.

WAG. That follows not necessary by force of argument, that you,
being licentiate, should stand upon't: therefore, acknowledge
your error and be attentive.

2 SCHOL. Why, didst thou not say thou knew'st?

WAG. Have you any witness on't?

1 SCHOL. Yes, sirrah, I heard you.

WAG. Ask my fellow if I be a thief.

2 SCHOL. Well, you will not tell us?

WAG. Yes, sir, I will tell you; yet if you were not dunces, you
would never ask me such a question; for is not he *corpus natu-*
*rale*?[2] and is not that *mobile?* Then wherefore should you ask

---

[26] Fine point.

[1] "Thus I prove" —a common formula in scholastic discussions.

[2] *'Corpus naturale seu mobile'* (literally, "natural or movable body") was the
scholastic expression for the subject-matter of Physics.

me such a question? But that I am by nature phlegmatic, slow to wrath, and prone to lechery (to love, I would say), it were not for you to come within forty foot of the place of execution, although I do not doubt to see you both hang'd the next sessions. Thus having triumph'd over you, I will set my countenance like a precisian,[3] and begin to speak thus: —Truly, my dear brethren, my master is within at dinner, with Valdes and Cornelius, as this wine, if it could speak, would inform your worships; and so the Lord bless you, preserve you, and keep you, my dear brethren, my dear brethren. *Exit.*

1 SCHOL. Nay, then, I fear he has fallen into that damned Art, for which they two are infamous through the world.

2 SCHOL. Were he a stranger, and not allied to me, yet should I grieve for him. But come, let us go and inform the Rector, and see if he by his grave counsel can reclaim him.

1 SCHOL. O, I fear me nothing can reclaim him.

2 SCHOL. Yet let us try what we can do. *Exeunt*

# SCENE III.

## *A Grove.*

### *Enter* FAUSTUS *to conjure.*

FAUSTUS. Now that the gloomy shadow of the earth
  Longing to view Orion's drizzling look,
  Leaps from th' antarctic world unto the sky,
  And dims the welkin with her pitchy breath,
  Faustus, begin thine incantations,
  And try if devils will obey thy hest,
  Seeing thou hast pray'd and sacrific'd to them.
  Within this circle is Jehovah's name,
  Forward and backward anagrammatis'd,
  The breviated names of holy saints,
  Figures of every adjunct[1] to the Heavens,
  And characters of signs and erring stars,[2]

---

[3] Puritan.
[1] Every star belonging to.
[2] Planets.

By which the spirits are enforc'd to rise:
Then fear not, Faustus, but be resolute,
And try the uttermost magic can perform.

*Sint mihi Dei Acherontis propitii! Valeat numen triplex Jehovae!
Ignei, aerii, aquatani spiritus, salvete! Orientis princeps Belzebub,
infemi ardentis monarcha, et Demogorgon, propitiamus vos, ut
appareat et surgat Mephistophilis. Quid tu moraris? Per Jehovam,
Gehennam, et consecratum aquam quam nunc spargo, signumque
crucis quod nunc facio, et per vota nostra, ipse nunc surgat nobis
dicatus Mephistophilis!³*

*Enter* [MEPHISTOPHILIS] *a Devil.*

I charge thee to return and change thy shape;
Thou art too ugly to attend on me.
Go, and return an old Franciscan friar;
That holy shape becomes a devil best.

*Exit Devil.*

I see there's virtue in my heavenly words;
Who would not be proficient in this art?
How pliant is this Mephistophilis,
Full of obedience and humility!
Such is the force of magic and my spells.
[Now,] Faustus, thou art conjuror laureate,
Thou canst command great Mephistophilis:
*Quin regis Mephistophilis fratris imagine.*⁴

*Re-enter* MEPHISTOPHILIS [*like a Franciscan* Friar].

MEPH. Now, Faustus, what would'st thou have me do?
FAUSTUS. I charge thee wait upon me whilst I live,
To do whatever Faustus shall command,
Be it to make the moon drop from her sphere,
Or the ocean to overwhelm the world.
MEPH. I am a servant to great Lucifer,
And may not follow thee without his leave;

---

³ "Be propitious to me, gods of Acheron! May the triple deity of Jehovah prevail!
Spirits of fire, air, water, hail! Belzebub, Prince of the East, monarch of
burning hell, and Demogorgon, we propitiate ye, that Mephistophilis may
appear and rise. Why dost thou delay? By Jehovah, Gehenna, and the holy
water which now I sprinkle, and the sign of the cross which now I make,
and by our prayer, may Mephistophilis now summoned by us arise!"

⁴ "For indeed thou hast power in the image of thy brother Mephistophilis."

No more than he commands must we perform.

FAUSTUS. Did he not charge thee to appear to me?

MEPH. No, I came hither of mine own accord.

FAUSTUS. Did not my conjuring speeches raise thee? Speak:

MEPH. That was the cause, but yet *per accidens;*
      For when we hear one rack[5] the name of God,
      Abjure the Scriptures and his Saviour Christ,
      We fly in hope to get his glorious soul;
      Nor will we come, unless he use such means
      Whereby he is in danger to be damn'd:
      Therefore the shortest cut for conjuring
      Is stoutly to abjure the Trinity,
      And pray devoutly to the Prince of Hell.

FAUSTUS. So Faustus hath
      Already done; and holds this principle,
      There is no chief but only Belzebub,
      To whom Faustus doth dedicate himself.
      This word "damnation" terrifies not him,
      For he confounds hell in Elysium;[6]
      His ghost be with the old philosophers!
      But, leaving these vain trifles of men's souls,
      Tell me what is that Lucifer thy lord?

MEPH. Arch-regent and commander of all spirits.

FAUSTUS. Was not that Lucifer an angel once?

MEPH. Yes, Faustus, and most dearly lov'd of God.

FAUSTUS. How comes it then that he is Prince of devils?

MEPH. O, by aspiring pride and insolence;
      For which God threw him from the face of Heaven.

FAUSTUS. And what are you that you live with Lucifer?

MEPH. Unhappy spirits that fell with Lucifer,
      Conspir'd against our God with Lucifer,
      And are for ever damn'd with Lucifer.

FAUSTUS. Where are you damn'd?

MEPH. In hell.

FAUSTUS. How comes it then that thou art out of hell?

MEPH. Why this is hell, nor am I out of it.
      Think'st thou that I who saw the face of God,

---

[5] Twist in anagrams.

[6] Heaven and hell are indifferent to him.

And tasted the eternal joys of Heaven,
Am not tormented with ten thousand hells,
In being depriv'd of everlasting bliss?
O Faustus! leave these frivolous demands,
Which strike a terror to my fainting soul.

FAUSTUS. What, is great Mephistophilis so passionate[7]
For being depriv'd of the joys of Heaven?
Learn thou of Faustus manly fortitude,
And scorn those joys thou never shalt possess.
Go bear these tidings to great Lucifer:
Seeing Faustus hath incurr'd eternal death
By desperate thoughts against Jove's deity,
Say he surrenders up to him his soul,
So he will spare him four and twenty years,
Letting him live in all voluptuousness;
Having thee ever to attend on me;
To give me whatsoever I shall ask,
To tell me whatsoever I demand,
To slay mine enemies, and aid my friends,
And always be obedient to my will.
Go and return to mighty Lucifer,
And meet me in my study at midnight,
And then resolve[8] me of thy master's mind.

MEPH. I will, Faustus.                                    *Exit.*

FAUSTUS. Had I as many souls as there be stars,
I'd give them all for Mephistophilis.
By him I'll be great Emperor of the world,
And make a bridge through the moving air,
To pass the ocean with a band of men;
I'll join the hills that bind the Afric shore,
And make that [country] continent to Spain,
And both contributory to my crown.
The Emperor shall not live but by my leave,
Nor any potentate of Germany.
Now that I have obtain'd what I desire,
I'll live in speculation[9] of this art
Till Mephistophilis return again.                        *Exit*

[7] Sorrowful.
[8] Inform.
[9] Study

# SCENE IV.

## *A Street.*

### *Enter* WAGNER *and the* CLOWN.

WAG. Sirrah, boy, come hither.

CLOWN. How, boy! Swowns, boy! I hope you have seen many
boys with such pickadevaunts[1] as I have. Boy, quotha!

WAG. Tell me, sirrah, hast thou any comings in?

CLOWN. Ay, and goings out too. You may see else.

WAG. Alas, poor slave! See how poverty jesteth in his nakedness!
The villain is bare and out of service, and so hungry that I
know he would give his soul to the devil for a shoulder of
mutton, though it were blood-raw.

CLOWN. How? My soul to the Devil for a shoulder of mutton,
though 'twere blood-raw! Not so, good friend. By 'r Lady, I
had need have it well roasted and good sauce to it, if I pay so
dear.

WAG. Well, wilt thou serve me, and I'll make thee go like *Qui
mihi discipulus?*[2]

CLOWN. How, in verse?

WAG. No, sirrah; in beaten silk and stavesacre.[3]

CLOWN. How, how, Knave's acre![4] Ay, I thought that was all
the land his father left him. Do you hear? I would be sorry to
rob you of your living.

WAG. Sirrah, I say in stavesacre.

CLOWN. Oho! Oho! Stavesacre! Why, then, belike if I were your
man I should be full of vermin.

WAG. So thou shalt, whether thou beest with me or no. But,
sirrah, leave your jesting, and bind yourself presently unto me
for seven years, or I'll turn all the lice about thee into familiars,
and they shall tear thee in pieces.

CLOWN. Do you hear, sir? You may save that labour; they are
too familiar with me already. Swowns! they are as bold with
my flesh as if they had paid for [their] meat and drink.

---

[1] Beards cut to a sharp point (Fr. *pic-à-devant*).

[2] "Whoever is my disciple," the first words of W. Lily's *"Ad discipulos carmen
de moribus"* (Ode to His Disciples on Morality).

[3] A kind of larkspur, used for destroying lice.

[4] A mean street in London.

WAG. Well, do you hear, sirrah? Hold, take these guilders.

[*Gives money.*]

CLOWN. Gridirons! what be they?

WAG. Why, French crowns.

CLOWN. Mass, but for the name of French crowns, a man were as good have as many English counters. And what should I do with these?

WAG. Why, now, sirrah, thou art at an hour's warning, whensoever and wheresoever the Devil shall fetch thee.

CLOWN. No, no. Here, take your gridirons again.

WAG. Truly I'll none of them.

CLOWN. Truly but you shall.

WAG. Bear witness I gave them him.

CLOWN. Bear witness I give them you again.

WAG. Well, I will cause two devils presently to fetch thee away— Baliol and Belcher.

CLOWN. Let your Baliol and your Belcher come here, and I'll knock them, they were never so knockt since they were devils. Say I should kill one of them, what would folks say? "Do you see yonder tall fellow in the round slop?[5] — he has kill'd the devil." So I should be call'd Kill-devil all the parish over.

*Enter two* DEVILS: *the* Clown *runs up and down crying.*

WAG. Baliol and Belcher! Spirits, away!          *Exeunt* Devils.

CLOWN. What, are they gone? A vengeance on them, they have vile long nails! There was a he-devil, and a she-devil! I'll tell you how you shall know them: all he-devils has horns, and all she-devils has clifts and cloven feet.

WAG. Well, sirrah, follow me.

CLOWN. But, do you hear — if I should serve you, would you teach me to raise up Banios and Belcheos?

WAG. I will teach thee to turn thyself to anything; to a dog, or a cat, or a mouse, or a rat, or anything.

CLOWN. How! a Christian fellow to a dog or a cat, a mouse or a rat! No, no, sir. If you turn me into anything, let it be in the likeness of a little pretty frisky flea, that I may be here and there and everywhere. Oh, I'll tickle the pretty wenches' plackets; I'll be amongst them, i' faith.

WAG. Well, sirrah, come.

---

[5] Short wide breeches.

CLOWN. But, do you hear, Wagner?

WAG. HOW! — Baliol and Belcher!

CLOWN. O Lord! I pray, sir, let Banio and Belcher go sleep.

WAG. Villain—call me Master Wagner, and let thy left eye be
diametarily[6] fixt upon my right heel, with *quasi vestigias nostras
insistere*.[7]                                                    Exit.

CLOWN. God forgive me, he speaks Dutch fustian. Well, I'll follow him, I'll serve him, that's flat.                             Exit.


# SCENE V.

*Enter* FAUSTUS *in his study*.

FAUSTUS. NOW, Faustus, must
    Thou needs be damn'd, and canst thou not be sav'd:
    What boots it then to think of God or Heaven?
    Away with such vain fancies, and despair:
    Despair in God, and trust in Belzebub.
    Now go not backward: no, Faustus, be resolute.
    Why waverest thou? O, something soundeth in mine ears
    "Abjure this magic, turn to God again!"
    Ay, and Faustus will turn to God again.
    To God? —He loves thee not—
    The God thou serv'st is thine own appetite,
    Wherein is fix'd the love of Belzebub;
    To him I'll build an altar and a church,
    And offer lukewarm blood of new-born babes.

*Enter* GOOD ANGEL *and* EVIL [ANGEL.]

G. ANG. Sweet Faustus, leave that execrable art.

FAUSTUS. Contrition, prayer, repentance! What of them?

G. ANG. O, they are means to bring thee unto Heaven.

E. ANG. Rather illusions, fruits of lunacy,
    That makes men foolish that do trust them most.

G. ANG. Sweet Faustus, think of Heaven, and heavenly things.

E. ANG. No, Faustus, think of honour and of wealth.

                                            *Exeunt* [ANGELS.]

---

[6] For *diametrically*.

[7] "As if to tread in my tracks."

FAUSTUS. Of wealth!

    Why, the signiory of Emden[1] shall be mine.

    When Mephistophilis shall stand by me,

    What God can hurt thee, Faustus? Thou art safe;

    Cast no more doubts. Come, Mephistophilis,

    And bring glad tidings from great Lucifer; —

    Is't not midnight? Come, Mephistophilis;

    *Veni, veni, Mephistophile!*

### *Enter* MEPHISTOPHILIS.

Now tell me, what says Lucifer thy lord?

MEPH. That I shall wait on Faustus whilst he lives,

    So he will buy my service with his soul.

FAUSTUS. Already Faustus hath hazarded that for thee.

MEPH. But, Faustus, thou must bequeath it solemnly,

    And write a deed of gift with thine own blood,

    For that security craves great Lucifer.

    If thou deny it, I will back to hell.

FAUSTUS. Stay, Mephistophilis! and tell me what good

    Will my soul do thy Lord.

MEPH.                  Enlarge his kingdom.

FAUSTUS. Is that the reason why he tempts us thus?

MEPH. *Solamen miseris socios habuisse doloris.*[2]

FAUSTUS. Why, have you any pain that torture others?

MEPH. As great as have the human souls of men.

But tell me, Faustus, shall I have thy soul?

    And I will be thy slave, and wait on thee,

    And give thee more than thou hast wit to ask.

FAUSTUS. Ay, Mephistophilis, I give it thee.

MEPH. Then Faustus, stab thine arm courageously.

    And bind thy soul that at some certain day

    Great Lucifer may claim it as his own;

    And then be thou as great as Lucifer.

FAUSTUS. [*Stabbing his arm.*] Lo, Mephistophilis, for love of thee,

    I cut mine arm, and with my proper blood

    Assure my soul to be great Lucifer's,

    Chief lord and regent of perpetual night!

---

[1] Emden, near the mouth *of* the river Ems, was an important commercial town in Elizabethan times.

[2] "Misery loves company."

View here the blood that trickles from mine arm.
And let it be propitious for my wish.
MEPH. But, Faustus, thou must
Write it in manner of a deed of gift.
FAUSTUS. Ay, so I will. [*Writes.*] But, Mephistophilis,
My blood congeals, and I can write no more.
MEPH. I'll fetch thee fire to dissolve it straight.                    *Exit.*
FAUSTUS. What might the staying of my blood portend?
Is it unwilling I should write this bill?
Why streams it not that I may write afresh?
*Faustus gives to thee his soul.* Ah, there it stay'd.
Why should'st thou not? Is not thy soul thine own?
Then write again, *Faustus gives to thee his soul.*

    *Re-enter* MEPHISTOPHILIS *with a chafer of coals.*

MEPH. Here's fire. Come, Faustus, set it on.
FAUSTUS. So now the blood begins to clear again;
Now will I make an end immediately. [*Writes.*]
MEPH. [*Aside.*] O what will not I do to obtain his soul.
FAUSTUS. *Consummatum est:*[3] this bill is ended,
And Faustus hath bequeath'd his soul to Lucifer —
But what is this inscription on mine arm?
*Homo, fuge!*[4] Whither should I fly?
If unto God, he'll throw me down to hell.
My senses are deceiv'd; here's nothing writ: —
I see it plain; here in this place is writ
*Homo, fuge!* Yet shall not Faustus fly.
MEPH. I'll fetch him somewhat to delight his mind.            *Exit.*

    *Re-enter* [MEPHISTOPHILIS] *with* Devils, *giving crowns
and rich apparel to* FAUSTUS, *and dance,
and then depart.*

FAUSTUS. Speak, Mephistophilis, what means this show?
MEPH. Nothing, Faustus, but to delight thy mind withal,
And to show thee what magic can perform.
FAUSTUS. But may I raise up spirits when I please?
MEPH. Ay, Faustus, and do greater things than these.

---

[3] "It is finished."
[4] "Man, fly!"

FAUSTUS. Then there's enough for a thousand souls.
Here, Mephistophilis, receive this scroll,
A deed of gift of body and of soul:
But yet conditionally that thou perform
All articles prescrib'd between us both.

MEPH. Faustus, I swear by hell and Lucifer
To effect all promises between us made.

FAUSTUS. Then hear me read them: *On these conditions following.
First, that Faustus may be a spirit in form and substance. Secondly,
that Mephistophilis shall be his servant, and at his command. Thirdly,
that Mephistophilis shall do for him and bring him whatsoever [he
desires]. Fourthly, that he shall be in his chamber or house invisible.
Lastly, that he shall appear to the said John Faustus, at all times, in
what form or shape soever he pleases. I, John Faustus, of Wittenberg,
Doctor, by these presents do give both body and soul to Lucifer, Prince
of the East, and his minister, Mephistophilis; and furthermore grant
unto them, that twenty-four years being expired, the articles above
written inviolate, full power to fetch or carry the said John Faustus,
body and soul, flesh, blood, or goods, into their habitation wheresoever.
By me, John Faustus.*

MEPH. Speak, Faustus, do you deliver this as your deed?

FAUSTUS. Ay, take it, and the Devil give thee good on 't.

MEPH. Now, Faustus, ask what thou wilt.

FAUSTUS. First will I question with thee about hell.
Tell me where is the place that men call hell?

MEPH. Under the heavens.

FAUSTUS. Ay, but whereabout?

MEPH. Within the bowels of these elements,
Where we are tortur'd and remain for ever;
Hell hath no limits, nor is circumscrib'd
In one self place; for where we are is hell,
And where hell is there must we ever be:
And, to conclude, when all the world dissolves,
And every creature shall be purified,
All places shall be hell that is not Heaven.

FAUSTUS. Come, I think hell's a fable.

MEPH. Ay, think so still, till experience change thy mind.

FAUSTUS. Why, think'st thou then that Faustus shall be damn'd?

MEPH. Ay, of necessity, for here's the scroll
Wherein thou hast given thy soul to Lucifer.

FAUSTUS. Ay, and body too; but what of that?
  Think'st thou that Faustus is so fond[5] to imagine
  That, after this life, there is any pain?
  Tush; these are trifles, and mere old wives' tales.
MEPH. But, Faustus, I am an instance to prove the contrary,
  For I am damned, and am now in hell.
FAUSTUS. HOW! now in hell!
  Nay, an this be hell, I'll willingly be damn'd here;
  What? walking, disputing, &c.?
  But, leaving off this, let me have a wife,
  The fairest maid in Germany;
  For I am wanton and lascivious,
  And cannot live without a wife.
MEPH. How —a wife?
  I prithee, Faustus, talk not of a wife.
FAUSTUS. Nay, sweet Mephistophilis, fetch me one, for I will
  have one.
MEPH. Well— thou wilt have one. Sit there till I come:
  I'll fetch thee a wife in the Devil's name.          [*Exit.*]

    *Re-enter* MEPHISTOPHILIS *with a* Devil *dressed like*
              *a woman, with fireworks.*

MEPH. Tell [me,] Faustus, how dost thou like thy wife?
FAUSTUS. A plague on her for a hot whore!
MEPH. Tut, Faustus,
  Marriage is but a ceremonial toy;
  And if thou lovest me, think no more of it.
  I'll cull thee out the fairest courtesans,
  And bring them every morning to thy bed;
  She whom thine eye shall like, thy heart shall have,
  Be she as chaste as was Penelope,
  As wise as Saba,[6] or as beautiful
  As was bright Lucifer before his fall.
  Here, take this book, peruse it thoroughly:     [*Gives a book.*]
  The iterating[7] of these lines brings gold;
  The framing of this circle on the ground
  Brings whirlwinds, tempests, thunder and lightning;

---

[5] Foolish.
[6] The Queen of Sheba.
[7] Repeating.

Pronounce this thrice devoutly to thyself,
And men in armour shall appear to thee,
Ready to execute what thou desir'st.

FAUSTUS. Thanks, Mephistophilis; yet fain would I have a book wherein I might behold all spells and incantations, that I might raise up spirits when I please.

MEPH. Here they are, in this book.     *Turns to them.*

FAUSTUS. Now would I have a book where I might see all characters and planets of the heavens, that I might know their motions and dispositions.

MEPH. Here they are too.     *Turns to them.*

FAUSTUS. Nay, let me have one book more, —and then I have done, —wherein I might see all plants, herbs, and trees that grow upon the earth.

MEPH. Here they be.

FAUSTUS. O, thou art deceived.

MEPH. Tut, I warrant thee.     *Turns to them.* [*Exeunt.*]

## SCENE VI.

### *The Same.*

*Enter* FAUSTUS *and* MEPHISTOPHILIS.

FAUSTUS. When I behold the heavens, then I repent,
And curse thee, wicked Mephistophilis,
Because thou hast depriv'd me of those joys.

MEPH. Why, Faustus,
Thinkest thou Heaven is such a glorious thing?
I tell thee 'tis not half so fair as thou,
Or any man that breathes on earth.

FAUSTUS. How provest thou that?

MEPH. 'Twas made for man, therefore is man more excellent.

FAUSTUS. If it were made for man, 'twas made for me;
I will renounce this magic and repent.

*Enter* GOOD ANGEL *and* EVIL ANGEL.

G. ANG. Faustus, repent; yet God will pity thee.

E. ANG. Thou art a spirit; God cannot pity thee.

FAUSTUS. Who buzzeth in mine ears I am a spirit?

Be I a devil, yet God may pity me;
Ay, God will pity me if I repent.

E. ANG. Ay, but Faustus never shall repent.

*Exeunt* [ANGELS.]

FAUSTUS. My heart's so hard'ned I cannot repent.
Scarce can I name salvation, faith, or heaven,
But fearful echoes thunder in mine ears
"Faustus, thou art damn'd!" Then swords and knives,
Poison, gun, halters, and envenom'd steel
Are laid before me to despatch myself,
And long ere this I should have slain myself,
Had not sweet pleasure conquer'd deep despair.
Have I not made blind Homer sing to me
Of Alexander's love and Œnon's death?
And hath not he that built the walls of Thebes
With ravishing sound of his melodious harp,
Made music with my Mephistophilis?
Why should I die then, or basely despair?
I am resolv'd: Faustus shall ne'er repent.
Come, Mephistophilis, let us dispute again,
And argue of divine astrology.
Tell me, are there many heavens above the moon?
Are all celestial bodies but one globe,
As is the substance of this centric earth?

MEPH. As are the elements, such are the spheres
Mutually folded in each other's orb,
And, Faustus,
All jointly move upon one axletree
Whose terminine is term'd the world's wide pole;
Nor are the names of Saturn, Mars, or Jupiter
Feign'd, but are erring stars.

FAUSTUS. But tell me, have they all one motion, both *situ et
tempore?*[1]

MEPH. All jointly move from east to west in twenty-four hours
upon the poles of the world; but differ in their motion upon
the poles of the zodiac.

FAUSTUS. Tush!
These slender trifles Wagner can decide;
Hath Mephistophilis no greater skill?

---

[1] "In direction and in time?"

Who knows not the double motion of the planets?

The first is finish'd in a natural day;

The second thus: as Saturn in thirty years; Jupiter in twelve;
Mars in four; the Sun, Venus, and Mercury in a year; the
moon in twenty-eight days. Tush, these are freshmen's sup-
positions. But tell me, hath every sphere a dominion or
*intelligentia*?

MEPH. Ay.

FAUSTUS. How many heavens, or spheres, are there?

MEPH. Nine: the seven planets, the firmament, and the empyreal
heaven.

FAUSTUS. Well, resolve me in this question: Why have we not
conjunctions, oppositions, aspects, eclipses, all at one time, but
in some years we have more, in some less?

MEPH. *Per inæqualem motum respecta totius.*[2]

FAUSTUS. Well, I am answered. Tell me who made the world.

MEPH. I will not.

FAUSTUS. Sweet Mephistophilis, tell me.

MEPH. Move me not, for I will not tell thee.

FAUSTUS. Villain, have I not bound thee to tell me anything?

MEPH. Ay, that is not against our kingdom; but this is.
Think thou on hell, Faustus, for thou art damn'd.

FAUSTUS. Think, Faustus, upon God that made the world.

MEPH. Remember this.

FAUSTUS. Ay, go, accursed spirit, to ugly hell.
'Tis thou hast damn'd distressed Faustus' soul.
Is't not too late?

*Re-enter* GOOD ANGEL *and* EVIL ANGEL.

E. ANG. Too late.

G. ANG. Never too late, if Faustus can repent.

E. ANG. If thou repent, devils shall tear thee in pieces.

G. ANG. Repent, and they shall never raze thy skin.

*Exeunt* [ANGELS.]

FAUSTUS. Ah, Christ, my Saviour,
Seek to save distressed Faustus' soul.

*Enter* LUCIFER, BELZEBUB, *and* MEPHISTOPHILIS.

LUC. Christ cannot save thy soul, for he is just;

---

[2] "On account of their unequal motion in relation to the whole."

There's none but I have interest in the same.

FAUSTUS. O, who art thou that look'st so terrible?

Luc. I am Lucifer,
    And this is my companion-prince in hell.

FAUSTUS. O Faustus! they are come to fetch away thy soul!

Luc. We come to tell thee thou dost injure us;
    Thou talk'st of Christ contrary to thy promise;
    Thou should'st not think of God: think of the Devil,
    And of his dam, too.

FAUSTUS. Nor will I henceforth: pardon me in this,
    And Faustus vows never to look to Heaven,
    Never to name God, or to pray to him,
    To burn his Scriptures, slay his ministers,
    And make my spirits pull his churches down.

Luc. Do so, and we will highly gratify thee. Faustus, we are come
    from hell to show thee some pastime. Sit down, and thou shalt
    see all the Seven Deadly Sins appear in their proper shapes.

FAUSTUS. That sight will be pleasing unto me,
    As Paradise was to Adam the first day
    Of his creation.

Luc. Talk not of Paradise nor creation, but mark this show: talk
    of the Devil, and nothing else.—Come away!

*Enter the* SEVEN DEADLY SINS.

Now, Faustus, examine them of their several names and dis-
    positions.

FAUSTUS. What art thou—the first?

PRIDE. I am Pride. I disdain to have any parents. I am like to
    Ovid's flea: I can creep into every corner of a wench; some-
    times, like a periwig, I sit upon her brow; or like a fan of
    feathers, I kiss her lips; indeed I do—what do I not? But, fie,
    what a scent is here! I'll not speak another word, except the
    ground were perfum'd, and covered with cloth of arras.

FAUSTUS. What art thou—the second?

COVET. I am Covetousness, begotten of an old churl in an old
    leathern bag; and might I have my wish I would desire that
    this house and all the people in it were turn'd to gold, that I
    might lock you up in my good chest. O, my sweet gold!

FAUSTUS. What art thou—the third?

WRATH. I am Wrath. I had neither father nor mother: I leapt out
    of a lion's mouth when I was scarce half an hour old; and ever

since I have run up and down the world with this case[3] of
rapiers wounding myself when I had nobody to fight withal.
I was born in hell; and look to it, for some of you shall be my
father.

FAUSTUS. What art thou—the fourth?

ENVY. I am Envy, begotten of a chimney sweeper and an oyster-
wife. I cannot read, and therefore wish all books were burnt.
I am lean with seeing others eat. O that there would come a
famine through all the world, that all might die, and I live
alone! then thou should'st see how fat I would be. But must
thou sit and I stand! Come down with a vengeance!

FAUSTUS. Away, envious rascal! What art thou—the fifth?

GLUT. Who, I, sir? I am Gluttony. My parents are all dead, and
the devil a penny they have left me, but a bare pension, and
that is thirty meals a day and ten bevers[4]—a small trifle to suffice nature. O, I come of a royal parentage! My grandfather
was a Gammon of Bacon, my grandmother a Hogshead of
Claret-wine; my godfathers were these, Peter Pickleherring,
and Martin Martlemas-beef.[5] O, but my godmother, she was
a jolly gentlewoman, and well beloved in every good town
and city; her name was Mistress Margery Marchbeer. Now,
Faustus, thou hast heard all my progeny, wilt thou bid me to
supper?

FAUSTUS. No, I'll see thee hanged: thou wilt eat up all my vict-
uals.

GLUT. Then the Devil choke thee!

FAUSTUS. Choke thyself, glutton! Who art thou—the sixth?

SLOTH. I am Sloth. I was begotten on a sunny bank, where I have
lain ever since; and you have done me great injury to bring
me from thence: let me be carried thither again by Gluttony
and Lechery. I'll not speak another word for a king's ransom.

FAUSTUS. What are you, Mistress Minx, the seventh and last?

LECH. Who, I, sir? I am one that loves an inch of raw mutton
better than an ell of fried stockfish; and the first letter of my
name begins with Lechery.

LUC. Away to hell, to hell!                    (*Exeunt the* SINS.)

---

[3] Pair.

[4] Refreshments between meals.

[5] Martlemas or Martinmas was the customary time for hanging up provisions
*to* dry which had been salted for the winter.

—Now, Faustus, how dost thou like this?

FAUSTUS. O, this feeds my soul!

LUC. Tut, Faustus, in hell is all manner of delight.

FAUSTUS. O might I see hell, and return again.
How happy were I then!

LUC. Thou shalt; I will send for thee at midnight.
In meantime take this book; peruse it throughly,
And thou shalt turn thyself into what shape thou wilt.

FAUSTUS. Great thanks, mighty Lucifer!
This will I keep as chary as my life.

LUC. Farewell, Faustus, and think on the Devil.

FAUSTUS. Farewell, great Lucifer! Come, Mephistophilis.

*Exeunt omnes.*

*Enter* WAGNER.

WAG. Learned Faustus,
To know the secrets of astronomy,
Graven in the book of Jove's high firmament,
Did mount himself to scale Olympus' top,
Being seated in a chariot burning bright,
Drawn by the strength of yoky dragons' necks.
He now is gone to prove cosmography,
And, as I guess, will first arrive at Rome,
To see the Pope and manner of his court,
And take some part of holy Peter's feast,
That to this day is highly solemnis'd. *Exit.*

# SCENE VII.

## *The Pope's Privy-chamber.*

*Enter* FAUSTUS *and* MEPHISTOPHILIS.

FAUSTUS. Having now, my good Mephistophilis,
Past with delight the stately town of Trier,[1]
Environ'd round with airy mountain-tops,
With walls of flint, and deep entrenched lakes,
Not to be won by any conquering prince;

---

[1] Treves.

From Paris next, coasting the realm of France,
We saw the river Maine fall into Rhine,
Whose banks are set with groves of fruitful vines;
Then up to Naples, rich Campania,
Whose buildings fair and gorgeous to the eye,
The streets straight forth, and pav'd with finest brick,
Quarter the town in four equivalents.
There saw we learned Maro's[2] golden tomb,
The way he cut, an English mile in length,
Thorough a rock of stone in one night's space;
From thence to Venice, Padua, and the rest,
In one of which a sumptuous temple stands,
That threats the stars with her aspiring top,
Thus hitherto has Faustus spent his time:
But tell me, now, what resting-place is this?
Hast thou, as erst I did command,
Conducted me within the walls of Rome?

MEPH. Faustus, I have; and because we will not be unprovided,
I have taken up[3] his Holiness' privy-chamber for our use.

FAUSTUS. I hope his Holiness will bid us welcome.

MEPH. Tut, 'tis no matter, man, we'll be bold with his good
cheer.
And now, my Faustus, that thou may'st perceive
What Rome containeth to delight thee with,
Know that this city stands upon seven hills
That underprop the groundwork of the same.
[Just through the midst runs flowing Tiber's stream,
With winding banks that cut it in two parts:]
Over the which four stately bridges lean,
That make safe passage to each part of Rome:
Upon the bridge call'd Ponto Angelo
Erected is a castle passing strong,
Within whose walls such store of ordnance are,
And double cannons, fram'd of carved brass,
As match the days within one cómplete year;
Besides the gates and high pyramides,
Which Julius Cæsar brought from Africa.

FAUSTUS. Now by the kingdoms of infernal rule,

---

[2] Virgil, who was reputed a magician in the Middle Ages, was buried at Naples.
[3] Engaged

Of Styx, of Acheron, and the fiery lake
Of ever-burning Phlegethon, I swear
That I do long to see the monuments
And situation of bright-splendent Rome:
Come therefore, let's away.

MEPH. Nay, Faustus, stay; I know you'd fain see the Pope,
And take some part of holy Peter's feast,
Where thou shalt see a troop of bald-pate friars,
Whose *summum bonum* is in belly-cheer.

FAUSTUS. Well, I'm content to compass then some sport,
And by their folly make us merriment.
Then charm me, [Mephistophilis,] that I
May be invisible, to do what I please
Unseen of any whilst I stay in Rome.

[MEPHISTOPHILIS *charms him.*]

MEPH. So, Faustus, now
Do what thou wilt, thou shalt not be discern'd.

*Sound a sennet.*[4] *Enter the* POPE *and the* CARDINAL *of*
LORRAIN *to the banquet, with* FRIARS *attending.*

POPE. My Lord of Lorrain, wilt please you draw near?

FAUSTUS. Fall to, and the devil choke you an[5] you spare!

POPE. How now! Who's that which spake? — Friars, look about.

1 FRIAR. Here's nobody, if it like your Holiness.

POPE. My lord, here is a dainty dish was sent me from the Bishop
of Milan.

FAUSTUS. I thank you, sir.                              *Snatches it*

POPE. How now! Who's that which snatch'd the meat from me?
Will no man look? My Lord, this dish was sent me from the
Cardinal of Florence.

FAUSTUS. You say true; I'll ha't.              [*Snatches it.*]

POPE. What, again! My lord, I'll drink to your Grace.

FAUSTUS. I'll pledge your Grace.              [*Snatches the cup.*]

C.OF LOR. My lord, it may be some ghost newly crept out of
purgatory, come to beg a pardon of your Holiness.

POPE. It may be so. Friars, prepare a dirge to lay the fury of this
ghost. Once again, my lord, fall to.

*The* POPE *crosseth himself.*

---

[4] A particular set of notes on the trumpet or cornet, different from a flourish.
[5] If.

FAUSTUS. What, are you crossing of yourself? Well, use that trick no more I would advise you.

> [*The Pope*] *crosses* [*himself*] *again.*

Well, there's the second time. Aware the third, I give you fair warning.

> [*The* POPE] *crosses* [*himself*] *again,*
> *and* FAUSTUS *hits him a box of the*
> *ear; and they all run away.*

Come on, Mephistophilis, what shall we do?

MEPH. Nay, I know not. We shall be curs'd with bell, book, and candle.

FAUSTUS. How! bell, book, and candle, —candle, book, and bell,
Forward and backward to curse Faustus to hell!
Anon you shall hear a hog grunt, a calf bleat, and an ass bray,
Because it is Saint Peter's holiday.

> *Re-enter all the* FRIARS *to sing the Dirge.*

1 FRIAR. Come, brethren, let's about our business with good devotion.

*They sing:*

   Cursed be he that stole away his Holiness' meat from the table!
      *Maledicat Dominus!*[6]
   Cursed be he that struck his Holiness a blow on the face!
      *Maledicat Dominus!*
   Cursed be he that took Friar Sandelo a blow on the pate!
      *Maledicat Dominus!*
   Cursed be he that disturbeth our holy dirge! *Maledicat Dominus!*
   Cursed be he that took away his Holiness' wine! *Maledicat*
      *Dominus! Et omnes sancti!*[7] *Amen!*

> [MEPHISTOPHILIS *and* FAUSTUS] *beat the* FRIARS, *and fling fireworks*
> *among them: and so exeunt.*

> *Enter* CHORUS.

CHORUS. When Faustus had with pleasure ta'en the view
   Of rarest things, and royal courts of kings,
   He stay'd his course, and so returned home;
   Where such as bear his absence but with grief,
   I mean his friends, and near'st companions,

---

[6] "May the Lord curse him."
[7] "And all the saints."

Did gratulate his safety with kind words,
And in their conference of what befell,
Touching his journey through the world and air,
They put forth questions of Astrology,
Which Faustus answer'd with such learned skill,
As they admir'd and wond'red at his wit.
Now is his fame spread forth in every land;
Amongst the rest the Emperor is one,
Carolus the Fifth, at whose palace now
Faustus is feasted 'mongst his noblemen.
What there he did in trial of his art,
I leave untold —your eyes shall see perform'd.     *Exit.*

# SCENE VIII.

## *An Inn-yard.*

*Enter* ROBIN *the Ostler with a book in his hand.*

ROBIN. O, this is admirable! here I ha' stolen one of Dr. Faustus'
conjuring books, and i' faith I mean to search some circles for
my own use. Now will I make all the maidens in our parish
dance at my pleasure, stark naked before me; and so by that
means I shall see more than e'er I felt or saw yet.

*Enter* RALPH *calling* ROBIN.

RALPH. Robin, prithee come away; there's a gentleman tarries
to have his horse, and he would have his things rubb'd and
made clean. He keeps such a chafing with my mistress about
it; and she has sent me to look thee out. Prithee come away.

ROBIN. Keep out, keep out, or else you are blown up; you are
dismemb'red, Ralph: keep out, for I am about a roaring piece
of work.

RALPH. Come, what dost thou with that same book? Thou canst
not read.

ROBIN. Yes, my master and mistress shall find that I can read, he
for his forehead, she for her private study; she's born to bear
with me, or else my art fails.

RALPH. Why, Robin, what book is that?

ROBIN. What book! Why, the most intolerable book for conjuring that e'er was invented by any brimstone devil.

RALPH. Canst thou conjure with it?

ROBIN. I can do all these things easily with it: first, I can make thee drunk with ippocras[1] at any tabern in Europe for nothing; that's one of my conjuring works.

RALPH. Our Master Parson says that's nothing.

ROBIN. True, Ralph; and more, Ralph, if thou hast any mind to Nan Spit, our kitchenmaid, then turn her and wind her to thy own use as often as thou wilt, and at midnight.

RALPH. O brave Robin, shall I have Nan Spit, and to mine own use?

On that condition I'll feed thy devil with horsebread as long as he lives, of free cost.

ROBIN. No more, sweet Ralph: let's go and make clean our boots, which lie foul upon our hands, and then to our conjuring in the Devil's name.                           *Exeunt.*

# SCENE IX.

## *An Inn.*

*Enter* ROBIN *and* RALPH *with a silver goblet*

ROBIN. Come, Ralph, did not I tell thee we were for ever made by this Doctor Faustus' book? *Ecce signum,*[1] here's a simple purchase[2] for horsekeepers; our horses shall eat no hay as long as this lasts.

*Enter the* VLNTNER.

RALPH. But, Robin, here comes the vintner.

ROBIN. Hush! I'll gull him supernaturally. Drawer, I hope all is paid: God be with you. Come, Ralph.

VLNT. Soft, sir; a word with you. I must yet have a goblet paid from you, ere you go.

ROBIN. I, a goblet, Ralph; I, a goblet! I scorn you, and you are but a[3] &c. I, a goblet! search me.

VLNT. I mean so, sir, with your favour. [*Searches him.*]

---

[1] Wine mixed with sugar and spices.

[1] "Behold the sign."

[2] Gain.

[3] The abuse was left to the actor's inventiveness.

ROBIN. How say you now?

VLNT. I must say somewhat to your fellow. You, sir!

RALPH. Me, sir! me, sir! search your fill. [VLNTNER *searches him.*]
   Now, sir, you may be ashamed to burden honest men with a
   matter of truth.

VLNT. Well, t' one of you hath this goblet about you.

ROBIN. [*Aside.*] You lie, drawer, 'tis afore me. —Sirrah you,
   I'll teach ye to impeach honest men; stand by; — I'll scour
   you for a goblet! —stand aside you had best, I charge you in
   the name of Belzebub. [*Aside to* RALPH.] Look to the goblet,
   Ralph.

VLNT. What mean you, sirrah?

ROBIN. I'll tell you what I mean. *Reads* [*from a book.*] *Sanctobulorum,
   Periphrasticon* — Nay, I'll tickle you, vintner. [*Aside to* RALPH.]
   Look to the goblet, Ralph. [*Reads.*] *Polypragmos Belseborams
   framanto pacostiphos tostu, Mephistophilis, &c.*

*Enter* MEPHISTOPHILIS, *sets squibs at their backs,* [*and then exit*].
*They run about.*

VLNT. O *nomine Domini!*[4] what meanest thou, Robin? Thou hast
   no goblet.

RALPH. *Peccatum peccatorum*[5] Here's thy goblet, good vintner.
                     [*Gives the goblet to* VINTNER, *who exit*]

ROBIN. *Misericordia pro nobis!*[6] What shall I do? Good Devil,
   forgive me now, and I'll never rob thy library more.

*Re-enter to them* MEPHISTOPHILIS.

MEPH. Monarch of hell, under whose black survey
   Great potentates do kneel with awful fear,
   Upon whose altars thousand souls do lie,
   How am I vexed with these villains' charms?
   From Constantinople am I hither come
   Only for pleasure of these damned slaves.

ROBIN. How from Constantinople? You have had a great journey. Will you take sixpence in your purse to pay for your
   supper, and begone?

---

[4] "In the name of the Lord."

[5] "Sin of sins."

[6] "Mercy on us."

MEPH. Well, villains, for your presumption, I transform thee into
    an ape, and thee into a dog; and so begone.                    *Exit.*
ROBIN. How, into an ape? That's brave! I'll have fine sport with
    the boys. I'll get nuts and apples enow.
RALPH. And I must be a dog.
ROBIN. I' faith thy head will never be out of the pottage pot.
                                                          *Exeunt.*


# SCENE X.

## *The Court of the Emperor.*

*Enter* EMPEROR, FAUSTUS, *and a* KNIGHT *with attendants.*

EMP. Master Doctor Faustus, I have heard strange report of thy
    knowledge in the black art, how that none in my empire nor
    in the whole world can compare with thee for the rare effects
    of magic; they say thou hast a familiar spirit, by whom thou
    canst accomplish what thou list. This, therefore, is my request,
    that thou let me see some proof of thy skill, that mine eyes
    may be witnesses to confirm what mine ears have heard
    reported; and here I swear to thee by the honour of mine
    imperial crown, that, whatever thou doest, thou shalt be no
    ways prejudiced or endamaged.
KNIGHT. [Aside.] I' faith he looks much like a conjuror.
FAUSTUS. My gracious sovereign, though I must confess myself
    far inferior to the report men have published, and nothing
    answerable[1] to the honour of your imperial majesty, yet for
    that love and duty binds me thereunto, I am content to do
    whatsoever your majesty shall command me.
EMP. Then, Doctor Faustus, mark what I shall say.
    As I was sometime solitary set
    Within my closet, sundry thoughts arose
    About the honour of mine ancestors,
    How they had won by prowess such exploits,
    Got such riches, subdued so many kingdoms,
    As we that do succeed, or they that shall

---

[1] Proportionate.

Hereafter possess our throne, shall
(I fear me) ne'er attain to that degree
Of high renown and great authority;
Amongst which kings is Alexander the Great,
Chief spectacle of the world's pre-eminence,
The bright shining of whose glorious acts
Lightens the world with his[2] reflecting beams,
As, when I heard but motion[3] made of him,
It grieves my soul I never saw the man.
If, therefore, thou by cunning of thine art
Canst raise this man from hollow vaults below,
Where lies entomb'd this famous conqueror,
And bring with him his beauteous paramour,
Both in their right shapes, gesture, and attire
They us'd to wear during their time of life,
Thou shalt both satisfy my just desire,
And give me cause to praise thee whilst I live.

FAUSTUS. My gracious lord, I am ready to accomplish your request so far forth as by art, and power of my Spirit, I am able to perform.

KNIGHT. [*Aside.*] I' faith that's just nothing at all.

FAUSTUS. But, if it like your Grace, it is not in my ability to present before your eyes the true substantial bodies of those two deceased princes, which long since are consumed to dust.

KNIGHT. [*Aside.*] Ay, marry, Master Doctor, now there's a sign of grace in you, when you will confess the truth.

Faustus. But such spirits as can lively resemble Alexander and his paramour shall appear before your Grace in that manner that they best liv'd in, in their most flourishing estate; which I doubt not shall sufficiently content your imperial majesty.

EMP. Go to, Master Doctor, let me see them presently.

Knight. Do you hear, Master Doctor? You bring Alexander and his paramour before the Emperor!

FAUSTUS. How then, sir?

KNIGHT. I' faith that's as true as Diana turn'd me to a stag!

FAUSTUS. No, sir, but when Actæon died, he left the horns for you.

---

[2] Its.

[3] Mention.

Mephistophilis, begone.                    *Exit* MEPHISTOPHILIS.

FAUSTUS. Nay, an you go to conjuring, I'll begone.          *Exit*.

FAUSTUS. I'll meet with you anon for interrupting me so. Here they are, my gracious lord.

> *Re-enter* MEPHISTOPHILIS *and* [SPIRITS *in the shape of*]
> ALEXANDER *and his* PARAMOUR.

EMP. Master Doctor, I heard this lady while she liv'd had a wart or mole in her neck: how shall I know whether it be so or no?

FAUSTUS. Your Highness may boldly go and see.

                                   *Exeunt* [Spirits.]

EMP. Sure these are no spirits, but the true substantial bodies of those two deceased princes.

FAUSTUS. Will't please your Highness now to send for the knight that was so pleasant with me here of late?

EMP. One of you call him forth.                    [*Exit* Attendant.]

> *Re-enter the* KNIGHT *with a pair of horns on his head.*

How now, sir knight! why I had thought thou had'st been a bachelor, but now I see thou hast a wife, that not only gives thee horns, but makes thee wear them. Feel on thy head.

KNIGHT. Thou damned wretch and execrable dog,
Bred in the concave of some monstrous rock,
How darest thou thus abuse a gentleman?
Villain, I say, undo what thou hast done!

FAUSTUS. O, not so fast, sir; there's no haste; but, good, are you rememb'red how you crossed me in my conference with the Emperor? I think I have met with you for it.

EMP. Good Master Doctor, at my entreaty release him; he hath done penance sufficient.

FAUSTUS. My gracious lord, not so much for the injury he off'red me here in your presence, as to delight you with some mirth, hath Faustus worthily requited this injurious knight; which, being all I desire, I am content to release him of his horns: and, sir knight, hereafter speak well of scholars. Mephistophilis, transform him straight. [MEPHISTOPHILIS *removes the horns.*] Now, my good lord, having done my duty I humbly take my leave.

EMP. Farewell, Master Doctor; yet, ere you go,
Expect from me a bounteous reward.                    *Exeunt*.

# SCENE XI

## *A Green; afterwards, the House of Faustus.*

[*Enter* FAUSTUS *and* MEPHISTOPHILIS.]

FAUSTUS. Now, Mephistophilis, the restless course
    That Time doth run with calm and silent foot,
    Short'ning my days and thread of vital life,
    Calls for the payment of my latest years;
    Therefore, sweet Mephistophilis, let us
    Make haste to Wittenberg.
MEPH. What, will you go on horseback or on foot?
FAUSTUS. Nay, till I'm past this fair and pleasant green.
    I'll walk on foot.

*Enter a* HORSE-COURSER.

HORSE-C. I have been all this day seeking one Master Fustian:
    mass, see where he is! God save you, Master Doctor!
FAUSTUS. What, horse-courser! You are well met.
HORSE-C. Do you hear, sir? I have brought you forty dollars for
    your horse.
FAUSTUS. I cannot sell him so: if thou likest him for fifty, take
    him.
HORSE-C. Alas, sir, I have no more.—I pray you speak for me.
MEPH. I pray you let him have him: he is an honest fellow, and
    he has a great charge, neither wife nor child.
FAUSTUS. Well, come, give me your money. [HORSE-COURSER
    *gives* FAUSTUS *the money*.] My boy will deliver him to you. But
    I must tell you one thing before you have him; ride him not
    into the water at any hand.
HORSE-C. Why, sir, will he not drink of all waters?
FAUSTUS. O yes, he will drink of all waters, but ride him not into
    the water: ride him over hedge or ditch, or where thou wilt,
    but not into the water.
HORSE-C. Well, sir.—Now I am made man forever. I'll not leave
    my horse for forty. [*Aside.*] If he had but the quality of hey-
    ding-ding, hey-ding-ding, I'd make a brave living on him: he
    has a buttock as slick as an eel. Well, God b' wi'ye, sir, your
    boy will deliver him me: but hark ye, sir; if my horse be sick
    or ill at ease, if I bring his water to you, you'll tell me what it
    is?                                      *Exit* HORSE-COURSER.

FAUSTUS. Away, you villain; what, dost think I am a horse-doctor?

What art thou, Faustus, but a man condemn'd to die?
Thy fatal time doth draw to final end;
Despair doth drive distrust unto my thoughts:
Confound these passions with a quiet sleep:
Tush, Christ did call the thief upon the cross;
Then rest thee, Faustus, quiet in conceit.

*Sleeps in his chair.*

*Re-enter* HORSE-COURSER, *all wet, crying.*

HORSE-C. Alas, alas! Doctor Fustian, quotha? Mass, Doctor Lopus[1] was never such a doctor. Has given me a purgation has purg'd me of forty dollars; I shall never see them more. But yet, like an ass as I was, I would not be ruled by him, for he bade me I should ride him into no water. Now I, thinking my horse had had some rare quality that he would not have had me known of, I, like a venturous youth, rid him into the deep pond at the town's end. I was no sooner in the middle of the pond, but my horse vanish'd away, and I sat upon a bottle of hay, never so near drowning in my life. But I'll seek out my Doctor, and have my forty dollars again, or I'll make it the dearest horse!—O, yonder is his snipper-snapper.—Do you hear? You heypass,[2] where's your master?

MEPH. Why, sir, what would you? You cannot speak with him.

HORSE-C. But I will speak with him.

MEPH. Why, he's fast asleep. Come some other time.

HORSE-C. I'll speak with him now, or I'll break his glass windows about his ears.

MEPH. I tell thee he has not slept this eight nights.

HORSE-C. An he have not slept this eight weeks, I'll speak with him.

MEPH. See where he is, fast asleep.

Horse-C. Ay, this is he. God save you, Master Doctor! Master Doctor, Master Doctor Fustian!—Forty dollars, forty dollars for a bottle of hay!

MEPH. Why, thou seest he hears thee not.

HORSE-C. So ho, ho!—so, ho, ho! (*Hollas in his ear.*) No, will you not wake? I'll make you wake ere I go. (*Pulls* FAUSTUS

---

[1] Dr. Lopez, physician to Queen Elizabeth, hanged in 1594 on the charge of conspiring to poison the Queen.

[2] A juggler's term, like "presto, fly!" Hence applied to the juggler himself.

*by the leg, and pulls it away.*) Alas, I am undone! What shall I do?

FAUSTUS. O my leg, my leg! Help, Mephistophilis! call the officers. My leg, my leg!

MEPH. Come, villain, to the constable.

HORSE-C. O lord, sir, let me go, and I'll give you forty dollars more.

MEPH. Where be they?

HORSE-C. I have none about me. Come to my ostry[3] and I'll give them you.

MEPH. Begone quickly.                    HORSE-COURSER *runs away.*

FAUSTUS. What, is he gone? Farewell he! Faustus has his leg again, and the horse-courser, I take it, a bottle of hay for his labour. Well, this trick shall cost him forty dollars more.

*Enter* WAGNER.

How now, Wagner, what's the news with thee?

WAG. Sir, the Duke of Vanholt doth earnestly entreat your company.

FAUSTUS. The Duke of Vanholt! an honourable gentleman, to whom I must be no niggard of my cunning. Come, Mephistophilis, let's away to him.                    *Exeunt.*

## SCENE XII.

### *The Court of the Duke of Vanholt.*

*Enter the* DUKE [OF VANHOLT], *the* DUCHESS, [FAUSTUS, *and* MEPHISTOPHILIS.]

DUKE. Believe me, Master Doctor, this merriment hath much pleased me.

FAUSTUS. My gracious lord, I am glad it contents you so well. — But it may be, madam, you take no delight in this. I have heard that great-bellied women do long for some dainties or other. What is it, madam? Tell me, and you shall have it.

DUCHESS. Thanks, good Master Doctor; and for I see your courteous intent to pleasure me, I will not hide from you the thing

---

[3] Inn.

my heart desires; and were it now summer, as it is January and
the dead time of the winter, I would desire no better meat
than a dish of ripe grapes.

FAUSTUS. Alas, madam, that's nothing! Mephistophilis, begone.
(*Exit* MEPHISTOPHILIS.) Were it a greater thing than this, so it
would content you, you should have it.

*Re-enter* MEPHISTOPHILIS *with the grapes*.

Here they be, madam; wilt please you taste on them?

DUKE. Believe me, Master Doctor, this makes me wonder above
the rest, that being in the dead time of winter, and in the month
of January, how you should come by these grapes.

FAUSTUS. If it like your Grace, the year is divided into two circles
over the whole world, that, when it is here winter with us, in
the contrary circle it is summer with them, as in India, Saba,
and farther countries in the East; and by means of a swift spirit
that I have, I had them brought hither, as ye see. — How do
you like them, madam; be they good?

DUCHESS. Believe me, Master Doctor, they be the best grapes
that I e'er tasted in my life before.

FAUSTUS. I am glad they content you so, madam.

DUKE. Come, madam, let us in, where you must well reward
this learned man for the great kindness he hath show'd to you.

DUCHESS. And so I will, my lord; and whilst I live, rest beholding for this courtesy.

FAUSTUS. I humbly thank your Grace.

DUKE. Come, Master Doctor, follow us and receive your reward.

*Exeunt*.

# SCENE XIII.

## *A Room in the House of Faustus.*

*Enter* WAGNER, *solus*.

WAG. I think my master means to die shortly,
For he hath given to me all his goods;
And yet, methinks, if that death were near,
He would not banquet and carouse and swill
Amongst the students, as even now he doth,

Who are at supper with such belly-cheer
As Wagner ne'er beheld in all his life.
See where they come! Belike the feast is ended.

*Enter* FAUSTUS, *with two or three* SCHOLARS
[*and* MEPHISTOPHILIS.]

1 SCHOL. Master Doctor Faustus, since our conference about fair
ladies, which was the beautifullest in all the world, we have
determined with ourselves that Helen of Greece was the admi-
rablest lady that ever lived: therefore, Master Doctor, if you
will do us that favour, as to let us see that peerless dame of
Greece, whom all the world admires for majesty, we should
think ourselves much beholding unto you.

FAUSTUS. Gentlemen,
For that I know your friendship is unfeigned,
And Faustus' custom is not to deny
The just requests of those that wish him well,
You shall behold that peerless dame of Greece,
No otherways for pomp and majesty
Than when Sir Paris cross'd the seas with her,
And brought the spoils to rich Dardania.
Be silent, then, for danger is in words.

*Music* sounds, *and* HELEN *passeth over the stage.*

2 SCHOL. Too simple is my wit to tell her praise,
Whom all the world admires for majesty.

3 SCHOL. No marvel though the angry Greeks pursu'd
With ten years' war the rape of such a queen,
Whose heavenly beauty passeth all compare.

1 SCHOL. Since we have seen the pride of Nature's works,
And only paragon of excellence,

*Enter an* OLD MAN.

Let us depart; and for this glorious deed
Happy and blest be Faustus evermore.

FAUSTUS. Gentlemen, farewell —the same I wish to you.

*Exeunt* SCHOLARS [*and* WAGNER].

OLD MAN. Ah, Doctor Faustus, that I might prevail
To guide thy steps unto the way of life,
By which sweet path thou may'st attain the goal
That shall conduct thee to celestial rest!
Break heart, drop blood, and mingle it with tears,

Tears falling from repentant heaviness
Of thy most vile and loathsome filthiness,
The stench whereof corrupts the inward soul
With such flagitious crimes of heinous sins
As no commiseration may expel,
But mercy, Faustus, of thy Saviour sweet,
Whose blood alone must wash away thy guilt.

FAUSTUS. Where art thou, Faustus? Wretch, what hast thou done?
Damn'd art thou, Faustus, damn'd; despair and die!
Hell calls for right, and with a roaring voice
Says "Faustus! come! thine hour is [almost] come!"
And Faustus [now] will come to do thee right.

                        MEPHISTOPHILIS *gives him a dagger.*

OLD MAN. Ah stay, good Faustus, stay thy desperate steps!
I see an angel hovers o'er thy head,
And, with a vial full of precious grace,
Offers to pour the same into thy soul:
Then call for mercy, and avoid despair.

FAUSTUS. Ah, my sweet friend, I feel
Thy words do comfort my distressed soul.
Leave me a while to ponder on my sins.

OLD MAN. I go, sweet Faustus, but with heavy cheer,
Fearing the ruin of thy hopeless soul.                    [*Exit.*]

FAUSTUS. Accursed Faustus, where is mercy now?
I do repent; and yet I do despair;
Hell strives with grace for conquest in my breast:
What shall I do to shun the snares of death?

MEPH. Thou traitor, Faustus, I arrest thy soul
For disobedience to my sovereign lord;
Revolt, or I'll in piecemeal tear thy flesh.

FAUSTUS. Sweet Mephistophilis, entreat thy lord
To pardon my unjust presumption,
And with my blood again I will confirm
My former vow I made to Lucifer.

MEPH. Do it now then quickly, with unfeigned heart,
Lest danger do attend thy drift.

          [FAUSTUS *stabs his arm and writes on a paper with his blood.*]

FAUSTUS. Torment, sweet friend, that base and crooked age,[1]
That durst dissuade me from my Lucifer,
With greatest torments that our hell affords.

MEPH. His faith is great, I cannot touch his soul;

But what I may afflict his body with
I will attempt, which is but little worth.

FAUSTUS. One thing, good servant, let me crave of thee,
To glut the longing of my heart's desire, —
That I might have unto my paramour
That heavenly Helen, which I saw of late,
Whose sweet embracings may extinguish clean
These thoughts that do dissuade me from my vow,
And keep mine oath I made to Lucifer.

MEPH. Faustus, this or what else thou shalt desire
Shall be perform'd in twinkling of an eye.

*Re-enter* HELEN.

FAUSTUS. Was this the face that launch'd a thousand ships,
And burnt the topless[2] towers of Ilium?
Sweet Helen, make me immortal with a kiss.       [*Kisses her.*]
Her lips suck forth my soul; see where it flies! —
Come, Helen, come, give me my soul again.
Here will I dwell, for Heaven be in these lips,
And all is dross that is not Helena.

*Enter* OLD MAN.

I will be Paris, and for love of thee,
Instead of Troy, shall Wittenberg be sack'd;
And I will combat with weak Menelaus,
And wear thy colours on my plumed crest;
Yea, I will wound Achilles in the heel,
And then return to Helen for a kiss.
Oh, thou art fairer than the evening air
Clad in the beauty of a thousand stars;
Brighter art thou than flaming Jupiter
When he appear'd to hapless Semele:
More lovely than the monarch of the sky
In wanton Arethusa's azur'd arms:
And none but thou shalt be my paramour.        *Exeunt.*

OLD MAN. Accursed Faustus, miserable man,
That from thy soul exclud'st the grace of Heaven,

---

[1] Old Man.
[2] Unsurpassed in height.

And fly'st the throne of his tribunal seat!

*Enter* DEVILS.

Satan begins to sift me with his pride:
As in this furnace God shall try my faith,
My faith, vile hell, shall triumph over thee.
Ambitious fiends! see how the heavens smiles
At your repulse, and laughs your state to scorn!
Hence, hell! for hence I fly unto my God.          *Exeunt.*

# SCENE XIV.

## *The Same.*

*Enter* FAUSTUS *with the* SCHOLARS.

FAUSTUS. Ah, gentlemen!

1 SCHOL. What ails Faustus?

FAUSTUS. Ah, my sweet chamber-fellow, had I lived with thee,
then had I lived still! but now I die eternally. Look, comes he
not, come he not?

2 SCHOL. What means Faustus?

3 SCHOL. Belike he is grown into some sickness by being over
solitary.

1 SCHOL. If it be so, we'll have physicians to cure him. 'Tis but
a surfeit. Never fear, man.

FAUSTUS. A surfeit of deadly sin that hath damn'd both body and
soul.

2 SCHOL. Yet, Faustus, look up to Heaven; remember God's
mercies are infinite.

FAUSTUS. But Faustus' offences can never be pardoned: the serpent
that tempted Eve may be sav'd, but not Faustus. Ah, gentlemen, hear me with patience, and tremble not at my speeches!
Though my heart pants and quivers to remember that I have
been a student here these thirty years, oh, would I had never
seen Wittenberg, never read book! And what wonders I have
done, all Germany can witness, yea, the world; for which
Faustus hath lost both Germany and the world, yea Heaven
itself, Heaven, the seat of God, the throne of the blessed, the

kingdom of joy; and must remain in hell for ever, hell, ah, hell, for ever! Sweet friends! what shall become of Faustus being in hell for ever?

3 SCHOL. Yet, Faustus, call on God.

FAUSTUS. On God, whom Faustus hath abjur'd! on God, whom Faustus hath blasphemed! Ah, my God, I would weep, but the Devil draws in my tears. Gush forth blood instead of tears! Yea, life and soul! Oh, he stays my tongue! I would lift up my hands, but see, they hold them, they hold them!

ALL. Who, Faustus?

FAUSTUS. Lucifer and Mephistophilis. Ah, gentlemen, I gave them my soul for my cunning!

ALL. God forbid!

FAUSTUS. God forbade it indeed; but Faustus hath done it. For vain pleasure of twenty-four years hath Faustus lost eternal joy and felicity. I writ them a bill with mine own blood: the date is expired; the time will come, and he will fetch me.

1 SCHOL. Why did not Faustus tell us of this before, that divines might have prayed for thee?

FAUSTUS. Oft have I thought to have done so; but the Devil threat'ned to tear me in pieces if I nam'd God; to fetch both body and soul if I once gave ear to divinity: and now 't is too late. Gentlemen, away! lest you perish with me.

2 SCHOL. Oh, what shall we do to save Faustus?

FAUSTUS. Talk not of me, but save yourselves, and depart.

3 SCHOL. God will strengthen me. I will stay with Faustus.

1 SCHOL. Tempt not God, sweet friend; but let us into the next room, and there pray for him.

FAUSTUS. Ay, pray for me, pray for me! and what noise soever ye hear, come not unto me, for nothing can rescue me.

2 SCHOL. Pray thou, and we will pray that God may have mercy upon thee.

FAUSTUS. Gentlemen, farewell! If I live till morning I'll visit you: if not—Faustus is gone to hell.

ALL. Faustus, farewell!

*Exeunt* SCHOLARS. *The clock strikes eleven.*

FAUSTUS. Ah, Faustus,
Now hast thou but one bare hour to live,
And then thou must be damn'd perpetually!
Stand still, you ever-moving spheres of Heaven,
That time may cease, and midnight never come;

Fair Nature's eye, rise, rise again and make
Perpetual day; or let this hour be but
A year, a month, a week, a natural day,
That Faustus may repent and save his soul!
O *lente, lente, currite noctis equi!*[1]
The stars move still,[2] time runs, the clock will strike,
The Devil will come, and Faustus must be damn'd.
O, I'll leap up to my God! Who pulls me down?
See, see where Christ's blood streams in the firmament!
One drop would save my soul— Half a drop: ah, my Christ!
Ah, rend not my heart for naming of my Christ!
Yet will I call on him: O spare me, Lucifer! —
Where is it now? 'Tis gone; and see where God
Stretcheth out his arm, and bends his ireful brows!
Mountain and hills come, come and fall on me,
And hide me from the heavy wrath of God!
No! no!
Then will I headlong run into the earth;
Earth gape! O no, it will not harbour me!
You stars that reign'd at my nativity,
Whose influence hath allotted death and hell,
Now draw up Faustus like a foggy mist
Into the entrails of yon labouring clouds,
That when they vomit forth into the air,
My limbs may issue from their smoky mouths,
So that my soul may but ascend to Heaven.

> *The watch strikes [the half hour].*

Ah, half the hour is past! Twill all be past anon!
O God!
If thou wilt not have mercy on my soul,
Yet for Christ's sake whose blood hath ransom'd me,
Impose some end to my incessant pain;
Let Faustus live in hell a thousand years —
A hundred thousand, and at last be sav'd!
O, no end is limited to damned souls!
Why wert thou not a creature wanting soul?
Or why is this immortal that thou hast?
Ah, Pythagoras' metempsychosis! were that true,

---

[1] "Run softly, softly, horses of the night." — Ovid*'s Amores,* i. 13.
[2] Without ceasing.

This soul should fly from me, and I be chang'd
Unto some brutish beast! All beasts are happy,
For, when they die,
Their souls are soon dissolv'd in elements;
But mine must live, still to be plagu'd in hell.
Curst be the parents that engend'red me!
No, Faustus: curse thyself: curse Lucifer
That hath depriv'd thee of the joys of Heaven.

                                        *The clock striketh twelve.*

O, it strikes, it strikes! Now, body, turn to air,
Or Lucifer will bear thee quick to hell.

                                        *Thunder and lightning.*

O soul, be chang'd into little water-drops,
And fall into the ocean — ne'er be found.
My God! my God! look not so fierce on me!

                        *Enter* DEVILS.

Adders and serpents, let me breathe awhile!
Ugly hell, gape not! come not, Lucifer!
I'll burn my books! —Ah Mephistophilis!

                        *Exeunt* [DEVILS *with* FAUSTUS.]

                        *Enter* CHORUS.

[CHO.] Cut is the branch that might have grown full straight,
    And burned is Apollo's laurel bough,
    That sometimes grew within this learned man.
    Faustus is gone; regard his hellish fall,
    Whose fiendful fortune may exhort the wise
    Only to wonder at unlawful things,
    Whose deepness doth entice such forward wits
    To practise more than heavenly power permits.

                                              [*Exit.*]

*Terminat hora diem, terminat author opus.*[3]

---

[3] "The hour ends the day, the author ends his work."

# A WOMAN KILLED WITH KINDNESS

## Thomas Heywood

# CHARACTERS

SIR FRANCIS ACTON, *brother of* MISTRESS FRANKFORD
SIR CHARLES MOUNTFORD
MASTER FRANKFORD
MASTER WENDOLL, *friend to* FRANKFORD
MASTER MALBY, *friend to* SIR FRANCIS
MASTER CRANWELL
SHAFTON, *a false friend to* SIR CHARLES
OLD MOUNTFORD, *uncle to* SIR CHARLES
TIDY, *cousin to* SIR CHARLES
SANDY,
RODER,
NICHOLAS,
JENKIN,
ROGER BRICKBAT, } *servants to* FRANKFORD
JACK SLIME,
SPIGOT, *a butler,*
SHERIFF
A SERJEANT, A KEEPER, OFFICERS, FALCONERS, HUNTSMEN, A
    COACHMAN, CABTERS, SERVANTS, MUSICIANS
MISTRESS FRANKFORD
SUSAN, *sister of* SIR CHARLES
CICELY, *maid to* MISTRESS FRANKFORD
WOMEN SERVANTS

SCENE—*The North of England.*

# ACT I

## SCENE I—*A room in* FRANKFORD'S *house.*

[*Enter* MASTER FRANKFORD, MISTRESS FRANKFORD, SIR FRANCIS ACTON, SIR CHARLES MOUNTFORD, MASTER MALBY, MASTER WENDOLL, *and* MASTER CRANWELL.]

SIR FRANCIS. Some music there: none lead the bride a dance?

SIR CHARLES. Yes, would she dance "The Shaking of the Sheets";
But that's the dance her husband means to lead her.

WENDOLL. That's not the dance that every man must dance,
According to the ballad.

SIR FRANCIS. Music, ho!
By your leave, sister;—by your husband's leave,
I should have said: the hand that but this day
Was given you in the church I'll borrow: sound!
This marriage music hoists me from the ground.

FRANKFORD. Ay, you may caper, you are light and free:
Marriage hath yoked my heels; pray then pardon me.

SIR FRANCIS. I'll have you dance too, brother.

SIR CHARLES. Master Frankford,
You are a happy man, sir; and much joy
Succeed your marriage mirth! you have a wife
So qualified, and with such ornaments
Both of the mind and body. First, her birth
Is noble, and her education such
As might become the daughter of a prince:
Her own tongue speaks all tongues, and her own hand
Can teach all strings to speak in their best grace,
From the shrillest treble to the hoarsest base.

139

To end her many praises in one word,
She's beauty and perfection's eldest daughter,
Only found by yours, though many a heart hath sought her.
   FRANKFORD. But that I know your virtues and chaste thoughts,
I should be jealous of your praise, Sir Charles.
   CRANWELL. He speaks no more than you approve.
   MALBY. Nor flatters he that gives to her her due.
   MISTRESS FRANKFORD. I would your praise could find a fitter
     theme
Than my imperfect beauties to speak on:
Such as they be, if they my husband please,
They suffice me now I am marrièd:
His sweet content is like a flattering glass,
To make my face seem fairer to mine eye;
But the least wrinkle from his stormy brow
Will blast the roses in my cheeks that grow.
   SIR FRANCIS. A perfect wife already, meek and patient:
How strangely the word "husband" fits your mouth,
Not married three hours since! Sister, 'tis good;
You, that begin betimes thus, must needs prove
Pliant and duteous in your husband's love.—
Gramercies, brother, wrought her to't already;
Sweet husband, and a curtsey, the first day!
Mark this, mark this, you that are bachelors,
And never took the grace of honest man;
Mark this, against you marry, this one phrase:
"In a good time that man both wins and woos,
That takes his wife down in her wedding shoes."
   FRANKFORD. Your sister takes not after you, Sir Francis;
All his wild blood your father spent on you:
He got her in his age, when he grew civil:
All his mad tricks were to his land entailed,
And you are heir to all; your sister, she
Hath to her dower her mother's modesty.
   SIR CHARLES. Lord, sir, in what a happy state live you!
This morning, which to many seems a burden
Too heavy to bear, is unto you a pleasure.
This lady is no clog, as many are:
She doth become you like a well-made suit,
In which the tailor hath used all his art;
Not like a thick coat of unseasoned frieze,

Forced on your back in summer. She's no chain
To tie your neck, and curb you to the yoke;
But she's a chain of gold to adorn your neck.
You both adorn each other, and your hands,
Methinks, are matches: there's equality
In this fair combination; you are both
Scholars, both young, both being descended nobly.
There's music in this sympathy; it carries
Consort, and expectation of much joy,
Which God bestow on you, from this first day
Until your dissolution; that's for aye.

   SIR FRANCIS. We keep you here too long, good brother
     Frankford.
Into the hall; away! go cheer your guests.
What, bride and bridegroom both withdrawn at once?
If you be missed, the guests will doubt their welcome,
And charge you with unkindness.

   FRANKFORD. To prevent it,
I'll leave you here, to see the dance within.

   MISTRESS FRANKFORD. And so will I.

[*Exeunt* FRANKFORD *and* MISTRESS FRANKFORD.]

   SIR FRANCIS. To part you, it were sin.
Now, gallants, while the town-musicians
Finger their frets within; and the mad lads
And country-lasses, every mother's child,
With nosegays and bridelaces in their hats,
Dance all their country measures, rounds, and jigs,
What shall we do? Hark, they are all on the hoigh;
They toil like mill-horses, and turn as round,—
Marry, not on the toe. Ay, and they caper,
Not without cutting; you shall see, to-morrow,
The hall-floor pecked and dinted like a mill-stone,
Made with their high shoes; though their skill be small,
Yet they tread heavy where their hobnails fall.

   SIR CHARLES. Well, leave them to their sports. Sir Francis
Acton,
I'll make a match with you; meet to-morrow
At Chevy-chase, I'll fly my hawk with yours.

   SIR FRANCIS. For what? For what?

   SIR CHARLES. Why, for a hundred pound.

SIR FRANCIS. Pawn me some gold of that.

SIR CHARLES. Here are ten angels;
I'll make them good a hundred pound to-morrow
Upon my hawk's wing.

SIR FRANCIS. 'Tis a match, 'tis done.
Another hundred pound upon your dogs;
Dare ye, Sir Charles?

SIR CHARLES. I dare: were I sure to lose,
I durst do more than that: here is my hand,
The first course for a hundred pound.

SIR FRANCIS. A match.

WENDOLL. Ten angels on Sir Francis Acton's hawk;
As much upon his dogs.

CRANWELL. I am for Sir Charles Mountford; I have seen
His hawk and dog both tried. What, clap you hands?
Or is't no bargain?

WENDOLL. Yes, and stake them down:
Were they five hundred, they were all my own.

SIR FRANCIS. Be stirring early with the lark to-morrow;
I'll rise into my saddle ere the sun
Rise from his bed.

SIR CHARLES. If there you miss me, say
I am no gentleman: I'll hold my day.

SIR FRANCIS. It holds on all sides. Come, to-night let's dance,
Early to-morrow let's prepare to ride;
We had need be three hours up before the bride.          [*Exeunt.*]


## SCENE II—*A Yard.*

[*Enter* NICHOLAS, JENKIN, JACK SLIME, *and* ROGER BRICKBAT,
    *with* COUNTRY WENCHES, *and two or three* MUSICIANS.]


JENKIN. Come, Nick, take you Joan Miniver to trace withal;
    Jack Slime, traverse you with Cicely Milk-pail: I will take
    Jane Trubkin, and Roger Brickbat shall have Isbel Motley;
    and now that they are busy in the parlour, come, strike up;
    we'll have a crash here in the yard.

NICHOLAS. My humour is not compendious; dancing I possess
    not, though I can foot it; yet, since I am fallen into the hands
    of Cicely Milk-pail, I consent.

SLIME. Truly Nick, though we were never brought up like serving courtiers, yet we have been brought up with serving creatures, ay, and God's creatures too; for we have been brought up to serve sheep, oxen, horses, hogs, and such like: and, though we be but country fellows, it may be in the way of dancing we can do the horse-trick as well as serving-men.

BRICKBAT. Ay, and the cross-point too.

JENKIN. O Slime, O Brickbat, do not you know that comparisons are odious? now we are odious ourselves too, therefore there are no comparisons to be made betwixt us.

NICHOLAS. I am sudden, and not superfluous;

I am quarrelsome, and not seditious;

I am peaceable, and not contentious;

I am brief, and not compendious.

SLIME. Foot it quickly: if the music overcome not my melancholy, I shall quarrel; and if they do not suddenly strike up, I shall presently strike them down.

JENKIN. No quarrelling, for God's sake: truly, if you do, I shall set a knave between ye.

SLIME. I come to dance, not to quarrel. Come, what shall it be? "Rogero?"

JENKIN. "Rogero!" no; we will dance "The Beginning of the World."

CICELY. I love no dance so well as "John come kiss me now."

NICHOLAS. I, that have ere now deserved a cushion, call for the "Cushion-dance."

BRICKBAT. For my part, I like nothing so well as "Tom Tyler."

JENKIN. No; we'll have "The Hunting of the Fox."

SLIME. "The Hay," "The Hay"; there's nothing like "The Hay."

NICHOLAS. I have said, I do say, and I will say again—

JENKIN. Every man agree to have it as Nick says.

ALL. Content.

NICHOLAS. It hath been, it now is, and it shall be—

CICELY. What, Master Nicholas, what?

NICHOLAS. "Put on your smock a' Monday."

JENKIN. So the dance will come cleanly off. Come, for God's sake agree of something: if you like not that, put it to the musicians; or let me speak for all, and we'll have "Sellenger's round."

ALL. That, that, that.

NICHOLAS. No, I am resolved, thus it shall be:
First take hands, then take ye to your heels.

JENKIN. Why, would ye have us run away?

NICHOLAS. No; but I would have you shake your heels.
Music, strike up!

[*They dance.* NICHOLAS *whilst dancing speaks stately and scurvily,
the rest after the country fashion.*]

JENKIN. Hey! lively, my lasses! here's a turn for thee! [*Exeunt.*]

## SCENE III—*The open country.*

[*Horns wind. Enter* SIR CHARLES MOUNTFORD, SIR FRANCIS
ACTON, MALBY, CRANWELL, WENDOLL, FALCONERS,
*and* HUNTSMEN.]

SIR CHARLES. So; well cast off: aloft, aloft! well flown!
Oh, now she takes her at the souwse, and strikes her
Down to the earth, like a swift thunderclap.

WENDOLL. She hath struck ten angels out of my way.

SIR FRANCIS. A hundred pound from me.

SIR CHARLES. What, falconer!

FALCONER. At hand, sir.

SIR CHARLES. Now she hath seized the fowl, and 'gins to plume
　　her,
Rebeck her not: rather stand still and check her.
So, seize her gets, her jesses, and her bells:
Away!

SIR FRANCIS. My hawk killed too.

SIR CHARLES. Ay, but 'twas at the querre,
Not at the mount, like mine.

SIR FRANCIS. Judgment, my masters.

CRANWELL. Yours missed her at the ferre.

WENDOLL. Ay, but our merlin first had plumed the fowl,
And twice renewed her from the river too;
Her bells, Sir Francis, had not both one weight,
Nor was one semi-tune above the other:
Methinks these Milan bells do sound too full,
And spoil the mounting of your hawk.

SIR CHARLES. 'Tis lost.

SIR FRANCIS. I grant it not. Mine likewise seized a fowl
Within her talons; and you saw her paws
Full of the feathers: both her petty singles,
And her long singles gripped her more than other;
The terrials of her legs were stained with blood:
Not of the fowl only, she did discomfit
Some of her feathers; but she brake away.
Come, come, your hawk is but a rifler.

SIR CHARLES. How!

SIR FRANCIS. Ay, and your dogs are trindle-tails and curs.

SIR CHARLES. You stir my blood.
You keep not one good hound in all your kennel,
Nor one good hawk upon your perch.

SIR FRANCIS. How, knight!

SIR CHARLES. So, knight: you will not swagger, sir?

SIR FRANCIS. Why, say I did?

SIR CHARLES. Why, sir,
I say you would gain as much by swaggering,
As you have got by wagers on your dogs:
You will come short in all things.

SIR FRANCIS. Not in this:
Now I'll strike home.

SIR CHARLES. Thou shalt to thy long home,
Or I will want my will.

SIR FRANCIS. All they that love Sir Francis, follow me.

SIR CHARLES. All that affect Sir Charles, draw on my part.

CRANWELL. On this side heaves my hand.

WENDOLL. Here goes my heart.

[*They divide themselves.* SIR CHARLES MOUNTFORD, CRANWELL,
FALCONER, *and* HUNTSMAN, *fight against* SIR FRANCIS ACTON,
WENDOLL, *his* FALCONER, *and* HUNTSMAN; *and* SIR CHARLES'S
*side gets the better, beating the others away, and killing both of* SIR
FRANCIS'S *men. Exeunt all except* SIR CHARLES.]

SIR CHARLES. My God! what have I done? what have I done?
My rage hath plunged into a sea of blood,
In which my soul lies drowned. Poor innocents,
For whom we are to answer! Well, 'tis I done,
And I remain the victor. A great conquest,
When I would give this right hand, nay, this head,

To breathe in them new life whom I have slain!
Forgive me, God! 'twas in the heat of blood,
And anger quite removes me from myself:
It was not I, but rage, did this vile murder;
Yet I, and not my rage, must answer it.
Sir Francis Acton he is fled the field;
With him all those that did partake his quarrel,
And I am left alone with sorrow dumb,
And in my height of conquest overcome.

[*Enter* SUSAN.]

SUSAN. O God! my brother wounded 'mong the dead!
Unhappy jest, that in such earnest ends:
The rumour of this fear stretched to my ears,
And I am come to know if you be wounded.
  SIR CHARLES. Oh! sister, sister, wounded at the heart.
  SUSAN. My God forbid!
  SIR CHARLES. In doing that thing which He forbad,
I am wounded, sister.
  SUSAN. I hope not at the heart.
  SIR CHARLES. Yes, at the heart.
  SUSAN. O God! a surgeon there!
  SIR CHARLES. Call me a surgeon, sister, for my soul;
The sin of murder it hath pierced my heart,
And made a wide wound there: but for these scratches,
They are nothing, nothing.
  SUSAN. Charles, what have you done?
Sir Francis hath great friends, and will pursue you
Unto the utmost danger of the law.
  SIR CHARLES. My conscience is become mine enemy,
And will pursue me more than Acton can.
  SUSAN. Oh, fly, sweet brother.
  SIR CHARLES. Shall I fly from thee?
Why, Sue, art weary of my company?
  SUSAN. Fly from your foe.
  SIR CHARLES. YOU, sister, are my friend;
And, flying you, I shall pursue my end.
  SUSAN. Your company is as my eye-ball dear;
Being far from you, no comfort can be near;
Yet fly to save your life: what would I care
To spend my future age in black despair,

So you were safe? and yet to live one week
Without my brother Charles, through every cheek
My streaming tears would downwards run so rank,
Till they could set on either side a bank,
And in the midst a channel; so my face
For two salt-water brooks shall still find place.

SIR CHARLES. Thou shalt not weep so much, for I will stay
In spite of danger's teeth: I'll live with thee,
Or I'll not live at all. I will not sell
My country and my father's patrimony,
Nor thy sweet sight, for a vain hope of life.

[*Enter* SHERIFF, *with* OFFICERS.]

SHERIFF. Sir Charles, I am made the unwilling instrument
Of your attach and apprehension:
I'm sorry that the blood of innocent men
Should be of you exacted. It was told me
That you were guarded with a troop of friends,
And therefore I come thus armed.

SIR CHARLES. O, Master Sheriff,
I came into the field with many friends,
But see, they all have left me: only one
Clings to my sad misfortune, my dear sister.
I know you for an honest gentleman;
I yield my weapons, and submit to you;
Convey me where you please.

SHERIFF. To prison then,
To answer for the lives of these dead men.

SUSAN. O God! O God!

SIR CHARLES. Sweet sister, every strain
Of sorrow from your heart augments my pain;
Your grief abounds, and hits against my breast.

SHERIFF. Sir, will you go?

SIR CHARLES. Even where it likes you best. [*Exeunt.*]

# ACT II

## Scene I—Frankford's *study*.

[*Enter* FRANKFORD.]

FRANKFORD. How happy am I amongst other men,
That in my mean estate embrace content!
I am a gentleman, and by my birth,
Companion with a king; a king's no more.
I am possessed of many fair revenues,
Sufficient to maintain a gentleman.
Touching my mind, I am studied in all arts;
The riches of my thoughts, and of my time,
Have been a good proficient; but the chief
Of all the sweet felicities on earth,
I have a fair, a chaste, and loving wife;
Perfection all, all truth, all ornament
If man on earth may truly happy be,
Of these at once possessed, sure I am he.

[*Enter* NICHOLAS.]

NICHOLAS. Sir, there's a gentleman attends without
To speak with you.
FRANKFORD. On horseback?
NICHOLAS. Yes, on horseback.
FRANKFORD. Entreat him to alight, I will attend him.
Know'st thou him, Nick?
NICHOLAS. Know him! yes, his name's Wendoll:
It seems he comes in haste: his horse is booted
Up to the flank in mire, himself all spotted

And stained with plashing. Sure he rid in fear,
Or for a wager: horse and man both sweat;
I ne'er saw two in such a smoking heat.

 FRANKFORD. Entreat him in: about it instantly.

[Exit NICHOLAS.]

This Wendoll I have noted, and his carriage
Hath pleased me much: by observation
I have noted many good deserts in him:
He's affable, and seen in many things,
Discourses well, a good companion;
And though of small means, yet a gentleman
Of a good house, though somewhat pressed by want:
I have preferred him to a second place
In my opinion, and my best regard.

 [Enter WENDOLL, MISTRESS FRANKFORD, and NICHOLAS.]

 MISTRESS FRANKFORD. O Master Frankford, Master Wendoll
  here
Brings you the strangest news that e'er you heard.

 FRANKFORD. What news, sweet wife?
What news, good Master Wendoll?

 WENDOLL. You knew the match made 'twixt Sir Francis Acton
And Sir Charles Mountford.

 FRANKFORD. True, with their hounds and hawks.

 WENDOLL. The matches were both played.

 FRANKFORD. Ha! and which won?

 WENDOLL. Sir Francis, your wife's brother, had the worst.
And lost the wager.

 FRANKFORD. Why, the worse his chance:
Perhaps the fortune of some other day
Will change his luck.

 MISTRESS FRANKFORD. Oh, but you hear not all.
Sir Francis lost, and yet was loth to yield:
At length the two knights grew to difference,
From words to blows, and so to banding sides;
Where valorous Sir Charles slew in his spleen
Two of your brother's men; his falconer,
And his good huntsman, whom he loved so well:
More men were wounded, no more slain outright.

 FRANKFORD. Now, trust me, I am sorry for the knight;

But is my brother safe?

WENDOLL. All whole and sound,
His body not being blemished with one wound:
But poor Sir Charles is to the prison led,
To answer at the assize for them that's dead.

FRANKFORD. I thank your pains, sir; had the news been better
Your will was to have brought it, Master Wendoll.
Sir Charles will find hard friends; his case is heinous,
And will be most severely censured on:
I'm sorry for him. Sir, a word with you
I know you, sir, to be a gentleman
In all things; your possibilities but mean:
Please you to use my table and my purse,
They are yours.

WENDOLL. O Lord, sir, I shall never deserve it.

FRANKFORD. O sir, disparage not your worth too much:
You are full of quality and fair desert:
Choose of my men which shall attend on you,
And he is yours. I will allow you, sir,
Your man, your gelding, and your table, all
At my own charge; be my companion.

WENDOLL. Master Frankford, I have oft been bound to you
By many favours; this exceeds them all,
That I shall never merit your least favour:
But, when your last remembrance I forget,
Heaven at my soul exact that weighty debt!

FRANKFORD. There needs no protestation; for I know you
Virtuous, and therefore grateful. Pr'ythee, Nan,
Use him with all thy loving'st courtesy.

MISTRESS FRANKFORD. As far as modesty may well extend,
It is my duty to receive your friend.

FRANKFORD. To dinner, come, sir; from this present day,
Welcome to me for ever; come, away.

[*Exeunt* FRANKFORD, MISTRESS FRANKFORD,
*and* WENDOLL.]

NICHOLAS. I do not like this fellow by no means:
I never see him but my heart still yearns:
Zounds! I could fight with him, yet know not why:
The devil and he are all one in my eye.

[*Enter* JENKIN.]

JENKIN. O Nick, what gentleman is that comes to lie at our
    house? my master allows him one to wait on him, and I
    believe it will fall to thy lot.
NICHOLAS. I love my master; by these hilts I do!
But rather than I'll ever come to serve him,
I'll turn away my master.

[*Enter* CICELY.]

CICELY. Nich'las, where are you, Nich'las? you must come
    in, Nich'las, and help the young gentleman off with his
    boots.
NICHOLAS. If I pluck off his boots, I'll eat the spurs,
And they shall stick fast in my throat like burs.
CICELY. Then, Jenkin, come you.
JENKIN. Nay, 'tis no boot for me to deny it. My master hath
    given me a coat here, but he takes pains himself to brush it
    once or twice a day with a hollywand.
CICELY. Come, come, make haste, that you may wash your
    hands again, and help to serve in dinner.
JENKIN. You may see, my masters, though it be afternoon with
    you, 'tis but early days with us, for we have not dined yet:
    stay a little, I'll but go in and help to bear up the first course,
    and come to you again presently.

[*Exeunt.*]

## SCENE II—*A room in the gaol.*

[*Enter* MALBY *and* CRANWELL.]

MALBY. This is the sessions-day; pray can you tell me
How young Sir Charles hath sped? Is he acquit,
Or must he try the law's strict penalty?
CRANWELL. He's cleared of all, spite of his enemies,
Whose earnest labour was to take his life:
But in this suit of pardon he hath spent
All the revenues that his father left him;
And he is now turned a plain countryman,
Reformed in all things. See, sir, here he comes.

[*Enter* SIR CHARLES *and* KEEPER.]

KEEPER. Discharge your fees, and you are then at freedom.

SIR CHARLES. Here, Master Keeper, take the poor remainder
Of all the wealth I have: my heavy foes
Have made my purse light; but, alas! to me
'Tis wealth enough that you have set me free.

MALBY. God give you joy of your delivery!
I am glad to see you abroad, Sir Charles.

SIR CHARLES. The poorest knight in England, Master Malby:
My life hath cost me all my patrimony
My father left his son: well, God forgive them
That are the authors of my penury.

[*Enter* SHAFTON.]

SHAFTON. Sir Charles! a hand, a hand! at liberty?
Now, by the faith I owe, I am glad to see it.
What want you? wherein may I pleasure you?

SIR CHARLES. O me! O most unhappy gentleman!
I am not worthy to have friends stirred up,
Whose hands may help me in this plunge of want.
I would I were in Heaven, to inherit there
The immortal birth-right which my Saviour keeps,
And by no unthrift can be bought and sold;
For here on earth what pleasures should we trust?

SHAFTON. To rid you from these contemplations,
Three hundred pounds you shall receive of me;
Nay, five for fail. Come, sir; the sight of gold
Is the most sweet receipt for melancholy,
And will revive your spirits: you shall hold law
With your proud adversaries. Tush, let Frank Acton
Wage with his knighthood like expense with me,
And he will sink, he will. Nay, good Sir Charles,
Applaud your fortune, and your fair escape
From all these perils.

SIR CHARLES. O sir, they have undone me.
Two thousand and five hundred pound a year
My father, at his death, possessed me of;
All which the envious Acton made me spend.
And, notwithstanding all this large expense,
I had much ado to gain my liberty:

And I have only now a house of pleasure,
With some five hundred pounds, reserved
Both to maintain me and my loving sister.

    SHAFTON [*aside*]. That must I have, it lies convenient for me:
If I can fasten but one finger on him,
With my full hand I'll gripe him to the heart.
'Tis not for love I proffered him this coin,
But for my gain and pleasure. [*Aloud.*] Come, Sir Charles,
I know you have need of money; take my offer.

    SIR CHARLES. Sir, I accept it, and remain indebted
Even to the best of my unable power.
Come, gentlemen, and see it tendered down.        [*Exeunt.*]


## SCENE III—*A room in* FRANKFORD'S *house.*

[*Enter* WENDOLL *melancholy.*]

    WENDOLL. I am a villain if I apprehend
But such a thought: then, to attempt the deed,—
Slave, thou art damned without redemption.
I'll drive away this passion with a song.
A song! ha, ha: a song! as if, fond man,
Thy eyes could swim in laughter, when thy soul
Lies drenched and drownèd in red tears of blood.
I'll pray, and see if God within my heart
Plant better thoughts. Why, prayers are meditations;
And when I meditate (O God, forgive me!)
It is on her divine perfections.
I will forget her; I will arm myself
Not to entertain a thought of love to her:
And, when I come by chance into her presence,
I'll hale these balls until *my* eye-strings crack,
From being pulled and drawn to look that way.

[*Enter over the stage,* FRANKFORD, MISTRESS FRANKFORD,
*and* NICHOLAS.]

O God! O God! with what a violence
I'm hurried to mine own destruction.
There goest thou, the most perfectest man
That ever England bred a gentleman;

And shall I wrong his bed? Thou God of thunder!
Stay in thy thoughts of vengeance and of wrath,
Thy great, almighty, and all-judging hand
From speedy execution on a villain:
A villain, and a traitor to his friend.

[*Enter* JENKIN.]

JENKIN. Did your worship call?
WENDOLL. He doth maintain me, he allows me largely
Money to spend——
JENKIN. By my faith, so do not you me; I cannot get a cross of
you.
WENDOLL. My gelding, and my man——
JENKIN. That's Sorrell and I.
WENDOLL. This kindness grows of no alliance 'twixt us——
JENKIN. Nor is my service of any great acquaintance.
WENDOLL. I never bound him to me by desert:
Of a mere stranger, a poor gentleman,
A man by whom in no kind he could gain,
He hath placed me in the height of all his thoughts,
Made me companion with the best and chiefest
In Yorkshire. He cannot eat without me,
Nor laugh without me: I am to his body
As necessary as his digestion,
And equally do make him whole or sick:
And shall I wrong this man? Base man! ingrate
Hast thou the power straight with thy gory hands
To rip thy image from his bleeding heart?
To scratch thy name from out the holy book
Of his remembrance; and to wound his name
That holds thy name so dear? or rend his heart
To whom thy heart was knit and joined together?
And yet I must: then, Wendoll, be content;
Thus villains, when they would, cannot repent.
JENKIN. What a strange humour is my new master in! pray God
    he be not mad: if he should be so, I should never have any
    mind to serve him in Bedlam. It may be he's mad for miss-
    ing of me.
WENDOLL [*seeing* JENKIN]. What, Jenkin, where's your mistress?
JENKIN. Is your worship married?
WENDOLL. Why dost thou ask?

JENKIN. Because you are my master; and if I have a mistress, I
   would be glad, like a good servant, to do my duty to her.
WENDOLL. I mean Mistress Frankford.
JENKIN. Marry, sir, her husband is riding out of town, and she
   went very lovingly to bring him on his way to horse. Do
   you see, sir? here she comes, and here I go.
WENDOLL. Vanish.                                    [*Exit* JENKIN.]

                [*Reënter* MISTRESS FRANKFORD.]

MISTRESS FRANKFORD. You are well met, sir; now, in troth,
   my husband,
Before he took horse, had a great desire
To speak with you: we sought about the house,
Hollaed into the fields, sent every way,
But could not meet you: therefore he enjoined me
To do unto you his most kind commends.
Nay, more; he wills you, as you prize his love,
Or hold in estimation his kind friendship,
To make bold in his absence, and command
Even as himself were present in the house:
For you must keep his table, use his servants,
And be a present Frankford in his absence.
   WENDOLL. I thank him for his love.—
Give me a name, you whose infectious tongues
Are tipped with gall and poison: as you would
Think on a man that had your father slain,
Murdered your children, made your wives base strumpets,
So call me, call me so: print in my face
The most stigmatic title of a villain,
For hatching treason to so true a friend.
                                                       [*Aside.*]
   MISTRESS FRANKFORD. Sir, you are much beholding to my
      husband;
You are a man most dear in his regard.
   WENDOLL [*aside*]. I am bound unto your husband, and you
      too.
   I will not speak to wrong a gentleman
   Of that good estimation, my kind friend:
   I will not; zounds! I will not. I may choose,
And I will choose. Shall I be so misled?
   Or shall I purchase to my father's crest

The motto of a villain? If I say
I will not do it, what thing can enforce me?
What can compel me? What sad destiny
Hath such command upon my yielding thoughts?
I will not—Ha! some fury pricks me on,
The swift Fates drag me at their chariot-wheel,
And hurry me to mischief. Speak I must;
Injure myself, wrong her, deceive his trust.
    MISTRESS FRANKFORD. Are you not well, sir, that you seem
        thus trou bled?
There is sedition in your countenance.
    WENDOLL. And in my heart, fair angel, chaste and wise.
I love you: start not, speak not, answer not.
I love you: nay, let me speak the rest:
Bid me to swear, and I will call to record
The host of Heaven.
    MISTRESS FRANKFORD. The host of Heaven forbid
Wendoll should hatch such a disloyal thought!
    WENDOLL. Such is my fate; to this suit I was born,
To wear rich pleasure's crown, or fortune's scorn.
    MISTRESS FRANKFORD. My husband loves you.
    WENDOLL. I know it.
    MISTRESS FRANKFORD. He esteems you
Even as his brain, his eye-ball, or his heart.
    WENDOLL. I have tried it.
    MISTRESS FRANKFORD. His purse is your exchequer, and his
        table
Doth freely serve you.
    WENDOLL. So I have found it.
    MISTRESS FRANKFORD. O! with what face of brass, what brow
        of steel,
Can you, unblushing, speak this to the face
Of the espoused wife of so dear a friend?
It is my husband that maintains your state;
Will you dishonour him that in your power
Hath left his whole affairs? I am his wife,
It is to me you speak.
    WENDOLL. O speak no more!
For more than this I know, and have recorded
Within the red-leaved table of my heart.
Fair, and of all beloved, I was not fearful
Bluntly to give my life into your hand,

And at one hazard all my earthly means.
Go, tell your husband; he will turn me off,
And I am then undone. I care not, I;
'Twas for your sake. Perchance in rage he'll kill me:
I care not, 'twas for you. Say I incur
The general name of villain through the world,
Of traitor to my friend; I care not, I.
Beggary, shame, death, scandal, and reproach,
For you I'll hazard all: why, what care I?
For you I'll live, and in your love I'll die.

   MISTRESS FRANKFORD. You move me, sir, to passion and to
     pity.
The love I bear my husband is as precious
As my soul's health.

   WENDOLL. I love your husband too,
And for his love I will engage my life:
Mistake me not, the augmentation
Of my sincere affection borne to you
Doth no whit lessen my regard of him.
I will be secret, lady, close as night;
And not the light of one small glorious star
Shall shine here in my forehead, to bewray
That act of night.

   MISTRESS FRANKFORD. What shall I say?
My soul is wandering, and hath lost her way.
Oh, Master Wendoll! Oh!

   WENDOLL. Sigh not, sweet saint;
For every sigh you breathe draws from my heart
A drop of blood.

   MISTRESS FRANKFORD. I ne'er offended yet:
My fault, I fear, will in my brow be writ.
Women that fall, not quite bereft of grace,
Have their offences noted in their face.
I blush and am ashamed. Oh, Master Wendoll,
Pray God I be not born to curse your tongue,
That hath enchanted me! This maze I am in
I fear will prove the labyrinth of sin.

       *[Reënter* NICHOLAS *behind.]*

   WENDOLL. The path of pleasure, and the gate to bliss,
Which on your lips I knock at with a kiss.

   NICHOLAS *[aside].* I'll kill the rogue.

WENDOLL. Your husband is from home, your bed's no blab.
Nay, look not down and blush.

[*Exeunt* WENDOLL *and* MISTRESS FRANKFORD.]

NICHOLAS. Zounds! I'll stab.
Ay, Nick, was it thy chance to come just in the nick?
I love my master, and I hate that slave:
I love my mistress, but these tricks I like not.
My master shall not pocket up this wrong;
I'll eat my fingers first. What say'st thou, metal?
Does not the rascal Wendoll go on legs
That thou must cut off? Hath he not ham strings
That thou must hough? Nay, metal, thou shalt stand
To all I say. I'll henceforth turn a spy,
And watch them in their close conveyances.
I never looked for better of that rascal,
Since he came miching first into our house:
It is that Satan hath corrupted her,
For she was fair and chaste. I'll have an eye
In all their gestures. Thus I think of them,
If they proceed as they have done before:
Wendoll's a knave, my mistress is a——

[*Exit.*]

# ACT III

## Scene I—*A room in* Sir Charles Mountford's *house.*

[*Enter* Sir Charles Mountford *and* Susan.]

Sir Charles. Sister, you see we are driven to hard shift
To keep this poor house we have left unsold;
I am now enforced to follow husbandry,
And you to milk; and do we not live well?
Well, I thank God.
    Susan. O brother, here's a change.
Since old Sir Charles died, in our father's house!
    Sir Charles. All things on earth thus change, some up, some
      down;
Content's a kingdom, and I wear that crown.

[*Enter* Shafton *with a* Serjeant.]

Shafton. Good morrow, morrow, Sir Charles: what, with
    your sister,
Plying your husbandry?—Serjeant, stand off.—
You have a pretty house here, and a garden,
And goodly ground about it. Since it lies
So near a lordship that I lately bought,
I would fain buy it of you. I will give you——
    Sir Charles. O, pardon me: this house successively
Hath 'longed to me and my progenitors
Three hundred years. My great-great-grandfather,
He in whom first our gentle style began,
Dwelt here; and in this ground, increased this mole-hill

Unto that mountain which my father left me.
Where he the first of all our house began,
I now the last will end, and keep this house,
This virgin title, never yet deflowered
By any unthrift of the Mountfords' line.
In brief, I will not sell it for more gold
Than you could hide or pave the ground withal.

    SHAFTON. Ha, ha! a proud mind and a beggar's purse!
Where's my three hundred pounds, besides the use?
I have brought it to an execution
By course of law: what, is my moneys ready?

    SIR CHARLES. An execution, sir, and never tell me
You put my bond in suit! you deal extremely.

    SHAFTON. Sell me the land, and I'll acquit you straight.

    SIR CHARLES. Alas, alas! 'tis all trouble hath left me
To cherish me and my poor sister's life.
If this were sold, our names should then be quite
Razed from the bed-roll of gentility.
You see what hard shift we have made to keep it
Allied still to our own name. This palm, you see,
Labour hath glowed within: her silver brow,
That never tasted a rough winter's blast
Without a mask or fan, doth with a grace
Defy cold winter, and his storms out-face.

    SUSAN. Sir, we feed sparing, and we labour hard,
We lie uneasy, to reserve to us
And our succession this small plot of ground.

    SIR CHARLES. I have so bent my thoughts to husbandry,
That I protest I scarcely can remember
What a new fashion is; how silk or satin
Feels in my hand: why, pride is grown to us
A mere, mere stranger. I have quite forgot
The names of all that ever waited on me;
I cannot name ye any of my hounds,
Once from whose echoing mouths I heard all music
That e'er my heart desired. What should I say?
To keep this place I have changed myself away.

    SHAFTON [*to the* SERJEANT]. Arrest him at my suit. Actions and
        actions
Shall keep thee in perpetual bondage fast:

Nay, more, I'll sue thee by a late appeal,
And call thy former life in question.
The keeper is my friend, thou shalt have irons,
And usage such as I'll deny to dogs:
Away with him!

    SIR CHARLES [*to* SUSAN], You are too timorous:
But trouble is my master,
And I will serve him truly.——My kind sister,
Thy tears are of no force to mollify
This flinty man. Go to my father's brother,
My kinsmen and allies; entreat them for me,
To ransom me from this injurious man,
That seeks my ruin.

    SHAFTON. Come, irons, irons! come away;
I'll see thee lodged far from the sight of day.

    [*Exeunt* SHAFTON *and* SERJEANT *with* SIR CHARLES.]

    SUSAN. My heart's so hardened with the frost of grief,
Death cannot pierce it through. Tyrant too fell!
So lead the fiends condemned souls to hell.

    [*Enter* SIR FRANCIS ACTON *and* MALBY.]

    SIR FRANCIS. Again to prison! Malby, hast thou seen
A poor slave better tortured? Shall we hear
The music of his voice cry from the grate,
"Meat for the Lord's sake"? No, no, yet I am not
Throughly revenged. They say he hath a pretty wench
Unto his sister: shall I, in mercy-sake
To him and to his kindred, bribe the fool
To shame herself by lewd dishonest lust?
I'll proffer largely; but, the deed being done,
I'll smile to see her base confusion.

    MALBY. Methinks, Sir Francis, you are full revenged
For greater wrongs than he can proffer you.
See where the poor sad gentlewoman stands.

    SIR FRANCIS. Ha, ha! now will I flout her poverty,
Deride her fortunes, scoff her base estate;
My very soul the name of Mountford hates.
But stay, my heart! oh, what a look did fly
To strike my soul through with thy piercing eye!

I am enchanted; all my spirits are fled,
And with one glance my envious spleen struck dead.
    SUSAN. Acton! that seeks our blood.

                                           *[Runs away.]*

    SIR FRANCIS. O chaste and fair!
    MALBY. Sir Francis, why, Sir Francis, zounds! in a trance?
Sir Francis, what cheer, man? Come, come, how is't?
    SIR FRANCIS. Was she not fair? Or else this judging eye
Cannot distinguish beauty.
    MALBY. She was fair.
    SIR FRANCIS. She was an angel in a mortal's shape,
And ne'er descended from old Mountford's line.
But soft, soft, let me call *my* wits together.
A poor, poor wench, to my great adversary
Sister, whose very souls denounce stern war,
One against other. How now, Frank, turned fool
Or madman, whether? But no; master of
My perfect senses and directest wits.
Then why should I be in this violent humour
Of passion and of love; and with a person
So different every way, and so opposed
In all contractions, and still-warring actions?
Fie, fie; how I dispute against my soul!
Come, come; I'll gain her, or in her fair quest
Purchase my soul free and immortal rest.

                                           *[Exeunt.]*

## SCENE II—*A sitting-room in* FRANKFORD'S *house.*

*[Enter* SERVING-MEN, *one with a voider and a wooden knife to take away; another with the salt and bread; another with the table-cloth and napkins; another with the carpet:* JENKIN *follows them with two lights.]*

    JENKIN. So, march in order, and retire in battle array. My master and the guests have supped already, all's taken way: here, now spread for the servingmen in the hall. Butler, it belongs to your office.

BUTLER. I know it, Jenkin. What d'ye call the gentleman that
   supped there to-night?

JENKIN. Who, my master?

BUTLER. No, no; Master Wendoll, he's a daily guest: I mean
   the gentleman that came but this afternoon.

JENKIN. His name's Master Cranwell. God's light, hark, within
   there, my master calls to lay more billets upon the fire. Come,
   come! Lord, how we that are in office here in the house are
   troubled! One spread the carpet in the parlour, and stand
   ready to snuff the lights; the rest be ready to prepare their
   stomachs. More lights in the hall there. Come, Nich'las.

[*Exeunt all but* NICHOLAS.]

NICHOLAS. I cannot eat, but had I Wendoll's heart
I would eat that; the rogue grows impudent.
Oh, I have seen such vile notorious tricks,
Ready to make my eyes dart from my head.
I'll tell my master, by this air I will!
Fall what may fall, I'll tell him. Here he comes.

[*Enter* FRANKFORD, *brushing the crumbs from his clothes with a napkin, as newly risen from supper.*]

FRANKFORD. Nicholas, what make you here? why are not you
At supper in the hall among your fellows?

NICHOLAS. Master, I stayed your rising from the board,
To speak with you.

FRANKFORD. Be brief, then, gentle Nicholas;
My wife and guests attend me in the parlour.
Why dost thou pause? Now, Nicholas, you want money,
And, unthrift-like, would eat into your wages
Ere you have earned it: here, sir, 's half a crown;
Play the good husband, and away to supper.

NICHOLAS. By this hand, an honourable gentleman! I will not
   see him wronged. —Sir, I have served you long; you enter-
   tained me seven years before your beard. You knew me, sir,
   before you knew my mistress.

FRANKFORD. What of this, good Nicholas?

NICHOLAS. I never was a make-bate or a knave;
I have no fault but one: I'm given to quarrel,
But not with women. I will tell you, master,

That which will make your heart leap from your breast,
Your hair to startle from your head, your ears to tingle.

  FRANKFORD. What preparation's this to dismal news?

  NICHOLAS. 'Sblood, sir! I love you better than your wife;
I'll make it good.

  FRANKFORD. You are a knave, and I have much ado
With wonted patience to contain my rage,
And not to break thy pate. Thou art a knave:
I'll turn you, with your base comparisons,
Out of my doors.

  NICHOLAS. Do, do: there is not room
For Wendoll and for me both in one house.
O master, master, that Wendoll is a villain.

  FRANKFORD. Ay, saucy!

  NICHOLAS. Strike, strike; do, strike; yet hear me: I am no fool,
I know a villain, when I see him act
Deeds of a villain. Master, master, that base slave
Enjoys my mistress, and dishonours you.

  FRANKFORD. Thou hast killed me with a weapon whose sharp
    point
Hath pricked quite through and through my shivering heart:
Drops of cold sweat sit dangling on my hairs,
Like morning's dew upon the golden flowers,
And I am plunged into strange agonies.
What didst thou say? If any word that touched
His credit or her reputation,
It is as hard to enter my belief
As Dives into heaven.

  NICHOLAS. I can gain nothing;
They are two that never wronged me. I knew before
'Twas but a thankless office, and perhaps
As much as is my service, or my life
Is worth. All this I know; but this and more,
More by a thousand dangers, could not hire me
To smother such a heinous wrong from you.
I saw, and I have said.

  FRANKFORD [*aside*]. 'Tis probable; though blunt, yet he is
    honest:
Though I durst pawn my life, and on their faith
Hazard the dear salvation of my soul,

Yet in my trust I may be too secure.
May this be true? O, may it, can it be?
Is it by any wonder possible?
Man, woman, what thing mortal may we trust,
When friends and bosom wives prove so unjust?—
[*To* NICHOLAS.] What instance hast thou of this strange report?
    NICHOLAS. Eyes, eyes.
    FRANKFORD. Thy eyes may be deceived, I tell thee:
For, should an angel from the heavens drop down,
And preach this to me that thyself hast told,
He should have much ado to win belief;
In both their loves I am so confident.
    NICHOLAS. Shall I discourse the same by circumstance?
    FRANKFORD. No more! to supper, and command your fel-
       lows
To attend us and the strangers. Not a word,
I charge thee on thy life: be secret then,
For I know nothing.
    NICHOLAS. I am dumb; and, now that I have eased my stomach,
I will go fill my stomach.
    FRANKFORD. Away; be gone.            [*Exit* NICHOLAS.]
She is well born, descended nobly;
Virtuous her education, her repute
Is in the general voice of all the country
Honest and fair; her carriage, her demeanour,
In all her actions that concern the love
To me her husband, modest, chaste, and godly.
Is all this seeming gold plain copper?
But he, that Judas that hath borne my purse,
And sold me for a sin!—O God! O God!
Shall I put up these wrongs? No. Shall I trust
The bare report of this suspicious groom,
Before the double-gilt, the well-hatched ore
Of their two hearts? No, I will lose these thoughts:
Distraction I will banish from my brow,
And from my looks exile sad discontent,
Their Wonted favours in my tongue shall flow;
Till I know all, I'll nothing seem to know.
Lights and a table there! Wife, Master Wendoll,
And gentle Master Cranwell.

[*Enter* MISTRESS FRANKFORD, WENDOLL, CRANWELL,
NICHOLAS, *and* JENKIN, *with cards, carpets, stools,
and other necessaries.*]

FRANKFORD. O Master Cranwell, you are a stranger here,
And often baulk my house: faith, y'are a churl:
Now we have supped, a table, and to cards.

JENKIN. A pair of cards, Nicholas, and a carpet to cover the
table. Where's Cicely with her counters and her box? Candles
and candlesticks there! Fie, we have such a household of
serving creatures! unless it be Nick and I, there's not one
amongst them all can say bo to a goose. Well said, Nick.
[*They spread a carpet, set down lights and cards.*]

MISTRESS FRANKFORD. Come, Master Frankford, who shall take
my part?

FRANKFORD. Marry, that will I, sweet wife.

WENDOLL. No, by my faith, sir; when you are together I sit
out: it must be Mistress Frankford and I, or else it is no
match.

FRANKFORD. I do not like that match.

NICHOLAS [*aside*]. You have no reason, marry, knowing all.

FRANKFORD. 'Tis no great matter neither. Come, Master
Cranwell, shall you and I take them up?

CRANWELL. At your pleasure, sir.

FRANKFORD. I must look to you, Master Wendoll, for you will
be playing false; nay, so will my wife too.

NICHOLAS [*aside*]. Ay, I will be sworn she will.

MISTRESS FRANKFORD. Let them that are taken playing false,
forfeit the set.

FRANKFORD. Content; it shall go hard but I'll take you.

CRANWELL. Gentlemen, what shall our game be?

WENDOLL. Master Frankford, you play best at noddy.

FRANKFORD. You shall not find it so; indeed you shall not.

MISTRESS FRANKFORD. I can play at nothing so well as double
ruff.

FRANKFORD. If Master Wendoll and my wife be together, there's
no playing against them at double hand.

NICHOLAS. I can tell you, sir, the game that Master Wendoll
is best at.

WENDOLL. What game is that, Nick?

NICHOLAS. Marry, sir, knave out of doors.

WENDOLL. She and I will take you at lodam.

MISTRESS FRANKFORD. Husband, shall we play at saint?

FRANKFORD. My saint's turned devil. No, we'll none of saint:
You are best at new-cut, wife; you'll play at that.

WENDOLL. If you play at new-cut, I am soonest hitter of any
    here, for a wager.

FRANKFORD. 'Tis me they play on. Well, you may draw out.
For all your cunning, 'twill be to your shame;
I'll teach you, at your new-cut, a new game.
Come, come.

CRANWELL. If you cannot agree upon the game, to post and
    pair.

WENDOLL. We shall be soonest pairs; and my good host,
When he comes late home, he must kiss the post.

FRANKFORD. Whoever wins, it shall be thy cost.

CRANWELL. Faith, let it be vide-ruff, and let's make honours.

FRANKFORD. If you make honours, one thing let me crave:
Honour the king and queen; except the knave.

WENDOLL. Well, as you please for that.
Lift who shall deal.

MISTRESS FRANKFORD. The least in sight: what are you, Master
    Wendoll?

WENDOLL. I am a knave.

NICHOLAS [aside]. I'll swear it.

MISTRESS FRANKFORD. I a queen.

FRANKFORD [aside]. A quean thou shouldst say. [Aloud.] Well,
    the cards are mine;
They are the grossest pair that e'er I felt.

MISTRESS FRANKFORD. Shuffle, I'll cut: would I had never dealt.

FRANKFORD. I have lost my dealing.

WENDOLL. Sir, the fault's in me:
This queen I have more than mine own, you see.
Give me the stock.

FRANKFORD. My mind's not on my game.
Many a deal I have lost; the more's your shame.
You have served me a bad trick, Master Wendoll.

WENDOLL. Sir, you must take your lot. To end this strife,
I know I have dealt better with your wife.

FRANKFORD. Thou hast dealt falsely, then.

MISTRESS FRANKFORD. What's trumps?

WENDOLL. Hearts: partner, I rub.

FRANKFORD [*aside*]. Thou robb'st me of my soul, of her chaste
    love;
In thy false dealing thou hast robbed my heart.
[*Aloud.*] Booty you play; I like a loser stand,
Having no heart, or here or in my hand.
I will give o'er the set; I am not well.
Come, who will hold my cards?
    MISTRESS FRANKFORD. Not well, sweet Master Frankford!
Alas, what ail you? 'Tis some sudden qualm.
    WENDOLL. How long have you been so, Master Frankford?
    FRANKFORD. Sir, I was lusty, and I had my health,
But I grew ill when you began to deal.
Take hence this table. Gentle Master Cranwell,
You are welcome; see your chamber at your pleasure.
I'm sorry that this meagrim takes me so,
I cannot sit and bear you company.
Jenkin, some lights, and show him to his chamber.

                              [*Exeunt* CRANWELL *and* JENKIN.]
    MISTRESS FRANKFORD. A night-gown for my husband; quickly
        there:
It is some rheum or cold.
    WENDOLL. Now, in good faith, this illness you have got
By sitting late without your gown.
    FRANKFORD. I know it, Master Wendoll.
Go, go to bed, lest you complain like me.
Wife, prythee, wife, into my bed-chamber;
The night is raw and cold, and rheumatic:
Leave me my gown and light; I'll walk away my fit.
    WENDOLL. Sweet sir, good night.
    FRANKFORD. Myself, good night.

                                            [*Exit* WENDOLL.]
    MISTRESS FRANKFORD. Shall I attend you, husband?
    FRANKFORD. No, gentle wife, thou'lt catch cold in thy head;
Prythee, be gone, sweet; I'll make haste to bed.
    MISTRESS FRANKFORD. No sleep will fasten on mine eyes, you
        know,
Until you come.
    FRANKFORD. Sweet Nan, I prythee go.—

                                [*Exit* MISTRESS FRANKFORD.]
I have bethought me: get me, by degrees,
The keys of all my doors, which I will mould

In wax, and take their fair impression,
To have by them new keys. This being compassed,
At a set hour a letter shall be brought me,
And, when they think they may securely play,
They nearest are to danger. Nick, I must rely
Upon thy trust and faithful secrecy.

   NICHOLAS. Build on my faith.

   FRANKFORD. To bed then, not to rest:
Care lodges in my brain, grief in my breast.       [Exeunt.]

## ACT IV

### SCENE I—*A room in old* MOUNTFORD'S *house.*

[*Enter* SUSAN, OLD MOUNTFORD, SANDY, RODER, *and* TIDY.]

OLD MOUNTFORD. You say my nephew is in great distress:
Who brought it to him, but his own lewd life?
I cannot spare a cross. I must confess
He was my brother's son: why, niece, what then?
This is no world in which to pity men.

SUSAN. I was not born a beggar, though his extremes
Enforce this language from me: I protest
No fortune of mine own could lead my tongue
To this base key. I do beseech you, uncle,
For the name's sake, for Christianity,
Nay, for God's sake, to pity his distress:
He is denied the freedom of the prison,
And in the hole is laid with men condemned;
Plenty he hath of nothing but of irons,
And it remains in you to free him thence.

OLD MOUNTFORD. Money I cannot spare; men should take heed;
He lost my kindred when he fell to need.          [*Exit.*]

SUSAN. Gold is but earth, thou earth enough shalt have,
When thou hast once took measure of thy grave.
You know me, Master Sandy, and my suit.

SANDY. I knew you, lady, when the old man lived;
I knew you ere your brother sold his land;
Then you sung well, played sweetly on the lute;
But now I neither know you nor your suit.          [*Exit.*]

SUSAN. You, Master Roder, was my brother's tenant,
Rent-free he placed you in that wealthy farm,
Of which you are possessed.

RODER. True, he did;
And have I not there dwelt still for his sake?
I have some business now; but, without doubt,
They that have hurled him in will help him out.

[*Exit.*]

SUSAN. Cold comfort still: what say you, cousin Tidy?

TIDY. I say this comes of roysting, swaggering.
Call me not cousin: each man for himself.
Some men are born to mirth, and some to sorrow.
I am no cousin unto them that borrow.           [*Exit.*]

SUSAN. O charity! why art thou fled to heaven,
And left all things upon this earth uneven?
Their scoffing answers I will ne'er return;
But to myself his grief in silence mourn.

[*Enter* SIR FRANCIS ACTON *and* MALBY.]

SIR FRANCIS. She is poor, I'll therefore tempt her with this
    gold.
Go, Malby, in my name deliver it,
And I will stay thy answer.

MALBY. Fair mistress, as I understand, your grief
Doth grow from want, so I have here in store
A means to furnish you, a bag of gold,
Which to your hands I freely tender you.

SUSAN. I thank you, Heavens! I thank you, gentle sir:
God make me able to requite this favour!

MALBY. This gold Sir Francis Acton sends by me,
And prays you——

SUSAN. Acton! O God! that name I am born to curse:
Hence, bawd! hence, broker! see, I spurn his gold;
My honour never shall for gain be sold.

SIR FRANCIS. Stay, lady, stay.

SUSAN. From you I'll posting hie,
Even as the doves from feathered eagles fly.

[*Exit.*]

SIR FRANCIS. She hates *my* name, my face: how should I
    woo?
I am disgraced in every thing I do.

The more she hates me, and disdains my love,
The more I am rapt in admiration
Of her divine and chaste perfections.
Woo her with gifts I cannot, for all gifts
Sent in my name she spurns: with looks I cannot,
For she abhors my sight; nor yet with letters,
For none she will receive. How then, how then?
Well, I will fasten such a kindness on her
As shall o'ercome her hate and conquer it.
Sir Charles, her brother, lies in execution
For a great sum of money; and, besides,
The appeal is sued still for my huntsman's death,
Which only I have power to reverse:
In her I'll bury all my hate of him.
Go seek the keeper, Malby, bring him to me:
To save his body, I his debts will pay;
To save his life, I his appeal will stay.

                                                      [*Exeunt.*]


## SCENE II—*A prison cell.*

[*Enter* SIR CHARLES MOUNTFORD, *with irons, his feet bare,
his garments all ragged and torn.*]


SIR CHARLES. Of all on the earth's face most miserable,
Breathe in this hellish dungeon thy laments,
Thus like a slave ragged, like a felon gyved.
What hurls thee headlong to this base estate?
O unkind uncle! O my friends ingrate!
Unthankful kinsmen! Mountford's all too base,
To let thy name be fettered in disgrace!
A thousand deaths here in this grave I die;
Fear, hunger, sorrow, cold, all threat my death,
And join together to deprive my breath.
But that which most torments me, my dear sister
Hath left to visit me, and from my friends
Hath brought no hopeful answer: therefore I
Divine they will not help my misery.
If it be so, shame, scandal, and contempt

Attend their covetous thoughts; need make their graves!
Usurers they live, and may they die like slaves!

[*Enter* KEEPER.]

KEEPER. Knight, be of comfort, for I bring thee freedom
From all thy troubles.
    SIR CHARLES. Then I am doomed to die;
Death is the end of all calamity.
    KEEPER. Live: your appeal is stayed; the execution
Of all your debts discharged; your creditors
Even to the utmost penny satisfied.
In sign whereof, your shackles I knock off;
You are not left so much indebted to us
As for your fees; all is discharged, all paid.
Go freely to your house, or where you please,
After long miseries, embrace your ease.
    SIR CHARLES. Thou grumblest out the sweetest music to me
That ever organ played. Is this a dream
Or do my waking senses apprehend
The pleasing taste of these applausive news?
Slave that I was, to wrong such honest friends,
My loving kinsmen, and my near allies.
Tongue, I will bite thee for the scandal breathed
Against such faithful kinsmen: they are all
Composed of pity and compassion,
Of melting charity, and of moving ruth.
That which I spake before was in my rage;
They are my friends, the mirrors of this age,
Bounteous and free. The noble Mountford's race,
Ne'er bred a covetous thought, or humour base.

[*Enter* SUSAN.]

SUSAN. I can no longer stay from visiting
My woful brother: while I could, I kept
My hapless tidings from his hopeful ear.
    SIR CHARLES. Sister, how much am I indebted to thee,
And to thy travel!
    SUSAN. What, at liberty?
    SIR CHARLES. Thou seest I am, thanks to thy industry:
Oh! unto which of all my courteous friends

Am I thus bound? My uncle Mountford, he
Even of an infant loved me: was it he?
So did my cousin Tidy; was it he?
So Master Roder, Master Sandy too:
Which of all these did this high kindness do?

   SUSAN. Charles, can you mock me in your poverty,
Knowing your friends deride your misery?
Now, I protest I stand so much amazed
To see your bonds free, and your irons knocked off,
That I am rapt into a maze of wonder:
The rather for I know not by what means
This happiness hath chanced.

   SIR CHARLES. Why, by my uncle,
My cousins, and my friends: who else, I pray,
Would take upon them all my debts to pay?

   SUSAN. O brother, they are men all of flint,
Pictures of marble, and as void of pity
As chased bears. I begged, I sued, I kneeled,
Laid open all your griefs and miseries,
Which they derided; more than that, denied us
A part in their alliance; but, in pride,
Said that our kindred with our plenty died.

   SIR CHARLES. Drudges too much—what did they? oh, known
    evil!
Rich fly the poor, as good men shun the devil.
Whence should my freedom come? of whom alive,
Saving of those, have I deserved so well?
Guess, sister, call to mind, remember me:
These I have raised; they follow the world's guise;
Whom rich in honour, they in woe despise.

   SUSAN. My wits have lost themselves, let's ask the keeper.

SIR CHARLES. Gaoler!

KEEPER. At hand, sir.

   SIR CHARLES. Of courtesy resolve me one demand.
What was he took the burthen of my debts
From off my back, stayed my appeal to death,
Discharged my fees, and brought me liberty?

   KEEPER. A courteous knight, one called Sir Francis Acton.

   SIR CHARLES. Ha! Acton! O me, more distressed in this
Than all my troubles! hale me back,

Double my irons, and my sparing meals
Put into halves, and lodge me in a dungeon
More deep, more dark, more cold, more comfortless.
By Acton freed! not all thy manacles
Could fetter so my heels as this one word
Hath thralled my heart; and it must now lie bound
In more strict prison than thy stony gaol.
I am not free; I go but under bail.

   KEEPER. My charge is done, sir, now I have my fees;
As we get little, we will nothing leese.

                                [*Exit.*]

   SIR CHARLES. By Acton freed, my dangerous opposite!
Why, to what end? on what occasion? ha!
Let me forget the name of enemy,
And with indifference balance this high favour:
Ha!

   SUSAN [*aside*]. His love to me? upon my soul 'tis so:
That is the root from whence these strange things grow.

   SIR CHARLES. Had this proceeded from my father, he
That by the law of nature is most bound
In offices of love, it had deserved
My best employment to requite that grace:
Had it proceeded from my friends or him,
From them this action had deserved my life:
And from a stranger more; because from such
There is less expectation of good deeds.
But he, nor father, nor ally, nor friend,
More than a stranger, both remote in blood
And in his heart opposed my enemy,—
That this high bounty should proceed from him,—
Oh, there I lose myself! What should I say,
What think, what do, his bounty to repay?

   SUSAN. You wonder, I am sure, whence this strange kind-
       ness
Proceeds in Acton. I will tell you, brother:
He dotes on me, and oft hath sent me gifts,
Letters and tokens: I refused them all.

   SIR CHARLES. I have enough, though poor; my heart is set,
In one rich gift to pay back all my debt.

                                [*Exeunt.*]

## Scene III—*A room in* Frankford's *house.*

[*Enter* Frankford, *and* Nicholas *with keys.*]

Frankford. This is the night that I must play my part
To try two seeming angels. Where's my keys?

Nicholas. They are made according to your mould in wax:
I bade the smith be secret, gave him money,
And here they are. The letter, sir.

Frankford. True, take it, there it is;

[*Gives him letter.*]

And when thou seest me in my pleasant'st vein,
Ready to sit to supper, bring it me.

Nicholas. I'll do't, make no more question but I'll do't.

[*Exit.*]

[*Enter* Mistress Frankford, Cranwell, Wendoll, *and*
Jenkin.]

Mistress Frankford. Sirrah, 'tis six o'clock already struck!
Go bid them spread the cloth and serve in supper.

Jenkin. It shall be done, forsooth, mistress. Where's
Spigot, the butler, to give us our salt and trenchers?

[*Exit.*]

Wendoll. We that have been a-hunting all the day
Come with prepared stomachs. Master Frankford,
We wished you at our sport.

Frankford. My heart was with you, and my mind was on you.
Fie, Master Cranwell! you are still thus sad?
A stool, a stool. Where's Jenkin, and where's Nick?
'Tis supper-time at least an hour ago.
What's the best news abroad?

Wendoll. I know none good.

Frankford. But I know too much bad.

[*Aside.*]

[*Enter* Jenkin *and* Butler *with a tablecloth, bread,*
*trenchers, and salt.*]

Cranwell. Methinks, sir, you might have that interest
In your wife's brother, to be more remiss

In his hard dealing against poor Sir Charles,
Who, as I hear, lies in York Castle, needy,
And in great want.

[*Exeunt* JENKIN *and* BUTLER.]

FRANKFORD. Did not more weighty business of my own
Hold me away, I would have laboured peace
Betwixt them, with all care; indeed I would, sir.

MISTRESS FRANKFORD. I'll write unto my brother earnestly
In that behalf.

WENDOLL. A charitable deed,
And will beget the good opinion
Of all your friends that love you, Mistress Frankford.

FBANKFORD. That's you for one; I know you love Sir Charles,
And my wife too, well.

WENDOLL. He deserves the love
Of all true gentlemen; be yourselves judge.

FRANKFORD. But supper, ho! Now as thou lov'st me, Wendoll,
Which I am sure thou dost, be merry, pleasant,
And frolic it to-night. Sweet Master Cranwell,
Do you the like. Wife, I protest my heart
Was ne'er more bent on sweet alacrity.
Where be those lazy knaves to serve in supper?

[*Reënter* NICHOLAS.]

NICHOLAS. Here's a letter, sir.

FRANKFORD. Whence comes it? and who brought it?

NICHOLAS. A stripling that below attends your answer,
And, as he tells me, it is sent from York.

FRANKFORD. Have him into the cellar; let him taste
A cup of our March beer: go, make him drink.

[*Reads the letter.*]

NICHOLAS. I'll make him drunk, if he be a Trojan.

FRANKFORD. My boots and spurs! where' Jenkin? God forgive
  me,
How I neglect my business! Wife, look here;
I have a matter to be tried to-morrow
By eight o'clock, and my attorney writes me,
I must be there betimes with evidence,
Or it will go against me. Where's my boots?

[*Reënter* JENKIN *with boots and spurs.*] MISTRESS FRANKFORD. I
           hope your business craves no such despatch
That you must ride to-night.

WENDOLL [*aside*]. I hope it doth.

FRANKFORD. God's me! no such despatch!
Jenkin, my boots. Where's Nick? Saddle my roan,
And the grey dapple for himself. Content ye,
It much concerns me. Gentle Master Cranwell,
And Master Wendoll, in my absence use
The very ripest pleasures of my house.

WENDOLL. Lord! Master Frankford, will you ride to-night?
The ways are dangerous.

FRANKFORD. Therefore will I ride
Appointed well; and so shall Nick my man.

MISTRESS FRANKFORD. I'll call you up by five o'clock to-
           morrow.

FRANKFORD. No, by my faith, wife, I'll not trust to that;
'Tis not such easy rising in a morning
From one I love so dearly: no, by my faith,
I shall not leave so sweet a bedfellow,
But with much pain. You have made me a sluggard
Since I first knew you.

MISTRESS FRANKFORD. Then, if you needs will go
This dangerous evening, Master Wendoll,
Let me entreat you bear him company.

WENDOLL. With all my heart, sweet mistress. My boots there!

FRANKFORD. Fie, fie, that for my private business
I should disease my friend, and be a trouble
To the whole house! Nick!

NICHOLAS. Anon, sir.

FRANKFORD. Bring forth my gelding.

[*Exit* NICHOLAS.]

As you love me, sir,
Use no more words: a hand, good Master Cranwell.

CRANWELL. Sir, God be your good speed!

FRANKFORD. Good night, sweet Nan; nay, nay, a kiss and part.
[*Aside.*] Dissembling lips, you suit not with my heart.

[*Exit.*]

WENDOLL. How business, time, and hours, all gracious prove,
And are the furtherers to my new-born love!
I am husband now in Master Frankford's place,

And must command the house. My pleasure is
We will not sup abroad so publicly,
But in your private chamber, Mistress Frankford.

MISTRESS FRANKFORD. O, sir, you are too public in your love,
And Master Frankford's wife——

CRANWELL. Might I crave favour,
I would entreat you I might see my chamber;
am on the sudden grown exceeding ill,
And would be spared from supper.

WENDOLL. Light there, ho!
See you want nothing, sir; for, if you do,
You injure that good man, and wrong me too.

CRANWELL. I will make bold: good night.        [Exit.]

WENDOLL. How all conspire
To make our bosom sweet, and full entire!
Come, Nan, I pr'ythee let us sup within.

MISTRESS FRANKFORD. Oh, what a clog unto the soul is sin!
We pale offenders are still full of fear;
Every suspicious eye brings danger near,
When they whose clear hearts from offence are free
Despise report, base scandals do outface,
And stand at mere defiance with disgrace.

WENDOLL. Fie, fie! you talk too like a puritan.

MISTRESS FRANKFORD. YOU have tempted me to mischief,
    Master Wendoll:
I have done I know not what. Well, you plead custom;
That which for want of wit I granted erst,
I now must yield through fear. Come, come, let's in;
Once o'er shoes, we are straight o'er head in sin.

WENDOLL. My jocund soul is joyful above measure;
I'll be profuse in Frankford's richest treasure.        [Exeunt.]


## SCENE IV—*Another part of the house.*

[*Enter* CICELY, JENKIN, *and* BUTLER.]

JENKIN. My mistress and Master Wendoll, my master, sup in
    her chamber to-night. Cicely, you are preferred from being
    the cook to be chambermaid: of all the loves betwixt thee
    and me, tell me what thou thinkest of this?

CICELY. Mum; there's an old proverb,—"when the cat's away, the mouse may play."

JENKIN. Now you talk of a cat, Cicely, I smell a rat.

CICELY. Good words, Jenkin, lest you be called to answer them.

JENKIN. Why, God make my mistress an honest woman! are not these good words? Pray God my new master play not the knave with my old master! is there any hurt in this? God send no villainy intended! and, if they do sup together, pray God they do not lie together! God make my mistress chaste, and make us all His servants! what harm is there in all this? Nay, more; here is my hand, thou shalt never have my heart unless thou say Amen.

CICELY. Amen, I pray God, I say.

[*Enter* SERVING-MAN.]

SERVING-MAN. My mistress sends that you should make less noise, to lock up the doors, and see the household all got to bed: you, Jenkin, for this night are made the porter to see the gates shut in.

JENKIN. Thus, by little and little, I creep into office. Come, to kennel, my masters, to kennel; 'tis eleven o'clock, already.

SERVING-MAN. When you have locked the gates in, you must send up the keys to my mistress.

CICELY. Quickly, for God's sake, Jenkin, for I must carry them. I am neither pillow nor bolster, but I know more than both.

JENKIN. To bed, good Spigot; to bed, good honest serving-creatures; and let us sleep as snug as pigs in pease-straw.

[*Exeunt.*]


## SCENE V—*Outside* FRANKFORD'S *house.*

[*Enter* FRANKFORD *and* NICHOLAS.]

FRANKFORD. Soft, soft; we have tied our geldings to a tree,
Two flight-shot off, lest by their thundering hoofs
They blab our coming back. Hear'st thou no noise?

NICHOLAS. Hear! I hear nothing but the owl and you.

FRANKFORD. So; now my watch's hand points upon twelve,
And it is dead midnight. Where are my keys?

NICHOLAS. Here, sir.

FRANKFORD. This is the key that opes my outward gate;
This is the hall-door; this the withdrawing chamber;
But this, that door that's bawd unto my shame,
Fountain and spring of all my bleeding thoughts,
Where the most hallowed order and true knot
Of nuptial sanctity hath been profaned;
It leads to my polluted bed-chamber,
Once my terrestrial heaven, now my earth's hell,
The place where sins in all their ripeness dwell.
But I forget myself: now to my gate.

NICHOLAS. It must ope with far less noise than Cripple-gate,
or your plot's dashed.

FRANKFORD. So, reach me my dark lanthorn to the rest;
Tread softly, softly.

NICHOLAS. I will walk on eggs this pace.

FRANKFORD. A general silence hath surprised the house,
And this is the last door. Astonishment,
Fear, and amazement play against my heart,
Even as a madman beats upon a drum.
Oh, keep my eyes, you Heavens, before I enter,
From any sight that may transfix my soul;
Or, if there be so black a spectacle,
Oh, strike mine eyes stark blind; or, if not so,
Lend me such patience to digest my grief
That I may keep this white and virgin hand
From any violent outrage or red murder!
And with that prayer I enter.                    [*Exeunt.*]


## SCENE VI—*The hull of* FRANKFORD'S *house.*

[NICHOLAS *discovered.*]

NICHOLAS. Here's a circumstance.
A man be made cuckold in the time
That he's about it. An the case were mine,
As 'tis my master's,—'sblood that he makes me swear!—
I would have placed his action, entered there;
I would, I would.

[*Enter* FRANKFORD.]

FRANKFORD. Oh! oh!

NICHOLAS. Master, 'sblood! master! master!

FBANKFORD. O me unhappy! I have found them lying
Close in each other's arms, and fast asleep.
But that I would not damn two precious souls,
Bought with my Saviour's blood, and send them, laden
With all their scarlet sins upon their backs,
Unto a fearful judgment, their two lives
Had met upon my rapier.

   NICHOLAS. 'Sblood, master, what, have you left them sleeping
     still? let me go wake them.

   FBANKFORD. Stay, let me pause a while.
O God! O God! that it were possible
To undo things done; to call back yesterday!
That Time could turn up his swift sandy glass,
To untell the days, and to redeem these hours!
Or that the sun
Could, rising from the west, draw his coach backward,
Take from the account of time so many minutes,
Till he had all these seasons called again,
Those minutes, and those actions done in them,
Even from her first offence; that I might take her
As spotless as an angel in my arms!
But, oh! I talk of things impossible,
And cast beyond the moon. God give me patience!
For I will in and wake them.                              [*Exit.*]

   NICHOLAS. Here's patience perforce;
He needs must trot afoot that tires his horse.

[*Enter* WENDOLL, *running over the stage in a night-gown,*
FRANKFORD *after him with a sword drawn; a* MAID-SERVANT
*in her smock stays his hand, and clasps hold on him.*
FRANKFORD *pauses for a while.*]

FRANKFORD. I thank thee, maid; thou, like the angel's hand,
Hast stayed me from a bloody sacrifice.

[*Exit* MAID-SERVANT.]

Go, villain, and my wrongs sit on thy soul
As heavy as this grief doth upon mine!
When thou record'st my many courtesies,

And shalt compare them with thy treacherous heart,
Lay them together, weigh them equally,
'Twill be revenge enough. Go, to thy friend
A Judas: pray, pray, lest I live to see
Thee, Judas-like, hanged on an elder-tree.

[*Enter* MISTRESS FRANKFORD *in her night attire.*]

MISTRESS FRANKFORD. Oh, by what word, what title, or what
     name,
Shall I entreat your pardon? Pardon! oh!
I am as far from hoping such sweet grace
As Lucifer from heaven. To call you husband—
O me, most wretched! I have lost that name,
I am no more your wife.
     NICHOLAS. 'Sblood, sir, she swoons.
     FRANKFORD. Spare thou thy tears, for I will weep for thee:
And keep thy countenance, for I'll blush for thee.
Now, I protest, I think 'tis I am tainted,
For I am most ashamed; and 'tis more hard
For me to look upon thy guilty face,
Than on the sun's clear brow. What wouldst thou speak?
     MISTRESS FRANKFORD. I would I had no tongue, no ears, no eyes,
No apprehension, no capacity.
When do you spurn me like a dog? when tread me
Under your feet? when drag me by the hair?
Though I deserve a thousand thousand fold
More than you can inflict: yet, once my husband,
For womanhood, to which I am a shame,
Though once an ornament—even for His sake
That hath redeemed our souls, mark not my face
Nor hack me with your sword; but let me go
Perfect and undeformèd to my tomb.
I am not worthy that I should prevail
In the least suit; no, not to speak to you,
Nor look on you, nor to be in your presence.
Yet, as an abject, this one suit I crave;
This granted, I am ready for my grave.

                                                    [*Kneels.*]

     FRANKFORD. My God, with patience arm me! Rise, nay, rise,
And I'll debate with thee. Was it for want
Thou playedst the strumpet? Wast thou not supplied

With every pleasure, fashion, and new toy
Nay, even beyond my calling?
   MISTRESS FRANKFORD. I was.
   FRANKFORD. Was it then disability in me;
Or in thine eye seemed he a properer man?
MISTRESS FRANKFORD. Oh, no.
   FRANKFORD. Did not I lodge thee in my bosom?
Wear thee here in my heart?
   MISTRESS FRANKFORD. You did.
   FRANKFORD. I did, indeed; witness my tears I did.
Go, bring my infants hither.

           [*Enter* SERVANT *with two* CHILDREN.]

                          O Nan! O Nan!
If neither fear of shame, regard of honour,
The blemish of my house, nor my dear love
Could have withheld thee from so lewd a fact,
Yet for these infants, these young harmless souls,
On whose white brows thy shame is charactered,
And grows in greatness as they wax in years,—
Look but on them, and melt away in tears.
Away with them! lest, as her spotted body
Hath stained their names with stripe of bastardy,
So her adulterous breath may blast their spirits
With her infectious thoughts. Away with them.

           [*Exeunt* SERVANT *and* CHILDREN.]

   MISTRESS FRANKFORD. In this one life I die ten thousand deaths.
   FRANKFORD. Stand up, stand up; I will do nothing rashly;
I will retire a while into my study,
And thou shalt hear thy sentence presently.      [*Exit.*]
   MISTRESS FRANKFORD. 'Tis welcome, be it death. O me, base
     strumpet,
That, having such a husband, such sweet children,
Must enjoy neither! Oh, to redeem my honour,
I would have this hand cut off, these my breasts seared,
Be racked, strappadoed, put to any torment:
Nay, to whip but this scandal out, I would hazard
The rich and dear redemption of my soul.
He cannot be so base as to forgive me;
Nor I so shameless to accept his pardon.

O women, women, you that yet have kept
Your holy matrimonial vow unstained,
Make me your instance: when you tread awry,
Your sins, like mine, will on your conscience lie.

[*Enter* CICELY, JENKIN, *and all the* SERVING-MEN
*as newly come out of bed.*]

ALL. O mistress, mistress, what have you done, mistress?
  NICHOLAS. 'Sblood, what a caterwauling keep you here!
  JENKIN. O Lord, mistress, how comes this to pass? My master
    is run away in his shirt, and never so much as called me to
    bring his clothes after him.
  MISTRESS FRANKFORD. See what guilt is! here stand I in this
    place,
Ashamed to look my servants in the face.

[*Enter* FRANKFORD *and* CRANWELL, *whom seeing
she falls on her knees.*]

  FRANKFORD. My words are registered in Heaven already,
With patience hear me. I'll not martyr thee,
Nor mark thee for a strumpet; but with usage
Of more humility torment thy soul,
And kill thee even with kindness.
  CRANWELL. Master Frankford——
  FRANKFORD. Good Master Cranwell. Woman, hear thy judg-
    ment.
Go make thee ready in thy best attire;
Take with thee all thy gowns, all thy apparel;
Leave nothing that did ever call thee mistress.
Or by whose sight, being left here in the house,
I may remember such a woman by.
Choose thee a bed and hangings for thy chamber;
Take with thee every thing that hath thy I mark,
And get thee to my manor seven mile off,
Where live; 'tis thine; I freely give it thee.
My tenants by shall furnish thee with wains
To carry all thy stuff, within two hours,—
No longer will I limit thee my sight.
Choose which of all my servants thou likest best,
And they are thine to attend thee.
  MISTRESS FRANKFORD. A mild sentence.

FRANKFORD. But, as thou hopest for Heaven, as thou believest
Thy name's recorded in the book of life,
I charge thee never, after this sad day,
To see me, or to meet me, or to send
By word or writing, gift, or otherwise,
To move me, by thyself, or by thy friends;
Nor challenge any part in my two children.
So, farewell, Nan! for we will henceforth be
As we had never seen, ne'er more shall see.

   MISTRESS FRANKFORD. How full my heart is, in mine eyes
     appears;
What wants in words, I will supply in tears.

   FRANKFORD. Come, take your coach, your stuff; all must along;
Servants and all, make ready; all be gone.
It was thy hand cut two hearts out of one.

                                   *[Exeunt.]*

# ACT V

## SCENE I—*The entrance to* SIR FRANCIS ACTON'S *house.*

[*Enter* SIR CHARLES MOUNTFORD, *and* SUSAN, *both well dressed.*]

SUSAN. Brother, why have you tricked me like a bride,
Bought me this gay attire, these ornaments?
Forget you our estate, our poverty?

SIR CHARLES. Call me not brother, but imagine me
Some barbarous outlaw, or uncivil kern;
For if thou shutt'st thy eye, and only hearest
The words that I shall utter, thou shalt judge me
Some staring ruffian, not thy brother Charles.
O sister!——

SUSAN. O brother, what doth this strange language mean?

SIR CHARLES. Dost love me, sister? wouldst thou see me live
A bankrupt beggar in the world's disgrace,
And die indebted to my enemies?
Wouldst thou behold me stand like a huge beam
In the world's eye, a bye-word and a scorn?
It lies in thee of these to acquit me free,
And all my debt I may out-strip by thee.

SUSAN. By me! why, I have nothing, nothing left;
I owe even for the clothes upon my back;
I am not worth——

SIR CHARLES. O sister, say not so;
It lies in you my downcast state to raise,
To make me stand on even points with the world.
Come, sister, you are rich; indeed you are;

187

And in your power you have, without delay,
Acton's five hundred pound back to repay.

  SUSAN. Till now I had thought you had loved me. By my
     honour
(Which I have kept as spotless as the moon),
I ne'er was mistress of that single doit
Which I reserved not to supply your wants;
And do you think that I would hoard from you?
Now, by my hopes in Heaven, knew I the means
To buy you from the slavery of your debts
(Especially from Acton, whom I hate),
I would redeem it with my life or blood.

  SIR CHARLES. I challenge it; and, kindred set apart,
Thus, ruffian-like, I lay siege to your heart.
What do I owe to Acton?

  SUSAN. Why some five hundred pounds; towards which, I
     swear,
In all the world I have not one denier.

  SIR CHARLES. It will not prove so. Sister, now resolve me:
What do you think (and speak your conscience)
Would Acton give, might he enjoy your bed?

  SUSAN. He would not shrink to spend a thousand pound,
To give the Mountfords' name so deep a wound.

  SIR CHARLES. A thousand pound! I but five hundred owe;
Grant him your bed, he's paid with interest so.

  SUSAN. O brother!

  SIR CHARLES. O sister! only this one way,
With that rich jewel you my debts may pay.
In speaking this my cold heart shakes with shame;
Nor do I woo you in a brother's name,
But in a stranger's. Shall I die in debt
To Acton, my grand foe, and you still wear
The precious jewel that he holds so dear?

  SUSAN. My honour I esteem as dear and precious
As my redemption.

  SIR CHARLES. I esteem you, sister,
As dear, for so dear prizing it.

  SUSAN. Will Charles
Have me cut off my hands, and send them Acton?
Rip up my breast, and with my bleeding heart
Present him as a token?

SIR CHARLES. Neither, sister:
But hear me in my strange assertion.
Thy honour and my soul are equal in my regard;
Nor will thy brother Charles survive thy shame.
His kindness, like a burthen hath surcharged me,
And under his good deeds I stooping go,
Not with an upright soul. Had I remained
In prison still, there doubtless I had died:
Then, unto him that freed me from that prison,
Still do I owe this life. What moved my foe
To enfranchise me? 'Twas, sister, for your love,
With full five hundred pounds he bought your love,
And shall he not enjoy it? Shall the weight
Of all this heavy burthen lean on me,
And will not you bear part? You did partake
The joy of my release; will you not stand
In joint-bond bound to satisfy the debt?
Shall I be only charged?

   SUSAN. But that I know
These arguments come from an honoured mind.
As in your most extremity of need
Scorning to stand in debt to one your hate,—
Nay, rather would engage your unstained honour
Than to be held ingrate,—I should condemn you.
I see your resolution, and assent;
So Charles will have me, and I am content.

   SIR CHARLES. For this I tricked you up.

   SUSAN. But here's a knife,
To save mine honour, shall slice out my life.

   SIR CHARLES. Ay! know thou pleasest me a thousand times
More in that resolution than thy grant.—
Observe her love; to soothe it to my suit,
Her honour she will hazard, though not lose:
To bring me out of debt, her rigorous hand
Will pierce her heart. O wonder! that will choose,
Rather than stain her blood, her life to lose.—
Come, you sad sister to a woful brother,
This is the gate: I'll bear him such a present,
Such an acquittance for the knight to seal,
As will amaze his senses, and surprise
With admiration all his fantasies.

SUSAN. Before his unchaste thoughts shall seize on me,
'Tis here shall my imprisoned soul set free.

[*Enter* SIR FRANCIS ACTON *and* MALBY.]

SIR FRANCIS. HOW! Mountford with his sister, hand in hand!
What miracle's afoot?

MALBY.                          It is a sight
Begets in me much admiration.

SIR CHARLES. Stand not amazed to see me thus attended:
Acton, I owe thee money, and being unable
To bring thee the full sum in ready coin,
Lo! for thy more assurance, here's a pawn,—
My sister, my dear sister, whose chaste honour
I prize above a million: here, nay, take her;
She's worth your money, man; do not forsake her.

SIR FRANCIS. I would he were in earnest!

SUSAN. Impute it not to my immodesty:
My brother being rich in nothing else
But in his interest that he hath in me,
According to his poverty hath brought you
Me, all his store; whom howsoe'er you prize
As forfeit to your hand, he values highly,
And would not sell, but to acquit your debt,
For any emperor's ransom.

SIR FRANCIS. Stern heart, relent;
Thy former cruelty at length repent.
Was ever known, in any former age,
Such honourable wrested courtesy?
Lands, honours, life, and all the world forego,
Rather than stand engaged to such a foe.          [*Aside.*]

SIR CHARLES. Acton, she is too poor to be thy bride,
And I too much opposed to be thy brother.
There, take her to thee: if thou hast the heart
To seize her as a rape, or lustful prey;
To blur our house, that never yet was stained;
To murder her that never meant thee harm;
To kill me now, whom once thou savedst from death,
Do them at once: on her all these rely,
And perish with her spotted chastity.

SIR FRANCIS. YOU overcome me in your love, Sir Charles;
I cannot be so cruel to a lady

I love so dearly. Since you have not spared
To engage your reputation to the world,
Your sister's honour, which you prize so dear,
Nay, all the comforts which you hold on earth,
To grow out of my debt, being your foe,
Your honoured thoughts, lo! thus I recompense:
Your metamorphosed foe receives your gift
In satisfaction of all former wrongs.
This jewel I will wear here in my heart;
And, where before I thought her for her wants
Too base to be my bride, to end all strife,
I seal you my dear brother, her my wife.

SUSAN. You still exceed us: I will yield to fate,
And learn to love, where I till now did hate.

SIR CHARLES. With that enchantment you have charmed my
    soul,
And made me rich even in those very words:
I pay no debt, but am indebted more;
Rich in your love, I never can be poor.

SIR FRANCIS. All's mine is yours; we are alike in state,
Let's knit in love what was opposed in hate.
Come! for our nuptials we will straight provide,
Blest only in our brother and fair bride.       *[Exeunt.]*


# SCENE II—*A room in* FRANKFORD'S *house*.

*[Enter* CRANWELL, FRANKFORD, *and* NICHOLAS.]

CRANWELL. Why do you search each room about your house.
Now that you have despatched your wife away?

FRANKFORD. O sir, to see that nothing may be left
That ever was my wife's. I loved her dearly,
And when I do but think of her unkindness,
My thoughts are all in hell; to avoid which torment,
I would not have a bodkin or a cuff,
A bracelet, necklace, or rebato wire;
Nor any thing that ever was called hers,
Left me, by which I might remember her.
Seek round about.

NICHOLAS. 'Sblood, master! here's her lute flung in a corner.

FRANKFORD. Her lute! O God! upon this instrument
Her fingers have run quick division,
Sweeter than that which now divides our hearts.
These frets have made me pleasant, that have now
Frets of ray heart-strings made. O Master Cranwell,
Oft hath she made this melancholy wood,
Now mute and dumb for her disastrous chance,
Speak sweetly many a note, sound many a strain
To her own ravishing voice, which being well strung,
What pleasant strange airs have they jointly rung!
Post with it after her. Now nothing's left;
Of her and hers, I am at once bereft.
    NICHOLAS. I'll ride and overtake her; do my message,
And come back again.                       *[Exit.]*
    CRANWELL. Mean time, sir, if you please,
I'll to Sir Francis Acton, and inform him
Of what hath passed betwixt you and his sister.
    FRANKFORD. Do as you please. How ill am I bested,
    To be a widower ere my wife be dead!      *[Exeunt.]*


## SCENE III—*A country road.*

[*Enter* MISTRESS FRANKFOLD, *with* JENKIN, CICELY, *a*
COACHMAN, *and three* CARTERS.]


MISTRESS FRANKFORD. Bid my coach stay: why should I ride
    in state,
Being hurled so low down by the hand of fate?
A seat like to my fortunes let me have;
Earth for my chair, and for my bed a grave.
    JENKIN. Comfort, good mistress; you have watered your coach
    with tears already: you have but two mile now to go to your
    manor. A man cannot say by my old master Frankford as he
    may say by me, that he wants manors; for he hath three or
    four, of which this is one that we are going to now.
    CICELY. Good mistress, be of good cheer; sorrow, you see,
    hurts you, but helps you not: we all mourn to see you so
    sad.
    CARTER. Mistress, I spy one of my landlord's men
Come riding post: 'tis like he brings some news.

MISTRESS FRANKFORD. Comes he from Master Frankford, he
   is welcome;
So are his news because they come from him.

[*Enter* NICHOLAS.]

NICHOLAS [*presenting lute*]. There.
   MISTRESS FRANKFORD. I know the lute; oft have I sung to thee:
We both are out of tune, both out of time.
   NICHOLAS. Would that had been the worst instrument that
      e'er you played on. My master commends him to ye; there's
      all he can find that was ever yours: he hath nothing left that
      ever you could lay claim to but his own heart, and he could
      afford you that. All that I have to deliver you is this: he prays
      you to forget him, and so he bids you farewell.
   MISTRESS FRANKFORD. I thank him: he is kind, and ever was.
All you that have true feeling of my grief,
That know my loss, and have relenting hearts,
Gird me about, and help me with your tears
To wash my spotted sins: my lute shall groan;
It cannot weep, but shall lament my moan.

[*Enter* WENDOLL.]

WENDOLL. Pursued with horror of a guilty soul,
And with the sharp scourge of repentance lashed
I fly from my own shadow. O my stars!
What have my parents in their lives deserved,
That you should lay this penance on their son?
When I but think of Master Frankford's love,
And lay it to my treason, or compare
My murdering him for his relieving me,
It strikes a terror like a lightning's flash
To scorch my blood up. Thus I, like the owl,
Ashamed of day, live in these shadowy woods,
Afraid of every leaf or murmuring blast,
Yet longing to receive some perfect knowledge
How he hath dealt with her. [*Sees* MISTRESS FRANKFORD.] O my
   sad fate!
Here, and so far from home, and thus attended!
O God! I have divorced the truest turtles
That ever lived together; and, being divided
In several places, make their several moan;

She in the fields laments, and he at home.
So poets write that Orpheus made the trees
And stones to dance to his melodious harp,
Meaning the rustic and the barbarous hinds,
That had no understanding part in them:
So she from these rude carters tears extracts,
Making their flinty hearts with grief to rise,
And draw down rivers from their rocky eyes.

   MISTRESS FRANKFORD [*to* NICHOLAS]. If you return unto your
      master, say
(Though not from me; for I am all unworthy
To blast his name so with a strumpet's tongue)
That you have seen me weep, wish myself dead:
Nay, you may say too, for my vow is passed,
Last night you saw me eat and drink my last.
This to your master you may say and swear;
For it is writ in Heaven, and decreed here.

   NICHOLAS. I'll say you wept: I'll swear you made me sad.
Why how now, eyes? what now? what's here to do?
I'm gone, or I shall straight turn baby too.

   WENDOLL. I cannot weep, my heart is all on fire:
Curst be the fruits of my unchaste desire!

   MISTRESS FRANKFORD. Go, break this lute upon my coach's
      wheel,
As the last music that I e'er shall make;
Not as my husband's gift, but my farewell
To all earth's joy; and so your master tell.

   NICHOLAS. If I can for crying.

   WENDOLL. Grief, have done,
Or like a madman I shall frantic run.

   MISTRESS FRANKFORD. You have beheld the wofullest wretch
      on earth;
A woman made of tears: would you had words
To express but what you see! My inward grief
No tongue can utter; yet unto your power
You may describe my sorrow, and disclose
To thy sad master my abundant woes.

   NICHOLAS. I'll do your commendations.

   MISTRESS FRANKFORD. O no:
I dare not so presume; nor to my children:
I am disclaimed in both; alas, I am.

Oh, never teach them, when they come to speak,
To name the name of mother; chide their tongue,
If they by chance light on that hated word;
Tell them 'tis naught; for, when that word they name,
Poor pretty souls! they harp on their own shame.
    WENDOLL. To recompense her wrongs, what canst thou do?
Thou hast made her husbandless and childless too.
    MISTRESS FRANKFORD. I have no more to say. Speak not for
        me;
Yet you may tell your master what you see.
    NICHOLAS. I'll do't.                              [*Exit.*]
    WENDOLL. I'll speak to her, and comfort her in grief.
Oh! but her wound cannot be cured with words.
No matter though, I'll do my best goodwill
To work a cure on her whom I did kill.
    MISTRESS FRANKFORD. So, now unto my coach, then to my
        home,
So to my death-bed; for from this sad hour
I never will nor eat, nor drink, nor taste
Of any cates that may preserve my life:
I never will nor smile, nor sleep, nor rest;
But when my tears have washed my black soul white,
Sweet Saviour, to Thy hands I yield my sprite.
    WENDOLL. O Mistress Frankford—
    MISTRESS FRANKFORD. Oh, for God's sake fly!
The devil doth come to tempt me ere I die.
My coach! this fiend, that with an angel's face
Conjured mine honour, till he sought *my* wrack,
In my repentant eyes seems ugly black.
                    [*Exeunt all, except* WENDOLL *and* JENKIN;
                         *the* CARTERS *whistling.*]
    JENKIN. What, my young master that fled in his shirt! How
      come you by your clothes again? You have made our house
      in a sweet pickle, ha' ye not, think you? What, shall I serve
      you still, or cleave to the old house?
    WENDOLL. Hence, slave! away with thy unseasoned mirth!
Unless thou canst shed tears, and sigh, and howl,
Curse thy sad fortunes, and exclaim on fate,
Thou art not for my turn.
    JENKIN. Marry, an you will not, another will: farewell, and be
      hanged! Would you had never come to have kept this coil

within our doors; we shall ha' you run away like a sprite
again.

                                                              [*Exit.*]

WENDOLL. She's gone to death; I live to want and woe;
Her life, her sins, and all upon my head.
And I must now go wander, like a Cain,
In foreign countries and remoted climes,
Where the report of my ingratitude
Cannot be heard. I'll over first to France,
And so to Germany and Italy;
Where when I have recovered, and by travel
Gotten those perfect tongues, and that these rumours
May in their height abate, I will return:
And I divine (however now dejected)
My worth and parts being by some great man praised,
At my return I may in court be raised.

                                                              [*Exit.*]


## SCENE IV—*Before the manor.*

[*Enter* SIR FRANCIS ACTON, SUSAN, SIR CHARLES MOUNTFORD,
CRANWELL, *and* MALBY.]

SIR FRANCIS. Brother, and now my wife, I think these troubles
Fall on my head by justice of the Heavens,
For being so strict to you in your extremities:
But we are now atoned. I would my sister
Could with like happiness o'ercome her griefs,
As we have ours.

SUSAN. You tell us, Master Cranwell, wondrous things,
Touching the patience of that gentleman,
With what strange virtue he demeans his grief.

CRANWELL. told you what I was a witness of;
It was my fortune to lodge there that night.

SIR FRANCIS. O that same villain Wendoll! 'twas his tongue
That did corrupt her; she was of herself
Chaste, and devoted well. Is this the house?

CRANWELL. Yes, sir, I take it here your sister lies.

SIR FRANCIS. My brother Frankford showed too mild a spirit
In the revenge of such a loathèd crime;

Less than he did, no man of spirit could do:
I am so far from blaming his revenge,
That I commend it. Had it been my case,
Their souls at once had from their breasts been freed:
Death to such deeds of shame is the due meed.

                              [*They enter the house.*]


## SCENE V—*A room in the manor.*

[*Enter* SIR FRANCIS ACTON, SUSAN, SIR CHARLES MOUNTFORD,
  CRANWELL, *and* MALBY; JENKIN *and* CICELY *following them.*]

JENKIN. O my mistress, my mistress, my poor mistress.
CICELY. Alas that ever I was born! what shall I do for my poor
    mistress?
SIR CHARLES. Why, what of her?
JENKIN. O Lord, sir, she no sooner heard that her brother and
    his friends were come to see how she did, but she, for very
    shame of her guilty conscience, fell into such a swoon, that
    we had much ado to get life into her.
SUSAN. Alas that she should bear so hard a fate!
Pity it is repentance comes too late.
SIR FRANCIS. Is she so weak in body?
JENKIN. O sir, I can assure you there's no hope of life in her,
    for she will take no sustenance: she hath plainly starved
    herself, and now she is as lean as a lath. She ever looks for
    the good hour. Many gentlemen and gentlewomen of the
    country are come to comfort her.                [*Exeunt.*]


## SCENE VI—MISTRESS FRANKFORD'S
## *bed-chamber.*

[MISTRESS FRANKFORD *in bed; enter* SIR CHARLES MOUNTFORD,
  SIR FRANCIS ACTON, MALBY, CRANWELL, *and* SUSAN.]

MALBY. How fare you, Mistress Frankford?
MISTRESS FRANKFORD. Sick, sick, oh, sick. Give me some air,
I pray you.
Tell me, oh, tell me where is Master Frankford?

Will not he deign to see me ere I die?

    MALBY. Yes, Mistress Frankford: divers gentlemen,
Your loving neighbours, with that just request
Have moved, and told him of your weak estate:
Who, though with much ado to get belief,
Examining of the general circumstance,
Seeing your sorrow and your penitence,
And hearing therewithal the great desire
You have to see him ere you left the world,
He gave to us his faith to follow us,
And sure he will be here immediately.

    MISTRESS FRANKFORD. You have half revived me with those
        pleasing news:
Raise me a little higher in my bed.
Blush I not, brother Acton? Blush I not, Sir Charles?
Can you not read my fault writ in my cheek?
Is not *my* crime there? tell me, gentlemen.

    SIR CHARLES. Alas! good mistress, sickness hath not left you
Blood in your face enough to make you blush.

    MISTRESS FRANKFORD. Then sickness, like a friend, my fault
        would hide.
Is my husband come? My soul but tarries
His arrive, then I am fit for Heaven.

    SIR FRANCIS. I came to chide you; but my words of hate
Are turned to pity and compassionate grief.
I came to rate you; but my brawls, you see,
Melt into tears, and I must weep by thee,
Here's Master Frankford now.

              [*Enter* FRANKFORD.]

    FRANKFORD. Good-morrow, brother; morrow, gentlemen:
God, that hath laid this cross upon our heads,
Might (had He pleased) have made our cause of meeting
On a more fair and more contented ground;
But He that made us, made us to this woe.

    MISTRESS FRANKFORD. And is he come?
Methinks that voice I know.

    FRANKFORD. How do you, woman?

    MISTRESS FRANKFORD. Well, Master Frankford, well; but shall
        be better,
I hope, within this hour. Will you vouch-safe,

Out of your grace and your humanity,
To take a spotted strumpet by the hand?
   FRANKFORD. This hand once held my heart in faster bonds
Than now 'tis gripped by me. God pardon them
That made us first break hold!
   MISTRESS FRANKFORD. Amen, amen.
Out of my zeal to Heaven, whither I'm now bound,
I was so impudent to wish you here;
And once more beg your pardon. O good man,
And father to my children, pardon me,
Pardon, oh, pardon me! My fault so heinous is,
That if you in this world forgive it not,
Heaven will not clear it in the world to come.
Faintness hath so usurped upon my knees
That kneel I cannot, but on my heart's knees
My prostrate soul lies thrown down at your feet
To beg your gracious pardon. Pardon, oh, pardon me!
   FRANKFORD. As freely, from the low depth of my soul,
As my Redeemer hath forgiven His death,
I pardon thee. I will shed tears for thee, pray with thee;
And, in mere pity of thy weak estate,
I'll wish to die with thee.
ALL. So do we all.
   NICHOLAS. So will not I;
I'll sigh and sob, but, by my faith, not die.
   SIR FRANCIS. O Master Frankford, all the near alliance
I lose by her shall be supplied in thee:
You are my brother by the nearest way;
Her kindred hath fallen off, but yours doth stay.
   FRANKFORD. Even as I hope for pardon at that day
When the great Judge of Heaven in scarlet sits,
So be thou pardoned. Though thy rash offence
Divorced our bodies, thy repentant tears
Unite our souls.
   SIR CHARLES. Then comfort, Mistress Frankford;
You see your husband hath forgiven your fall;
Then rouse your spirits, and cheer your fainting soul.
   SUSAN. How is it with you?
   SIR FRANCIS. How do ye feel yourself?
   MISTRESS FRANKFORD. Not of this world.
   FRANKFORD. I see you are not, and I weep to see it.

My wife, the mother to my pretty babes!
Both those lost names I do restore thee back,
And with this kiss I wed thee once again:
Though thou art wounded in thy honoured name,
And with that grief upon thy death-bed liest,
Honest in heart, upon my soul, thou diest.

    MISTRESS FRANKFORD. Pardoned on earth, soul, thou in Heaven
       art free
Once more: thy wife dies thus embracing thee.     [*Dies.*]

    FRANKFORD. New married, and new widowed. Oh! she's dead,
And a cold grave must be her nuptial bed.

    SIR CHARLES. Sir, be of good comfort; and your heavy sorrow
Part equally amongst us: storms divided
Abate their force, and with less rage are guided.

    CRANWELL. Do, Master Frankford: he that hath least part
Will find enough to drown one troubled heart.

    SIR FRANCIS. Peace with thee, Nan. Brothers, and gentlemen,
All we that can plead interest in her grief,
Bestow upon her body funeral tears.
Brother, had you with threats and usage bad
Punished her sin, the grief of her offence
Had not with such true sorrow touched her heart.

    FRANKFORD. I see it had not: therefore on her grave
Will I bestow this funeral epitaph,
Which on her marble tomb shall be engraved.
In golden letters shall these words be filled,
"Here lies she whom her husband's kindness killed."

# THE TRAGEDIE OF MARIAM

## Elizabeth Cary

# TO DIANAES EARTHLIE DEPVTESSE,

### and my worthy Sister,
### Mistris Elizabeth Carye.

When cheerful *Phœbus* his full course hath run,
His sisters fainter beams our harts doth cheere:
So your faire Brother is to mee the Sunne,
And you his Sister as my Moone appeere.

You are my next belou'd, my second Friend,
For when my *Phœbus* absence makes it Night,
Whilst to th' *Antipodes* his beames do bend,
From you my *Phœbe,* shines my second Light.

Hee like to *SOL,* cleare-fighted, constant, free,
You *LV* NA-like, vnspotted, chast, diuine:
Hee shone on *Sicily,* you destin'd bee,
T'illumine the now obscurde *Palestine.*
My first was consecrated to *Apollo,*
My second to *DIANA* now shall follow.

E. C.

# THE NAMES OF THE SPEAKERS.

*Herod, King of Iudea.*
*Doris, his first Wife.*
*Mariam, his second Wife.*
*Salome, Herods Sister.*
*Antipater his sonne by Salome.*
*Alexandra, Mariams mother.*
*Sillius, Prince of Arabia.*
*Constabarus, husband to Salome.*
*Phœroras, Herods Brother.*
*Graphina, his Loue.*
*Babus first Sonne.*
*Babus second Sonne.*
*Annanell, the high Priest.*
*Sohemus, a Counsellor to Herod.*
*Nuntio.*
*Bu. another Messenger.*
*Chorus, a Companie of Iewes.*

# ACTUS PRIMUS.

## SCŒNA PRIMA.

*Mariam sola.*

How oft haue I with publike voyce runne on?
To censure *Romes* last *Hero* for deceit:
Because he wept when *Pompeis* life was gone,
Yet when he liu'd, hee thought his Name too great.
But now I doe recant, and *Roman* Lord
Excufe too rash a judgement in a woman:
My Sexe pleads pardon, pardon then afford,
Mistaking is with vs, but too too common.
Now doe I finde by selfe Experience taught,
One Object yeelds both griefe and ioy:
You wept indeed, when on his worth you thought,
But ioyd that slaughter did your Foe destroy.
So at his death your Eyes true droppes did raine,
Whom dead, you did not wish aliue againe.
When *Herod* liu'd, that now is done to death,
Oft haue I wisht that I from him were free:
Oft haue I wisht that he might lose his breath,
Oft haue I wisht his Carkas dead to see.
Then Rage and Scorne had put my loue to flight,
That Loue which once on him was firmely set:
Hate hid his true affection from my sight,
And kept my heart from paying him his debt.
And blame me not, for *Herods* Iealousie
Had power euen constancie it selfe to change:
For hee by barring me from libertie,
To shunne my ranging, taught me first to range.

205

But yet too chast a Scholler was my hart,
To learne to loue another then my Lord:
To leaue his Loue, my lessons former part,
I quickly learn'd, the other I abhord.
But now his death to memorie doth call,
The tender loue, that he to *Mariam* bare:
And mine to him, this makes those riuers fall.
Which by an other thought vnmoistned are.
For *Ariftobolus* the lowlyest youth
That euer did in Angels shape appeare:
The cruell *Herod* was not mou'd to ruth,
Then why grieues *Mariam Herods* death to heare?
Why ioy I not the tongue no more shall speake,
That yeelded forth my brothers latest dome:
Both youth and beautie might thy furie breake,
And both in him did ill befit a Tombe.
And worthy Grandsire ill did he requite,
His high Affent alone by thee procur'd,
Except he murdred thee to free the spright
Which still he thought on earth too long immur'd.
How happie was it that *Sohemus* maide
Was mou'd to pittie my distrest estate?
Might *Herods* life a trustie seruant finde,
My death to his had bene vnseparate.                    (beare,
These thoughts haue power, his death to make me
Nay more, to wish the newes may firmely hold:
Yet cannot this repulse some falling teare,
That will against my will some griefe vnfold.
And more I owe him for his loue to me,
The deepest loue that euer yet was seene:
Yet had I rather much a milke-maide bee,
Then be the Monarke of *Iudeas* Queene.
It was for nought but loue, he wisht his end
Might to my death, but the vaunt-currier proue:
But I had rather still be foe then friend,
To him that saues for hate, and kills for loue.
Hard-hearted *Mariam,* at thy discontent,
What flouds of teares haue drencht his manly face?
How canst thou then so faintly now lament,
Thy truest louers death, a deaths disgrace:
I now mine eyes you do begin to right

The wrongs of your admirer. And my Lord,
Long since you should haue put your smiles to flight,
Ill doth a widowed eye with ioy accord.
Why now me thinkes the loue I bare him then,
When virgin freedome left me vnrestraind:
Doth to my heart begin to creepe agen,
My passion now is far from being faind.
But teares flie backe, and hide you in your bankes,
You must not be to *Alexandra* seene:
For if my mone be spide, but little thankes
Shall *Mariam* haue, from that incensed Queene.

## ACTUS PRIMUS: SCŒNA SECUNDA.

*Mariam. Alexandra.*

                              *Alex:*                    (mistake,
What meanes these teares? my *Mariam* doth
The newes we heard did tell the *Tyrants* end:
What weepst thou for, thy brothers murthers sake,
Will euer wight a teare for *Herod* spend?
My curie pursue his breathles trunke and spirit,
Base *Edomite* the damned *Esaus* heire:
Must he ere *Iacobs* child the crowne inherit?
Must he vile wretch be set in *Dauids* chaire?
No *Dauids* soule within the bosome plac'te,
Of our forefather *Abram* was asham'd:
To see his seat with such a toade disgrac'te,
That seat that hath by *Iudas* race bene fain'd.
Thou fatall enemie to royall blood,
Did not the murther of my boy suffice,
To stop thy cruell mouth that gaping stood?
But must thou dim the milde *Hercanus* eyes?
My gratious father, whose too readie hand
Did lift this *Idumean* from the dust:
And he vngratefull catiffe did withstand,
The man that did in him most friendly trust.
What kingdomes right could cruell *Herod* claime,
Was he not *Esaus* Issue, heyre of hell?
Then what succession can he haue but shame?

Did not his Ancestor his birth-right sell?
O yes, he doth from *Edoms* name deriue,
His cruell nature which with blood is fed:
That made him me of Sire and sonne depriue,
He euer thirsts for blood, and blood is red.
Weepst thou because his loue to thee was bent?
And readst thou loue in crimson caracters?
Slew he thy friends to worke thy hearts content?
No: hate may Iustly call that action hers.
He gaue the sacred Priesthood for thy sake,
To *Aristobolus.* Yet doomde him dead:
Before his backe the *Ephod* warme could make,
And ere the *Myter* setled on his head:
Oh had he giuen my boy no lesse then right,
The double oyle should to his forehead bring:
A double honour, shining doubly bright,
His birth annoynted him both Priest and King.
And say my father, and my sonne he slewe,
To royalize by right your Prince borne breath:
Was loue the cause, can *Mariam* deeme it true,
That *Mariam* gaue commandment for her death?
I know by fits, he shewd some signes of loue,
And yet not loue, but raging lunacie:
And this his hate to thee may iustly proue,
That sure he hates *Hercanus* familie.
Who knowes if he vnconstant wauering Lord,
His loue to *Doris* had renew'd againe?
And that he might his bed to her afford,
Perchance he wisht that *Mariam* might be slaine,
   *Nun: Doris,* Alas her time of loue was past,
Those coales were rakte in embers long agoe:
If *Mariams* loue and she was now disgrast,
Nor did I glorie in her ouerthrowe.
He not a whit his first borne sonne esteem'd,
Because as well as his he was not mine:
My children onely for his owne he deem'd,
These boyes that did descend from royall line.
These did he stile his heyres to *Dauids* throne,
My *Alexander* if he liue, shall sit
In the Maiesticke seat of *Salamon,*
To will it so, did *Herod* thinke it fit.
   *Alex.* Why? who can claime from *Alexanders* brood

That Gold adorned Lyon-guarded Chaire?
Was *Alexander* not of *Dauids* blood?
And was not *Mariam Alexanders* heire?
What more then right could *Herod* then bestow,
And who will thinke except for more then right,
He did not raise them, for they were not low,
But borne to weare the Crowne in his despight:
Then send those teares away that are not sent
To thee by reason, but by passions power:
Thine eyes to cheere, thy cheekes to smiles be bent,
And entertaine with ioy this happy houre.
Felicitie, if when shee comes, she findes
A mourning habite, and a cheerlesse looke,
Will thinke she is not welcome to thy minde,
And so perchance her lodging will not brooke.
Oh keepe her whilest thou hast her, if she goe
She will not easily returne againe:
Full many a yeere haue I indur'd in woe,
Yet still haue sude her presence to obtaine:
And did not I to her as presents send
A Table, that best Art did beautifie
Of two, to whom Heauen did best feature lend,
To woe her loue by winning *Anthony*:
For when a Princes fauour we doe craue,
We first their Mynions loues do seeke to winne:
So I, that sought Felicitie to haue,
Did with her Mynion *Anthony* beginne,
With double slight I sought to captiuate
The warlike louer, but I did not right:
For if my gift had borne but halfe the rate,
The *Roman* had beene ouer-taken quite.
But now he fared like a hungry guest,
That to some plenteous festiuall is gone,
Now this, now that, hee deems to eate were best,
Such choice doth make him let them all alone.
The boyes large forehead first did fayrest seeme,
Then glaunst his eye vpon my *Mariams* cheeke:
And that without companion did deeme,
What was in eyther but he most did leeke.
And thus distracted, eythers beauties might
Within the others excellence was drown'd:
Too much delight did bare him from delight,

For eithers loue, the others did confound.
Where if thy portraiture had onely gone,
His life from *Herod*, *Anthony* had taken:
He would haue loued thee, and thee alone,
And left the browne *Egyptian* cleane forsaken.
And *Cleopatra* then to seeke had bene,
So firme a louer of her wayned face:
Then great *Anthonius* fall we had not seene,
By her that fled to haue him holde the chase.
Then *Mariam* in a *Romans* Chariot set,
In place of *Cleopatra* might haue showne;
A mart of Beauties in her visage met,
And part in this, that they were all her owne.

   *Ma.* Not to be Emprise of aspiring *Rome*,
Would *Mariam* like to *Cleopatra* liue:
With purest body will I presse my Toome,
And wish no fauours *Anthony* could giue.

   *Alex.* Let vs retire vs, that we may resolue
How now to deale in this reuerfed ftate:
Great are th'affaires that we must now reuolue,
And great affaires must not be taken late.

## ACTUS PRIMUS. SCŒNA TERTIA.

*Mariam. Alexandra. Salome.*

*Salome.*

More plotting yet? Why? now you haue the thing
For which so oft you spent your supliant breath:
And *Mariam* hopes to haue another King,
Her eyes doe sparkle ioy for *Herods* death.

   *Alex.* If she desir'd another King to haue,
She might before she came in *Herods* bed
Haue had her wish. More Kings then one did craue,
For leaue to set a Crowne vpon her head.
I thinke with more then reason she laments,
That she is freed from such a sad annoy:
Who ist will weepe to part from discontent,
And if she ioy, she did not causelesse ioy.

*Sal.* You durst not thus haue giuen your tongue the
If noble *Herod* still remaind in life:                    (raine,
Your daughters betters farre I dare maintaine,
Might haue reioyc'd to be my brothers wife.

*Mar.* My betters farre, bafe woman t'is vntrue,
You scarce haue euer my superiors seene:
For *Mariams* seruants were as good as you,
Before she came to be *Iudeas* Queene.

*Sal.* Now stirs the tongue that is so quickly mou'd,
But more then once your collor haue I borne:
Your fumish words are sooner sayd then prou'd,
And *Salomes* reply is onely scorne.

*Mar.* Scorne those that are for thy companions
Though I thy brothers face had neuer seene,          (held,
My birth, thy baser birth so farre exceld,
I had to both of you the Princesse bene.
Thou party Iew, and party Edomite,
Thou Mongrell: issu'd from reiected race,
Thy Ancestors against the Heauens did fight,
And thou like them wilt heauenly birth disgrace.

*Sal.* Still twit you me with nothing but my birth,
What ods betwixt your ancestors and mine?
Both borne of *Adam,* both were made of Earth,
And both did come from holy *Abrahams* line.

*Mar.* I fauour thee when nothing else I say,
With thy blacke acts ile not pollute my breath:
Else to thy charge I might full iustly lay
A shamefull life, besides a husbands death.

*Sal.* Tis true indeed, I did the plots reueale,
That past betwixt your fauorites and you:
I ment not I, a traytor to conceale.
Thus *Salome* your Mynion *Ioseph* slue.

*Mar.* Heauen, dost thou meane this Infamy to smo-
Let flandred *Mariam* ope thy closed eare:          (ther?
Selfe-guilt hath euer bene suspitious mother,
And therefore I this speech with patience beare.
No, had not *Salomes* vnstedfast heart,
In *Iofepbus* stead her *Constabarus* plast,
To free her selfe, she had not vsde the art,
To slander haplesse *Mariam* for vnchast..

*Alex.* Come *Mariam,* let vs goe: it is no boote

To let the head contend against the foote.


## ACTUS PRIMUS. SCŒNA QUARTA.

*Salome, Sola.*

Liues *Salome,* to get to base a stile
As foote, to the proud *Mariam Herods* spirit:
In happy time for her endured exile,
For did he liue she should not misse her merit:
But he is dead: and though he were my Brother,
His death such store of Cinders cannot cast
My Coales of loue to quench: for though they smo-
The flames a while, yet will they out at last.          (ther
Oh blest *Arabia,* in best climate plast,
I by the Fruit will censure of the Tree:
Tis not in vaine, thy happy name thou hast,
If all *Arabians* like *Silleus* bee:
Had not my Fate bene too too contrary,
When I on *Constabarus* first did gaze,
*Silleus* had beene obiect to mine eye:
Whose lookes and personage must allyes amaze.
But now ill Fated *Salome,* thy tongue
To *Constabarus* by it selfe is tide:
And now except I doe the Ebrew wrong
I cannot be the faire *Arabian* Bride:
What childish *lets* are these? Why stand I now
On honourable points? Tis long agoe
Since shame was written on my tainted brow:
And certaine tis, that shame is honours foe.
Had I vpon my reputation stood,
Had I affected an vnspotted life,
*Iosephus* vaines had still bene stuft with blood,
And I to him had liu'd a sober wife.
Then had I neuer cast an eye of loue,
On *Constabarus* now detested face,
Then had I kept my thoughts without remoue:
And blusht at motion of the least disgrace:
But shame is gone, and honour wipt away,
And Impudencie on my forehead sits:

She bids me worke my will without delay,
And for my will I will imploy my wits.
He loues, I loue; what then can be the cause,
Keepes me for being the *Arabians* wife?
It is the principles of *Moses* lawes,
For *Constabarus* still remaines in life,
If he to me did beare as Earnest hate,
As I to him, for him there were an ease,
A separating bill might free his fate:
From such a yoke that did so much displease.
Why should such priuiledge to man be giuen?
Or giuen to them, why bard from women then?
Are men then we in greater grace with Heauen?
Or cannot women hate as well as men?
Ile be the custome-breaker: and beginne
To shew my Sexe the way to freedomes doore,
And with an offring will I purge my sinne,
The lawe was made for none but who are poore.
If *Herod* had liu'd, I might to him accuse
My present Lord. But for the futures sake
Then would I tell the King he did refuse
The sonnes of *Baba* in his power to take.
But now I must diuorse him from my bed,
That my *Silleus* may possesse his roome:
Had I not begd his life he had bene dead,
I curse my tongue the hindrer of his doome,
But then my wandring heart to him was fast,
Nor did I dreame of chaunge: *Silleus* said,
He would be here, and see he comes at last,
Had I not nam'd him longer had he staid.


## ACTUS PRIMUS. SCŒNA QUINTA.

*Salome, Silleus.*

*Silleus.* Well found faire *Salome Iudæas* pride,
Hath thy innated wisedome found
To make *Silleus* deeme him deified,                    (the way
By gaining thee a more then precious pray?
     *Salo.* I haue deuisde the best I can deuise,

A more imperfect meanes was neuer found:
But what cares *Salome,* it doth suffice
If our indeuours with their end be crown'd.
In this our land we haue an ancient vse,
Permitted first by our law-giuers head:
Who hates his wife, though for no iust abuse,
May with a bill diuorce her from his bed.
But in this custome women are not free,
Yet I for once will wrest it, blame not thou
The ill I doe, since what I do'es for thee,
Though others blame, *Silleus* should allow.

   *Solleus.* Thinkes *Salome, Silleus* hath a tongue
To censure her faire actions: let my blood
Bedash my proper brow, for such a wrong,
The being yours, can make euen vices good:
*Arabia* ioy, prepare thy earth with greene,
Thou neuer happie wert indeed till now:
Now shall thy ground be trod by beauties Queene,
Her foote is destin'd to depresse thy brow.
Thou shalt faire *Salome* commaund as much
As if the royall ornament were thine:
The weaknes of *Arabias* King is such,
The kingdome is not his so much as mine.
My mouth is our *Obodas* oracle,
Who thinkes not ought but what *Silleus* will?
And thou rare creature. *Asias* miracle,
Shalt be to me as It: *Obodas* still.

   *Salome.* Tis not for glory I thy loue accept,
*Iudea* yeelds me honours worthy store:
Had not affection in my bosome crept,
My natiue country should my life deplore.
Were not *Silleus* he with home I goe,
I would not change my *Palastine* for *Rome:*
Much lesse would I a glorious state to shew,
Goe far to purchase an *Arabian* toome.

   *Silleus.* Far be it from *Silleus* so to thinke,
I know it is thy gratitude requites
The loue that is in me, and shall not shrinke
Till death doe seuer me from earths delights.       (talke,

   *Salom.* But whist; me thinkes the wolfe is in our
Be gone *Silleus,* who doth here arriue?

Tis *Constabarus* that doth hither walke,
Ile find a quarrell, him from me to driue.

   *Sille.* Farewell, but were it not for thy commaund,
In his despight *Silleus* here would stand.

## ACTUS PRIMUS: SCŒNA SEXTA.

### *Salome: Constabarus.*

   *Const:* Oh *Salome,* how much you wrong your name,
Your race, your country, and your husband
A straungers priuate conference is shame,        (most?
I blush for you, that haue your blushing lost.
Oft haue I found, and found you to my griefe,
Consorted with this base *Arabian* heere;
Heauen knowes that you haue bin my comfort chiefe,
Then doe not now my greater plague appeare.
Now by the stately Carued edifice
That on Mount *Sion* makes so faire a show,
And by the Altar fit for sacrifice,
I loue thee more then thou thy selfe doest know.
Oft with a silent sorrow haue I heard
How ill *Iudeas* mouth doth censure thee:
And did I not thine honour much regard,
Thou shouldst not be exhorted thus for mee.
Didst thou but know the worth of honest fame,
How much a vertuous woman is esteem'd,
Thou wouldest like hell eschew deserued shame,
And seeke to be both chast and chastly deem'd.
Our wisest Prince did say, and true he said,
A vertuous woman crownes her husbands head.

   *Salome.* Did I for this, vpreare thy lowe estate?
Did I for this requitall begge thy life,
That thou hadst forfeited haples fate?
To be to such a thankles wretch the wife.
This hand of mine hath lifted vp thy head,
Which many a day agoe had falne full lowe,
Because the sonnes of *Baba* are not dead,
To me thou doest both life and fortune owe.

   *Const.* You haue my patience often exercisde,

Vse make my choller keepe within the bankes:
Yet boast no more, but be by me aduisde.
A benefit vpbraided, forfeits thankes:
I prethy *Salome* dismisse this mood,
Thou doest not know how ill it fits thy place:
My words were all intended for thy good,
To raise thine honour and to stop disgrace.

   *Sa.* To stop disgrace? take thou no care for mee,
Nay do thy worst, thy worst I fet not by:
No shame of mine is like to light on thee,
Thy loue and admonitions I defie.
Thou shalt no hower longer call me wife,
Thy Iealousie procures my hate so deepe:
That I from thee doe meane to free my life,
By a diuorcing bill before I sleepe.

   *Const.* Are Hebrew women now trãsform'd to men?
Why do you not as well our battels fight,
And weare our armour? suffer this, and then
Let all the world be topsie turued quite.
Let fishes graze, beastes, swine, and birds descend,
Let fire burne downewards whilst the earth aspires:
Let Winters heat and Summers cold offend,
Let Thiftels growe on Vines, and Grapes on Briers,
Set vs to Spinne or Sowe, or at the best
Make vs Wood-hewers, Waters-bearing wights:
For sacred seruice let vs take no rest,
Vse vs as *Ioshua* did the *Gibonites.*

   *Salom.* Hold on your talke, till it be time to end,
For me I am resolu'd it shall be so:
Though I be first that to this course do bend,
I shall not be the last full well I know.

   *Const.* Why then be witnesse Heau'n, the Iudge of
Be witnesse Spirits that eschew the darke:     (sinnes,
Be witnesse Angels, witnesse Cherubins,
Whose semblance sits vpon the holy Arke:
Be witnesse earth, be witnesse *Palestine,*
Be witnesse *Dauids* Citie, if my heart
Did euer merit such an act of thine:
Or if the fault be mine that makes vs part,
Since mildest *Moses* friend vnto the Lord,

Did worke his wonders in the land of *Ham*,
And slew the first-borne Babes without a sword,
In signe whereof we eate the holy Lambe:
Till now that foureteene hundred yeeres are past,
Since first the Law with vs hath beene in force:
You are the first, and will I hope, be last,
That euer sought her husband to diuorce.

   *Salom.* I meane not to be led by president,
My will shall be to me in stead of Law.

   *Const.* I feare me much you will too late repent,
That you haue euer liu'd so void of awe:
This is *Silleus* loue that makes you thus
Reuerse all order; you must next be his.
But if my thoughts aright the cause discusse,
In winning you, he gaines no lasting blisse,
I was *Silleus*, and not long agoe
*Iosephus* then was *Constabarus* now:
When you became my friend you prou'd his foe,
As now for him you breake to me your vowd.

   *Sal.* If once I lou'd you, greater is your debt:
For certaine tis that you deserued it not.
And vndeserued loue we soone forget,
And therefore that to me can be no blot
But now fare ill my once beloued Lord,
Yet neuer more belou'd then now abhord.

   *Const.* Yet *Constabarus* biddeth thee farewell.
Farewell light creature. Heauen forgiue thy sinne:
My prophecying spirit doth foretell
Thy wauering thoughts doe yet but new beginne.
Yet I haue better scap'd then *Ioseph* did,
But if our *Herods* death had bene delayd,
The valiant youths that I so long haue hid,
Had bene by her, and I for them betrayd.
Therefore in happy houre did *Cæsar* giue
The fatall blow to wanton *Anthony*:
For had he liued, our *Herod* then should liue,
But great *Anthonius* death made *Herod* dye.
Had he enioyed his breath, not I alone
Had beene in danger of a deadly fall:
But *Mariam* had the way of perill gone,

Though by the Tyrant most belou'd of all.
The sweet fac'd *Mariam* as free from guilt
As Heauen from spots, yet had her Lord come backe
Her purest blood had bene vniustly spilt.
And *Salome* it was would worke her wracke.
Though all *Iudea* yeeld her innocent,
She often hath bene neere to punishment.

*Chorus.*

Those mindes that wholy dote vpon delight,
Except they onely ioy in inward good:
Still hope at last to hop vpon the right,
And so from Sand they leape in loathsome mud.
Fond wretches, seeking what they cannot finde,
For no content attends a wauering minde.
If wealth they doe desire, and wealth attaine,
Then wondrous faine would they to honor lep:
Of meane degree they doe in honor gaine,
They would but wish a little higher step.
    Thus step to step, and wealth to wealth they ad,
    Yet cannot all their plenty make them glad.

Yet oft we see that some in humble state,
Are chreefull, pleasant, happy, and content:
When those indeed that are of higher state,
With vaine additions do their thoughts torment,
    Th'one would to his minde his fortune binde,
    T'hother to his fortune frames his minde.

To wish varietie is signe of griefe,
For if you like your state as now it is,
Why should an alteration bring reliefe?
Nay change would then be fear'd as losse of blis.
    That man is onely happy in his Fate,
    That is delighted in a setled state.

Still *Mariam* wisht she from her Lord were free,
For expectation of varietie:
Yet now she sees her wishes prosperous bee,
She grieues, because her Lord so soone did die.

Who can those vast imaginations feede,
Where in a propertie, contempt doth breede?

Were *Herod* now perchance to liue againe,
She would againe as much be grieued at that;
All that she may, she euer doth disdaine,
Her wishes guide her to she knowes not what.
    And sad must be their lookes, their honor sower,
    That care for nothing being in their power.

# ACTUS SECUNDUS.

## Scœna prima.

*Pheroras and Graphina.*

*Pher.* Tis true *Graphina,* now the time drawes nye
Wherin the holy Priest with hallowed right,
The happy long desired knot shall tie,
*Pheroras* and *Graphina* to vnite:
How oft haue I with lifted hands implor'd
This blessed houre, till now implord in vaine,
Which hath my wished libertie restor'd,
And made my subiect selfe my owne againe.
Thy loue faire Mayd vpon mine eye doth sit,
Whose nature hot doth dry the moysture all,
Which were in nature, and in reason fit
For my monachall Brothers death to fall:
Had *Herod* liu'd, he would haue pluckt my hand
From faire *Graphinas* Palme perforce: and tide
The same in hatefull and despised band,
For I had had a Baby to my Bride:
Scarce can her Infant tongue with easie voice
Her name distinguish to anothers eare:
Yet had he liu'd, his power, and not my choise
Had made me solembly the contract sweare.
Haue I not cause in such a change to ioy?
What? though she be my Neece, a Princesse borne:
Neere bloods without respect: high birth a toy.
Since Loue can teach blood and kindreds scorne.
What booted it that he did raise my head,

To be his Realmes Copartner, Kingdomes mate,
Withall, he kept *Graphina* from my bed,
More wisht by me then thrice *Iudeas* state.
Oh, could not he be skilfull Iudge in loue,
That doted so vpon his *Mariams* face?
He, for his passion, *Doris* did remoue.
I needed not a lawfull Wife displace,
It could not be but he had power to iudge,
But he that neuer grudg'd a Kingdomes share,
This well knowne happinesse to me did grudge:
And ment to be therein without compare.
Else had I bene his equall in loues hoast,
For though the Diadem on *Mariams* head
Corrupt the vulgar iudgements, I will boast
*Graphinas* brow's as white, her cheekes as red.
Why speaks thou not faire creature? moue thy tongue,
For Silence is a signe of discontent:
It were to both our loues too great a wrong
If now this hower do find thee sadly bent.
    *Graph.* Mistake me not my Lord, too oft haue I
Desir'd this time to come with winged feete,
To be inwrapt with griefe when tis too nie,
You know my wishes euer yours did meete:
If I be filent, tis no more but feare
That I should say too little when I speake:
But since you will my imperfections beare,
In spight of doubt I will my silence breake:
Yet might amazement tie my mouing tongue,
But that I know before *Pheroras* minde,
I haue admired your affection long:
And cannot yet therein a reason finde.
Your hand hath lifted me from lowest state,
To highest eminencie wondrous grace,
And me your hand-maid haue you made your mate,
Though all but you alone doe count me base.
You haue preserued me pure at my request,
Though you so weake a vassaile might constraine
To yeeld to your high will, then last not best
In my respect a Princesse you disdaine,
Then need not all these fauours studie craue,

To be requited by a simple maide:
And studie still you know must silence haue,
Then be my cause for silence iustly waide,
But studie cannot boote nor I requite,
Except your lowly hand-maides steadfast loue
And fast obedience may your mind delight,
I will not promise more then I can proue.

   *Phero.* That studie needs not let *Graphina* smile,
And I desire no greater recompence:
I cannot vaunt me in a glorious stile,
Nor shew my loue in far-fetcht eloquence:
But this beleeue me, neuer *Herods* heart
Hath held his Prince-borne beautie famed wife
In neerer place then thou faire virgin art,
To him that holds the glory of his life.
Should *Herods* body leaue the Sepulcher,
And entertaine the seuer'd ghoft againe:
He should not be my nuptiall hinderer,
Except he hindred it with dying paine.
Come faire *Graphina,* let vs goe in slate,
This wish-indeered time to celebrate.


# ACTUS 2. SCÆNA. 2.

*Constabarus* and *Babus Sonnes.*

### *Babus.* 1. *Sonne.*

Now valiant friend you haue our liues redeem'd,
Which liues as sau'd by you, to you are due:
Command and you shall see your selfe esteem'd,
Our liues and liberties belong to you.
This twice sixe yeares with hazard of your life,
You haue conceal'd vs from the tyrants sword:
Though cruell *Herods* sister were your wife,
You durst in scorne of feare this grace afford.
In recompence we know not what to say,
A poore reward were thankes for fuch a merit,
Our truest friendship at your feete we lay,

The beſt requitall to a noble spirit.                    (youth,
     *Const.* Oh how you wrong our friendship valiant
With friends there is not such a word as det;
Where amitie is tide with bond of truth,
All benefits are there in common set.
Then is the golden age with them renew'd,
All names of properties are banisht quite:
Diuision, and distinction, are eschew'd:
Each hath to what belongs to others right.
And tis not sure so full a benefit,
Freely to giue, as freely to require:
A bountious act hath glory following it,
They cause the glory that the act desire.
All friendship should the patterne imitate,
Of *Iesses* Sonne and valiant *Ionathan*:
For neither Soueraignes nor fathers hate,
A friendship fixt on vertue seuer can.
Too much of this, tis written in the heart,
And need no amplifying with the tongue:
Now may you from your liuing tombe depart,
Where *Herods* life hath kept you ouer long.
Too great an iniury to a noble minde,
To be quicke buried, you had purchast fame,
Some yeares a goe, but that you were confinde.
While thousand meaner did aduance their name.
Your best of life the prime of all your yeares,
Your time of action is from you bereft.
Twelue winters haue you operpast in feares:
Yet if you vse it well, enough is left.
And who can doubt but you will vse it well?
The sonnes of *Babus* haue it by descent:
In all their thoughts each action to excell,
Boldly to act, and wisely to inuent.

### Babus 2. Sonne.

Had it not like the hatefull cuckoe beene,
Whose riper age his infant nurse doth kill:
So long we had not kept our selues vnseene,
But *Constabarus* safely crost our will:
For had the Tyrant fixt his cruell eye,

On our concealed feces wrath had swaide
His Iustice so, that he had forst vs die.
And dearer price then life we should haue paid,
For you our truest friend had falne with vs:
And we much like a house on pillers set,
Had cleane deprest our prop, and therefore thus
Our readie will with our concealement met.
But now that you faire Lord are daungerlesse,
The Sonnes of *Baba* shall their rigor show:
And proue it was not basenes did oppresse
Our hearts so long, but honour kept them low.

    *Ba.* 1. *Sonne.* Yet do I feare this tale of *Herods* death,
At last will proue a very tale indeed;
It giues me strongly in my minde, his breath
Will be preseru'd to make a number bleed:
I wish not therefore to be set at large,
Yet perill to my selfe I do not leare:
Let vs for fome daies longer be your charge,
Till we of *Herods* state the truth do heare.

    *Const.* What art thou turn'd a coward noble youth,
That thou beginst to doubt, vndoubted truth?

    *Babus.* I. *Son.* Were it my brothers tongue that cast
I frõ his hart would haue the question out:    (this doubt,
With this keene fauchion, but tis you my Lord
Against whose head I must not lift a sword:
I am so tide in gratitude *Const.* belieue
You haue no cause to take it ill,
If any word of mine your heart did grieue
The word discented from the speakers will,
I know it was not feare the doubt begun,
But rather valour and your care of me,
A coward could not be your fathers sonne,
Yet know I doubts vnnecessarie be:
For who can thinke that in *Anthonius* fall,
*Herod* his bosome friend should scape vnbrusde:
Then *Cæsar* we might thee an idiot call,
If thou by him should'st be so farre abusde.

    *Babus.* 2. *Sonne.* Lord *Constab:* let me tell you this,
Vpon submission *Cæfar* will forgiue:
And therefore though the tyrant did amisse,

It may fall out that he will let him liue.
Not many yeares agone it is since I
Directed thither by my fathers care,
In famous *Rome* for twice twelue monthes did liue,
My life from *Hebrewes* crueltie to spare,
There though I were but yet of boyish age,
I bent mine eye to marke, mine eares to heare.
Where I did see *Octauious* then a page,
When first he did to *Iulions* sight appeare:
Me thought I saw such mildnes in his face,
And such a sweetnes in his lookes did grow,
Withall, commixt with so maiesticke grace,
His Phisnomy his Fortune did foreshow:
For this I am indebted to mine eye,
But then mine eare receiu'd more euidence,
By that I knew his loue to clemency,
How he with hottest choller could dispence.

    *Const.* But we haue more then barely heard the news,
It hath bin twice confirm'd. And though some tongue
Might be so false, with false report t'abuse,
A false report hath neuer lasted long.
But be it so that *Herod* haue his life,
Concealement would not then a whit auaile:
For certaine t'is, that she that was my wife,
Would not to set her accusation faile.
And therefore now as good the venture giue,
And free our selues from blot of cowardise:
As show a pittifull desire to liue,
For, who can pittie but they must despise?

*Babus first sonne.*

I yeeld, but to necessitie I yeeld,
I dare vpon this doubt ingage mine arme:
That *Herod* shall againe this kingdome weeld,
And proue his death to be a false alarme.

*Babus second sonne.*

I doubt it too: God grant it be an error,
Tis best without a cause to be in terror:
And rather had I, though my soule be mine,

My soule should lie, then proue a true diuine,
   *Const.* Come, come, let feare goe seeke a dastards
Vndanted courage lies in a noble brest.          (nest,

## ACTUS 2. SCŒNA 3.

*Doris and Antipater*

   *Dor.* Your royall buildings bow your loftie side,
And scope to her that is by right your Queen:
Let your humilitie vpbraid the pride
Of those in whom no due respect is seene:
Nine times haue we with Trumpets haughtie sound,
And banishing sow's Leauen from our taste:
Obseru'd the feast that takes the fruit from ground.
Since I faire Citie did behold thee last,
So long it is since *Mariams* purer cheeke
Did rob from mine the glory. And so long
Since I returnd my natiue Towne to seeke:
And with me nothing but the sence of wrong.
And thee my Boy, whose birth though great it were,
Yet haue thy after fortunes prou'd but poore:
When thou wert borne how little did I feare
Thou shouldst be thrust from forth thy Fathers doore.
Art thou not *Herods* right begotten Sonne?
VVas not the haples *Doris, Herods* wife?
Yes: ere he had the Hebrew kingdome wonne,
I was companion to his priuate life.
VVas I not faire enough to be a Queene?
Why ere thou wert to me false Monarch tide,
My lake of beauty might as well be seene,
As after I had liu'd fiue yeeres thy Bride.
Yet then thine oath came powring like the raine,
Which all affirm'd my face without compare:
And that if thou might'st *Doris* loue obtaine,
For all the world besides thou didst not care.
Then was I yong, and rich, and nobly borne,
And therefore worthy to be *Herods* mate:
Yet thou vngratefull cast me off with scorne,

When Heauens purpose raisd your meaner fate.
Oft haue I begd for vengeance for this fact,
And with deiected knees, aspiring hands
Haue prayd the highest power to inact
The fall of her that on my Trophee stands,
Reuenge I haue according to my will,
Yet where I wisht this vengeance did not light:
I wisht it should high-hearted *Mariam* kill.
But it against my whilome Lord did fight
With thee sweet Boy I came, and came to try
If thou before his bastards might be plac'd
In *Herods* royall seat and dignitie.
But *Mariams* infants here are onely grac'd,
And now for vs there doth no hope remaine:
Yet we will not returne till *Herods* end
Be more confirmd, perchance he is not slaine.
So glorious Fortunes may my Boy attend,
For if he liue, hee'll thinke it doth suffice,
That he to *Doris* shows such crueltie:
For as he did my wretched life dispise,
So doe I know I shall despised die.
Let him but proue as naturall to thee,
As cruell to thy miserable mother:
His crueltie shall not vpbraided bee
But in thy fortunes. I his faults will smother.

   *Antipat.* Each mouth within the Citie loudly cries
That *Herods* death is certaine; therefore wee
Had best some subtill hidden plot deuise,
That *Mariams* children might subuerted bee,
By poisons drinke, or else by murtherous Knife,
So we may be aduanc'd, it skils not how:
They are but Bastards, you were *Herods* wife,
And foule adultery blotteth *Mariams* brow.

   *Doris.* They are too strong to be by vs remou'd,
Or elfe reuenges foulest spotted face:
By our detested wrongs might be approu'd,
But weakenesse must to greater power giue place.
But let vs now retire to grieue alone,
For solitarines best fitteth mone.

## Actus secundus. Scœna 4.

*Silleus and Constabarus.*

*Silleus.* Well met *Iudean* Lord, the onely wight
*Silleus* wisht to see. I am to call
Thy tongue to strict account. *Const.* For what despight
I ready am to heare, and answere all.
But if directly at the cause I gesse
That breeds this challenge, you must pardon me:
And now some other ground of fight professe,
For I haue vow'd, vowes must vnbroken be.
   *Sill.* What may be your expectation? let me know.
   *Const.* Why? ought concerning *Salom,* my sword
Shall not be welded for a cause so low,
A blow for her my arme will scorne t'afford.
   *Sill.* It is for slandering her vnspotted name,
And I will make thee in thy vowes despight,
Sucke vp the breath that did my Mistris blame,
And swallow it againe to doe her right.
   *Const.* I prethee giue some other quarrell ground
To finde beginning, raile against my name:
Or strike me first, or let some scarlet wound
Inflame my courage, giue me words of shame,
Doe thou our *Moses* sacred Lawes disgrace,
Depraue our nation, doe me some despight:
I'm apt enough to fight in any case,
But yet for *Salome* I will not fight.
   *Sill.* Nor I for ought but *Salome:* My sword
That owes his seruice to her sacred name:
Will not an edge for other cause afford,
In other fight I am not sure of fame.
   *Const.* For her, I pitty thee enough already,
For her, I therefore will not mangle thee:
A woman with a heart so most vnsteady,
Will of her selfe sufficient torture bee.
I cannot enuy for so light a gaine,
Her minde with such vnconstancie doth runne:
As with a word thou didst her loue obtaine,
So with a word she will from thee be wonne.
So light as her possessions for most day
Is her affections lost, to me tis knowne:

As good goe hold the winde as make her stay,
Shee neuer loues, but till she call her owne.
She meerly is a painted sepulcher,
That is both faire, and vilely foule at once:
Though on her out-side graces garnish her,
Her mind is fild with worse then rotten bones.
And euer readie lifted is her hand,
To aime destruction at a husbands throat:
For proofes, *Iosephus* and my selfe do stand,
Though once on both of vs, she seem'd to doat.
Her mouth though serpent-like it neuer hisses,
Yet like a Serpent, poysons where it kisses,                    (bite.
  *Silleus.* Well *Hebrew* well, thou bark'st, but wilt not
  *Const.* I tell thee still for her I will not fight.          (heart
  *Sille:* Why then I call thee coward. *Conft:* From my
I giue thee thankes. A cowards hatefull name,
Cannot to valiant mindes a blot impart,
And therefore I with ioy receiue the same.
Thou know'st I am no coward: thou wert by
At the *Arabian* battaile th'other day:
And saw'st my sword with daring valiancy,
Amongst the faint *Arabians* cut my way.
The blood of foes no more could let it shine,
And twas inameled with some of thine.
But now haue at thee, not for *Salome*
I fight: but to discharge a cowards stile:
Here gins the fight that shall not parted be,
Before a soule or two indure exile.                    (my blood,
  *Silleus.* Thy sword hath made some windowes for
To shew a horred crimson phisnomie:
To breath for both of vs me thinkes twere good,
The day will giue vs time enough to die.                    (time,
  *Const:* With all my hart take breath, thou shalt haue
And if thou list a twelue month, let vs end:
Into thy cheekes there doth a palenes clime,
Thou canst not from my sword thy selfe defend.
What needest thou for *Salome* to fight,                    (her:
Thou hast her, and may'st keepe her, none striues for
I willingly to thee resigne my right,
For in my very soule I do abhorre her.
Thou feest that I am fresh, vnwounded yet,
Then not for feare I do this offer make:

Thou art with losse of blood, to fight vnfit,
For here is one, and there another take.

    *Silleus.* I will not leaue, as long as breath remaines
Within my wounded body: spare your words,
My heart in bloods stead, courage entertaines,
*Salomes* loue no place for feare affords.

    *Const:* Oh could thy soule but prophesie like mine,
I would not wonder thou should'st long to die:
For *Salome* if I aright diuine
Will be then death a greater miserie.         (will,

    *Sille:* Then list, Ile breath no longer, *Const:* Do thy
I hateles fight, and charitably kill. I, I, they fight,
Pittie thy selfe *Silleus,* let not death
Intru'd before his time into thy hart:
Alas it is too late to feare, his breath
Is from his body now about to part.
How far'st thou braue *Arabian? Silleus* very well,
My legge is hurt, I can no longer fight:
It onely grieues me, that so soone I fell,
Before faire *Saloms* wrongs I came to right.      (feare,

    *Const:* Thy wounds are lesse then mortall. Neuer
Thou shalt a safe and quicke recouerie finde:
Come, I will thee vnto my lodging beare,
I hate thy body, but I loue thy minde.

    *Silleus.* Thankes noble Iew, I see a courtious foe,
Sterne enmitie to friendship can no art:
Had not my heart and tongue engagde me so,
I would from thee no foe, but friend depart.
My heart to *Salome* is tide so fast,
To leaue her loue for friendship, yet my skill
Shall be imploy'd to make your fauour last,
And I will honour *Constabarus* still.

    *Const:* I ope my bosome to thee, and will take
Thee in, as friend, and grieue for thy complaint:
But if we doe not expedition make,
Thy losse of blood I feare will make thee faint.

*Chorus.*

To heare a tale with eares preiudicate,
It spoiles the iudgement, and corrupts the sence:
That humane error giuen to euery state,

Is greater enemie to innocence.
　　It makes vs foolish, heddy, rash, vniust,
　　It makes vs neuer try before we trust.

It will confound the meaning, change the words,
For it our sence of hearing much deceiues:
Besides no time to Iudgement it affords,
To way the circumstance our eare receiues.
　　The ground of accidents it neuer tries,
　　But makes vs take for truth ten thousand lies.

Our eares and hearts are apt to hold for good,
That we our selues doe most desire to bee:
And then we drowne obiections in the flood
Of partialitie, tis that we see
　　That makes false rumours long with credit past,
　　Though they like rumours must conclude at last.

The greatest part of vs preiudicate,
With wishing *Herods* death do hold it true:
The being once deluded doth not bate,
The credit to a better likelihood due.
　　Those few that wish it not the multitude,
　　Doe carrie headlong, so they doubts conclude.

They not obiect the weake vncertaine ground,
Whereon they built this tale of *Herods* end:
Whereof the Author scarcely can be found,
And all because their wishes that way bend.
　　They thinke not of the perill that ensu'th,
　　If this should proue the contrary to truth.

On this same doubt, on this so light a breath,
They pawne their liues, and fortunes. For they all
Behaue them as the newes of *Herods* death,
They did of most vndoubted credit call;
　　But if their actions now doe rightly hit,
　　Let them commend their fortune, not their wit.

# ACTUS TERTIUS

## Scœna prima.

*Pheroras: Salome.*

*Phero.* Vrge me no more *Graphina* to forsake,
Not twelue howers since I married her
And doe you thinke a sisters power cane mak      (for loue:
A resolute decree, so soone remoue?      (affects.
    *Salome.* Poore minds they are that honour not
    *Phero:* Who hunts for honour, happines neglects.
    *Salom.* You might haue bene both of felicitie,
And honour too in equall measure seasde.
    *Phero:* It is not you can tell so well as I,
What tis can make me happie, or displeasde.
    *Salome.* To match for neither beautie nor respects
One meane of birth, but yet of meaner minde,
A woman full of naturall defects,
I wonder what your eye in her could finde.      (wit,
    *Phero:* Mine eye found louelines, mine eare found
To please the one, and to enchant the other;
Grace on her eye, mirth on her tongue doth sit,
In lookes a child, in wisedomes house a mother,      (elfe,
    *Salom:* But say you thought her faire, as none thinks
Knowes not *Pheroras,* beautie is a blast:
Much like this flower which to day excels,
But longer then a day it will not last.      (show
    *Phero:* Her wit exceeds her beautie, *Salo:* Wit may
The way to ill, as well as good you know.
    *Phero:* But wisedome is the porter of her head,
And bares all wicked words from issuing thence.

*Sal.* But of a porter, better were you sped,
If she against their entrance made defence.
   *Phero.* But wherefore comes the sacred *Ananell*,
That hitherward his hastie steppes doth bend?
Great sacrificer y'are arriued well,
Ill newes from holy mouth I not attend.


## ACTUS TERTIUS. SCŒNA 2.

*Pheroras. Salome. Ananell.*


*Ananell.*

My lippes, my sonne, with peacefull tidings blest,
Shall vtter Honey to your listning eare:
A word of death comes not from Priestly brest,
I speake of life: in life there is no feare.
And for the newes I did the Heauens salute,
And fill'd the Temple with my thankfull voice:
For though that mourning may not me pollute,
At pleasing accidents I may reioyce.
   *Pheror.* Is *Herod* then reuiu'd from certaine death?
   *Sall.* What? can your news restore my brothers breath?
   *Ana.* Both so, and so, the King is safe and sound,
And did such grace in royall *Cæsar* meet:
That he with larger stile then euer crownd,
Within this houre Ierusalem will greet.
I did but come to tell you, and must backe
To make preparatiues for sacrifice:
I knew his death, your hearts like mine did racke,
Though to conceale it, prou'd you wise.
   *Salom.* How can my ioy sufficiently appeare?
   *Phero.* A heauier tale did neuer pierce mine eare.
   *Salo.* Now *Salome* of happinesse may boast.
   *Pheror.* But now *Pheroras* is in danger most,
   *Salom.* I shall enioy the comfort of my life.
   *Pheror.* And I shall loose it, loosing of my wife.
   *Salom.* Ioy heart, for *Constan:* shall be slaine.
   *Phero.* Grieue soule, *Graphina* shall from me be tane.
   *Salom.* Smile cheekes, the faire *Silleus* shall be mine.

 *Phero*. Weepe eyes, for I must with a child combine.

 *Salom*. Well brother, cease your mones, on one con-
Ile vndertake to winne the Kings consent:   (dition
*Graphina* still shall be in your tuition,
And her with you be nere the lesse content.

 *Phero*. What's the condition? let me quickly know,
That I as quickly your command may act:
Were it to see what Hearbs in *Ophir* grow,
Or that the lofty *Tyrus* might be sackt.

 *Salom*. Tis no so hard a taske: It is no more,
But tell the King that *Consta:* hid
The sonnes of *Baba,* done to death before:
And tis no more then *Consta,* did.
And tell him more that he for *Herods* sake,
Not able to endure his brothers foe:
Did with a bill our separation make,
Though loth from *Consta:* else to goe.

 *Phero*. Beleeue this tale for told, Ile goe from hence,
In *Herods* eare the Hebrew to deface:
And I that neuer studied eloquence,
Doe meane with eloquence this tale to grace.   *Exit.*

 *Salom*. This will be *Constabarus* quicke dispatch,
Which from my mouth would lesser credit finde:
Yet shall he not decease without a match,
For *Mariam* shall not linger long behinde.
First Iealousie, if that auaile not, feare
Shalbe my minister to worke her end;
A common error moues not *Herods* eare,
Which doth so firmly to his *Mariam* bend.
She shall be charged with so horrid crime,
As *Herods* feare shall turne his loue to hate:
Ile make some sweare that she desires to clime,
And seekes to poyson him for his estate.
I scorne that she should liue my birth t'vpbraid,
To call me base and hungry Edomite:
With patient show her choller I betrayd,
And watcht the time to be reueng'd by slite.
Now tongue of mine with scandall load her name,
Turne hers to fountaines, *Herods* eyes to flame:
Yet first I will begin *Pheroras* suite,
That he my earnest businesse may effect:

And I of *Mariam* will keepe me mute,
Till first some other doth her name detect.
Who's there, *Silleus* man? How fares your Lord?
That your aspects doe beare the badge of sorrow?

### *Silleus man.*

He hath the marks of *Constabarus* sword,
And for a while desires your sight to borrow.
   *Salom.* My heauy curse the hatefull sword pursue,
My heauier curse on the more hatefull arme
That wounded my *Silleus*. But renew
Your tale againe. Hath he no mortall harme?

### *Silleus man.*

No signe of danger doth in him appeare,
Nor are his wounds in place of perill seene:
Hee bides you be assured you need not feare,
He hopes to make you yet *Arabias* Queene.
   *Salom.* Commend my heart to be *Silleus* charge,
Tell him, my brothers suddaine comming now;
Will giue my foote no roome to walke at large,
But I will see him yet ere night I vow.

## ACTUS 3. SCŒNA 3.

### *Mariam and Sohemus.*

### *Mariam.*

*Sohemus*, tell me what the newes may be
That makes your eyes so full, your cheeks so blew?
   *Sohem.* I know not how to call them. Ill for me
Tis sure they are: not so I hope for you.
   *Herod. Mari.* Oh, what *Herod*? *Sohem. Herod* liues.
How! liues? What in some Caue or forrest hid?
   *Sohem.* Nay, backe return'd with honor. *Cæsar giues*
Him greater grace then ere *Anthonius* did.
   *Mari.* Foretell the ruine of my family,
Tell me that I shall see our Citie burnd:
Tell me I shall a death disgracefull die,

But tell me not that *Herod is* returnd.

    *Sohem.* Be not impatient Madam, be but milde,
His loue to you againe will soone be bred:

    *Mar.* I will not to his loue be reconcilde,
With solemne vowes I haue forsworne his Bed.

    *Sohem.* But you must breake those vowes.

    *Mar.* Ile rather breake
The heart of *Mariam.* Cursed is my Fate:
But speake no more to me, in vaine ye speake
To liue with him I so profoundly hate.

    *Sohem.* Great Queene, you must to me your pardon
*Sohemus* cannot now your will obey:            (giue,
If your command should me to silence driue,
It were not to obey, but to betray.
Reiect, and slight my speeches, mocke my faith,
Scorne my obseruance, call my counsell nought;
Though you regard not what *Sohemus* saith,
Yet will I euer freely speake my thought.
I feare ere long I shall faire *Mariam* see
In wofull state, and by her selfe vndone:
Yet for your issues sake more temp'rate bee,
The heart by affabilitie is wonne.

    *Mari.* And must I to my Prison turne againe?
Oh, now I see I was an hypcorite:
I did this morning for his death complaine,
And yet doe mourne, because he liues ere night.
When I his death beleeu'd, compassion wrought,
And was the stickler twixt my heart and him:
But now that Curtaine's drawne from off my thought,
Hate doth appeare againe with visage grim:
And paints the face of *Herod in* my heart,
In horred colours with detested looke:
Then feare would come, but scorne doth play her part,
And saith that scorne with feare can neuer brooke.
I know I could inchaine him with a smile:
And lead him captiue with a gentle word,
I scorne my looke should euer man beguile,
Or other speech, then meaning to afford.
Else *Salome* in vaine might spend her winde,
In vaine might *Herods* mother whet her tongue:

In vaine had they complotted and combinde,
For I could ouerthrow them all ere long.
Oh what a shelter is mine innocence,
To shield me from the pangs of inward griefe:
Gainst all mishaps it is my faire defence,
And to my sorrowes yeelds a large reliefe.
To be commandresse of the triple earth,
And sit in safetie from a fell secure:
To haue all nations celebrate my birth,
I would not that my spirit were impure.
Let my distressed state vnpittied bee,
Mine innocence is hope enough for mee.                    *Exit*

   *Sobem:* Poore guiltles Queene. Oh that my wish
A little temper now about thy heart:                    (might place
Vnbridled speech is *Mariams* worst disgrace,
And will indanger her without desart.
I am in greater hazard. O're my head,
The fattall axe doth hang vnstedily:
My disobedience once discouered,
Will shake it downe: *Sohemus so* shall die.
For when the King shall find, we thought his death
Had bene as certaine as we see his life:
And markes withall I slighted so his breath,
As to preserue aliue his matchles wife.
Nay more, to giue to *Alexanders* hand
The regall dignitie. The soueraigne power,
How I had yeelded vp at her command,
The strength of all the citie, *Dauids* Tower.
What more then common death may I expect,
Since I too well do know his crueltie:
Twere death, a word of *Herods* to neglect,
What then to doe directly contrarie?
Yet life I quite thee with a willing spirit,
And thinke thou could'st not better be imploi'd:
I forfeit thee for her that more doth merit,
Ten such were better dead then she destroi'd.
But fare thee well chast Queene, well may I see
The darknes palpable, and riuers part:
The sunne stand still. Nay more retorted bee,
But neuer woman with so pure a heart.

Thine eyes graue maiestie keepes all in awe,
And cuts the winges of euery loose desire:
Thy brow is table to the modest lawe,
Yet though we dare not loue, we may admire.
And if I die, it shall my soule content,
My breath *in Mariams* seruice shall be spent.

### Chorus.

Tis not enough for one that is a wife
To keepe her spotles from an act of ill:
But from suspition she should free her life,
And bare her selfe of power as well as will.
Tis not so glorious for her to be free,
As by her proper selfe restrain'd to bee.

When she hath spatious ground to walke vpon,
Why on the ridge should she desire to goe?
It is no glory to forbeare alone,
Those things that may her honour ouerthrowe.
But tis thanke-worthy, if she will not take
All lawfull liberties for honours sake.

That wife her hand against her fame doth reare,
That more then to her Lord alone will giue
A priuate word to any second eare,
And though she may with reputation liue.
Yet though most chast, she doth her glory blot,
And wounds her honour, though she killes it not.

When to their Husbands they themselues doe bind,
Doe they not wholy giue themselues away?
Or giue they but their body not their mind,
Reseruing that though best, for others pray?
No sure, their thoughts no more can be their owne,
And therefore should to none but one be knowne.

Then she vsurpes vpon anothers right,
That seekes to be by publike language grac't:
And though her thoughts reflect with purest light,
Her mind if not peculiar is not chast.

    For in a wife it is no worse to finde,
    A common body, then a common minde.

And euery mind though free from thought of ill,
That out of glory seekes a worth to show:
When any's eares but one therewith they fill,
Doth in a sort her purenes ouerthrow.
    Now *Mariam* had, (but that to this she bent)
    Beene free from feare, as well as innocent.

# ACTUS QUARTUS:

## SCŒNA PRIMA.

*Enter Herod and his attendants.*

*Herod.*

Haile happie citie, happie in thy store,
And happy that thy buildings such we see;
   More happie in the Temple where w'adore,
But most of all that *Mariam* liues in thee.
Art thou return'd? how fares my *Mariam? Enter Nutio.*
   *Nutio.* She's well my Lord, and will anon be here
As you commanded. *Her:* Muffle vp thy browe
Thou daies darke taper. *Mariam* will appeare.
And where she shines, we need not thy dimme light,
Oh hast thy steps rare creature, speed thy pace:
And let thy presence make the day more bright,
And cheere the heart of *Herod with* thy face.
It is an age since I from *Mariam* went,
Me thinkes our parting was in *Dauids* daies;
The houres are so increast by discontent,
Deepe sorrow, *Iosua* like the season staies:
But when I am with *Mariam,* time runnes on,
Her sight, can make months, minutes, daies of weekes:
An hower is then no sooner come then gon.
When in her face mine eye for wonders seekes.
You world commanding citie, *Europes* grace,
Twice hath my curious eye your streets suruai'd,
And I haue seene the statue filled place,
That once if not for griefe had bene betrai'd.

240

I all your *Roman* beauties haue beheld,
And seene the showes your *Ediles* did prepare,
I saw the sum of what in you exceld,
Yet saw no miracle like *Mariam* rare.
The faire and famous *Liuia, Cæsars* loue,
The worlds commaunding Mistresse did I see:
Whose beauties both the world and *Rome* approue,
Yet *Mariam: Liuia* is not like to thee.
Be patient but a little, while mine eyes
Within your compass limits be contain'd:
That obiect straight shall your desires suffice,
From which you were so long a while restrain'd.
How wisely *Mariam* doth the time delay,
Least suddaine ioy my sence should suffocate:
I am prepar'd, thou needst no longer stay:
Whose there, my *Mariam*, more then happie fate?
Oh no, it is *Pheroras,* welcome Brother,
Now for a while, I must my passion smother.

## ACTUS QUARTUS. SCŒNA FECUNDA.

*Herod. Pheroras.*

*Pheroras.*

All health and safetie waite vpon my Lord,
And may you long in prosperous fortunes liue
With *Rome* commanding *Cæsar;* at accord,
And haue all honors that the world can giue.
   *Herod.* Oh brother, now thou speakst not from thy
No, thou hast strooke a blow at *Herods* loue:    (hart,
That cannot quickly from my memory part,
Though *Salome* did me to pardon moue.
Valiant *Phasaelus,* now to thee farewell,
Thou wert my kinde and honorable brother:
Oh haples houre, when you selfe striken fell,
Thou fathers Image, glory of thy mother.
Had I defir'd a greater sute of thee,
Then to withhold thee from a harlots bed,
Thou wouldst haue granted it: but now I see

All are not like that in a wombe are bred.
Thou wouldst not, hadst thou heard of *Herods* death,
Haue made his buriall time, thy bridall houre:
Thou wouldst with clamours, not with ioyfull breath,
Haue show'd the newes to be not sweet but soure.

　　*Phero.* *Phasaelus* great worth I know did staine
*Pheroras* petty valour: but they lie
(Excepting you your selfe) that dare maintaine,
That he did honor *Herod* more then I.
For what I showd, loues power constraind me show,
And pardon louing faults for *Mariams* sake.

　　*Herod. Mariam,* where is she? *Phero.* Nay, I do not
But absent vse of her faire name I make:　　　　　　(know,
You haue forgiuen greater faults then this,
For *Constabarus* that against you will
Preseru'd the sonnes of *Baba,* liues in blisse,
Though you commanded him the youths to kill.

　　*Herod.* Goe, take a present order for his death,
And let those traytors feele the worst of feares:
Now *Salome* will whine to begge his breath,
But Ile be deafe to prayers: and blind to teares.

　　*Phero.* He is my Lord from *Salom* diuorst,
Though her affection did to leaue him grieue:
Yet was she by her loue to you inforst,
To leaue the man that would your foes relieue.

　　*Herod.* Then haste them to their death. I will requite
Thee gentle *Mariam. Salom.* I meane
The thought of *Mariam* doth so steale my spirit,
My mouth from speech of her I cannot weane.　　　　*Exit.*

## ACTUS 4. SCŒNA 3.

### *Herod. Mariam.*

### *Herod.*

And heere she comes indeed: happily met
　　My best, and deerest halfe: what ailes my deare?
　　Thou doest the difference certainly forget
Twixt Duskey habits, and a time so cleare.

　　*Mar.* My Lord, I suit my garment to my minde,

And there no cheerfull colours can I finde.

   *Herod.* Is this my welcome? haue I longd so much
To see my dearest *Mariam* discontent?
What ist that is the cause thy heart to touch?
Oh speake, that I thy sorrow may preuent.
Art thou not *Iuries* Queene, and *Herods* too?
Be my Commandres, be my Soueraigne guide:
To be by thee directed I will woo,
For in thy pleasure lies my highest pride.
Or if thou thinke *Iudæas* narrow bound,
Too strict a limit for thy great command:
Thou shalt be Empresse of *Arabia* crownd,
For thou shalt rule, and I will winne the Land.
Ile robbe the holy *Dauids* Sepulcher
To giue thee wealth, if thou for wealth do care:
Thou shalt haue all, they did with him inter,
And I for thee will make the Temple bare.

   *Mar.* I neither haue of power nor riches want,
I haue enough, nor doe I wish for more:
Your offers to my heart no ease can grant,
Except they could my brothers life restore.
No, had you wifht the wretched *Mariam* glad,
Or had your loue to her bene truly tide:
Nay, had you not defir'd to make her fad,
My brother nor my Grandfyre had not dide.

   *Her.* Wilt thou beleeue no oathes to cleere thy Lord?
How oft haue I with execration sworne:
Thou art by me belou'd, by me ador'd,
Yet are my protestations heard with scorne.
*Hercanus* plotted to depriue my head
Of this long setled honor that I weare:
And therefore I did iustly doome him dead,
To rid the Realme from perill, me from feare.
Yet I for *Mariams* sake doe so repent
The death of one: whose blood she did inherit:
I wish I had a Kingdomes treasure spent,
So I had nere expeld *Hercanus* spirit.
As I affected that same noble youth,
In lasting infamie my name inrole:
If I not mournd his death with heartie truth.
Did I not shew to him my earnest loue,
When I to him the Priesthood did restore?

And did for him a liuing Priest remoue,
Which neuer had bene done but once before.

    *Mariam*. I know that mou'd by importunitie,
You made him Priest, and shortly after die.

    *Herod*. I will not speake, vnles to be beleeu'd,
This froward humor will not doe you good:
It hath too much already *Herod* grieu'd,
To thinke that you on termes of hate haue stood.
Yet smile my dearest *Mariam,* doe but smile,
And I will all vnkind conceits exile.

    *Mari*. I cannot frame disguise, nor neuer taught
My face a looke dissenting from my thought.

    *Herod*. By heau'n you vexe me, build not on my loue.

    *Mari*. I wil not build on so vnstable ground.

    *Herod*. Nought is so fixt, but peeuishnes may moue.

    *Mar*. Tis better sleightest cause then none were foūd.

    *Herod*. Be iudge your selfe, if euer *Herod* sought
Or would be mou'd a cause of change to finde:
Yet let your looke declare a milder thought,
My heart againe you shall to *Mariam* binde.
How oft did I for you my Mother chide,
Reuile my Sister, and my brother rate:
And tell them all my *Mariam* they belide,
Distrust me still, if these be signes of hate.

## Actus 4. Sccena 4.

*Herod.*

VVhat hast thou here? *Bu.* A drinke procuring
The Queene defir'd me to deliuer it.                    (loue,

    *Mar*. Did I; some hatefull practise this will proue,
Yet can it be no worse then Heauens permit.

    *Herod*. Confesse the truth thou wicked instrument,
To her outragious will, tis passion sure:
Tell true, and thou shalt scape the punishment,
Which if thou doe conceale thou shalt endure.

    *Bu*. I know not, but I doubt it be no lesse,
Long since the hate of you her heart did cease.

    *Herod*. Know'st thou the cause thereof? *Bu.* My Lord
*Sohemus* told the tale that did displease.              (I geffe,

*Herod.* Oh Heauen! *Sohemus* false! Goe let him die,
Stay not to suffer him to speake a word:
Oh damned villaine, did he falsifie
The oath he swore eu'n of his owne accord?
Now doe I know thy falshood, painted Diuill
Thou white Inchantres. Oh thou art so foule,
That Ysop cannot clense thee worst of euill.
A beautious body hides a loathsome soule,
Your loue *Sobemus* mou'd by his affection,
Though he haue euer heretofore bene true:
Did blab forfooth, that I did giue direction,
If we were put to death to slaughter you.
And you in blacke reuenge attended now
To adde a murther to your breach of vow.
    *Mar.* Is this a dream? *Her.* Oh Heauen, that t'were no
Ile giue my Realme to who can proue it so:            (more,
I would I were like any begger poore,
So I for false my *Mariam* did not know.
Foule pith contain'd in the fairest rinde,
That euer grac'd a Cædar. Oh thine eye
Is pure as heauen, but impure thy minde,
And for impuritie shall *Mariam* die.
Why didst thou loue *Sohemus? Mar:* they can tell
That say I lou'd him, *Mariam* saies not so.
    *Herod.* Oh cannot impudence the coales expell,
That for thy loue in *Herods* bosome glowe:
It is as plaine as water, and deniall
Makes of thy falsehood but a greater triall.
Haft thou beheld thy selfe, and couldst thou staine
So rare perfection: euen for loue of thee
I doe profoundly hate thee. Wert thou plaine,
Thou shoul'dst the wonder of *Iudea* bee.
But oh thou art not. Hell it selfe lies hid
Beneath thy heauenly show. Yet neuer wert thou chast:
Thou might'st exalt, pull downe, command, forbid,
And be aboue the wheele of fortune plast.
Hadst thou complotted *Herods* massacre,
That so thy sonne a Monarch might be stilde,
Not halfe so grieuous such an action were,
As once to thinke, that *Mariam* is defilde.
Bright workmanship of nature sulli'd ore,
With pitched darknes now thine end shall bee:

Thou shalt not liue faire fiend to cozen more,
With heauy semblance, as thou cousnedst mee.
Yet must I loue thee in despight of death,
And thou shalt die in the dispight of loue:
For neither shall my loue prolong thy breath,
Nor shall thy losse of breath my loue remoue.
I might haue seene thy falsehood in thy face,
Where coul'dst thou get thy stares that seru'd for eyes?
Except by theft, and theft is foule disgrace:
This had appear'd before were *Herod* wise,
But I'me a sot, a very sot, no better:
My wisedome long agoe a wandring fell,
Thy face incountring it, my wit did fetter,
And made me for delight my freedome sell.
Giue me my heart false creature, tis a wrong,
My guliltles heart should now with thine be slaine:
Thou hadst no right to looke it vp so long,
And with vsurpers name I *Mariam* staine.

*Enter Bu:*

He: Haue you design'd *Sobemus* to his end?          (guard
Bu: I haue my Lord. *Herod:* Then call our royall
To doe as much for *Mariam,* they offend
Leaue ill vnblam'd, or good without reward.
Here take her to her death. Come backe, come backe,
What ment I to depriue the world of light:
To muffle *Iury* in the foulest blacke,
That euer was an opposite to white.
Why whither would you carrie her: *Sould:* you bad
We should conduct her to her death my Lord.
Hero: Wie sure I did not, *Herod* was not mad,
Why should she feele the furie of the sword?
Oh now the griefe returnes into my heart,
And pulles me peecemeale: loue and hate doe fight:
And now hath boue acquir'd the greater part,
Yet now hath hate, affection conquer'd quite.
And therefore beare her hence: and *Hebrew* why
Seaze you with Lyons pawes the fairest lam
Of all the flocke? she must not, shall not, die,
Without her I most miserable am.
And with her more then most, away, away,
But beare her but to prison not to death:

And is she gon indeed, stay villaines stay,
Her lookes alone preseru'd your Soueraignes breath.
Well let her goe, but yet she shall not die,
I cannot thinke she ment to poison me:
But certaine tis she liu'd too wantonly,
And therefore shall she neuer more be free.

## ACTUS 4. SCŒNA 5.

*Bu.* Foule villaine, can thy pitchie coloured soule
    Permit thine eare to heare her caules doome?
And not inforce thy tongue that tale controule,
That must vniustly bring her to her toome.
Oh *Salome* thou hast thy selfe repaid,
For all the benefits that thou hast done:
Thou art the cause I haue the queene betraid,
Thou hast my hart to darkest false-hood wonne,
I am condemn'd, heau'n gaue me not my tongue
To slander innocents, to lie, deceiue:
To be the hatefull instrument to wrong,
The earth of greatest glory to bereaue.
My sinne ascends and doth to heau'n crie,
It is the blackest deed that euer was:
And there doth sit an Angell notarie,
That doth record it downe in leaues of brasse.
Oh how my heart doth quake: *Achitophel*,
Thou founds a meanes thy selfe from shame to free:
And sure my soule approues thou didst not well,
All follow some, and I will follow thee.

## ACTUS 4. SCŒNA 6.

*Constabarus, Babus Sonnes, and their guard.*

*Const:* Now here we step our last, the way to death,
    We must not tread this way a second time:
    Yet let vs resolutely yeeld our breath,
Death is the onely ladder, Heau'n to clime.            (resigne,
    *Babus* 1. *Sonne.* With willing mind I could my selfe
But yet it grieues me with a griefe vntold:

Our death should be accompani'd with thine,
Our frendship we to thee haue dearely sold.

   *Const.* Still wilt thou wrong the sacred name of friend?
Then should'st thou neuer stile it friendship more:
But base mechanicke traffique that doth lend,
Yet will be sure they shall the debt restore.
I could with needlesse complement returne,
Tis for thy ceremonie I could say;
Tis I that made the fire your house to burne,
For but for me she would not you betray.
Had not the damned woman sought mine end,
You had not bene the subiect other hate:
You neuer did her hatefull minde offend,
Nor could your deaths haue freed your nuptiall fate.
Therefore faire friends, though you were still vnborne,
Some other subtiltie deuisde should bee:
Were by my life, though guiltles should be torne,
Thus haue I prou'd, tis you that die for mee.
And therefore should I weakely now lament,
You haue but done your duties, friends should die:
Alone their friends disaster to preuent,
Though not compeld by strong necessitie.
But now farewell faire citie, neuer more
Shall I behold your beautie shining bright:
Farewell of *Iewish* men the worthy store,
But no farewell to any female wight.
You wauering crue: my curse to you I leaue,
You had but one to giue you any grace:
And you your selues will *Mariams* life bereaue,
Your common-wealth doth innocencie chase.
You creatures made to be the humane curse,
You Tygers, Lyonesses, hungry Beares,
Teare massacring *Hienas:* nay far worse,
For they for pray doe shed their fained teares;
But you will weepe, (you creatures crosse to good)
For your vnquenched thirst of humane blood:
You were the Angels cast from heaue'n for pride,
And still doe keepe your Angels outward show,
But none of you are inly beautifide,
For still your heau'n depriuing pride doth grow.
Did not the sinnes of many require a scourge,
Your place on earth had bene by this withstood:

But since a flood no more the world must purge,
You staid in office of a second flood.
You giddy creatures, sowers of debate,
You'll loue to day, and for no other cause,
But for you yefterday did deply hate,
You are the wreake of order, breach of lawes.
You beft, are foolish, froward, wanton, vaine,
Your worft adulterous, murderous, cunning, proud:
And *Salome* attends the latter traine,
Or rather he their leader is allowd.
I do the sottishnesse of men bewaile,
That doe with following you inhance your pride:
T'were better that the humane race should faile,
Then be by such a mischiefe multiplide.
*Chams* seruile curse to all your sexe was giuen,
Because in Paradise you did offend:
Then doe we not resist the will of Heauen,
When on your willes like seruants we attend?
You are to nothing constant but to ill,
You are with nought but wickednesse indude:
Your loues are set on nothing but your will,
And thus my censure I of you conclude.
You are the least of goods, the worst of euils,
Your best are worse then men: your worst then diuels.

*Babus second sonne.*

Come let vs to our death: are we not blest?
Our death will freedome from these creatures giue:
Those trouble quiet sowers of vnrest,
And this I vow that had I leaue to liue,
I would for euer leade a single life,
And neuer venter on a diuellish wife.

# ACTUS 4. SCŒNA 7.

*Herod and Salome.*

*Herod.*

Nay, she shall die. Die quoth you, that she shall:
But for the meanes. The meanes! Me thinks tis

To finde a meanes to murther her withall,                    (hard
Therefore I am resolu'd she shall be spar'd.

   *Salom.* Why? let her be beheaded. *Her.* That were
Thinke you that swords are miracles like you:                (well,
Her skinne will eu'ry Curtlax edge refell,
And then your enterprise you well may rue.
What if the fierce Arabian notice take,
Of this your wretched weaponlesse estate:
They answere when we bid resistance make,
That *Mariams* skinne their fanchions did rebate.
Beware of this, you make a goodly hand,
If you of weapons doe depriue our Land.

   *Sal.* Why drowne her then. *Herod.* Indeed a sweet de-
Why? would not eu'ry Riuer turne her course               (uice,
Rather then doe her beautie preiudice?
And be reuerted to the proper sourse.
So not a drop of water should be found
In all Iudeas quondam firtill ground.

   *Sal.* Then let the fire deuoure her. *Her.* T'will not
Flame is from her deriu'd into my heart:                     (bee:
Thou nursest flame, flame will not murther thee,
My fairest *Mariam,* fullest of desert.

   *Salom.* Then let her liue for me. *Herod.* Nay, she shall
But can you liue without her? *Sal.* doubt you that?       (die:

   *Herod.* I'me sure I cannot, I beseech you trie:
I haue experience but I know not what.

   *Salom.* How should I try? *Her.* Why let my lone be
But if we cannot liue without her sight                      (slaine,
Youle finde the meanes to make her breathe againe,
Or else you will bereaue my comfort quite.

   *Sal.* Oh I; I warrant you. *Herod.* What is she gone?
And gone to bid the world be ouerthrowne:
What? is her hearts composure hardest stone?
To what a passe are cruell women growne?
She is return'd already: haue you done?
Ist possible you can command so soone?
A creatures heart to quench the flaming Sunne,
Or from the skie to wipe away the Moone.

   *Salo.* If *Mariam* be the Sunne and Moone, it is:
For I already haue commanded this.                           (times.

   *Her.* But haue you seene her cheek? *Sal.* A thousand

*Herod*. But did you marke it too? *Sal*. I very well.

*Herod*. What ist? *Sal*. A Crimson bush, that euer limes
The soule whose foresight doth not much excell.

*Herod*. Send word she shall not dye. Her cheek a bush,
Nay, then I see indeed you markt it not.

*Sal*. Tis very faire, but yet will neuer blush,
Though foule dishonors do her forehead blot

*Herod*. Then let her die, tis very true indeed,
And for this fault alone shall *Mariam* bleed.

*Sal*. What fault my Lord? *Herod*. What fault ist? you
If you be ignorant I know of none,                    (that aske:
To call her backe from death shall be your taske,
I'm glad that she for innocent is knowne.
For on the brow of *Mariam* hangs a Fleece,
Whose slenderest twine is strong enough to binde
The hearts of Kings, the pride and shame of *Greece*,
*Troy* flaming *Helens* not so fairely shinde.

*Salom*. Tis true indeed, she layes them out for nets,
To catch the hearts that doe not shune a baite:
Tis time to speake: for *Herod* sure forgets
That *Mariams* very tresses hide deceit.

*Her*. Oh doe they so? nay, then you doe but well,
Insooth I thought it had beene haire:
Nets call you them? Lord, how they doe excell,
I neuer saw a net that show'd so faire.
But haue you heard her speake? *Sal*. You know I haue.

*Her:* And were you not amaz'd? *Sal*. No, not a whit.

*Her*. Then t'was not her you heard, her life Ile faue,
For *Mariam* hath a world amazing wit.

*Salo*. She speaks a beautious language, hut within
Her heart is false as powder: and her tongue
Doth but allure the auditors to sinne,
And is the instrument to doe you wrong.

*Herod*. It may be so: nay, tis so: shee's vnehaste,
Her mouth will ope to eu'ry strangers eare:
Then let the executioner make haste,
Lest she inchant him, if her words he heare.
Let him be deafe, lest she do him surprise
That shall to free her spirit be assignde:
Yet what boots deafenes if he haue his eyes,
Her murtherer must be both deafe and blinde.

For if he see, he needs must see the starres
That shine on eyther side of *Mariams* face:
Whose sweet aspect will terminate the warres,
Wherewith he should a soule so precious chase.
Her eyes can speake, and in their speaking moue,
Oft did my heart with reuerence receiue
The worlds mandates. Pretty tales of loue
They vtter, which can humane bondage weaue.
But shall I let this heauens modell dye?
Which for a small selfe-portraiture she drew:
Her eyes like starres, her forehead like the skie,
She is like Heauen, and must be heauenly true.

    *Salom.* Your thoughts do raue with doating on the (Queen,
Her eyes are ebon hewde, and you'll confesse:
A sable starre hath beene but seldome seene,
Then speake of reason more, of *Mariam* lesse.

    *Herod.* Your selfe are held a goodly creature heere,
Yet so vnlike my *Mariam* in your shape:
That when to her you haue approached neere,
My selfe hath often tane you for an Ape.
And yet you prate of beautie: goe your waies,
You are to her a Sun-burnt Blackamore:
Your paintings cannot equall *Mariams* praise,
Her nature is so rich, you are so poore.
Let her be staide from death, for if she die,
We do we know not what to stop her breath:
A world cannot another *Mariam* buy,
Why stay you lingring? countermaund her death.

    *Salo.* Then youle no more remember what hath past,
*Sohemus* loue, and hers shall be forgot:
Tis well in truth: that fault may be her last,
And she may mend, though yet she loue you not.

    *Her:* Oh God: tis true. *Sohemus:* earth and heau'n,
Why did you both conspire to make me curst:
In cousning me with showes, and proofes vneu'n?
She show'd the best, and yet did proue the worst.
Her show was such, as had our singing king
The holy *Dauid*, *Mariams* beautie seene:
The *Hittits* had then felt no deadly sting,
Nor *Bethsabe* had neuer bene a Queene.
Or had his sonne the wisest man of men,

Whose fond delight did most consist in change:
Beheld her face, he had bene staid agen,
No creature hauing her, can wish to range.
Had *Asuerus* seene my *Mariams* brow,
The humble *Iewe,* she might haue walkt alone:
Her beautious vertue should haue staid below,
Whiles *Mariam* mounted to the Persian throne.
But what auailes it all: for in the waight
She is deceitfull, light as vanitie:
Oh she was made for nothing but a bait,
To traine some haples man to miserie.
I am the haples man that haue bene trainde,
To endles bondage. I will see her yet:
Me thinkes I should discerne her if she fainde,
Can humane eyes be dazde by womans wit?
Once more these eyes of mine with hers shall meet,
Before the headsman doe her life bereaue:
Shall I for euer part from thee my sweet?
Without the taking of my latest leaue.

   *Salo:* You had as good resolue to saue her now,
Ile stay her death, tis well determined:
For sure she neuer more will breake her vow,
*Sohemus* and *Iosepbus* both are dead.

   *Herod.* She shall not liue, nor will I see her face,
A long heald wound, a second time doth bleed:
With *Ioseph* I remember her disgrace,
A shamefull end ensues a shamefull deed.
Oh that I had not cald to minde anew,
The discontent of *Mariams* wauering hart:
Twas you: you foule mouth'd *Ate,* none but you,
That did the thought hereof to me impart.
Hence from my sight, my blacke tormenter hence,
For hadst not thou made *Herod* vnsecure:
I had not doubted *Mariams* innocence,
But still had held her in my heart for pure.

   *Salo:* Ile leaue you to your paffion: tis no time
To purge me now, though of a guiltles crime.    (*Exit.*

   *Herod.* Destruction take thee: thou hast made
As heauie as reuenge, I am so dull,      (my hart
Me thinkes I am not sensible of smart,
Though hiddious horrors at my bosome pull.

My head waies downwards: therefore will I goe
To try if I can sleepe away my woe.


### ACTUS 4. SCŒNA. 8.

*Mariam.*

Am I the *Mariam* that presum'd so much,                    (breath?
And deem'd my face must needes preserue my
I, I it was that thought my beautie such,
At it alone could countermaund my death.
Now death will teach me: he can pale aswell
A cheeke of roses, as a cheeke lesse bright:
And dim an eye whose shine doth most excell,
Assoone as one that casts a meaner light.
Had not my selfe against my selfe conspirde,
No plot: no aduersarie from without
Could *Herods* loue from *Mariam* haue retirde,
Or from his heart haue thrust my semblance out.
The wanton Queene that neuer lou'd for loue,
False *Cleopatra,* wholly set on gaine:
With all her slights did proue; yet vainly proue,
For her the loue of *Herod* to obtaine.
Yet her allurements, all her courtly guile,
Her smiles, her fauours, and her smooth deceit:
Could not my face from *Herods* minde exile,
But were with him of lesse then little weight.
That face and person that in *Asia* late
For beauties Goddesse *Paphos* Queene was tane:
That face that did captiue great *Iulius* fate,
That very face that was *Anthonius* bane.
That face that to be *Egipts* pride was borne,
That face that all the world esteem'd so rare:
Did *Herod* hate, despise, neglect, and scorne,
When with the same, he *Mariams* did compare.
This made that I improuidently wrought,
And on the wager euen my life did pawne:
Because I thought, and yet but truly thought,
That *Herods* loue could not from me be drawne.
But now though out of time, I plainly see

It could be drawne, though neuer drawne from me:
Had I but with humilitie bene grac'te,
As well as faire I might haue prou'd me wise:
But I did thinke because I knew me chaste,
One vertue for a woman, might suffice.
That mind for glory of our sexe might stand,
Wherein humilitie and chastitie
Doth march with equall paces hand in hand,
But one if single seene, who setteth by?
And I had singly one, but tis my ioy,
That I was euer innocent, though sower:
And therefore can they but my life destroy,
My Soule is free from aduersaries power.)          *Enter Doris.*
You Princes great in power, and high in birth,
Be great and high, I enuy not your hap:
Your birth must be from dust: your power on earth,
In heau'n shall *Mariam* sit in *Saraes* lap.          (thither,

     *Doris.* I heau'n, your beautie cannot bring you
Your soule is blacke and spotted, full of sinne:
You in adultry liu'd nine yeare together,
And heau'n will neuer let adultry in.

     *Mar:* What art thou that dost poore *Mariam* pursue?
Some spirit sent to driue me to dispaire:
Who sees for truth that *Mariam* is vntrue,
If faire she be, she is as chaste as faire.

     *Doris.* I am that *Doris* that was once belou'd,
Belou'd by *Herod: Herods* lawfull wife:
Twas you that *Doris* from his side remou'd,
And rob'd from me the glory of my life.

     *Mar:* Was that adultry: did not Moses say,
That he that being matcht did deadly hate:
Might by permission put his wife away,
And take a more belou'd to be his mate?

     *Doris.* What did he hate me for: for simple truth?
For bringing beautious babes for loue to him:
For riches: noble birth, or tender youth,
Or for no staine did *Doris* honour dim?
Oh tell me *Mariam*, tell me if you knowe,
Which fault of these made *Herod Doris* foe.
These thrice three yeares haue I with hands held vp,
And bowed knees fast nailed to the ground;

Besought for thee the dreggs of that same cup,
That cup of wrath that is for sinners found.
And now thou art to drinke it; *Doris* curse,
Vpon thy selfe did all this while attend,
But now it shall pursue thy children worse.

   *Mar:* Oh *Doris* now to thee my knees I bend,
That hart that neuer bow'd to thee doth bow:
Curse not mine infants, let it thee suffice,
That Heau'n doth punishment to me allow.
Thy curse is cause that guiltles *Mariam* dies.

   *Doris.* Had I ten thousand tongues, and eu'ry tongue
Inflam'd with poisons power, and steept in gall:
My curses would not answere for my wrong,
Though I in cursing thee imployd them all.
Heare thou that didst mount *Gerarim* command,
To be a place whereon with cause to curse:
Stretch thy reuenging arme: thrust forth thy hand,
And plague the mother much: the children worse.
Throw flaming fire vpon the baseborne heads
That were begotten in vnlawfull beds.
But let them liue till they haue sence to know
What tis to be in miserable state:
Then be their neerest friends their ouerthrow,
Attended be they by suspitious hate.
And *Mariam,* I doe hope this boy of mine
Shall one day come to be the death of thine.          *Exit.*

   *Mariam.* Oh ! Heauen forbid. I hope the world shall
This curse of thine shall be return'd on thee;          (see,
Now earth farewell, though I be yet but yong,
Yet I, me thinks, haue knowne thee too too long.          *Exit.*

### *Chorus.*

The fairest action of our humane life,
  Is scorniug to reuenge an iniurie;
  For who forgiues without a further strife,
His aduersaries heart to him doth tie.
    And tis a firmer conquest truely sed,
    To winne the heart, then ouerthrow the head.

If we a worthy enemie doe finde,
  To yeeld to worth, it must be nobly done:

But if of baser mettall be his minde,
In base reuenge there is no honor wonne.
  Who would a worthy courage ouerthrow,
  And who would wrastle with a worthles foe?

We say our hearts are great and cannot yeeld,
Because they cannot yeeld it proues them poore:
Great hearts are task't beyond their power, but seld
The weakest Lyon will the lowdest roare.
  Truths schoole for certaine doth this same allow,
  High hartednes doth sometimes teach to bow.

A noble heart doth teach a vertuous scorne,
To scorne to owe a dutie ouer-long:
To scorne to be for benefits forborne,
To scorne to lie, to scorne to doe a wrong.
  To scorne to beare an iniurie in minde,
  To scorne a free-borne heart slaue-like to binde.

But if for wrongs we needs reuenge must haue,
Then be our vengeance of the noblest kinde:
Doe we his body from our furie saue,
And let our hate preuaile against our minde?
  What can gainst him a greater vengeance bee,
  Then make his foe more worthy farre then hee?

Had *Mariam* scorn'd to leaue a due vnpaide,
Shee would to *Herod* then haue paid her loue:
And not haue bene by sullen passion swaide
To fixe her thoughts all iniurie aboue
  Is vertuous pride. Had *Mariam* thus bene prou'd,
  Long famous life to her had bene allowd.

# ACTUS QUINTUS.

## SCŒNA PRIMA.

### *Nuntio.*

When, sweetest friend, did I so farre offend
Your heauenly selfe: that you my fault to quit
Haue made me now relator of her end,
The end of beautie? Chastitie and wit,
Was none so haples in the fatall place,
But I, most wretched, for the Queene t'chuse,
Tis certaine I haue some ill boding face
That made me culd to tell this luckles newes.
And yet no news to *Herod:* were it new,
To him vnhappy t'had not bene at all:
Yet doe I long to come within his vew,
That he may know his wife did guiltles fall;
And heere he comes. Your *Mariam* greets you well.

### Enter Herod.

*Herod.* What? liues my *Mariam?* ioy, exceeding ioy.
She shall not die. *Nun.* Heau'n doth your will repell.
  *Herod.* Oh doe not with thy words my life destroy,
I prethy tell no dying-tale: thine eye
Without thy tongue doth tell but too too much:
Yet let thy tongues addition make me die,
Death welcome, comes to him whose griefe is such.
  *Nunti.* I went amongst the curious gazing troope,
To see the last of her that was the best:
To see if death had hart to make her stoope,
To see the Sunne admiring *Phœnix* nest.

When there I came, vpon the way I saw
The stately *Mariam* not debas'd by feare:
Her looke did seeme to keepe the world in awe,
Yet mildly did her face this fortune beare.

   *Herod.* Thou dost vsurpe my right, my tongue was
To be the instrument of *Mariams* praise:        (fram'd
Yet speake; she cannot be too often fam'd:
All tongues suffice not her sweet name to raise.

   *Nun.* But as she came she *Alexandra* met,
Who did her death (sweet Queene) no whit bewaile,
But as if nature she did quite forget,
She did vpon her daughter loudly raile.

   *Herod.* Why stopt you not her mouth? where had she
To darke that, that Heauen made so bright?        (words
Our sacred tongue no *Epthite* affords,
To call her other then the worlds delight.

   *Nun.* Shee told her that her death was too too good,
And that already she had liu'd too long:
She said, she sham'd to haue a part in blood
Of her that did the princely *Herod* wrong.        (glory,

   *Herod.* Base picke-thanke Diuell. Shame, twas all her
That she to noble *Mariam* was the mother:
But neuer shall it liue in any storie
Her name, except to infamy ile smother.
What answere did her princely daughter make?

   *Nun.* She made no answere, but she lookt the while,
As if thereof she scarce did notice take,
Yet smilde, a dutifull, though scornefull smile.

   *Her.* Sweet creature, I that looke to mind doe call,
Full oft hath *Herod* bene amaz'd withall.

   *Nun.* Go on, she came vnmou'd with pleasant grace,
As if to triumph her arriuall were:
In stately habite, and with cheefull face:
Yet eu'ry eye was moyst, but *Mariams* there.
When iustly opposite to me she came,
She pickt me out from all the crue:
She beckned to me, cald me by my name,
For she my name, my birth, and fortune knew.

   *Herod.* What did she name thee? happy, happy man,
Wilt thou not euer loue that name the better?
But what sweet tune did this faire dying Swan

Afford thine eare: tell all, omit no letter.

    *Nun.* Tell thou my Lord, said she. *Her.* Mee, ment she<br>
Ist true, the more my shame: I was her Lord,         (mee?<br>
Were I not made her Lord, I still should bee:<br>
But now her name must be by me ador'd.<br>
Oh say, what faid she more? each word she sed<br>
Shall be the food whereon my heart is fed.         (breath,<br>
    *Nun:* Tell thou my Lord thou saw'ft me loose my<br>
    *Herod.* Oh that I could that sentence now controule,<br>
    *Nun.* If guiltily eternall be my death,<br>
    *Her:* I hold her chast eu'n in my inmost soule.<br>
    *Nun:* By three daies hence if wishes could reuiue,<br>
I know himselfe would make me oft aliue.<br>
    *Herod.* Three daies: three houres, three minutes, not<br>
A minute in a thoufand parts diuided,         (so much,<br>
My penitencie for her death is such,<br>
As in the first I wisht she had not died.<br>
But forward in thy tale, *Nun:* Why on she went,<br>
And after she some silent praier had fed:<br>
She did as if to die she were content,<br>
And thus to heau'n her heau'nly soule is fled.<br>
    *Herod.* But art thou sure there doth no life remaine?<br>
Ist possible my *Mariam* should be dead,<br>
Is there no tricke to make her breathe againe?<br>
    *Nun:* Her body is diuided from her head.         (art,<br>
    *Her:* Why yet me thinkes there might be found by<br>
Strange waies of cure, tis sure rare things are don:<br>
By an inuentiue head, and willing heart.<br>
    *Nun:* Let not my Lord your fancies idlely run.<br>
It is as possible it should be seene,<br>
That we should make the holy Abraham liue,<br>
Though he intomb'd two thousand yeares had bene,<br>
As breath againe to slaughtred *Mariam* giue,<br>
But now for more assaults prepare your eares,<br>
    *Herod.* There cannot be a further cause of mone,<br>
This accident shall shelter me from feares:<br>
What can I feare? already *Mariams* gone.<br>
Yet tell eu'n what you will: *Nun:* As I came by,<br>
From *Mariams* death I saw vpon a tree,<br>
A man that to his necke a cord did tie:<br>
Which cord he had designd his end to bee.

When me he once discern'd, he downwards bow'd,
And thus with fearefull voyce she cride alowd,
Goe tell the King he trailed ere he tride,
I am the cause that *Mariam* causeles dide.

   *Herod.* Damnation take him, for it was the slaue
That said she ment with poisons deadly force
To end my life that she the Crowne might haue:
Which tale did *Mariam* from her selfe diuorce.
Oh pardon me thou pure vnspotted Ghost,
My punishment must needes sufficient bee,
In missing that content I valued most:
Which was thy admirable face to see.
I had but one inestimable Iewell,
Yet one I had no monarch had the like,
And therefore may I curse my selfe as cruell:
Twas broken by a blowe my selfe did strike.
I gaz'd thereon and neuer thought me blest,
But when on it my dazled eye might rest:
A pretious Mirror made by wonderous art,
I prizd it ten times dearer then my Crowne,
And laide it vp fast foulded in my heart;
Yet I in suddaine choler cast it downe.
And pasht it all to peeces: twas no foe,
That robd me of it; no *Arabian* host,
Nor no *Armenian* guide hath vsde me so:
But *Herods* wretched selfe hath *Herod* crost.
She was my gracefull moytie, me accurst,
To slay my better halfe and saue my worst.
But sure she is not dead you did but iest,
To put me in perplexitie a while,
Twere well indeed if I could so be drest:
I see she is aliue, me thinkes you smile.

   *Nun:* If sainted *Abel* yet deceased bee,
Tis certaine *Mariam* is as dead as hee.

   *Her:* Why then goe call her to me, bid her now
Put on faire habite, stately ornament:
And let no frowne oreshade her smoothest brow,
In her doth *Herod* place his whole content.

   *Nun:* Sheel come in stately weedes to please your (sence,
If now she come attirde in robe of heauen:
Remember you your selfe did send her hence,

And now to you she can no more be giuen.                                    faire,
    *Herod.* Shee's dead, hell take her murderers, she was
Oh what a hand she had, it was so white,
It did the whitenes of the snowe impaire:
I neuer more shall see so sweet a fight.                                    (hands;
    *Nun:* Tis true, her hand was rare. *Her:* her hand? her
She had not singly one of beautie rare,
But such a paire as heere where *Herod* stands,
He dares the world to make to both compare.
Accursed *Salome,* hadst thou bene still,
My *Mariam* had bene breathing by my side:
Oh neuer had I: had I had my will,
Sent forth command, that *Mariam* should haue dide.
But *Salome* thou didst with enuy vexe,
To see thy selfe out-matched in thy sexe:
Vpon your sexes forehead *Mariam* sat,
To grace you all like an imperiall crowne,
But you fond foole haue rudely pusht thereat,
And proudly puld your proper glory downe.
One smile of hers: Nay, not so much a: looke
Was worth a hundred thousand such as you,
*Iudea* how canst thou the wretches brooke,
That robd from thee the fairest of the crew?
You dwellers in the now depriued land,
Wherein the matchles *Mariam* was bred:
Why graspe not each of you a sword in hand,
To ayme at me your cruell Soueraignes head.
Oh when you thinke of *Herod* as your King,
And owner of the pride of *Palestine:*
This act to your remembrance likewise bring,
Tis I haue ouerthrowne your royall line.
Within her purer vaines the blood did run,
That from her Grandam *Sara* she deriu'd,
Whose beldame age the loue of Kings hath wonne,
Oh that her issue had as long bene li'ud.
But can her eye be made by death obscure?
I cannot thinke but it must sparkle still:
Foule sacriledge to rob those lights so pure,
From out a Temple made by heau'nly skill.
I am the Villaine that haue done the deed,
The cruell deed, though by anothers hand,

My word though not my sword made *Mariam* bleed,
*Hircanus* Grandchild did at my command.
That *Mariam* that I once did loue so deare,
The partner of my now detested bed,
Why shine you sun with an aspect so cleare?
I tell you once againe my *Mariams* dead.
You could but shine, if some *Egiptian* blows,
Or *Æthiopian* doudy lose her life:
This was, then wherefore bend you not your brows,
The King of *Iuries* faire and spotles wife.
Denie thy beames, and *Moone* refuse thy light,
Let all the starres be darke, let *Iuries* eye
No more distinguish which is day and night:
Since her best birth did in her bosome die.
Those fond Idolaters the men of *Greece*,
Maintaine these orbes are safely gouerned;
That each within themselues haue Gods a peece,
By whom their stedfast course is iustly led.
But were it so, as so it cannot bee,
They all would put their mourning garments on:
Not one of them would yeeld a light to mee,
To me that is the cause that *Mariams* gon.
For though they fame their *Saturne* melancholy,
Of sowre behauiours, and of angry moode:
They fame him likewise to be iust and holy,
And iustice needes must seeke reuenge for blood.
Their *Ioue,* if *Ioue* he were, would sure desire,
To punish him that slew so faire a lasse:
For *Lædaes* beautie set his heart on fire,
Yet she not halfe so faire as *Mariam* was.
And *Mars* would deeme his *Venus* had bene slaine,
*Sol* to recouer her would neuer sticke;
For if he want the power her life to gaine:
Then Physicks God is but an Empericke.
The Queene of loue would storme for beauties sake,
And *Hermes* too, since he bestow'd her wit,
The nights pale light for angrie griefe would shake,
To see chast *Mariam* die in age vnfit.
But oh I am deceiu'd, she past them all
In euery gift, in euery propertie:
Her Excellencies wrought her timeles fall,

And they reioyc'd, not grieu'd to see her die.
The *Paphian* Goddesse did repent her wast,
When me to one such beautie did allow:
*Mercurius* thought her wit his wit surpast,
And *Cinthia* enui'd *Mariams* brighter brow.
But these are fictions, they are voyd of sence,
The *Greekes* but dreame, and dreaming falsehoods tell:
They neither can offend nor giue defence,
And not by them it was my *Mariam* fell.
If she had bene like an *Egipttan* blacke,
And not so faire, she had bene longer liude:
Her ouerflow of beautie turned backe,
And drownde the spring from whence it was deriude.
Her heau'nly beautie twas that made me thinke
That it with chastitie could neuer dwell:
But now I see that heau'n in her did linke,
A spirit and a perfon to excell.
Ile muffle vp my selfe in endles night,
And neuer let mine eyes behold the light.
Retire thy selfe vile monster, worse then hee
That staind the virgin earth with brothers blood,
Still in some vault or denne inclosed bee,
Where with thy teares thou maist beget a flood,
Which flood in time may drowne thee: happie day
When thou at once shalt die and finde a graue,
A stone vpon the vault, some one shall lay,
Which monument shall an inscription haue.
And these shall be the words it shall containe,
*Heere* Herod *lies, that hath his Mariam slaine.*

### Chorus.

Who euer hath beheld with steadfast eye,
    The strange euents of this one onely day:
    How many were deceiu'd? How many die,
That once to day did grounds of safetie lay?
    It will from them all certaintie bereue,
    Since twice six houres so many can deceiue.


This morning *Herod* held for surely dead,
And all the *Iewes* on *Mariam* did attend:
And *Constabarus* rise from *Saloms* bed,

And neither dreamd of a diuorce or end.
    *Pheroras* ioyd that he might haue his wife,
    And *Babus* sonnes for safetie of their life.

To night our *Herod* doth aliue remaine,
The guiltles *Mariam* is depriu'd of breath:
Stout *Constabarus* both diuorst and slaine,
The valiant sonnes of *Baba* haue their death.
    *Pheroras* sure his loue to be bereft,
    If *Salome* her sute vnmade had left.

*Herod* this morning did expect with ioy,
To see his *Mariams* much beloued face:
And yet ere night he did her life destroy,
And surely thought she did her name disgrace.
    Yet now againe so short do humors last,
    He both repents her death and knowes her chast.

Had he with wisedome now her death delaide,
He at his pleasure might command her death:
But now he hath his power so much betraide,
As all his woes cannot restore her breath.
    Now doth he strangely lunatickly raue,
    Because his *Mariams* life he cannot saue.

This daies euents were certainly ordainde,
To be the warning to posteritie:
So many changes are therein containde,
So admirablie strange varietie.
    This day alone, our sagest *Hebrewes* shall
    In after times the schoole of wisedome call.

FINIS

# THE DUCHESS OF MALFI

## John Webster

# DRAMATIS PERSONAE

FERDINAND, *Duke of Calabria*

THE CARDINAL, *his brother*

ANTONIO BOLOGNA, *steward of the household to the Duchess*

DELIO, *his friend*

DANIEL DE BOSOLA, *gentleman of the horse to the Duchess*

CASTRUCCIO

MARQUIS OF PESCARA

COUNT MALATESTI

RODERIGO

SILVIO

GRISOLAN

DOCTOR

DUCHESS OF MALFI

CARIOLA, *her woman*

JULIA, *Castruccio's wife, and the Cardinal's mistress*

OLD LADY, LADIES, AND CHILDREN

*Several* MADMEN, PILGRIMS, EXECUTIONERS, OFFICERS, ATTENDANTS, &C.

SCENE: *Malfi, Rome, and Milan*

# ACT I

## SCENE I: *The presence-chamber in the* DUCHESS'S *palace at Malfi.*

### Enter ANTONIO *and* DELIO.

DELIO. You are welcome to your country, dear Antonio;
    You have been long in France, and you return
    A very formal Frenchman in your habit.
    How do you like the French court?
ANTONIO. I admire it;
    In seeking to reduce both state and people
    To a fixed order, their judicious king
    Begins at home; quits first his royal palace
    Of flattering sycophants, of dissolute
    And infamous persons,—which he sweetly terms
    His master's master-piece, the work of Heaven:
    Considering duly that a prince's court
    Is like a common fountain, whence should flow
    Pure silver drops in general, but if't chance
    Some cursed example poison 't near the head,
    Death and diseases through the whole land spread.
    And what is 't makes this blessed government
    But a most provident council, who dare freely
    Inform him the corruption of the times?
    Though some o' the court hold it presumption
    To instruct princes what they ought to do,
    It is a noble duty to inform them
    What they ought to foresee.—Here comes Bosola,
    The only court-gall; yet I observe his railing

Is not for simple love of piety:
Indeed, he rails at those things which he wants;
Would be as lecherous, covetous, or proud,
Bloody, or envious, as any man,
If he had means to be so.—Here's the cardinal.

*Enter* CARDINAL *and* BOSOLA.

BOSOLA. I do haunt you still.

CARDINAL. So.

BOSOLA. I have done you better service than to be slighted thus.
Miserable age, where only the reward of doing well is the
doing of it!

CARDINAL. You enforce your merit too much.

BOSOLA. I fell into the galleys in your service; where, for two
years together, I wore two towels instead of a shirt, with a
knot on the shoulder, after the fashion of a Roman mantle.
Slighted thus! I will thrive some way: blackbirds fatten best in
hard weather; why not I in these dog-days?

CARDINAL. Would you could become honest!

BOSOLA. With all your divinity do but direct me the way to it. I
have known many travel far for it, and yet return as arrant knaves
as they went forth, because they carried themselves always along
with them. [*Exit* CARDINAL] Are you gone? Some fellows, they
say, are possessed with the devil, but this great fellow were able
to possess the greatest devil, and make him worse.

ANTONIO. He hath denied thee some suit?

BOSOLA. He and his brother are like plum-trees that grow crooked
over standing-pools; they are rich and o'er-laden with fruit,
but none but crows, magpies, and caterpillars feed on them.
Could I be one of their flattering panders, I would hang on
their ears like a horseleech, till I were full, and then drop off.
I pray, leave me. Who would rely upon these miserable depen-
dancies, in expectation to be advanced tomorrow? what creatures ever fed worse than hoping Tantalus?[1] nor ever died any
man more fearfully than he had hoped for a pardon. There are
rewards for hawks and dogs when they have done us service;
but for a soldier that hazards his limbs in a battle, nothing but
a kind of geometry is his last supportation.

---

[1] Legendary king whose punishment in the lower world was to be unable to
slake his thirst or allay his hunger.

DELIO. Geometry!

BOSOLA. Ay, to hang in a fair pair of slings, take his latter swing in the world upon an honorable pair of crutches, from hospital to hospital. Fare ye well, sir: and yet do not you scorn us; for places in the court are but like beds in the hospital, where this man's head lies at that man's foot, and so lower and lower.    [*Exit.*

DELIO. I knew this fellow seven years in the galleys
   For a notorious murder; and 'twas thought
   The cardinal suborned it: he was released
   By the French general, Gaston de Foix,
   When he recovered Naples.

ANTONIO.  'Tis great pity
   He should be thus neglected: I have heard
   He's very valiant. This foul melancholy
   Will poison all his goodness; for, I'll tell you,
   If too immoderate sleep be truly said
   To be an inward rust into the soul,
   It then doth follow want of action
   Breeds all black malcontents; and their close rearing,
   Like moths in cloth, do hurt for want of wearing.

DELIO. The presence 'gins to fill: you promised me
   To make me the partaker of the natures
   Of some of your great courtiers.

ANTONIO. The lord cardinal's,
   And other strangers' that are now in court?
   I shall.—Here comes the great Calabrian duke.

*Enter* FERDINAND, CASTRUCCIO, SILVIO, RODERIGO,
GRISOLAN, *and* ATTENDANTS.

FERDINAND. Who took the ring oftenest?

SILVIO. Antonio Bologna, my lord.

FERDINAND. Our sister duchess's great-master of her household? give him the jewel.—When shall we leave this sportive action, and fall to action indeed?

CASTRUCCIO. Methinks, my lord, you should not desire to go to war in person.

FERDINAND. Now for some gravity:—why, my lord?

CASTRUCCIO. It is fitting a soldier arise to be a prince, but not necessary a prince descend to be a captain. FERDINAND. No?

CASTRUCCIO. No, my lord; he were far better do it by a deputy.
FERDINAND. Why should he not as well sleep or eat by a deputy?

This might take idle, offensive, and base office from him, whereas the other deprives him of honor.

CASTRUCCIO. Believe my experience, that realm is never long in quiet where the ruler is a soldier.

FERDINAND. Thou toldest me thy wife could not endure fighting.

CASTRUCCIO. True, my lord.

FERDINAND. And of a jest she broke of a captain she met full of wounds: I have forgot it.

CASTRUCCIO. She told him, my lord, he was a pitiful fellow, to lie, like the children of Ismael, all in tents.[2]

FERDINAND. Why, there's a wit were able to undo all the surgeons o' the city; for although gallants should quarrel, and had drawn their weapons, and were ready to go to it, yet her persuasions would make them put up.

CASTRUCCIO. That she would, my lord.—How do you like my Spanish jennet?[3]

RODERIGO. He is all fire.

FERDINAND. I am of Pliny's opinion,[4] I think he was begot by the wind; he runs as if he were ballasted with quicksilver.

SILVIO. True, my lord, he reels from the tilt often.

RODERIGO *and* GRISOLAN. Ha! ha! ha!

FERDINAND. Why do you laugh? methinks you that are courtiers should be my touchwood, take fire when I give fire; that is, laugh but when I laugh, were the subject never so witty.

CASTRUCCIO. True, my lord: I myself have heard a very good jest, and have scorned to seem to have so silly a wit as to understand it.

FERDINAND. But I can laugh at your fool, my lord.

CASTRUCCIO. He cannot speak, you know, but he makes faces: my lady cannot abide him.

FERDINAND. No?

CASTRUCCIO. Nor endure to be in merry company; for she says too much laughing, and too much company, fills her too full of the wrinkle.

FERDINAND. I would, then, have a mathematical instrument made for her face, that she might not laugh out of compass.—I shall shortly visit you at Milan, Lord Silvio.

SILVIO. Your grace shall arrive most welcome.

---

[2] A play upon the word "tent," which also means a bandage.

[3] A jennet was a small Spanish horse.

[4] Pliny the Elder (23-79 A.D.), Roman naturalist who authored the Historia Naturalis.

FERDINAND. You are a good horseman, Antonio: you have excellent riders in France: what do you think of good horsemanship?

ANTONIO. Nobly, my lord: as out of the Grecian horse[5] issued many famous princes, so out of brave horsemanship arise the first sparks of growing resolution that raise the mind to noble action.

FERDINAND. You have bespoke it worthily.

SILVIO. Your brother, the lord cardinal, and sister duchess.

## SCENE II

*Re-enter* CARDINAL *and* FERDINAND, *with* DUCHESS *and* CARIOLA.

CARDINAL. Are the galleys come about?

GRISOLAN. They are, my lord.

FERDINAND. Here's the Lord Silvio is come to take his leave.

DELIO. Now, sir, your promise; what's that cardinal?
    I mean his temper? they say he's a brave fellow,
    Will play his five thousand crowns at tennis, dance,
    Court ladies, and one that hath fought single combats.

ANTONIO. Some such flashes superficially hang on him for form; but observe his inward character: he is a melancholy churchman; the spring in his face is nothing but the engendering of toads; where he is jealous of any man, he lays worse plots for them than ever was imposed on Hercules, for he strews in his way flatterers, panders, intelligencers, atheists, and a thousand such political monsters. He should have been Pope; but instead of coming to it by the primitive decency of the church, he did bestow bribes so largely and so impudently as if he would have carried it away without Heaven's knowledge. Some good he hath done—

DELIO. You have given too much of him. What's his brother?

ANTONIO. The duke there? a most perverse and turbulent nature;
    What appears in him mirth is merely outside;
    If he laugh heartily, it is to laugh
    All honesty out of fashion.

DELIO. Twins?

ANTONIO. In quality.

---

[5] The wooden Trojan horse, described in the *Aeneid* and the *Odyssey*.

He speaks with others' tongues, and hears men's suits
With others' ears; will seem to sleep o' the bench
Only to entrap offenders in their answers;
Dooms men to death by information;
Rewards by hearsay.

DELIO. Then the law to him
Is like a foul black cobweb to a spider,—
He makes it his dwelling and a prison
To entangle those shall feed him.

ANTONIO. Most true:
He never pays debts unless they be shrewd turns,
And those he will confess that he doth owe.
Last, for his brother there, the cardinal,
They that do flatter him most say oracles
Hang at his lips; and verily I believe them,
For the devil speaks in them.
But for their sister, the right noble duchess,
You never fixed your eye on three fair medals
Cast in one figure, of so different temper.
For her discourse, it is so full of rapture,
You only will begin then to be sorry
When she doth end her speech, and wish, in wonder,
She held it less vain-glory to talk much,
Than your penance to hear her: whilst she speaks,
She throws upon a man so sweet a look,
That it were able to raise one to a galliard[6]
That lay in a dead palsy, and to dote
On that sweet countenance; but in that look
There speaketh so divine a continence
As cuts off all lascivious and vain hope.
Her days are practised in such noble virtue,
That sure her nights, nay, more, her very sleeps,
Are more in Heaven than other ladies' shrifts.
Let all sweet ladies break their flattering glasses,
And dress themselves in her.

DELIO. Fie, Antonio,
You play the wire-drawer with her commendations.

ANTONIO. I'll case the picture up: only thus much;
All her particular worth grows to this sum,—

---

[6] A dance.

She stains the time past, lights the time to come.

CARIOLA. You must attend my lady in the gallery,
   Some half an hour hence.

ANTONIO. I shall.

*Exeunt* ANTONIO *and* DELIO.

FERDINAND. Sister, I have a suit to you.

DUCHESS. To me, sir?

FERDINAND. A gentleman here, Daniel de Bosola,
   One that was in the galleys—

DUCHESS. Yes, I know him.

FERDINAND. A worthy fellow he is: pray, let me entreat for
   The provisorship of your horse.[7]

DUCHESS. Your knowledge of him
   Commends him and prefers him.

FERDINAND. Call him hither.

*Exit* ATTENDANT.

   We are now upon parting. Good Lord Silvio,
   Do us commend to all our noble friends
   At the leaguer.[8]

SILVIO. Sir, I shall.

FERDINAND. You are for Milan?

SILVIO. I am.

DUCHESS. Bring the caroches.[9] We'll bring you down to the
haven.

*Exeunt* DUCHESS, SILVIO, CASTRUCCIO, RODERIGO, GRISOLAN,
   CARIOLA, JULIA, *and* ATTENDANTS.

CARDINAL. Be sure you entertain that Bosola
   For your intelligence: I would not be seen in 't;
   And therefore many times I have slighted him
   When he did court our furtherance, as this morning.

FERDINAND. Antonio, the great-master of her household,
   Had been far fitter.

CARDINAL. You are deceived in him:
   His nature is too honest for such business.—
   He comes: I'll leave you.                          [*Exit*

---

[7] Stewardship of her horses.
[8] Camp; from the German *Lager*.
[9] Stately carriages.

*Re-enter* BOSOLA.

BOSOLA. I was lured to you.

FERDINAND. My brother, here, the cardinal, could never
 Abide you.

BOSOLA. Never since he was in my debt.

FERDINAND. May be some oblique character in your face
 Made him suspect you.

BOSOLA. Doth he study physiognomy?
 There's no more credit to be given to the face
 Than to a sick man's urine, which some call
 The physician's whore because she cozens him..
 He did suspect me wrongfully.

FERDINAND. For that
 You must give great men leave to take their times.
 Distrust doth cause us seldom be deceived:
 You see the oft shaking of the cedar-tree
 Fastens it more at root.

BOSOLA. Yet, take heed;
 For to suspect a friend unworthily
 Instructs him the next way to suspect you,
 And prompts him to deceive you.

FERDINAND. There's gold.

BOSOLA. So:
 What follows? never rained such showers as these
 Without thunderbolts i' the tail of them: whose throat must I
  cut?

FERDINAND. Your inclination to shed blood rides post
 Before my occasion to use you. I give you that
 To live i' the court here, and observe the duchess;
 To note all the particulars of her havior,
 What suitors do solicit her for marriage,
 And whom she best affects. She's a young widow:
 I would not have her marry again.

BOSOLA. No, sir?

FERDINAND. Do not you ask the reason; but be satisfied
 I say I would not.

BOSOLA. It seems you would create me
 One of your familiars.

FERDINAND. Familiar! what's that?

BOSOLA. Why, a very quaint invisible devil in flesh,

An intelligencer.

FERDINAND. Such a kind of thriving thing
 I would wish thee; and ere long thou mayest arrive
 At a higher place by 't.

BOSOLA. Take your devils,
 Which hell calls angels, these cursed gifts would make
 You a corrupter, me an impudent traitor;
 And should I take these, they'd take me to hell.

FERDINAND. Sir, I'll take nothing from you that I have given:
 There is a place that I procured for you
 This morning, the provisorship o' the horse;
 Have you heard on 't?

BOSOLA. No.

FERDINAND. 'Tis yours: is't not worth thanks?

BOSOLA. I would have you curse yourself now, that your bounty
 (Which makes men truly noble) e'er should make me
 A villain. O, that to avoid ingratitude
 For the good deed you have done me, I must do
 All the ill man can invent! Thus the devil
 Candies all sins o'er; and what Heaven terms vile,
 That names he complimental.

FERDINAND. Be yourself;
 Keep your old garb of melancholy; 'twill express
 You envy those that stand above your reach,
 Yet strive not to come near 'em: this will gain
 Access to private lodgings, where yourself
 May, like a politic dormouse—

BOSOLA. As I have seen some
 Feed in a lord's dish, half asleep, not seeming
 To listen to any talk; and yet these rogues
 Have cut his throat in a dream. What's my place?
 The provisorship o' the horse? say, then, my corruption
 Grew out of horse-dung: I am your creature.

FERDINAND. Away!

BOSOLA. Let good men, for good deeds, covet good fame,
 Since place and riches oft are bribes of shame:
 Sometimes the devil doth preach.                    [*Exit*

 *Re-enter* DUCHESS, CARDINAL, *and* CARIOLA.

CARDINAL. We are to part from you; and your own discretion
 Must now be your director.

FERDINAND. YOU are a widow:
    You know already what man is; and therefore
    Let not youth, high promotion, eloquence—
CARDINAL. NO,
    Nor any thing without the addition, honor,
    Sway your high blood.
FERDINAND. Marry! they are most luxurious[10]
    Will wed twice.
CARDINAL. O, fie!
FERDINAND. Their livers are more spotted
    Than Laban's sheep.
DUCHESS. Diamonds are of most value,
    They say, that have passed through most jewelers' hands.
FERDINAND. Whores by that rule are precious.
DUCHESS. Will you hear me?
    I'll never marry.
CARDINAL. SO most widows say;
    But commonly that motion lasts no longer
    Than the turning of an hour-glass: the funeral sermon
    And it end both together.
FERDINAND. NOW hear me:
    You live in a rank pasture, here, i' the court;
    There is a kind of honey-dew that's deadly;
    'Twill poison your fame; look to 't: be not cunning;
    For they whose faces do belie their hearts
    Are witches ere they arrive at twenty years,
    Ay, and give the devil suck.
DUCHESS. This is terrible good counsel.
FERDINAND. Hypocrisy is woven of a fine small thread, Subtler
than Vulcan's engine:[11] yet, believe 't,
    Your darkest actions, nay, your privat'st thoughts,
    Will come to light.
CARDINAL. YOU may flatter yourself,
    And take your own choice; privately be married
    Under the eaves of night—
FERDINAND. Think 't the best voyage
    That e'er you made; like the irregular crab,
    Which, though 't goes backward, thinks that it goes right

---

[10] Lecherous.
[11] The net that held Mars and Venus.

Because it goes its own way; but observe,
Such weddings may more properly be said
To be executed than celebrated.
CARDINAL. The marriage night
Is the entrance into some prison.
FERDINAND. And those joys,
Those lustful pleasures, are like heavy sleeps
Which do fore-run man's mischief.
CARDINAL. Fare you well.
Wisdom begins at the end: remember it.          [*Exit*
DUCHESS. I think this speech between you both was studied,
It came so roundly off.
FERDINAND. YOU are my sister;
This was my father's poniard, do you see?
I'd be loth to see 't look rusty, 'cause 'twas his.
I would have you give o'er these chargeable revels:
A visor and a mask are whispering-rooms
That were never built for goodness;—fare ye well;—
And women like that part which, like the lamprey,
Hath never a bone in 't.
DUCHESS. Fie, sir!
FERDINAND. Nay,
I mean the tongue; variety of courtship:
What cannot a neat knave with a smooth tale
Make a woman believe? Farewell, lusty widow.          [*Exit*
DUCHESS. Shall this move me? If all my royal kindred
Lay in my way unto this marriage,
I'd make them my low footsteps: and even now,
Even in this hate, as men in some great battles,
By apprehending danger, have achieved
Almost impossible actions (I have heard soldiers say so),
So I through frights and threatenings will assay
This dangerous venture. Let old wives report
I winked and chose a husband. —Cariola,
To thy known secrecy I have given up
More than my life—my fame.
CARIOLA. Both shall be safe;
For I'll conceal this secret from the world
As warily as those that trade in poison
Keep poison from their children.
DUCHESS. Thy protestation

Is ingenious and hearty: I believe it.
Is Antonio come?
CARIOLA. He attends you.
DUCHESS. Good, dear soul,
Leave me; but place thyself behind the arras,
Where thou may'st overhear us. Wish me good speed;
For I am going into a wilderness
Where I shall find nor path nor friendly clue
To be my guide.        [CARIOLA goes *behind the arras*[12]

*Enter* ANTONIO.

I sent for you: sit down;
Take pen and ink, and write: are you ready?
ANTONIO. Yes.
DUCHESS. What did I say?
ANTONIO. That I should write somewhat.
DUCHESS. O, I remember.
After these triumphs and this large expense,
It's fit, like thrifty husbands, we inquire
What's laid up for to-morrow.
ANTONIO. So please your beauteous excellence.
DUCHESS. Beauteous!
Indeed, I thank you: I look young for your sake;
You have ta'en my cares upon you.
ANTONIO. I'll fetch your grace
The particulars of your revenue and expense.
DUCHESS. O, you are
An upright treasurer: but you mistook;
For when I said I meant to make inquiry
What's laid up for to-morrow, I did mean
What's laid up yonder for me.
ANTONIO. Where?
DUCHESS. In Heaven.
I am making my will (as 'tis fit princes should,
In perfect memory), and, I pray, sir, tell me,
Were not one better make it smiling, thus,
Than in deep groans and terrible ghastly looks,
As if the gifts we parted with procured
That violent distraction?

---

[12] Tapestry screen.

ANTONIO. O, much better.

DUCHESS. If I had a husband now, this care were quit:
  But I intend to make you overseer.
  What good deed shall we first remember? say.

ANTONIO. Begin with that first good deed began i' the world
  After man's creation, the sacrament of marriage:
  I'd have you first provide for a good husband;
  Give him all.

DUCHESS. All!

ANTONIO. Yes, your excellent self.

DUCHESS. In a winding-sheet?

ANTONIO. In a couple.

DUCHESS. Saint Winifred, that were a strange will!

ANTONIO. 'Twere stranger if there were no will in you
  To marry again.

DUCHESS. What do you think of marriage?

ANTONIO. I take 't, as those that deny purgatory,
  It locally contains or Heaven or hell;
  There's no third place in 't.

DUCHESS. How do you affect it?

ANTONIO. My banishment, feeding my melancholy,
  Would often reason thus.

DUCHESS. Pray, let's hear it.

ANTONIO. Say a man never marry, nor have children,
  What takes that from him? only the bare name
  Of being a father, or the weak delight
  To see the little wanton ride a-cock-horse
  Upon a painted stick, or hear him chatter
  Like a taught starling.

DUCHESS. Fie, fie, what's all this?
  One of your eyes is blood-shot; use my ring to 't,
  They say 'tis very sovereign: 'twas my wedding-ring.
  And I did vow never to part with it
  But to my second husband.

ANTONIO. You have parted with it now.

DUCHESS. Yes, to help your eye-sight.

ANTONIO. You have made me stark blind.

DUCHESS. How?

ANTONIO. There is a saucy and ambitious devil
  Is dancing in this circle.

DUCHESS. Remove him.

ANTONIO. HOW?

DUCHESS. There needs small conjuration, when your finger
   May do it: thus; is it fit?

                         [*She puts the ring upon his finger; he kneels*

ANTONIO. What said you?

DUCHESS. Sir,
   This goodly roof of yours is too low built;
   I cannot stand upright in 't nor discourse,
   Without I raise it higher: raise yourself;
   Or, if you please, my hand to help you: so.     [*Raises him*

ANTONIO. Ambition, madam, is a great man's madness,
   That is not kept in chains and close-pent rooms,
   But in fair lightsome lodgings, and is girt
   With the wild noise of prattling visitants,
   Which makes it lunatic beyond all cure.
   Conceive not I am so stupid but I aim
   Whereto your favors tend: but he's a fool
   That, being a-cold, would thrust his hands i' the fire
   To warm them.

DUCHESS. So, now the ground's broke,
   You may discover what a wealthy mine
   I make you lord of.

ANTONIO. O my unworthiness!

DUCHESS. You were ill to sell yourself:
   This darkening of your worth is not like that
   Which tradesmen use i' the city; their false lights
   Are to rid bad wares off: and I must tell you,
   If you will know where breathes a complete man
   (I speak it without flattery), turn your eyes,
   And progress through yourself.

ANTONIO. Were there nor Heaven nor hell,
   I would be honest: I have long served virtue,
   And ne'er ta'en wages of her.

DUCHESS. Now she pays it.
   The misery of us that are borm great!
   We are forced to woo, because none dare woo us;
   And as a tyrant doubles with his words,
   And fearfully equivocates, so we
   Are forced to express our violent passions
   In riddles and in dreams, and leave the path

Of simple virtue, which was never made
To seem the thing it is not. Go, go brag
You have left me heartless; mine is in your bosom:
I hope 'twill multiply love there. You do tremble:
Make not your heart so dead a piece of flesh,
To fear more than to love me. Sir, be confident:
What is 't distracts you? This is flesh and blood, sir;
'Tis not the figure cut in alabaster
Kneels at my husband's tomb. Awake, awake, man!
I do here put off all vain ceremony,
And only do appear to you a young widow
That claims you for her husband, and, like a widow,
I use but half a blush in 't.
ANTONIO. Truth speak for me;
　I will remain the constant sanctuary
　Of your good name.
DUCHESS. I thank you, gentle love:
　And 'cause you shall not come to me in debt,
　Being now my steward, here upon your lips
　I sign your *Quietus est.*[13] This you should have begged now:
　I have seen children oft eat sweetmeats thus,
　As fearful to devour them too soon.
ANTONIO. But for your brothers?
DUCHESS. Do not think of them:
　All discord without this circumference
　Is only to be pitied, and not feared:
　Yet, should they know it, time will easily
　Scatter the tempest.
ANTONIO. These words would be mine,
　And all the parts you have spoke, if some part of it
　Would not have savored flattery.
DUCHESS. Kneel.

CARIOLA *comes from behind the arras.*

ANTONIO. Ha!
DUCHESS. Be not amazed; this woman's of my counsel:
　I have heard lawyers say, a contract in a chamber
　*Per verba presenti* is absolute marriage.

___
[13] Discharge.

*She and* ANTONIO *kneel.*

Bless, Heaven, this sacred gordian, which let violence
    Never untwine!
ANTONIO. And may our sweet affections, like the spheres,
    Be still in motion!
DUCHESS. Quickening, and make
    The like soft music!
ANTONIO. That we may imitate the loving palms,
    Best emblem of a peaceful marriage,
    That never bore fruit, divided!
DUCHESS. What can the church force more?
ANTONIO. That fortune may not know an accident,
    Either of joy or sorrow, to divide
    Our fixéd wishes!
DUCHESS. How can the church build faster?
    We now are man and wife, and 'tis the church
    That must but echo this.—Maid, stand apart:
    I now am blind.
ANTONIO. What's your conceit in this?
DUCHESS. I would have you lead your fortune by the hand
    Unto your marriage bed
    (You speak in me this, for we now are one):
    We'll only lie, and talk together, and plot
    To appease my humorous[14] kindred; and if you please,
    Like the old tale in Alexander and Lodowick,[15]
    Lay a naked sword between us, keep us chaste.
    O, let me shroud my blushes in your bosom,
    Since 'tis the treasury of all my secrets!

*Exeunt* DUCHESS *and* ANTONIO.

CARIOLA. Whether the spirit of greatness or of woman
    Reign most in her, I know not; but it shows
    A fearful madness: I owe her much of pity.                [*Exit*

---

[14] Having "humors" or moods.
[15] The heroes of an English ballad based on the medieval tale *Amis and Amiloun;*
    extraordinarily faithful friends who look alike. One friend marries a prin-
    cess in behalf of the other but places a naked sword between himself and
    the bride in the marriage bed.

# ACT II

## SCENE I: *An apartment in the palace of the* DUCHESS.

*Enter* BOSOLA *and* CASTRUCCIO.

BOSOLA. You say you would fain be taken for an eminent courtier?

CASTRUCCIO. 'Tis the very main of my ambition.

BOSOLA. Let me see: you have a reasonable good face for 't already, and your nightcap expresses your ears sufficient largely. I would have you learn to twirl the strings of your band with a good grace, and in a set speech, at the end of every sentence, to hum three or four times, or blow your nose till it smart again, to recover your memory. When you come to be a president in criminal causes, if you smile upon a prisoner, hang him, but if you frown upon him and threaten him, let him be sure to scape the gallows.

CASTRUCCIO. I would be a very merry president.

BOSOLA. Do not sup o' nights; 'twill beget you an admirable wit.

CASTRUCCIO. Rather it would make me have a good stomach to quarrel; for they say, your roaring boys[16] eat meat seldom, and that makes them so valiant. But how shall I know whether the people take me for an eminent fellow?

BOSOLA. I will teach a trick to know it: give out you lie a–dying, and if you hear the common people curse you, be sure you are taken for one of the prime nightcaps.[17] [*Enter an* OLD LADY] You come from painting now.

---

[16] Bullies.

[17] Lawyers.

OLD LADY. From what?

BOSOLA. Why, from your scurvy face-physic. To behold thee
not painted inclines somewhat near a miracle; these in thy face
here were deep ruts and foul sloughs the last progress.[18] There
was a lady in France that, having had the small-pox, flayed the
skin off her face to make it more level; and whereas before she
looked like a nutmeg-grater, after she resembled an abortive
hedge-hog.

OLD LADY. Do you call this painting?

OLD LADY. No no, but you call it careening of an old morphewed
lady, to make her disembogue[19] again: there's rough-cast phrase
to your plastic.

OLD LADY. It seems you are well acquainted with my closet.

BOSOLA. One would suspect it for a shop of witchcraft, to find in it
the fat of serpents, spawn of snakes, Jews' spittle, and their young
children's ordure; and all these for the face. I would sooner eat a
dead pigeon taken from the soles of the feet of one sick of the
plague than kiss one of you fasting. Here are two of you, whose
sin of your youth is the very patrimony of the physician; makes
him renew his foot-cloth with the spring, and change his high-
priced courtezan with the fall of the leaf. I do wonder you do not
loathe yourselves. Observe my meditation now.

What thing is in this outward form of man
To be beloved? We account it ominous,
If nature do produce a colt, or lamb,
A fawn, or goat, in any limb resembling
A man, and fly from 't as a prodigy:
 Man stands amazed to see his deformity
 In any other creature but himself.
But in our own flesh, though we bear diseases
Which have their true names only ta'en from beasts,—
As the most ulcerous wolf and swinish measle,—
Though we are eaten up of lice and worms,
And though continually we bear about us
A rotten and dead body, we delight
To hide it in rich tissue: all our fear,
Nay, all our terror, is lest our physician
Should put us in the ground to be made sweet.—

---

[18] As though a state procession had driven across it.
[19] Morphewed: scaly; disembogue: empty.

Your wife's gone to Rome: you two couple, and get you to
    the wells at Lucca to recover your aches. I have other work
    on foot.

*Exeunt* CASTRUCCIO *and* OLD LADY.

I observe our duchess
Is sick a-days, she pukes, her stomach seethes,
The fins of her eye-lids look most teeming blue,
She wanes i' the cheek, and waxes fat i' the flank,
And, contrary to our Italian fashion,
Wears a loose-bodied gown: there's somewhat in 't.
I have a trick may chance discover it,
A pretty one; I have bought some apricocks,
The first our spring yields.

*Enter* ANTONIO *and* DELIO.

DELIO. And so long since married!
    You amaze me.
ANTONIO. Let me seal your lips for ever:
    For, did I think that any thing but the air
    Could carry these words from you, I would wish
    You had no breath at all.—Now, sir, in your contemplation?
    You are studying to become a great wise fellow.
BOSOLA. O, sir, the opinion of wisdom is a foul tether that runs
    all over a man's body: if simplicity direct us to have no evil, it
    directs us to a happy being; for the subtlest folly proceeds from
    the subtlest wisdom: let me be simply honest.
ANTONIO. I do understand your inside.
BOSOLA. Do you so?
ANTONIO. Because you would not seem to appear to the world
    Puffed up with your preferment, you continue
    This out-of-fashion melancholy: leave it, leave it.
BOSOLA. Give me leave to be honest in any phrase, in any
    compliment whatsoever. Shall I confess myself to you? I look
    no higher than I can reach: they are the gods that must ride
    on winged horses. A lawyer's mule of a slow pace will both
    suit my disposition and business; for, mark me, when a man's
    mind rides faster than his horse can gallop, they quickly both
    tire.
ANTONIO. You would look up to Heaven, but I think
    The devil, that rules i' the air, stands in your light.

BOSOLA. O, sir, you are lord of the ascendant, chief man with the duchess; a duke was your cousin-german[20] removed. Say you are lineally descended from King Pepin, or he himself, what of this? search the heads of the greatest rivers in the world, you shall find them but bubbles of water. Some would think the souls of princes were brought forth by some more weighty cause than those of meaner persons: they are deceived, there's the same hand to them; the like passions sway them; the same reason that makes a vicar to go to law for a tithe-pig, and undo his neighbors, makes them spoil a whole province, and batter down goodly cities with the cannon.

*Enter* DUCHESS *and* LADIES.

DUCHESS. Your arm, Antonio: do I not grow fat?
I am exceeding short-winded.—Bosola,
I would have you, sir, provide for me a litter;
Such a one as the Duchess of Florence rode in.
BOSOLA. The duchess used one when she was great with child.
DUCHESS. I think she did.—Come hither, mend my ruff;
Here, when? thou art such a tedious lady; and
Thy breath smells of lemon-pills; would thou hadst done!
Shall I swoon under thy fingers! I am
So troubled with the mother![21]
BOSOLA. [Aside] I fear too much.
DUCHESS. I have heard you say that the French courtiers
Wear their hats on 'fore the king.
ANTONIO. I have seen it.
DUCHESS. In the presence?
ANTONIO. Yes.
DUCHESS. Why should not we bring up that fashion!
'Tis ceremony more than duty that consists
In the removing of a piece of felt:
Be you the example to the rest o' the court;
Put on your hat first.
ANTONIO. You must pardon me:
I have seen, in colder countries than in France,
Nobles stand bare to the prince; and the distinction
Methought showed reverently.
BOSOLA. I have a present for your grace.

---

[20] First cousin.
[21] The effects of female hormones.

DUCHESS. For me, sir?

BOSOLA. Apricocks, madam.

DUCHESS. O, sir, where are they?
  I have heard of none to-year.

BOSOLA. [Aside] Good; her color rises.

DUCHESS. Indeed, I thank you: they are wondrous fair ones.
  What an unskilful fellow is our gardener!
  We shall have none this month.

BOSOLA. Will not your grace pare them?

DUCHESS. No: they taste of musk, methinks; indeed they do.

BOSOLA. I know not: yet I wish your grace had pared 'em.

DUCHESS. Why?

BOSOLA. I forgot to tell you, the knave gardener,
  Only to raise his profit by them the sooner,
  Did ripen them in horse-dung.

DUCHESS. O, you jest—
  You shall judge: pray taste one.

ANTONIO. Indeed, madam,
  I do not love the fruit.

DUCHESS. Sir, you are loth
  To rob us of our dainties: 'tis a delicate fruit;
  They say they are restorative.

BOSOLA. 'Tis a pretty art,
  This grafting.

DUCHESS. 'Tis so; bettering of nature.

BOSOLA. To make a pippin grow upon a crab,
  A damson[22] on a blackthorn. — [Aside] How greedily she eats
    them!
  A whirlwind strike off these bawd farthingales![23]
  For, but for that and the loose-bodied gown,
  I should have discovered apparently
  The young springal[24] cutting a caper in her belly.

DUCHESS. I thank you, Bosola: they are right good ones,
  If they do not make me sick.

ANTONIO. How now, madam!

DUCHESS. This green fruit and my stomach are not friends:
  How they swell me!

BOSOLA. [Aside] Nay, you are too much swelled already.

---

[22] Plum.
[23] Hooped petticoats.
[24] Stripling, young man.

DUCHESS. O, I am in an extreme cold sweat!

BOSOLA. I am very sorry.

DUCHESS. Lights to my chamber!—O good Antonio, I fear I am
    undone!

DELIO. Lights there, lights!

*Exeunt* DUCHESS *and* LADIES.—Exit, *on the other side,* BOSOLA.

ANTONIO. O my trusty Delio, we are lost!
    I fear she's fall'n in labor; and there's left
    No time for her remove.

DELIO. Have you prepared
    Those ladies to attend her? and procured
    That politic safe conveyance for the midwife
    Your duchess plotted?

ANTONIO. I have.

DELIO. Make use, then, of this forced occasion:
    Give out that Bosola hath poisoned her
    With these apricocks; that will give some color
    For her keeping close.

ANTONIO. Fie, fie, the physicians
    Will then flock to her.

DELIO. For that you may pretend
    She'll use some prepared antidote of her own,
    Lest the physicians should re-poison her.

ANTONIO. I am lost in amazement: I know not what to think on 't.

                                                              [*Exeunt*


# SCENE II

## *A hall in the same palace.*

*Enter* BOSOLA.

BOSOLA. So, so, there's no question but her techiness and most
    vulturous eating of the apricocks are apparent signs of breed-
    ing.

*Enter an* OLD LADY.

OLD LADY. Now? I am in haste, sir.

BOSOLA. There was a young waiting-woman had a monstrous desire
    to see the glass-house—

OLD LADY. Nay, pray let me go.

BOSOLA. And it was only to know what strange instrument it was should swell up a glass to the fashion of a woman's belly.

OLD LADY. I will hear no more of the glass-house. You are still abusing women?

BOSOLA. Who, I? no; only, by the way now and then, mention your frailties. The orange-tree bears ripe and green fruit and blossoms all together; and some of you give entertainment for pure love, but more for more precious reward. The lusty spring smells well; but drooping autumn tastes well. If we have the same golden showers that rained in the time of Jupiter the thunderer, you have the same Danaës[25] still, to hold up their laps to receive them. Didst thou never study the mathematics?

OLD LADY. What's that, sir?

BOSOLA. Why to know the trick how to make a many lines meet in one centre. Go, go, give your foster-daughters good counsel: tell them, that the devil takes delight to hang at a woman's girdle, like a false rusty watch, that she cannot discern how the time passes.

Exit OLD LADY. *Enter* ANTONIO, DELIO, RODERIGO, *and* GRISOLAN.

ANTONIO. Shut up the court-gates.

RODERIGO. Why, sir? what's the danger?

ANTONIO. Shut up the posterns presently, and call
    All the officers o' the court.

GRISOLAN. I shall instantly.                                    [*Exit*

ANTONIO. Who keeps the key o' the park-gate?

RODERIGO. Forobosco.

ANTONIO. Let him bring 't presently.

*Re-enter* GRISOLAN *with* SERVANTS.

1ST SERVANT. O, gentlemen o' the court, the foul treason!

BOSOLA. [Aside] If that these apricocks should be poisoned now, Without my knowledge!

1ST SERVANT. There was taken even now a Switzer[26] in the duchess's bed-chamber—

2ND SERVANT. A Switzer!

---

[25] Jupiter (or Zeus) wooed the maiden Danaë by transforming himself into a golden shower, which dropped into her lap.

[26] Swiss.

1ST SERVANT. With a pistol in his great cod-piece.[27]

BOSOLA. Ha, ha, ha!

1ST SERVANT. The cod-piece was the case for 't.

2ND SERVANT. There was a cunning traitor: who would have searched his cod-piece?

1ST SERVANT. True, if he had kept out of the ladies' chambers: and all the moulds of his buttons were leaden bullets.

2ND SERVANT. O wicked cannibal! a firelock in 's cod-piece!

1ST SERVANT. 'Twas a French plot, upon my life.

2ND SERVANT. To see what the devil can do!

ANTONIO. Are all the officers here?

SERVANTS. We are.

ANTONIO. Gentlemen,
   We have lost much plate you know; and but this evening
   Jewels, to the value of four thousand ducats,
   Are missing in the duchess's cabinet.
   Are the gates shut?

SERVANTS. Yes.

ANTONIO. 'Tis the duchess's pleasure
   Each officer be locked into his chamber
   Till the sun-rising; and to send the keys
   Of all their chests and of their outward doors
   Into her bed-chamber. She is very sick.

RODERIGO. At her pleasure.

ANTONIO. She entreats you take 't not ill: the innocent
   Shall be the more approved by it.

BOSOLA. Gentlemen o' the wood-yard, where's your Switzer now?

1ST SERVANT. By this hand, 'twas credibly reported by one o' the blackguard.

*Exeunt all except* ANTONIO *and* DELIO.

DELIO. How fares it with the duchess? ANTONIO. She's exposed
   Unto the worst of torture, pain and fear.

DELIO. Speak to her all happy comfort.

ANTONIO. How I do play the fool with mine own danger!
   You are this night, dear friend, to post to Rome:
   My life lies in your service.

DELIO. Do not doubt me.

ANTONIO. O, 'tis far from me: and yet fear presents me

---

[27] An ornamented flap concealing the opening in the breeches.

Somewhat that looks like danger.
DELIO. Believe it,
  'Tis but the shadow of your fear, no more:
  How superstitiously we mind our evils!
  The throwing down salt, or crossing of a hare,
  Bleeding at nose, the stumbling of a horse,
  Or singing of a cricket, are of power
  To daunt whole man in us. Sir, fare you well:
  I wish you all the joys of a blessed father:
  And, for my faith, lay this unto your breast,—
  Old friends, like old swords, still are trusted best.     [Exit

*Enter* CARIOLA.

CARIOLA. Sir, you are the happy father of a son:
  Your wife commends him to you.
ANTONIO. Blessed comfort!—
  For Heaven's sake tend her well: I'll presently
  Go set a figure for 's nativity.[28]     [Exeunt

# SCENE III

## *The court of the same palace.*

*Enter* BOSOLA, *with a dark lantern.*

BOSOLA. Sure I did hear a woman shriek: list, ha!
  And the sound came, if I received it right,
  From the duchess's lodgings. There's some stratagem
  In the confining all our courtiers
  To their several wards: I must have part of it;
  My intelligence will freeze else. List, again!
  It may be 'twas the melancholy bird,
  Best friend of silence and of solitariness,
  The owl, that screamed so.—Ha! Antonio!

*Enter* ANTONIO.

ANTONIO. I heard some noisxe.—Who's there? what art thou?
speak.

---

[28] Cast a horoscope for the newborn baby.

BOSOLA. Antonio, put not your face nor body
　　To such a forced expression of fear:
　　I am Bosola, your friend.
ANTONIO. Bosola! —
　　[*Aside*] This mole does undermine me.—Heard you not
　　A noise even now?
BOSOLA. From whence?
ANTONIO. From the duchess's lodging.
BOSOLA. Not I: did you?
ANTONIO. I did, or else I dreamed.
BOSOLA. Let's walk towards it.
ANTONIO. No: it may be 'twas
　　But the rising of the wind.
BOSOLA. Very likely.
　　Methinks 'tis very cold, and yet you sweat:
　　You look wildly.
ANTONIO. I have been setting a figure
　　For the duchess's jewels.
BOSOLA. Ah, and how falls your question?
　　Do you find it radical?[29]
ANTONIO. What's that to you?
　　'Tis rather to be questioned what design,
　　When all men were commanded to their lodgings,
　　Makes you a night-walker.
BOSOLA. In sooth, I'll tell you:
　　Now all the court's asleep, I thought the devil
　　Had least to do here; I came to say my prayers;
　　And if it do offend you I do so,
　　You are a fine courtier.
ANTONIO. [*Aside*] This fellow will undo me. —
　　You gave the duchess apricocks to-day:
　　Pray Heaven they were not poisoned!
BOSOLA. Poisoned! A Spanish fig
　　For the imputation.
ANTONIO. Traitors are ever confident
　　Till they are discovered. There were jewels stol'n too:
　　In my conceit, none are to be suspected
　　More than yourself.
BOSOLA. You are a false steward.

---

[29] Fit to be judged.

ANTONIO. Saucy slave, I'll pull thee up by the roots.

BOSOLA. May be the ruin will crush you to pieces.

ANTONIO. You are an impudent snake indeed, sir:
  Are you scarce warm, and do you show your sting?
  You libel well, sir.

BOSOLA. No, sir: copy it out,
  And I will set my hand to 't.

ANTONIO. [Aside] My nose bleeds.
  One that were superstitious would count
  This ominous, when it merely comes by chance:
  Two letters, that are wrote here for my name,
  Are drowned in blood!
  Mere accident—For you, sir, I'll take order
  I' the morn you shall be safe: — [Aside] 'tis that must color
  Her lying-in:—sir, this door you pass not:
  I do not hold it fit that you come near
  The duchess's lodgings, till you have quit yourself —
  [Aside] The great are like the base, nay, they are the same,
  When they seek shameful ways to avoid shame.        [Exit

BOSOLA. Antonio hereabout did drop a paper:—
  Some of your help, false friend:—O, here it is.
  What's here? a child's nativity calculated! [Reads]
  "The duchess was delivered of a son, 'tween the hours twelve
    and one in the night, Anno Dom. 1504,"—that's this year—
    "decimo non Decembris"—that's this night,—"taken according
    to the meridian of Malfi,"—that's our duchess: happy dis-
    covery! -"The lord of the first house being combust in the
    ascendant, signifies short life; and Mars being in a human
    sign, joined to the tail of the Dragon, in the eighth house,
    doth threaten a violent death. Coetera non scrutantur"[30]
  Why, now 'tis most apparent: this precise fellow
  Is the duchess's bawd:[31]— I have it to my wish!
  This is a parcel of intelligency
  Our courtiers were cased up for: it needs must follow
  That I must be committed on pretence
  Of poisoning her; which I'll endure, and laugh at.
  If one could find the father now! but that
  Time will discover. Old Castruccio

---

[30] The rest is not investigated.
[31] Pander.

I' the morning posts to Rome: by him I'll send
A letter that shall make her brothers' galls
O'erflow their livers. This was a thrifty way.
Though lust do mask in ne'er so strange disguise,
She's oft found witty, but is never wise.                    [*Exit*

## SCENE IV

### *An apartment in the palace of the* CARDINAL *at Rome.*

*Enter* CARDINAL *and* JULIA.

CARDINAL. Sit: thou art my best of wishes. Prithee, tell me
  What trick didst thou invent to come to Rome
  Without thy husband.
JULIA. Why, my lord, I told him
  I came to visit an old anchorite
  Here for devotion.
CARDINAL. Thou art a witty false one,—
  I mean, to him.
JULIA. You have prevailed with me
  Beyond my strongest thoughts: I would not now
  Find you inconstant.
CARDINAL. Do not put yourself
  To such a voluntary torture, which proceeds
  Out of your own guilt.
JULIA. How, my lord!
CARDINAL. You fear
  My constancy, because you have approved
  Those giddy and wild turnings in yourself.
JULIA. Did you e'er find them?
CARDINAL. Sooth, generally for women,
  A man might strive to make glass malleable,
  Ere he should make them fixèd.
JULIA. So, my lord.
CARDINAL. We had need go borrow that fantastic glass
  Invented by Galileo the Florentine
  To view another spacious world i' the moon,
  And look to find a constant woman there.

JULIA. This is very well, my lord.
CARDINAL. Why do you weep?
  Are tears your justification? the self-same tears
  Will fall into your husband's bosom, lady,
  With a loud protestation that you love him
  Above the world. Come, I'll love you wisely,
  That's jealousy; since I am very certain
  You cannot make me cuckold.
JULIA. I'll go home
  To my husband.
CARDINAL. You may thank me, lady,
  I have taken you off your melancholy perch,
  Bore you upon my fist, and showed you game,
  And let you fly at it.—I pray thee, kiss me.—
  When thou wast with thy husband, thou wast watched
  Like a tame elephant:—still you are to thank me: —
  Thou hadst only kisses from him and high feeding;
  But what delight was that? 'twas just like one
  That hath a little fingering on the lute,
  Yet cannot tune it:—still you are to thank me.
JULIA. You told me of a piteous wound i' the heart
  And a sick liver, when you wooed me first,
  And spake like one in physic.
CARDINAL. Who's that?—

### Enter SERVANT.

  Rest firm, for my affection to thee,
  Lightning moves slow to 't.
SERVANT. Madam, a gentleman,
  That's come post from Malfi, desires to see you.
CARDINAL. Let him enter: I'll withdraw.                    [Exit
SERVANT. He says
  Your husband, old Castruccio, is come to Rome,
  Most pitifully tired with riding post.                   [Exit

### Enter DELIO.

JULIA. [Aside] Signior Delio! 'tis one of my old suitors.
DELIO. I was bold to come and see you.
JULIA. Sir, you are welcome.
DELIO. Do you lie here?
JULIA. Sure, your own experience

Will satisfy you no: our Roman prelates
Do not keep lodging for ladies.
DELIO. Very well:
  I have brought you no commendations from your husband,
  For I know none by him.
JULIA. I hear he's come to Rome.
DELIO. I never knew man and beast, of a horse and a knight,
  So weary of each other: if he had had a good back,
  He would have undertook to have borne his horse,
  His breech was so pitifully sore.
JULIA. Your laughter
  Is my pity.
DELIO. Lady, I know not whether
  You want money, but I have brought you some.
JULIA. From my husband?
DELIO. No, from mine own allowance.
JULIA. I must hear the condition, ere I be bound to take it.
DELIO. Look on 't, 'tis gold: hath it not a fine color?
JULIA. I have a bird more beautiful.
DELIO. Try the sound on 't.
JULIA. A lute-string far exceeds it:
  It hath no smell, like cassia or civet;
  Nor is it physical, though some fond doctors
  Persuade us seethe 't in cullises.[32] I'll tell you,
  This is a creature bred by-

                    Re-enter SERVANT.

SERVANT. Your husband's come,
  Hath delivered a letter to the Duke of Calabria
  That, to my thinking, hath put him out of his wits.        [*Exit*
JULIA. Sir, you hear:
  Pray, let me know your business and your suit
  As briefly as can be.
DELIO. With good speed: I would wish you,
  At such time as you are non-resident
  With your husband, my mistress.
JULIA. Sir, I'll go ask my husband if I shall,
  And straight return your answer.                           [*Exit*

---

[32] Strong broths. The old recipe-books recommend "pieces of gold" among
  the ingredients.

DELIO. Very fine!
Is this her wit, or honesty, that speaks thus?
I heard one say the duke was highly moved
With a letter sent from Malfi. I do fear
Antonio is betrayed: how fearfully
Shows his ambition now! unfortunate fortune!
They pass through whirlpools, and deep woes do shun,
Who the event weigh ere the action's done.          [*Exit*

# SCENE V

## *Another apartment in the same palace.*

*Enter* CARDINAL *and* FERDINAND *with a letter.*

FERDINAND. I have this night digged up a mandrake.
CARDINAL. Say you?
FERDINAND. And I am grown mad with 't.
CARDINAL. What's the prodigy?
FERDINAND. Read there,—a sister damned: she's loose i' the hilts;
Grown a notorious strumpet.
CARDINAL. Speak lower.
FERDINAND. Lower!
Rogues do not whisper 't now, but seek to publish 't
(As servants do the bounty of their lords)
Aloud; and with a covetous searching eye,
To mark who note them. O, confusion seize her!
She hath had most cunning bawds to serve her turn,
And more secure conveyances for lust
Than towns of garrison for service.
CARDINAL. Is 't possible?
Can this be certain?
FERDINAND. Rhubarb, O, for rhubarb
To purge this choler! here's the cursèd day
To prompt my memory; and here 't shall stick
Till of her bleeding heart I make a sponge
To wipe it out.
CARDINAL. Why do you make yourself
So wild a tempest?
FERDINAND. Would I could be one,

That I might toss her palace 'bout her ears,
Root up her goodly forests, blast her meads,
And lay her general territory as waste
As she hath done her honors.

CARDINAL. Shall our blood,
The royal blood of Aragon and Castile,
Be thus attainted?

FERDINAND. Apply desperate physic:
We must not now use balsamum, but fire,
The smarting cupping-glass, for that's the mean
To purge infected blood, such blood as hers.
There is a kind of pity in mine eye,—
I'll give it to my handkercher; and now 'tis here,
I'll bequeath this to her bastard.

CARDINAL. What to do?

FERDINAND. Why, to make soft lint for his mother's wounds,
When I have hewed her to pieces.

CARDINAL. Cursèd creature!
Unequal nature, to place women's hearts
So far upon the left side!

FERDINAND. Foolish men,
That e'er will trust their honor in a bark
Made of so slight weak bulrush as is woman,
Apt every minute to sink it!

CARDINAL. Thus
Ignorance, when it hath purchased honor,
It cannot wield it.

FERDINAND. Methinks I see her laughing—
Excellent hyena! Talk to me somewhat quickly,
Or my imagination will carry me
To see her in the shameful act of sin.

CARDINAL. With whom?

FERDINAND. Happily with some strong-thighed bargeman,
Or one o' the woodyard that can quoit the sledge
Or toss the bar, or else some lovely squire
That carries coals up to her privy lodgings.

CARDINAL. You fly beyond your reason.

FERDINAND. Go to, mistress!
'Tis not your whore's milk that shall quench my wild fire,
But your whore's blood.

CARDINAL. How idly shows this rage, which carries you,

As men conveyed by witches through the air,
On violent whirlwinds! this intemperate noise
Fitly resembles deaf men's shrill discourse,
Who talk aloud, thinking all other men
To have their imperfection.

FERDINAND. Have not you
My palsy?

CARDINAL. Yes, but I can be angry
Without this rupture: there is not in nature
A thing that makes man so deformed, so beastly,
As doth intemperate anger. Chide yourself.
You have divers men who never yet expressed
Their strong desire of rest but by unrest,
By vexing of themselves. Come, put yourself
In tune.

FERDINAND. So I will only study to seem
The thing I am not. I could kill her now,
In you, or in myself; for I do think
It is some sin in us Heaven doth revenge
By her.

CARDINAL. Are you stark mad?

FERDINAND. I would have their bodies
Burnt in a coal-pit with the ventage stopped,
That their cursed smoke might not ascend to Heaven
Or dip the sheets they lie in in pitch or sulphur,
Wrap them in 't, and then light them like a match;
Or else to boil their bastard to a cullis,
And give 't his lecherous father to renew
The sin of his back.

CARDINAL. I'll leave you.

FERDINAND. Nay, I have done.
I am confident, had I been damned in hell,
And should have heard of this, it would have put me
Into a cold sweat. In, in; I'll go sleep.
Till I know who leaps my sister, I'll not stir:
That known, I'll find scorpions to string my whips,
And fix her in a general eclipse.              [*Exeunt*

# ACT III

## SCENE I: *An apartment in the palace of the* DUCHESS.

*Enter* ANTONIO *and* DELIO.

ANTONIO. Our noble friend, my most belovèd Delio!
O, you have been a stranger long at court;
Came you along with the Lord Ferdinand?

DELIO. I did, sir: and how fares your noble duchess?

ANTONIO. Right fortunately well: she's an excellent
Feeder of pedigrees; since you last saw her,
She hath had two children more, a son and daughter.

DELIO. Methinks 'twas yesterday: let me but wink,
And not behold your face, which to mine eye
Is somewhat leaner, verily I should dream
It were within this half hour.

ANTONIO. You have not been in law, friend Delio,
Nor in prison, nor a suitor at the court,
Nor begged the reversion of some great man's place,
Nor troubled with an old wife, which doth make
Your time so insensibly hasten.

DELIO. Pray, sir, tell me,
Hath not this news arrived yet to the ear
Of the lord cardinal?

ANTONIO. I fear it hath:
The Lord Ferdinand, that's newly come to court,
Doth bear himself right dangerously.

DELIO. Pray, why?

ANTONIO. He is so quiet that he seems to sleep

The tempest out, as dormice do in winter:
Those houses that are haunted are most still
Till the devil be up.

DELIO. What say the common people?

ANTONIO. The common rabble do directly say
  She is a strumpet.

DELIO. And your graver heads
  Which would be politic, what censure they?

ANTONIO. They do observe I grow to infinite purchase,
  The left hand way, and all suppose the duchess
  Would amend it, if she could; for, say they,
  Great princes, though they grudge their officers
  Should have such large and unconfinèd means
  To get wealth under them, will not complain,
  Lest thereby they should make them odious
  Unto the people; for other obligation
  Of love or marriage between her and me
  They never dream of.

DELIO. The Lord Ferdinand
  Is going to bed.

*Enter* DUCHESS, FERDINAND, *and* ATTENDANTS.

FERDINAND. I'll instantly to bed,
  For I am weary.—I am to bespeak
  A husband for you.

DUCHESS. For me, sir! pray, who is 't?

FERDINAND. The great Count Malatesti.

DUCHESS. Fie upon him!
  A count! he's a mere stick of sugar-candy;
  You may look quite through him. When I choose
  A husband, I will marry for your honor.

FERDINAND. You shall do well in 't.—How is 't, worthy Antonio?

DUCHESS. But, sir, I am to have private conference with you
  About a scandalous report is spread
  Touching mine honor.

FERDINAND. Let me be ever deaf to 't:
  One of Pasquil's paper bullets,[33] court-calumny,
  A pestilent air, which princes' palaces
  Are seldom purged of. Yet say that it were true,

---

[33] Scurrilous verses.

I pour it in your bosom, my fixed love
Would strongly excuse, extenuate, nay, deny
Faults, were they apparent in you. Go, be safe
In your own innocency.

DUCHESS. [*Aside*] O blessed comfort!
This deadly air is purged.

*Exeunt* DUCHESS, ANTONIO, DELIO, *and* ATTENDANTS.

FERDINAND. Her guilt treads on
Hot-burning coulters.

*Enter* BOSOLA.

Now, Bosola,
How thrives our intelligence?

BOSOLA. Sir, uncertainly:
'Tis rumored she hath had three bastards, but
By whom we may go read i' the stars.

FERDINAND. Why, some
Hold opinion all things are written there.

BOSOLA. Yes, if we could find spectacles to read them.
I do suspect there hath been some sorcery
Used on the duchess.

FERDINAND. Sorcery! to what purpose?

BOSOLA. To make her dote on some desertless fellow
She shames to acknowledge.

FERDINAND. Can your faith give way
To think there's power in potions or in charms,
To make us love whether we will or no?

BOSOLA. Most certainly.

FERDINAND. Away! these are mere gulleries, horrid things,
Invented by some cheating mountebanks
To abuse us. Do you think that herbs or charms
Can force the will? Some trials have been made
In this foolish practice, but the ingredients
Were lenitive poisons, such as are of force
To make the patient mad; and straight the witch
Swears by equivocation they are in love.
The witchcraft lies in her rank blood. This night
I will force confession from her. You told me
You had got, within these two days, a false key
Into her bed-chamber.

BOSOLA. I have.

FERDINAND. As I would wish.

BOSOLA. What do you intend to do?

FERDINAND. Can you guess?

BOSOLA. No.

FERDINAND. Do not ask, then:
   He that can compass me, and know my drifts,
   May say he hath put a girdle 'bout the world,
   And sounded all her quicksands.

BOSOLA. I do not
   Think so.

FERDINAND. What do you think, then, pray?

BOSOLA. That you are
   Your own chronicle too much, and grossly
   Flatter yourself.

FERDINAND. Give me thy hand; I thank thee:
   I never gave pension but to flatterers,
   Till I entertainèd thee. Farewell.
   That friend a great man's ruin strongly checks,
   Who rails into his belief all his defects.          [*Exeunt*

## SCENE II

### *The bed-chamber of the* DUCHESS.

*Enter* DUCHESS, ANTONIO, *and* CARIOLA.

DUCHESS. Bring me the casket hither, and the glass.—You get
   no lodging here tonight, my lord.

ANTONIO. Indeed, I must persuade one.

DUCHESS. Very good:
   I hope in time 'twill grow into a custom,
   That noblemen shall come with cap and knee
   To purchase a night's lodging of their wives.

ANTONIO. I must lie here.

DUCHESS. Must! you are a lord of misrule.

ANTONIO. Indeed, my rule is only in the night.

DUCHESS. To what use will you put me?

ANTONIO. We'll sleep together.

DUCHESS. Alas,

What pleasure can two lovers find in sleep!

CARIOLA. My lord, I lie with her often; and I know
    She'll much disquiet you.

ANTONIO. See, you are complained of.

CARIOLA. For she's the sprawling'st bedfellow.

ANTONIO. I shall like her the better for that.

CARIOLA. Sir, shall I ask you a question?

ANTONIO. Ay, pray thee, Cariola.

CARIOLA. Wherefore still, when you lie with my lady,
    Do you rise so early?

ANTONIO. Laboring men
    Count the clock oftenest, Cariola,
    Are glad when their task's ended.

DUCHESS. I'll stop your mouth.                 [*Kisses him*

ANTONIO. Nay, that's but one; Venus had two soft doves
    To draw her chariot; I must have another—

                               [*She kisses him again*

    When wilt thou marry, Cariola?

CARIOLA. Never, my lord.

ANTONIO. O, fie upon this single life! forego it.
    We read how Daphne, for her peevish flight,
    Became a fruitless bay-tree; Syrinx turned
    To the pale empty reed; Anaxarete
    Was frozen into marble: whereas those
    Which married, or proved kind unto their friends,
    Were by a gracious influence transhaped
    Into the olive, pomegranate, mulberry,
    Became flowers, precious stones, or eminent stars.

CARIOLA. This is a vain poetry: but I pray you tell me,
    If there were proposed me, wisdom, riches, and beauty,
    In three several young men, which should I choose.

ANTONIO. 'Tis a hard question: this was Paris's case,
    And he was blind in 't, and there was great cause;
    For how was 't possible he could judge right,
    Having three amorous goddesses in view,
    And they stark naked? 'twas a motion
    Were able to benight the apprehension
    Of the severest counsellor of Europe.
    Now I look on both your faces so well formed,
    It puts me in mind of a question I would ask.

CARIOLA. What is 't?

ANTONIO. I do wonder why hard-favored ladies,
  For the most part, keep worse-favored waiting-women
  To attend them, and cannot endure fair ones.
DUCHESS. O, that's soon answered.
  Did you ever in your life know an ill painter
  Desire to have his dwelling next door to the shop
  Of an excellent picture-maker? 'twould disgrace
  His face-making, and undo him. I prithee,
  When were we so merry?—My hair tangles.
ANTONIO. Pray thee, Cariola, let's steal forth the room,
  And let her talk to herself: I have divers times
  Served her the like, when she hath chafed extremely.
  I love to see her angry. Softly, Cariola.

*Exeunt* ANTONIO *and* CARIOLA.

DUCHESS. Doth not the color of my hair 'gin to change?
  When I wax gray, I shall have all the court
  Powder their hair with arras,[34] to be like me.
  You have cause to love me; I entered you into my heart
  Before you would vouchsafe to call for the keys.

*Enter* FERDINAND *behind.*

  We shall one day have my brothers take you napping;
  Methinks his presence, being now in court,
  Should make you keep your own bed; but you'll say
  Love mixed with fear is sweetest. I'll assure you,
  You shall get no more children till my brothers
  Consent to be your gossips.[35] Have you lost your tongue?
  'Tis welcome:
  For know, whether I am doomed to live or die,
  I can do both like a prince.
FERDINAND. Die, then, quickly!          [Giving *her a poniard*
  Virtue, where art thou hid? what hideous thing
  Is it that doth eclipse thee?
DUCHESS. Pray, sir, hear me.
FERDINAND. Or is it true thou art but a bare name,
  And no essential thing?
DUCHESS. Sir,—

---

[34] Orrisroot, the rootstock of irises, used in perfumes.
[35] Godparents.

FERDINAND. Do not speak.

DUCHESS. No, sir:
  I will plant my soul in mine ears, to hear you.

FERDINAND. O most imperfect light of human reason,
  That mak'st us so unhappy to foresee
  What we can least prevent! Pursue thy wishes,
  And glory in them: there's in shame no comfort
  But to be past all bounds and sense of shame.

DUCHESS. I pray, sir, hear me: I am married.

FERDINAND. So!

DUCHESS. Happily, not to your liking: but for that,
  Alas, your shears do come untimely now
  To clip the bird's wing that's already flown!
  Will you see my husband?

FERDINAND. Yes, if I could change
  Eyes with a basilisk.

DUCHESS. Sure, you came hither
  By his confederacy.

FERDINAND. The howling of a wolf
  Is music to thee, screech-owl: prithee, peace.—
  Whate'er thou art that hast enjoyed my sister,
  For I am sure thou hear'st me, for thine own sake
  Let me not know thee. I came hither prepared
  To work thy discovery; yet am now persuaded
  It would beget such violent effects
  As would damn us both. I would not for ten millions
  I had beheld thee: therefore use all means
  I never may have knowledge of thy name;
  Enjoy thy lust still, and a wretched life,
  On that condition.—And for thee, vile woman,
  If thou do wish thy lecher may grow old
  In thy embracements, I would have thee build
  Such a room for him as our anchorites
  To holier use inhabit. Let not the sun
  Shine on him till he's dead; let dogs and monkeys
  Only converse with him, and such dumb things
  To whom nature denies use to sound his name;
  Do not keep a paraquito, lest she learn it;
  If thou do love him, cut out thine own tongue,
  Lest it bewray him.

DUCHESS. Why might not I marry?
  I have not gone about in this to create

Any new world or custom.

FERDINAND. Thou art undone;
    And thou hast ta'en that massy sheet of lead
    That hid thy husband's bones, and folded it
    About my heart.

DUCHESS. Mine bleeds for't.

FERDINAND. Thine! thy heart!
    What should I name 't unless a hollow bullet
    Filled with unquenchable wild-fire?

DUCHESS. YOU are in this
    Too strict; and were you not my princely brother,
    I would say, too wilful: my reputation
    Is safe.

FERDINAND. Dost thou know what reputation is?
    I'll tell thee,—to small purpose, since the instruction
    Comes now too late.
    Upon a time Reputation, Love, and Death,
    Would travel o'er the world; and it was concluded
    That they should part, and take three several ways.
    Death told them, they should find him in great battles,
    Or cities plagued with plagues: Love gives them counsel
    To inquire for him 'mongst unambitious shepherds,
    Where dowries were not talked of, and sometimes
    'Mongst quiet kindred that had nothing left
    By their dead parents: "Stay," quoth Reputation,
    "Do not forsake me; for it is my nature,
    If once I part from any man I meet,
    I am never found again." And so for you:
    You have shook hands with Reputation,
    And made him invisible. So, fare you well:
    I will never see you more.

DUCHESS. Why should only I,
    Of all the other princes of the world,
    Be cased up, like a holy relic? I have youth
    And a little beauty.

FERDINAND. So you have some virgins
    That are witches. I will never see thee more.     [*Exit*

        *Re-enter* ANTONIO *with a pistol, and* CARIOLA.

DUCHESS. YOU saw this apparition?

ANTONIO. Yes: we are
    Betrayed. How came he hither? I should turn

This to thee, for that.
CARIOLA. Pray, sir, do; and when
  That you have cleft my heart, you shall read there
  Mine innocence.
DUCHESS. That gallery gave him entrance.
ANTONIO. I would this terrible thing would come again,
  That, standing on my guard, I might relate
  My warrantable love.——

*She shows the poniard.*

Ha! what means this?
DUCHESS. He left this with me.
ANTONIO. And it seems did wish
  You would use it on yourself.
DUCHESS. His action
  Seemed to intend so much.
ANTONIO. This hath a handle to 't,
  As well as a point: turn it towards him,
  And so fasten the keen edge in his rank gall.

*Knocking within.*

How now! who knocks? more earthquakes?
DUCHESS. I stand
  As if a mine beneath my feet were ready
  To be blown up.
CARIOLA. 'Tis Bosola.
DUCHESS. Away!
  O misery! methinks unjust actions
  Should wear these masks and curtains, and not we.
  You must instantly part hence: I have fashioned it already.

*Exit* ANTONIO. *Enter* BOSOLA.

BOSOLA. The duke your brother is ta'en up in a whirlwind;
  Hath took horse, and 's rid post to Rome.
DUCHESS. So late?
BOSOLA. He told me, as he mounted into the saddle,
  You were undone.
DUCHESS. Indeed, I am very near it.
BOSOLA. What's the matter?
DUCHESS. Antonio, the master of our household,
  Hath dealt so falsely with me in 's accounts:

My brother stood engaged with me for money
Ta'en up of certain Neapolitan Jews,
And Antonio lets the bonds be forfeit.

BOSOLA. Strange! — [Aside] This is cunning.

DUCHESS. And hereupon
My brother's bills at Naples are protested
Against.—Call up our officers.

BOSOLA. I shall. [Exit

*Re-enter* ANTONIO.

DUCHESS. The place that you must fly to is Ancona:
Hire a house there; I'll send after you
My treasure and my jewels. Our weak safety
Runs upon enginous[36] wheels: short syllables
Must stand for periods. I must now accuse you
Of such a feignéd crime as Tasso calls
*Magnanima menzogna,* a noble lie,
'Cause it must shield our honors.—Hark! they are coming.

*Re-enter* BOSOLA *and* OFFICERS.

ANTONIO. Will your grace hear me?

DUCHESS. I have got well by you; you have yielded me
A million of loss: I am like to inherit
The people's curses for your stewardship.
You had the trick in audit-time to be sick,
Till I had signed your quietus;[37] and that cured you
Without help of a doctor.—Gentlemen,
I would have this man be an example to you all;
So shall you hold my favor; I pray, let him;
For he's done that, alas, you would not think of,
And, because I intend to be rid of him,
I mean not to publish.—Use your fortune elsewhere.

ANTONIO. I am strongly armed to brook my overthrow,
As commonly men bear with a hard year:
I will not blame the cause on 't; but do think
The necessity of my malevolent star
Procures this, not her humor. O, the inconstant
And rotten ground of service! you may see,

---

[36] Rapid.
[37] Here, death certificate; *Quietus* was used playfully in Act I, Scene I.

'Tis even like him, that in a winter night,
Takes a long slumber o'er a dying fire,
As loth to part from 't; yet parts thence as cold
As when he first sat down.

DUCHESS. We do confiscate,
Towards the satisfying of your accounts,
All that you have.

ANTONIO. I am all yours; and 'tis very fit
All mine should be so.

DUCHESS. So, sir, you have your pass.

ANTONIO. You may see, gentlemen, what 'tis to serve
A prince with body and soul.                    [*Exit*

BOSOLA. Here's an example for extortion: what moisture is drawn
out of the sea, when foul weather comes, pours down, and
runs into the sea again.

DUCHESS. I would know what are your opinions
Of this Antonio.

2ND OFFICER. He could not abide to see a pig's head gaping: I
thought your grace would find him a Jew.

3RD OFFICER. I would you had been his officer, for your own
sake.

4TH OFFICER. You would have had more money.

1ST OFFICER. He stopped his ears with black wool, and to those
came to him for money said he was thick of hearing.

2ND OFFICER. Some said he was an hermaphrodite, for he could
not abide a woman.

4TH OFFICER. How scurvy proud he would look when the treasury was full! Well, let him go.

1ST OFFICER. Yes, and the chippings of the butterfly after him,
to scour his gold chain.

DUCHESS. Leave us.

*Exeunt* OFFICERS.

What do you think of these?

BOSOLA. That these are rogues that in 's prosperity,
But to have waited on his fortune, could have wished
His dirty stirrup rivetted through their noses,
And followed after 's mule, like a bear in a ring;
Would have prostituted their daughters to his lust;
Made their first-born intelligencers; thought none happy
But such as were born under his blest planet,
And wore his livery: and do these lice drop off now?

Well, never look to have the like again:
He hath left a sort of flattering rogues behind him;
Their doom must follow. Princes pay flatterers
In their own money: flatterers dissemble their vices,
And they dissemble their lies; that's justice.
Alas, poor gentleman!

DUCHESS. Poor! he hath amply filled his coffers.

BOSOLA. Sure, he was too honest. Pluto, the god of riches,
When he's sent by Jupiter to any man,
He goes limping, to signify that wealth
That comes on God's name comes slowly; but when he's
    sent
On the devil's errand, he rides post and comes in by scuttles.[38]
Let me show you what a most unvalued jewel
You have in a wanton humor thrown away,
To bless the man shall find him. He was an excellent
Courtier and most faithful; a soldier that thought it
As beastly to know his own value too little
As devilish to acknowledge it too much.
Both his virtue and form deserved a far better fortune:
His discourse rather delighted to judge itself than show itself:
His breast was filled with all perfection,
And yet it seemed a private whispering-room,
It made so little noise of 't.

DUCHESS. But he was basely descended.

BOSOLA. Will you make yourself a mercenary herald,
Rather to examine men's pedigrees than virtues?
You shall want him:
For know an honest statesman to a prince
Is like a cedar planted by a spring;
The spring bathes the tree's root, the grateful tree
Rewards it with his shadow: you have not done so.
I would sooner swim to the Bermoothes[39] on
Two politicians' rotten bladders, tied
Together with an intelligencer's heartstring,
Than depend on so changeable a prince's favor.
Fare thee well, Antonio! since the malice of the world
Would needs down with thee, it cannot be said yet
That any ill happened unto thee, considering thy fall

---

[38] A quick run.
[39] Bermudas.

Was accompanied with virtue.

DUCHESS. O, you render me excellent music!

BOSOLA. Say you?

DUCHESS. This good one that you speak of is my husband.

BOSOLA. Do I not dream! can this ambitious age
   Have so much goodness in 't as to prefer
   A man merely for worth, without these shadows
   Of wealth and painted honors? possible?

DUCHESS. I have had three children by him.

BOSOLA. Fortunate lady!
   For you have made your private nuptial bed
   The humble and fair seminary of peace.
   No question but many an unbeneficed scholar
   Shall pray for you for this deed, and rejoice
   That some preferment in the world can yet
   Arise from merit. The virgins of your land
   That have no dowries shall hope your example
   Will raise them to rich husbands. Should you want
   Soldiers, 'twould make the very Turks and Moors
   Turn Christians, and serve you for this act.
   Last, the neglected poets of your time,
   In honor of this trophy of a man,
   Raised by that curious engine, your white hand,
   Shall thank you, in your grave, for 't; and make that
   More reverend than all the cabinets
   Of living princes. For Antonio.
   His fame shall likewise flow from many a pen,
   When heralds shall want coats to sell to men.

DUCHESS. As I taste comfort in this friendly speech,
   So would I find concealment.

BOSOLA. O, the secret of my prince,
   Which I will wear on the inside of my heart!

DUCHESS. You shall take charge of all my coin and jewels
   And follow him; for he retires himself
   To Ancona.

BOSOLA. So.

DUCHESS. Whither, within few days,
   I mean to follow thee.

BOSOLA. Let me think:
   I would wish your grace to feign a pilgrimage
   To our Lady of Loretto, scarce seven leagues

From fair Ancona; so may you depart
Your country with more honor, and your flight
Will seem a princely progress, retaining
Your usual train about you.

DUCHESS. Sir, your direction
Shall lead me by the hand.

CARIOLA. In my opinion,
She were better progress to the baths at Lucca,
Or go visit the Spa
In Germany; for, if you will believe me,
I do not like this jesting with religion,
This feignèd pilgrimage.

DUCHESS. Thou art a superstitious fool:
Prepare us instantly for our departure.
Past sorrows, let us moderately lament them;
For those to come, seek wisely to prevent them.

*Exeunt* DUCHESS *and* CARIOLA.

BOSOLA. A politician is the devil's quilted anvil;
He fashions all sins on him, and the blows
Are never heard: he may work in a lady's chamber,
As here for proof. What rests but I reveal
All to my lord? O, this base quality
Of intelligencer! why, every quality i' the world
Prefers but gain or commendation:
Now for this act I am certain to be raised,
And men that paint weeds to the life are praised.          [*Exit*

# SCENE III

## An apartment in the CARDINAL's palace at Rome.

*Enter* CARDINAL, FERDINAND, MALATESTI, PESCARA, DELIO,
*and* SILVIO.

CARDINAL. Must we turn soldier, then?

MALATESTI. The emperor,
Hearing your worth that way, ere you attained
This reverend garment, joins you in commission
With the right fortunate soldier the Marquis of Pescara,

And the famous Lannoy.

CARDINAL. He that had the honor
Of taking the French king prisoner?

MALATESTI. The same.
Here's a plot drawn for a new fortification
At Naples.

FERDINAND. This great Count Malatesti, I perceive,
Hath got employment?

DELIO. No employment, my lord;
A marginal note in the muster-book, that he is
A voluntary lord.

FERDINAND. He's no soldier.

DELIO. He has worn gunpowder in 's hollow tooth for the
toothache.

SILVIO. He comes to the leaguer[40] with a full intent
To eat fresh beef and garlic, means to stay
Till the scent be gone, and straight return to court.

DELIO. He hath read all the late service
As the city chronicle relates it;
And keeps two pewterers going, only to express
Battles in model.

SILVIO. Then he'll fight by the book.

DELIO. By the almanac, I think,
To choose good days and shun the critical;
That's his mistress's scarf.

SILVIO. Yes, he protests
He would do much for that taffeta.

DELIO. I think he would run away from a battle,
To save it from taking prisoner.

SILVIO. He is horribly afraid
Gunpowder will spoil the perfume on 't.

DELIO. I saw a Dutchman break his pate once
For calling him pot-gun; he made his head
Have a bore in 't like a musket.

SILVIO. I would he had made a touchhole to 't.
He is indeed a guarded sumpter-cloth,
Only for the remove of the court.

---

[40] Camp.

*Enter* BOSOLA.

PESCARA. Bosola arrived! what should be the business?
  Some falling-out amongst the cardinals.
  These factions amongst great men, they are like
  Foxes, when their heads are divided,
  They carry fire in their tails, and all the country
  About them goes to wreck for 't.
SILVIO. What's that Bosola?
DELIO. I knew him in Padua—a fantastical scholar, like such who
  study to know how many knots was in Hercules' club, of what
  color Achilles' beard was, or whether Hector were not troubled
  with the toothache. He hath studied himself half blear-eyed
  to know the true symmetry of Caesar's nose by a shoeing-horn;
  and this he did to gain the name of a speculative man.
PESCARA. Mark Prince Ferdinand:
  A very salamander lives in 's eye,
  To mock the eager violence of fire.
SILVIO. That cardinal hath made more bad faces with his oppres-
  sion than ever Michael Angelo made good ones: he lifts up's
  nose, like a foul porpoise before a storm.
PESCARA. The Lord Ferdinand laughs.
DELIO. Like a deadly cannon
  That lightens ere it smokes.
PESCARA. These are your true pangs of death,
  The pangs of life, that struggle with great statesmen.
DELIO. In such a deformed silence witches whisper their charms.
CARDINAL. Doth she make religion her riding-hood
  To keep her from the sun and tempest?
FERDINAND. That,
  That damns her. Methinks her fault and beauty,
  Blended together, show like leprosy,
  The whiter, the fouler. I make it a question
  Whether her beggarly brats were ever christened.
CARDINAL. I will instantly solicit the state of Ancona
  To have them banished.
FERDINAND. You are for Loretto:
  I shall not be at your ceremony; fare you well. ——
  Write to the Duke of Malfi, my young nephew
  She had by her first husband, and acquaint him

With 's mother's honesty.

BOSOLA. I will.

FERDINAND. Antonio!
 A slave that only smelled of ink and counters,
 And never in 's life looked like a gentleman,
 But in the audit-time.—Go, go presently,
 Draw me out an hundred and fifty of our horse,
 And meet me at the fort-bridge.     *[Exeunt*


# SCENE IV

## *The shrine of Our Lady of Loretto.*

*Enter* TWO PILGRIMS.

1ST PILGRIM. I have not seen a goodlier shrine than this;
 Yet I have visited many.

2ND PILGRIM. The Cardinal of Aragon
 Is this day to resign his cardinal's hat:
 His sister duchess likewise is arrived
 To pay her vow of pilgrimage. I expect
 A noble ceremony.

1ST PILGRIM. No question.—They come.

*Here the ceremony of the* CARDINAL'S *instalment, in the habit of a soldier, is performed by his delivering up his cross, hat, robes, and ring, at the shrine, and the investing of him with sword, helmet, shield, and spurs; then* ANTONIO, *the* DUCHESS, *and the* CHILDREN, *having presented themselves at the shrine, are, by a form of banishment in dumb-show expressed towards them by the* CARDINAL *and the state of Ancona, banished: during all which ceremony, this ditty is sung, to by divers churchmen.*


Arms and honors deck thy story,
To thy fame's eternal glory!
Adverse fortune ever fly thee;
No disastrous fate come nigh thee!
I alone will sing thy praises,

Whom to honor virtue raises;
And thy study, that divine is,
Bent to martial discipline is.
Lay aside all those robes lie by thee;
Crown thy arts with arms, they'll beautify thee.
O worthy of worthiest name, adorned in this manner,
Lead bravely thy forces on under war's warlike banner!
O, mayst thou prove fortunate in all martial courses!
Guide thou still by skill in arts and forces!
Victory attend thee nigh, whilst fame sings loud thy powers;
Triumphant conquest crown thy head, and blessings pour down
    showers!

*Exeunt all except the Two* PILGRIMS.

1ST PILGRIM. Here's a strange turn of state! who would have
    thought
    So great a lady would have matched herself
    Unto so mean a person? yet the cardinal
    Bears himself much too cruel.
2ND PILGRIM. They are banished.
1ST PILGRIM. But I would ask what power hath this state
    Of Ancona to determine of a free prince?
2ND PILGRIM. They are a free state, sir, and her brother showed
    How that the Pope, fore-hearing of her looseness,
    Hath seized into the protection of the church
    The dukedom which she held as dowager.
1ST PILGRIM. But by what justice?
2ND PILGRIM. Sure, I think by none,
    Only her brother's instigation.
1ST PILGRIM. What was it with such violence he took
    Off from her finger?
2ND PILGRIM. 'Twas her wedding-ring;
    Which he vowed shortly he would sacrifice
    To his revenge.
1ST PILGRIM. Alas, Antonio!
    If that a man be thrust into a well,
    No matter who sets hand to 't, his own weight
    Will bring him sooner to the bottom. Come, let's hence.
    Fortune makes this conclusion general,
    All things do help the unhappy man to fall.          [*Exeunt*

## SCENE V

### *Near Loretto.*

*Enter* DUCHESS, ANTONIO, CHILDREN, CARIOLA,
*and* SERVANTS.

DUCHESS. Banished Ancona!
ANTONIO. Yes, you see what power
  Lightens in great men's breath.
DUCHESS. Is all our train
  Shrunk to this poor remainder?
ANTONIO. These poor men,
  Which have got little in your service, vow
  To take your fortune: but your wiser buntings,[41]
  Now they are fledged, are gone.
DUCHESS. They have done wisely.
  This puts me in mind of death: physicians thus,
  With their hands full of money, use to give o'er
  Their patients.
ANTONIO. Right the fashion of the world:
  From decayed fortunes every flatterer shrinks;
  Men cease to build where the foundation sinks.
DUCHESS. I had a very strange dream tonight.
ANTONIO. What was 't?
DUCHESS. Methought I wore my coronet of state,
  And on a sudden all the diamonds
  Were changed to pearls.
ANTONIO. My interpretation
  Is, you'll weep shortly; for to me the pearls
  Do signify your tears.
DUCHESS. The birds that live i' the field
  On the wild benefit of nature live
  Happier than we; for they may choose their mates,
  And carol their sweet pleasures to the spring.

*Enter* BOSOLA *with a letter.*

BOSOLA. You are happily o'erta'en.
DUCHESS. From my brother?
BOSOLA. Yes, from the Lord Ferdinand your brother

---

[41] A bird that resembles a lark but does not possess its voice.

All love and safety.

DUCHESS. Thou dost blanch mischief,
    Wouldst make it white. See, see, like to calm weather
    At sea before a tempest, false hearts speak fair
    To those they intend most mischief.
    [Reads] "Send Antonio to me; I want his head in a business."
    A politic equivocation!
    He doth not want your counsel, but your head;
    That is, he cannot sleep till you be dead.
    And here's another pitfall that's strewed o'er
    With roses; mark it, 'tis a cunning one:
    [Reads] "I stand engaged for your husband for several debts at
    Naples: let not that trouble him; I had rather have his heart
      than his money":—
    And I believe so too.

BOSOLA. What do you believe?

DUCHESS. That he so much distrusts my husband's love,
    He will by no means believe his heart is with him
    Until he sees it: the devil is not cunning enough
    To circumvent us in riddles.

BOSOLA. Will you reject that noble and free league
    Of amity and love which I present you?

DUCHESS. Their league is like that of some politic kings,
    Only to make themselves of strength and power
    To be our after-ruin: tell them so.

BOSOLA. And what from you?

ANTONIO. Thus tell him; I will not come.

BOSOLA. And what of this?

ANTONIO. My brothers have dispersed
    Blood-hounds abroad; which till I hear are muzzled,
    No truce, though hatched with ne'er such politic skill,
    Is safe, that hangs upon our enemies' will.
    I'll not come at them.

BOSOLA. This proclaims your breeding:
    Every small thing draws a base mind to fear,
    As the adamant draws iron. Fare you well, sir:
    You shall shortly hear from 's.                    [Exit

DUCHESS. I suspect some ambush:
    Therefore by all my love I do conjure you
    To take your eldest son, and fly towards Milan.
    Let us not venture all this poor remainder
    In one unlucky bottom.

ANTONIO. You counsel safely.
  Best of my life, farewell, since we must part-Heaven hath a
    hand in 't; but no otherwise
  Then as some curious artist takes in sunder
  A clock or watch, when it is out of frame,
  To bring 't in better order.
DUCHESS. I know not which is best,
  To see you dead, or part with you.—Farewell, boy:
  Thou art happy that thou hast not understanding
  To know thy misery; for all our wit
  And reading brings us to a truer sense
  Of sorrow.—In the eternal church, sir,
  I do hope we shall not part thus.
ANTONIO. O, be of comfort!
  Make patience a noble fortitude,
  And think not how unkindly we are used:
  Man, like to cassia,[42] is proved best being bruised.
DUCHESS. Must I, like a slave-born Russian,
  Account it praise to suffer tyranny?
  And yet, O Heaven, thy heavy hand is in 't!
  I have seen my little boy oft scourge his top,
  And compared myself to 't: naught made me e'er
  Go right but Heaven's scourge-stick.
ANTONIO. Do not weep:
  Heaven fashioned us of nothing, and we strive
  To bring ourselves to nothing.—Farewell, Cariola,
  And thy sweet armful.—If I do never see thee more,
  Be a good mother to your little ones,
  And save them from the tiger: fare you well.
DUCHESS. Let me look upon you once more, for that speech
  Came from a dying father: your kiss is colder
  Than that I have seen a holy anchorite
  Give to a dead man's skull.
ANTONIO. My heart is turned to a heavy lump of lead,
  With which I sound my danger: fare you well.

*Exeunt* ANTONIO *and his* SON.

DUCHESS. My laurel is all withered.
CARIOLA. Look, madam, what a troop of armèd men

---

[42] A medicinal bark.

Make towards us.

DUCHESS. O, they are very welcome:
When Fortune's wheel is over-charged with princes,
The weight makes it move swift: I would have my ruin
Be sudden.

*Re-enter* BOSOLA *visarded,*[43] *with a* GUARD.

I am your adventure,[44] am I not?

BOSOLA. You are: you must see your husband no more.

DUCHESS. What devil art thou that counterfeit'st
Heaven's thunder?

BOSOLA. Is that terrible? I would have you tell me whether
Is that note worse that frights the silly birds
Out of the corn, or that which doth allure them
To the nets? you have hearkened to the last too much.

DUCHESS. O misery! like to a rusty o'ercharged cannon,
Shall I never fly in pieces?—Come, to what prison?

BOSOLA. To none.

DUCHESS. Whither, then?

BOSOLA. To your palace.

DUCHESS. I have heard
That Charon's boat serves to convey all o'er
The dismal lake, but brings none back again.

BOSOLA. Your brothers mean you safety and pity.

DUCHESS. Pity!
With such a pity men preserve alive
Pheasants and quails, when they are not fat enough
To be eaten.

BOSOLA. These are your children?

DUCHESS. Yes.

BOSOLA. Can they prattle?

DUCHESS. No;
But I intend, since they were born accursed,
Curses shall be their first language.

BOSOLA. Fie, madam!
Forget this base, low fellow, —

DUCHESS. Were I a man,
I'd beat that counterfeit face into thy other.

---

[43] Visored or masked.
[44] Quarry.

BOSOLA. One of no birth.

DUCHESS. Say that he was born mean,
   Man is most happy when 's own actions
   Be arguments and examples of his virtue.

BOSOLA. A barren, beggarly virtue.

DUCHESS. I prithee, who is greatest? can you tell?
   Sad tales befit my woe: I'll tell you one.
   A salmon, as she swam unto the sea,
   Met with a dog-fish, who encounters her
   With this rough language: "Why art thou so bold
   To mix thyself with our high state of floods,
   Being no eminent courtier, but one
   That for the calmest and fresh time o' the year
   Dost live in shallow rivers, rank'st thyself
   With silly smelts and shrimps? and darest thou
   Pass by our dog-ship without reverence?"
   "O!" quoth the salmon, "sister, be at peace:
   Thank Jupiter we both have passed the net!
   Our value never can be truly known,
   Till in the fisher's basket we be shown:
   I' the market then my price may be the higher,
   Even when I am nearest to the cook and fire."
   So to great men the moral may be stretched;
   Men oft are valued high, when they're most wretched.—
   But come, whither you please. I am armed 'gainst misery;
   Bent to all sways of the oppressor's will:
   There's no deep valley but near some great hill.          [*Exeunt*

# ACT IV

## SCENE I: *An apartment in the* DUCHESS'S *palace at Malfi.*

*Enter* FERDINAND *and* BOSOLA.

FERDINAND. How doth our sister duchess bear herself
    In her imprisonment?
BOSOLA. Nobly: I'll describe her.
    She's sad as one long used to 't, and she seems
    Rather to welcome the end of misery
    Than shun it; a behavior so noble
    As gives a majesty to adversity:
    You may discern the shape of loveliness
    More perfect in her tears than in her smiles:
    She will muse four hours together; and her silence,
    Methinks, expresseth more than if she spake.
FERDINAND. Her melancholy seems to be fortified
    With a strange disdain.
BOSOLA.     'Tis so; and this restraint,
    Like English mastiffs that grow fierce with tying,
    Makes her too passionately apprehend
    Those pleasures she's kept from.
FERDINAND. Curse upon her!
    I will no longer study in the book
    Of another's heart. Inform her what I told you.     [*Exit*

*Enter* DUCHESS.

BOSOLA. All comfort to your grace!
DUCHESS. I will have none.

Pray thee, why dost thou wrap thy poisoned pills
In gold and sugar?

BOSOLA. Your elder brother, the Lord Ferdinand,
Is come to visit you, and sends you word,
'Cause once he rashly made a solemn vow
Never to see you more, he comes i' the night;
And prays you gently neither torch nor taper
Shine in your chamber: he will kiss your hand,
And reconcile himself; but for his vow
He dares not see you.

DUCHESS. At his pleasure.—
Take hence the lights.—He's come.

*Enter* FERDINAND.

FERDINAND. Where are you?

DUCHESS. Here, sir.

FERDINAND. This darkness suits you well.

DUCHESS. I would ask your pardon.

FERDINAND. You have it;
For I account it the honorabl'st revenge,
Where I may kill, to pardon.—Where are your cubs?

DUCHESS. Whom?

FERDINAND. Call them your children;
For though our national law distinguish bastards
From true legitimate issue, compassionate nature
Makes them all equal.

DUCHESS. Do you visit me for this?
You violate a sacrament o' the church
Shall make you howl in hell for 't.

FERDINAND. It had been well,
Could you have lived thus always; for, indeed,
You were too much i' the light:—but no more:
I come to seal my peace with you. Here's a hand
                              [*Gives her a dead man's hand*
To which you have vowed much love; the ring upon 't
You gave.

DUCHESS. I affectionately kiss it.

FERDINAND. Pray, do, and bury the print of it in your heart.
I will leave this ring with you for a love-token;
And the hand as sure as the ring; and do not doubt
But you shall have the heart too: when you need a friend,

Send it to him that owned it; you shall see
Whether he can aid you.

DUCHESS. You are very cold:
I fear you are not well after your travel.—
Ha! lights!—O, horrible!

FERDINAND. Let her have lights enough.                    [Exit

DUCHESS. What witchcraft doth he practice, that he hath left
A dead man's hand here?

*Here is discovered, behind a traverse,*[45] *the artificial figures of*
ANTONIO *and his* CHILDREN, *appearing as if they were dead.*

BOSOLA. Look you, here's the piece from which 'twas ta'en.
He doth present you this sad spectacle,
That, now you know directly they are dead,
Hereafter you may wisely cease to grieve
For that which cannot be recoverèd.

DUCHESS. There is not between Heaven and earth one wish
I stay for after this: it wastes me more
Than were 't my picture, fashioned out of wax,
Stuck with a magical needle, and then buried
In some foul dunghill; and yond's an excellent property
For a tyrant, which I would account mercy.

BOSOLA. What's that?

DUCHESS. If they would bind me to that lifeless trunk,
And let me freeze to death.

BOSOLA. Come, you must live.

DUCHESS. That's the greatest torture souls feel in hell,
In hell, that they must live, and cannot die.
Portia,[46] I'll new kindle thy coals again,
And revive the rare and almost dead example
Of a loving wife.

BOSOLA. O, fie! despair? remember
You are a Christian.

DUCHESS. The church enjoins fasting:
I'll starve myself to death.

BOSOLA. Leave this vain sorrow.
Things being at the worst begin to mend: the bee

---

[45] A curtain.
[46] Brutus's wife, who committed suicide by casting burning coals into her mouth and choking herself with them after the death of Brutus at Philippi.

When he hath shot his sting into your hand,
  May then play with your eyelid.
DUCHESS. Good comfortable fellow,
  Persuade a wretch that's broke upon the wheel
  To have all his bones new set; entreat him live
  To be executed again. Who must despatch me?
  I account this world a tedious theater,
  For I do play a part in 't 'gainst my will.
BOSOLA. Come, be of comfort; I will save your life.
DUCHESS. Indeed, I have not leisure to tend
  So small a business.
BOSOLA. Now, by my life, I pity you.
DUCHESS. Thou art a fool, then,
  To waste thy pity on a thing so wretched
  As cannot pity itself. I am full of daggers.
  Puff, let me blow these vipers from me.

*Enter* SERVANT.

What are you?
SERVANT. One that wishes you long life.
DUCHESS. I would thou wert hanged for the horrible curse
  Thou hast given me: I shall shortly grow one
  Of the miracles of pity. I'll go pray;—
  No, I'll go curse.
BOSOLA. O, fie!
DUCHESS. I could curse the stars.
BOSOLA. O, fearful.
DUCHESS. And those three smiling seasons of the year
  Into a Russian winter: nay, the world
  To its first chaos.
BOSOLA. Look you, the stars shine still.
DUCHESS. O, but you must
  Remember, my curse hath a great way to go.—
  Plagues, that make lanes through largest families,
  Consume them!—
BOSOLA. Fie, lady!
DUCHESS. Let them, like tyrants,
  Never be remembered but for the ill they have done;
  Let all the zealous prayers of mortified
  Churchmen forget them!—
BOSOLA. O, uncharitable!

DUCHESS. Let Heaven a little while cease crowning martyrs,
  To punish them! —
  Go, howl them this, and say, I long to bleed:
  It is some mercy when men kill with speed.          [*Exit*

*Re-enter* FERDINAND.

FERDINAND. Excellent, as I would wish; she's plagued in art:
  These presentations are but framed in wax
  By the curious master in that quality,
  Vincentio Lauriola, and she takes them
  For true substantial bodies.
BOSOLA. Why do you do this?
FERDINAND. To bring her to despair.
BOSOLA. Faith, end here,
  And go no farther in your cruelty:
  Send her a penitential garment to put on
  Next to her delicate skin, and furnish her
  With beads and prayer-books.
FERDINAND. Damn her! that body of hers,
  While that my blood ran pure in 't, was more worth
  Than that which thou wouldst comfort, called a soul.
  I will send her masks of common courtezans,
  Have her meat served up by bawds and ruffians,
  And, 'cause she'll needs be mad, I am resolved
  To remove forth the common hospital
  All the mad-folk, and place them near her lodging;
  There let them practice together, sing and dance,
  And act their gambols to the full o' the moon:
  If she can sleep the better for it, let her.
  Your work is almost ended.
BOSOLA. Must I see her again?
FERDINAND. Yes.
BOSOLA. Never.
FERDINAND. You must.
BOSOLA. Never in mine own shape;
  That's forfeited by my intelligence
  And this last cruel lie: when you send me next,
  The business shall be comfort.
FERDINAND. Very likely;
  Thy pity is nothing of kin to thee. Antonio
  Lurks about Milan: thou shalt shortly thither,

To feed a fire as great as my revenge,
Which never will slack till it have spent his fuel:
Intemperate agues make physicians cruel.          [*Exeunt*

## SCENE II

### *Another room in the DUCHESS's lodging.*

*Enter DUCHESS and CARIOLA.*

DUCHESS. What hideous noise was that?
CARIOLA. 'Tis the wild consort
  Of madmen, lady, which your tyrant brother
  Hath placed about your lodging: this tyranny,
  I think, was never practiced till this hour.
DUCHESS. Indeed, I thank him: nothing but noise and folly
  Can keep me in my right wits; whereas reason
  And silence make me stark mad. Sit down;
  Discourse to me some dismal tragedy.
CARIOLA. O, 'twill increase your melancholy.
DUCHESS. Thou art deceived:
  To hear of greater grief would lessen mine.
  This is a prison?
CARIOLA. Yes, but you shall live
  To shake this durance off.
DUCHESS. Thou art a fool:
  The robin-redbreast and the nightingale
  Never live long in cages.
CARIOLA. Pray, dry your eyes.
  What think you of, madam?
DUCHESS. Of nothing;
  When I muse thus, I sleep.
CARIOLA. Like a madman, with your eyes open?
DUCHESS. Dost thou think we shall know one another
  In the other world?
CARIOLA. Yes, out of question.
DUCHESS. O, that it were possible we might
  But hold some two days' conference with the dead!
  From them I should learn somewhat, I am sure,
  I never shall know here. I'll tell thee a miracle;

I am not mad yet, to my cause of sorrow:
The Heaven o'er my head seems made of molten brass,
The earth of flaming sulphur, yet I am not mad.
I am acquainted with sad misery
As the tanned galley-slave is with his oar;
Necessity makes me suffer constantly,
And custom makes it easy. Who do I look like now?

CARIOLA. Like to your picture in the gallery,
A deal of life in show, but none in practice;
Or rather like some reverend monument
Whose ruins are even pitied.

DUCHESS. Very proper;
And Fortune seems only to have her eyesight
To behold my tragedy.—How now!
What noise is that?

*Enter* SERVANT.

SERVANT. I am come to tell you
Your brother hath intended you some sport.
A great physician, when the Pope was sick
Of a deep melancholy, presented him
With several sorts of madmen, which wild object
Being full of change and sport, forced him to laugh,
And so the imposthume[47] broke: the self-same cure
The duke intends on you.

DUCHESS. Let them come in.

SERVANT. There's a mad lawyer; and a secular priest;
A doctor that hath forfeited his wits
By jealousy; an astrologian
That in his works said such a day o' the month
Should be the day of doom, and, failing of 't,
Ran mad; an English tailor crazed i' the brain
With the study of new fashions; a gentleman-usher
Quite beside himself with care to keep in mind
The number of his lady's salutations
Or "How do you" she employed him in each morning;
A farmer, too, an excellent knave in grain,
Mad 'cause he was hindered transportation:
And let one broker that's mad loose to these,

---

[47] Ulcer.

You'd think the devil were among them.

DUCHESS. Sit, Cariola.—Let them loose when you please,
For I am chained to endure all your tyranny.

*Enter* MADMEN. *Here this song is sung to a dismal kind of music
by a* MADMAN.

O, let us howl some heavy note,
　Some deadly doggéd howl,
Sounding as from the threatening throat
　Of beasts and fatal fowl!
As ravens, screech-owls, bulls, and bears,
　Well bell, and bawl our parts,
Till irksome noise have cloyed your ears
　And córrosived your hearts.
At last, when as our choir wants breath,
　Our bodies being blest,
Well sing, like swans, to welcome death,
　And die in love and rest,

1ST MADMAN. Doom's-day not come yet! Ill draw it nearer by
a perspective, or make a glass that shall set all the world on fire
upon an instant. I cannot sleep; my pillow is stuffed with a
litter of porcupines.

2ND MADMAN. Hell is a mere glass-house, where the devils are
continually blowing up women's souls on hollow irons, and
the fire never goes out.

3RD MADMAN. I will lie with every woman in my parish the tenth
night; I will tythe them over like haycocks.

4TH MADMAN. Shall my pothecary out-go me because I am a
cuckold? I have found out his roguery; he makes alum of his
wife's urine, and sells it to Puritans that have sore throats with
overstraining.

1ST MADMAN. I have skill in heraldry.

2ND MADMAN. Hast?

1ST MADMAN. You do give for your crest a woodcock's head
with the brains picked out on 't; you are a very ancient gentleman.

3RD MADMAN. Greek is turned Turk: we are only to be saved
by the Helvetian translation.[48]

---

[48] The Genevan Bible, a translation made by Puritan exiles in 1560.

1st MADMAN. Come on, sir, I will lay the law to you.

2nd MADMAN. O, rather lay a corrosive: the law will eat to the bone.

3rd MADMAN. He that drinks but to satisfy nature is damned.

4th MADMAN. If I had my glass here, I would show a sight should make all the women here call me mad doctor.

1st MADMAN. What's he? a rope-maker?

2nd MADMAN. No, no, no, a snuffling knave that, while he shows the tombs, will have his hand in a wench's placket.

3rd MADMAN. Woe to the caroche that brought home my wife from the masque at three o'clock in the morning! it had a large feather-bed in it.

4th MADMAN. I have pared the devil's nails forty times, roasted them in raven's eggs, and cured agues with them.

3rd MADMAN. Get me three hundred milch-bats, to make possets to procure sleep.

4th MADMAN. All the college may throw their caps at me: I have made a soap-boiler costive;[49] it was my masterpiece.

*Here a dance of* EIGHT MADMEN, *with music answerable thereto; after which,* BOSOLA, *like an* OLD MAN, *enters.*

DUCHESS. Is he mad too?

SERVANT. Pray, question him. I'll leave you.

*Exeunt* SERVANT *and* MADMEN.

BOSOLA. I am come to make thy tomb.

DUCHESS. Ha! my tomb!
Thou speak 'st as if I lay upon my deathbed,
Gasping for breath: dost thou perceive me sick?

BOSOLA. Yes, and the more dangerously, since thy sickness is insensible.

DUCHESS. Thou art not mad, sure: dost know me?

BOSOLA. Yes.

DUCHESS. Who am I?

BOSOLA. Thou art a box of worm-seed, at best but a salvatory of green mummy. What's this flesh? a little crudded[50] milk, fantastical puff-paste. Our bodies are weaker than those paper-prisons boys use to keep flies in; more contemptible, since ours

---

[49] Constipated.
[50] Curdled.

is to preserve earthworms. Didst thou ever see a lark in a cage? Such is the soul in the body: this world is like her little turf of grass, and the Heaven o'er our heads, like her looking-glass, only gives us a miserable knowledge of the small compass of our prison.

DUCHESS. Am not I thy duchess?

BOSOLA. Thou art some great woman, sure, for riot begins to sit on thy forehead (clad in gray hairs) twenty years sooner than on a merry milkmaid's. Thou sleepest worse than if a mouse should be forced to take up her lodging in a cat's ear: a little infant that breeds its teeth, should it lie with thee, would cry out, as if thou wert the more unquiet bedfellow.

DUCHESS. I am Duchess of Malfi still.

BOSOLA. That makes thy sleeps so broken:
Glories, like glow-worms, afar off shine bright,
But looked to near, have neither heat nor light.

DUCHESS. Thou art very plain.

BOSOLA. My trade is to flatter the dead, not the living;
I am a tomb-maker.

DUCHESS. And thou comest to make my tomb?

BOSOLA. Yes.

DUCHESS. Let me be a little merry:—of what stuff wilt thou make it?

BOSOLA. Nay, resolve me first, of what fashion?

DUCHESS. Why do we grow fantastical in our deathbeds? do we affect fashion in the grave?

BOSOLA. Most ambitiously. Princes' images on their tombs do not lie, as they were wont, seeming to pray up to Heaven; but with their hands under their cheeks, as if they died of the toothache: they are not carved with their eyes fixed upon the stars; but as their minds were wholly bent upon the world, the self-same way they seem to turn their faces.

DUCHESS. Let me know fully therefore the effect
Of this thy dismal preparation,
This talk fit for a charnel.

BOSOLA. Now I shall:—

Enter EXECUTIONERS, *with a coffin, cords, and a bell.*

Here is a present from your princely brothers;
And may it arrive welcome, for it brings
Last benefit, last sorrow.

DUCHESS. Let me see it:
I have so much obedience in my blood,

I wish it in their veins to do them good.

BOSOLA. This is your last presence-chamber.

CARIOLA. O my sweet lady!

DUCHESS. Peace; it affrights not me.

BOSOLA. I am the common bellman,
That usually is sent to condemned persons
The night before they suffer.

DUCHESS. Even now thou said 'st
Thou wast a tomb-maker.

BOSOLA. 'Twas to bring you
By degrees to mortification. Listen.

Hark, now every thing is still
The screech-owl and the whistler shrill
Call upon our dame aloud,
And bid her quickly don her shroud!
Much you had of land and rent;
Your length in clay's now competent:
A long war disturbed your mind;
Here your perfect peace is signed.
Of what is 't fools make such vain keeping?
Sin their conception, their birth weeping,
Their life a general mist of error,
Their death a hideous storm of terror.
Strew your hair with powders sweet,
Don clean linen, bathe your feet,
And (the foul fiend more to check)
A crucifix let bless your neck:
'Tis now full tide 'tween night and day;
End your groan, and come away.

CARIOLA. Hence, villains, tyrants, murderers! alas!
What will you do with my lady?—Call for help.

DUCHESS. To whom? to our next neighbors? they are mad-folks.

BOSOLA. Remove that noise.

DUCHESS. Farewell, Cariola.
In my last will I have not much to give:
A many hungry guests have fed upon me;
Thine will be a poor reversion.[51]

CARIOLA. I will die with her.

---

[51] Residue.

DUCHESS. I pray thee, look thou giv'st my little boy
    Some syrup for his cold, and let the girl
    Say her prayers ere she sleep.

          CARIOLA *is forced out by the* EXECUTIONERS.

    Now what you please:
    What death?
BOSOLA. Strangling; here are your executioners.
DUCHESS. I forgive them:
    The apoplexy, catarrh, or cough o' the lungs
    Would do as much as they do.
BOSOLA. Doth not death fright you?
DUCHESS. Who would be afraid on 't,
    Knowing to meet such excellent company
    In the other world?
BOSOLA. Yet, methinks,
    The manner of your death should much afflict you:
    This cord should terrify you.
DUCHESS. Not a whit:
    What would it pleasure me to have my throat cut
    With diamonds? or to be smotherèd
    With cassia? or to be shot to death with pearls?
    I know death hath ten thousand several doors
    For men to take their exits; and 'tis found
    They go on such strange geometrical hinges,
    You may open them both ways; any way, for Heaven sake,
    So I were out of your whispering. Tell my brothers
    That I perceive death, now I am well awake,
    Best gift is they can give or I can take.
    I would fain put off my last woman's fault,
    I'd not be tedious to you.
1ST EXECUTIONER. We are ready.
DUCHESS. Dispose my breath how please you; but body
    Bestow upon my women, will you?
1ST EXECUTIONER. Yes.
DUCHESS. Pull, and pull strongly, for your able strength
    Must pull down Heaven upon me:—
    Yet stay; Heaven-gates are not so highly arched
    As princes' palaces; they that enter there
    Must go upon their knees. [Kneels]—Come, violent death,

Serve for mandragora to make me sleep! —
Go tell my brothers, when I am laid out,
They then may feed in quiet.

*The* EXECUTIONERS *strangle the* DUCHESS.

BOSOLA. Where's the waiting woman?
Fetch her: some other strangle the children.

CARIOLA *and* CHILDREN *are brought in by the* EXECUTIONERS;
*who presently strangle the* CHILDREN.

Look you, there sleeps your mistress.
CARIOLA. O, you are damned
Perpetually for this! My turn is next,
Is 't not so ordered?
BOSOLA. Yes, and I am glad
You are so well prepared for 't.
CARIOLA. You are deceived, sir,
I am not prepared for 't, I will not die;
I will first come to my answer, and know
How I have offended.
BOSOLA. Come, despatch her.—
You kept her counsel; now you shall keep ours.
CARIOLA. I will not die, I must not; I am contracted
To a young gentleman.
1ST EXECUTIONER. Here's your wedding-ring.
CARIOLA. Let me but speak with the duke; I'll discover
Treason to his person.
BOSOLA. Delays:—throttle her.
1ST EXECUTIONER. She bites and scratches.
CARIOLA. If you kill me now,
I am damned; I have not been at confession
This two years.
BOSOLA. [To EXECUTIONERS] When?
CARIOLA. I am quick with child.
BOSOLA. Why, then,
Your credit's saved.

*The* EXECUTIONERS *strangle* CARIOLA.

Bear her into the next room;
Let these lie still.

*Exeunt the* EXECUTIONERS *with the body of* CARIOLA.
*Enter* FERDINAND.

FERDINAND. Is she dead?
BOSOLA. She is what
 You'd have her. But here begin your pity.
                              [*Shows the* CHILDREN *strangled*
 Alas, how have these offended?
FERDINAND. The death
 Of young wolves is never to be pitied.
BOSOLA. Fix your eye here.
FERDINAND. Constantly.
BOSOLA. Do you not weep?
 Other sins only speak; murder shrieks out:
 The element of water moistens the earth,
 But blood flies upwards and bedews the heavens.
FERDINAND. Cover her face; mine eyes dazzle: she died young.
BOSOLA. I think not so; her infelicity
 Seemed to have years too many.
FERDINAND. She and I were twins;
 And should I die this instant, I have lived
 Her time to a minute.
BOSOLA. It seems she was born first:
 You have bloodily approved the ancient truth,
 That kindred commonly do worse agree
 Than remote strangers.
FERDINAND. Let me see her face
 Again. Why didst not thou pity her? what
 An excellent honest man mightst thou have been,
 If thou hadst borne her to some sanctuary!
 Or, bold in a good cause, opposed thyself,
 With thy advancèd sword above thy head,
 Between her innocence and my revenge!
 I bade thee, when I was distracted of my wits,
 Go kill my dearest friend, and thou hast done 't.
 For let me but examine well the cause:
 What was the meanness of her match to me?
 Only I must confess I had a hope,
 Had she continued widow, to have gained
 An infinite mass of treasure by her death:
 And what was the main cause? her marriage,

That drew a stream of gall quite through my heart.
For thee, as we observe in tragedies
That a good actor many times is cursed
For playing a villain's part, I hate thee for 't,
And, for my sake, say, thou hast done much ill well.

BOSOLA. Let me quicken your memory, for I perceive
You are falling into ingratitude: I challenge
The reward due to my service.

FERDINAND. I'll tell thee
What I'll give thee.

BOSOLA. Do.

FERDINAND. I'll give thee a pardon
For this murder.

BOSOLA. Ha!

FERDINAND. Yes, and 'tis
The largest bounty I can study to do thee.
By what authority didst thou execute
This bloody sentence?

BOSOLA. By yours.

FERDINAND. Mine! was I her judge?
Did any ceremonial form of law
Doom her to not-being? did a cómplete jury
Deliver her conviction up i' the court?
Where shalt thou find this judgment registered,
Unless in hell? See, like a bloody fool,
Thou'st forfeited thy life, and thou shalt die for 't.

BOSOLA. The office of justice is perverted quite
When one thief hangs another. Who shall dare
To reveal this?

FERDINAND. O, I'll tell thee;
The wolf shall find her grave, and scrape it up,
Not to devour the corpse, but to discover
The horrid murder.

BOSOLA. You, not I, shall quake for 't.

FERDINAND. Leave me.

BOSOLA. I will first receive my pension.

FERDINAND. You are a villain.

BOSOLA. When your ingratitude
Is judge, I am so.

FERDINAND. O horror,
That not the fear of him which binds the devils

Can prescribe man obedience!—
Never look upon me more.

BOSOLA. Why, fare thee well.
Your brother and yourself are worthy men:
You have a pair of hearts are hollow graves,
Rotten, and rotting others; and your vengeance,
Like two chained bullets, still goes arm in arm:
You may be brothers; for treason, like the plague,
Doth take much in a blood. I stand like one
That long hath ta'en a sweet and golden dream:
I am angry with myself, now that I wake.

FERDINAND. Get thee into some unknown part o' the world,
That I may never see thee.

BOSOLA. Let me know
Wherefore I should be thus neglected. Sir,
I served your tyranny, and rather strove
To satisfy yourself than all the world:
And though I loathed the evil, yet I loved
You that did counsel it; and rather sought
To appear a true servant than an honest man.

FERDINAND. I'll go hunt the badger by owl-light.
'Tis a deed of darkness.                                    [*Exit*

BOSOLA. He's much distracted. Off, my painted honor!
While with vain hopes our faculties we tire,
We seem to sweat in ice and freeze in fire.
What would I do, were this to do again?
I would not change my peace of conscience
For all the wealth of Europe.—She stirs; here's life:—
Return, fair soul, from darkness, and lead mine
Out of this sensible hell:—she's warm, she breathes:—
Upon thy pale lips I will melt my heart,
To store them with fresh color.—Who's there!
Some cordial drink!—Alas! I dare not call:
So pity would destroy pity.—Her eye opes,
And Heaven in it seems to ope, that late was shut,
To take me up to mercy.

DUCHESS. Antonio!

BOSOLA. Yes, madam, he is living;
The dead bodies you saw were but feigned statues:
He's reconciled to your brothers; the Pope hath wrought
The atonement.

DUCHESS. Mercy!                                         [*Dies*

BOSOLA. O, she's gone again! there the cords of life broke.
    O sacred innocence, that sweetly sleeps
    On turtles' feathers, whilst a guilty conscience
    Is a black register wherein is writ
    All our good deeds and bad, a perspective
    That shows us hell! That we cannot be suffered
    To do good when we have a mind to it!
    This is manly sorrow;
    These tears, I am very certain, never grew
    In my mother's milk: my estate has sunk
    Below the degree of fear: where were
    These penitent fountains while she was living?
    O, they were frozen up! Here is a sight
    As direful to my soul as is the sword
    Unto a wretch has slain his father. Come,
    I'll bear thee hence,
    And execute thy last will; that's deliver
    Thy body to the reverend dispose
    Of some good women: that the cruel tyrant
    Shall not deny me. Then I'll post to Milan,
    Where somewhat I will speedily enact
    Worth my dejection.                              [*Exit*

# ACT V

## SCENE I: *A public place in Milan.*

*Enter* ANTONIO *and* DELIO.

ANTONIO. What think you of my hope of reconcilement
   To the Araeonian brethren?
DELIO. I misdoubt it;
   For though they have sent their letters of safe-conduct
   For your repair to Milan, they appear
   But nets to entrap you. The Marquis of Pescara,
   Under whom you hold certain land in cheat,[52]
   Much 'gainst his noble nature hath been moved
   To seize those lands; and some of his dependents
   Are at this instant making it their suit
   To be invested in your revenues.
   I cannot think they mean well to your life
   That do deprive you of your means of life,
   Your living.
ANTONIO. You are still an heretic
   To any safety I can shape myself.
DELIO. Here comes the marquis: I will make myself
   Petitioner for some part of your land,
    To know whither it is flying.
ANTONIO. I pray do.

*Enter* PESCARA.

DELIO. Sir, I have a suit to you.

---

[52] Subject to escheat.

PESCARA. To me?

DELIO. An easy one:
     There is the citadel of Saint Bennet,
     With some demesnes, of late in the possession
     Of Antonio Bologna,—please you bestow them on me.

PESCARA. You are my friend; but this is such a suit,
     Nor fit for me to give, nor you to take.

DELIO. No, sir?

PESCARA. I will give you ample reason for 't
     Soon in private:—here's the cardinal's mistress.

*Enter* JULIA.

JULIA. My lord, I am grown your poor petitioner,
     And should be an ill beggar, had I not
     A great man's letter here, the cardinal's,
     To court you in my favor.                         [*Gives a letter*

PESCARA. He entreats for you
     The citadel of Saint Bennet, that belonged
     To the banished Bologna.

JULIA. Yes.

PESCARA. I could not have thought of a friend I could rather
     Pleasure with it: 'tis yours.

JULIA. Sir, I thank you;
     And he shall know how doubly I am engaged
     Both in your gift, and speediness of giving
     Which makes your grant the greater.                [*Exit*

ANTONIO. How they fortify
     Themselves with my ruin!

DELIO. Sir, I am
     Little bound to you.

PESCARA. Why?

DELIO. Because you denied this suit to me, and gave 't
     To such a creature.

PESCARA. Do you know what it was?
     It was Antonio's land; not forfeited
     By course of law, but ravished from his throat
     By the cardinal's entreaty: it were not fit
     I should bestow so main a piece of wrong
     Upon my friend; 'tis a gratification
     Only due to a strumpet, for it is injustice.

Shall I sprinkle the pure blood of innocents
To make those followers I call my friends
Look ruddier upon me? I am glad
This land, ta'en from the owner by such wrong,
Returns again unto so foul an use
As salary for his lust. Learn, good Delio,
To ask noble things of me, and you shall find
I'll be a noble giver.

DELIO. You instruct me well.

ANTONIO. Why, here's a man who would fright impudence
From sauciest beggars.

PESCARA. Prince Ferdinand's come to Milan,
Sick, as they give out, of an apoplexy;
But some say 'tis a frenzy: I am going
To visit him.

[*Exit*

ANTONIO. 'Tis a noble old fellow.

DELIO. What course do you mean to take, Antonio?

ANTONIO. This night I mean to venture all my fortune,
Which is no more than a poor lingering life,
To the cardinal's worst of malice: I have got
Private access to his chamber; and intend
To visit him about the mid of night,
As once his brother did our noble duchess.
It may be that the sudden apprehension
Of danger,—for I'll go in mine own shape,—
When he shall see it fraight with love and duty,
May draw the poison out of him, and work
A friendly reconcilement: if it fail,
Yet it shall rid me of this infamous calling;
For better fall once than be ever falling.

DELIO. I'll second you in all danger; and, howe'er,
My life keeps rank with yours.

ANTONIO. You are still my loved and best friend.

[*Exeunt*

## Scene II

*A gallery in the* Cardinal's *palace at Milan.*

*Enter* Pescara *and* Doctor.

Pescara. Now, doctor, may I visit your patient?
Doctor. If 't please your lordship: but he's instantly
  To take the air here in the gallery
  By my direction.
Pescara. Pray thee, what's his disease?
Doctor. A very pestilent disease, my lord,
  They call lycanthropia.
Pescara. What's that?
  I need a dictionary to 't.
Doctor. I'll tell you.
  In those that are possessed with 't there o'erflows
  Such melancholy humor they imagine
  Themselves to be transformed into wolves;
  Steal forth to churchyards in the dead of night,
  And dig dead bodies up: as two nights since
  One met the duke 'bout midnight in a lane
  Behind Saint Mark's church, with the leg of a man
  Upon his shoulder; and he howled fearfully;
  Said he was a wolf, only the difference
  Was, a wolfs skin was hairy on the outside,
  His on the inside; bade them take their swords,
  Rip up his flesh, and try: straight I was sent for,
  And, having ministered to him, found his grace
  Very well recovered.
Pescara. I am glad on 't.
Doctor. Yet not without some fear
  Of a relapse. If he grow to his fit again,
  I'll go a nearer way to work with him
  Than ever Paracelsus[53] dreamed of; if
  They'll give me leave, I'll buffet his madness out of him.
  Stand aside; he comes.

---

[53] Physician and alchemist (1493?—1541).

*Enter* FERDINAND, CARDINAL, MALATESTI, *and* BOSOLA.

FERDINAND. Leave me.

MALATESTI. Why doth your lordship love this solitariness?

FERDINAND. Eagles commonly fly alone; they are crows, daws, and starlings that flock together. Look, what's that follows me?

MALATESTI. Nothing, my lord.

FERDINAND. Yes.

MALATESTI. 'Tis your shadow.

FERDINAND. Stay it; let it not haunt me.

MALATESTI. Impossible, if you move, and the sun shine.

FERDINAND. I will throttle it.     [*Throws himself down on his shadow*

MALATESTI. O, my lord, you are angry with nothing.

FERDINAND. You are a fool: how is't possible I should catch my shadow, unless I fall upon 't? When I go to hell, I mean to carry a bribe; for, look you, good gifts evermore make way for the worst persons.

PESCARA. Rise, good my lord.

FERDINAND. I am studying the art of patience.

PESCARA. 'Tis a noble virtue.

FERDINAND. To drive six snails before me from this town to Moscow; neither use goad nor whip to them, but let them take their own time;—the patient'st man i' the world match me for an experiment;—and I'll crawl after like a sheep-biter.

CARDINAL. Force him up.

*They raise him.*

FERDINAND. Use me well, you were best. What I have done, I have done: I'll confess nothing.

DOCTOR. Now let me come to him.—Are you mad, my lord? are you out of your princely wits?

FERDINAND. What's he?

PESCARA. Your doctor.

FERDINAND. Let me have his beard sawed off, and his eyebrows filed more civil.

DOCTOR. I must do mad tricks with him, for that's the only way on't. — I have brought your grace a salamander's skin to keep you from sun-burning.

FERDINAND. I have cruel sore eyes.

DOCTOR. The white of a cockatrix's egg is present remedy.

FERDINAND. Let it be a new laid one, you were best.—
   Hide me from him: physicians are like kings,—
   They brook no contradiction.

DOCTOR. Now he begins to fear me: now let me alone with him.

CARDINAL. How now! put off your gown!

DOCTOR. Let me have some forty urinals filled with rose-water:
   he and I'll go pelt one another with them.—Now he begins
   to fear me.—Can you fetch a frisk, sir?—Let him go, let him
   go, upon my peril: I find by his eye he stands in awe of me;
   I'll make him as tame as a dormouse.

FERDINAND. Can you fetch your frisks, sir!—I will stamp him
   into a cullis, flay off his skin, to cover one of the anatomies[54]
   this rogue hath set i' the cold yonder in Barber-Surgeon's[55]
   hall—Hence, hence! you are all of you like beasts for sacrifice:
   there's nothing left of you but tongue and belly, flattery and
   lechery.                                                    [Exit

PESCARA. Doctor, he did not fear you thoroughly.

DOCTOR. True; I was somewhat too forward.

BOSOLA. Mercy upon me, what a fatal judgment
   Hath fall'n upon this Ferdinand!

PESCARA. Knows your grace
   What accident hath brought unto the prince
   This strange distraction?

CARDINAL. [Aside] I must feign somewhat.—Thus they say it
   grew.
   You have heard it rumored, for these many years
   None of our family dies but there is seen
   The shape of an old woman, which is given
   By tradition to us to have been murdered
   By her nephews for her riches. Such a figure
   One night, as the prince sat up late at's book,
   Appeared to him; when crying out for help,
   The gentlemen of 's chamber found his grace
   All on a cold sweat, altered much in face
   And language: since which apparition,
   He hath grown worse and worse, and I much fear
   He cannot live.

---

[54] Skeletons.
[55] The surgeons or barber-surgeons were given the bodies of four executed
criminals each year.

BOSOLA. Sir, I would speak with you.
PESCARA. We'll leave your grace,
    Wishing to the sick prince, our noble lord,
    All health of mind and body.
CARDINAL. You are most welcome.

*Exeunt* PESCARA, MALATESTI, *and* DOCTOR.

    Are you come? so.— [Aside] This fellow must not know
    By any means I had intelligence
    In our duchess's death; for, though I counselled it,
    The full of all the engagement seemed to grow
    From Ferdinand.—Now, sir, how fares our sister?
    I do not think but sorrow makes her look
    Like to an oft-dyed garment: she shall now
    Taste comfort from me. Why do you look so wildly?
    O, the fortune of your master here the prince
    Dejects you; but be you of happy comfort:
    If you'll do one thing for me I'll entreat,
    Though he had a cold tombstone o'er his bones,
    I'd make you what you would be.
BOSOLA. Any thing;
    Give it me in a breath, and let me fly to 't:
    They that think long small expedition win,
    For musing much o' the end cannot begin.

*Enter* JULIA.

JULIA. Sir, will you come in to supper?
CARDINAL. I am busy; leave me.
JULIA. [Aside] What an excellent shape hath that fellow!   [*Exit*
CARDINAL. 'Tis thus. Antonio lurks here in Milan:
    Inquire him out, and kill him. While he lives,
    Our sister cannot marry; and I have thought
    Of an excellent match for her. Do this, and style me
    Thy advancement.
BOSOLA. But by what means shall I find him out?
CARDINAL. There is a gentleman called Delio
    Here in the camp, that hath been long approved
    His loyal friend. Set eye upon that fellow;
    Follow him to mass; may be Antonio,
    Although he do account religion
    But a school-name, for fashion of the world

May accompany him; or else go inquire out
Delio's confessor, and see if you can bribe
Him to reveal it. There are a thousand ways
A man might find to trace him; as to know
What fellows haunt the Jews for taking up
Great sums of money, for sure he's in want;
Or else to go to the picture-makers, and learn
Who bought her picture lately: some of these
Happily may take.

BOSOLA. Well, I'll not freeze i' the business:
I would see that wretched thing, Antonio,
Above all sights i' the world.

CARDINAL. Do, and be happy.                    [*Exit*

BOSOLA. This fellow doth breed basilisks in 's eyes,
He's nothing else but murder; yet he seems
Not to have notice of the duchess's death.
'Tis his cunning: I must follow his example;
There cannot be a surer way to trace
Than that of an old fox.

*Re-enter* JULIA.

JULIA. So, sir, you are well met.

BOSOLA. How now!

JULIA. Nay, the doors are fast enough:
Now, sir, I will make you-confess your treachery.

BOSOLA. Treachery!

JULIA. Yes, confess to me
Which of my women 'twas you hired to put
Love-powder into my drink?

BOSOLA. Love-powder!

JULIA. Yes, when I was at Malfi.
Why should I fall in love with such a face else?
I have already suffered for thee so much pain,
The only remedy to do me good
Is to kill my longing.

BOSOLA. Sure, your pistol holds
Nothing but perfumes or kissing-comfits.[56]
Excellent lady!
You have a pretty way on 't to discover

---

[56] Perfumed sugar-plums, for sweetening the breath.

Your longing. Come, come, I'll disarm you,
And arm you thus: yet this is wondrous strange.

JULIA. Compare thy form and my eyes together,
You'll find my love no such great miracle.
Now you'll say
I am wanton: this nice modesty in ladies
Is but a troublesome familiar
That haunts them.

BOSOLA. Know you me, I am a blunt soldier.

JULIA. The better:
Sure, there wants fire where there are no lively sparks
Of roughness.

BOSOLA. And I want compliment.

JULIA. Why, ignorance
In courtship cannot make you do amiss,
If you have a heart to do well.

BOSOLA. You are very fair.

JULIA. Nay, if you lay beauty to my charge,
I must plead unguilty.

BOSOLA. Your bright eyes
Carry a quiver of darts in them sharper
Than sunbeams.

JULIA. You will mar me with commendation,
Put yourself to the charge of courting me,
Whereas now I woo you.

BOSOLA. [Aside] I have it, I will work upon this creature.—
Let us grow most amorously familiar:
If the great cardinal now should see me thus,
Would he not count me a villain?

JULIA. No; he might count me a wanton,
Not lay a scruple of offence on you;
For if I see and steal a diamond,
The fault is not i' the stone, but in me the thief
That purloins it. I am sudden with you:
We that are great women of pleasure use to cut off
These uncertain wishes and unquiet longings,
And in an instant join the sweet delight
And the pretty excuse together. Had you been i' the street,
Under my chamber-window, even there
I should have courted you.

BOSOLA. O, you are an excellent lady!

JULIA. Bid me do somewhat for you presently
  To express I love you.
BOSOLA. I will; and if you love me,
  Fail not to effect it.
  The cardinal is grown wondrous melancholy;
  Demand the cause, let him not put you off
  With feigned excuse; discover the main ground on 't.
JULIA. Why would you know this?
BOSOLA. I have depended on him,
  And I hear that he is fall'n in some disgrace
  With the emperor: if he be, like the mice
  That forsake falling houses, I would shift
  To other dependance.
JULIA. You shall not need
  Follow the wars: I'll be your maintenance.
BOSOLA. And I your loyal servant: but I cannot
  Leave my calling.
JULIA. Not leave an ungrateful
  General for the love of a sweet lady!
  You are like some cannot sleep in feather-beds,
  But must have blocks for their pillows.
BOSOLA. Will you do this?
JULIA. Cunningly.
BOSOLA. To-morrow I'll expect the intelligence.
JULIA. To-morrow! get you into my cabinet;
  You shall have it with you. Do not delay me,
  No more than I do you: I am like one
  That is condemned; I have my pardon promised,
  But I would see it sealed. Go, get you in:
  You shall see me wind my tongue about his heart
  Like a skein of silk.

                *Exit* BOSOLA. *Re-enter* CARDINAL.

CARDINAL. Where are you?

                *Enter* SERVANTS.

SERVANTS. Here.
CARDINAL. Let none, upon your lives, have conference
  With the Prince Ferdinand, unless I know it.—
  [*Aside*] In this distraction he may reveal
  The murder.

*Exeunt* SERVANTS.

Yond's my lingering consumption:
I am weary of her, and by any means
Would be quit of.

JULIA. How now, my lord! what ails you?

CARDINAL. Nothing.

JULIA. O, you are much altered:
Come, I must be your secretary, and remove
This lead from off your bosom: what's the matter?

CARDINAL. I may not tell you.

JULIA. Are you so far in love with sorrow
You cannot part with part of it? or think you
I cannot love your grace when you are sad
As well as merry? or do you suspect
I, that have been a secret to your heart
These many winters, cannot be the same
Unto your tongue?

CARDINAL. Satisfy thy longing,—
The only way to make thee keep my counsel
Is, not to tell thee.

JULIA. Tell your echo this,
Or flatterers, that like echoes still report
What they hear though most imperfect, and not me;
For if that you be true unto yourself,
I'll know.

CARDINAL. Will you rack me?

JULIA. No, judgment shall
Draw it from you: it is an equal fault,
To tell one's secrets unto all or none.

CARDINAL. The first argues folly.

JULIA. But the last tyranny.

CARDINAL. Very well: why, imagine I have committed
Some secret deed which I desire the world
May never hear of.

JULIA. Therefore may not I know it?
You have concealed for me as great a sin
As adultery. Sir, never was occasion
For perfect trial of my constancy
Till now: sir, I beseech you—

CARDINAL. You'll repent it.

JULIA. Never.

CARDINAL. It hurries thee to ruin: I'll not tell thee.
  Be well advised, and think what danger 'tis
  To receive a prince's secrets: they that do,
  Had need have their breasts hooped with adamant
  To contain them. I pray thee, yet be satisfied;
  Examine thine own frailty; 'tis more easy
  To tie knots than unloose them: 'tis a secret
  That, like a lingering poison, may chance lie
  Spread in thy veins, and kill thee seven year hence.

JULIA. Now you dally with me.

CARDINAL. No more; thou shalt know it.
  By my appointment the great Duchess of Malfi
  And two of her young children, four nights since,
  Were strangled.

JULIA. O Heaven! sir, what have you done!

CARDINAL. How now? how settles this? think you your bosom
  Will be a grave dark and obscure enough
  For such a secret?

JULIA. You have undone yourself, sir.

CARDINAL. Why?

JULIA. It lies not in me to conceal it.

CARDINAL. No?
  Come, I will swear you to 't upon this book.

JULIA. Most religiously.

CARDINAL. Kiss it.

*She kisses the book*

  Now you shall never utter it; thy curiosity
  Hath undone thee: thou 'rt poisoned with that book;
  Because I knew thou couldst not keep my counsel,
  I have bound thee to 't by death.

*Re-enter BOSOLA.*

BOSOLA. For pity-sake, hold!

CARDINAL. Ha, Bosola!

JULIA. I forgive you
  This equal piece of justice you have done;

For I betrayed your counsel to that fellow:
He overheard it; that was the cause I said
It lay not in me to conceal it.

BOSOLA. O foolish woman,
Couldst not thou have poisoned him?

JULIA. 'Tis weakness,
Too much to think what should have been done.
I go,
I know not whither.                                    [*Dies*

CARDINAL. Wherefore com'st thou hither?

BOSOLA. That I might find a great man like yourself,
Not out of his wits as the Lord Ferdinand,
To remember my service.

CARDINAL. I'll have thee hewed in pieces.

BOSOLA. Make not yourself such a promise of that life
Which is not yours to dispose of.

CARDINAL. Who placed thee here?

BOSOLA. Her lust, as she intended.

CARDINAL. Very well:
Now you know me for your fellow-murderer.

BOSOLA. And wherefore should you lay fair marble colors
Upon your rotten purposes to me?
Unless you imitate some that do plot great treasons,
And when they have done, go hide themselves i' the graves
Of those were actors in 't?

CARDINAL. No more; there is
A fortune attends thee.

BOSOLA. Shall I go sue to Fortune any longer?
'Tis the fool's pilgrimage.

CARDINAL. I have honors in store for thee.

BOSOLA. There are many ways that conduct to seeming honor,
And some of them very dirty ones.

CARDINAL. Throw to the devil
Thy melancholy. The fire burns well;
What need we keep a stirring of 't, and make
A greater smother? Thou wilt kill Antonio?

BOSOLA. Yes.

CARDINAL. Take up that body.

BOSOLA. I think I shall
Shortly grow the common bearer for churchyards.

CARDINAL. I will allow thee some dozen of attendants
  To aid thee in the murder.
BOSOLA. O, by no means. Physicians that apply horse-leeches to any
  rank swelling use to cut off their tails, that the blood may run
  through them the faster: let me have no train when I go to shed
  blood, lest it make me have a greater when I ride to the gallows.
CARDINAL. Come to me after midnight, to help to remove
  That body to her own lodging: I'll give out
  She died o' the plague; 'twill breed the less inquiry
  After her death.
BOSOLA. Where's Castruccio, her husband?
CARDINAL. He's rode to Naples, to take possession
  Of Antonio's citadel.
BOSOLA. Believe me, you have done a very happy turn.
CARDINAL. Fail not to come: there is the master-key
  Of our lodgings; and by that you may conceive
  What trust I plant in you.
BOSOLA. You shall find me ready.

*Exit* CARDINAL.

O poor Antonio, though nothing be so needful
To thy estate as pity, yet I find
Nothing so dangerous; I must look to my footing:
In such slippery ice-pavements men had need
To be frost-nailed well, they may break their necks.
The precedent's here afore me. How this man
Bears up in blood! seems fearless! Why, 'tis well: else;
Security some men call the suburbs of hell,
Only a dead wall between. Well, good Antonio,
I'll seek thee out; and all my care shall be
To put thee into safety from the reach
Of these most cruel biters that have got
Some of thy blood already. It may be,
I'll join with thee in a most just revenge:
The weakest arm is strong enough that strikes
With the sword of justice. Still methinks the duchess
Haunts me: there, there!—'Tis nothing but my melancholy.
O Penitence, let me truly taste thy cup,
That throws men down only to raise them up!

[*Exit*

# SCENE III

## *A fortification at Milan.*

Enter ANTONIO *and* DELIO.

DELIO. Yond's the cardinal's window. This fortification
    Grew from the ruins of an ancient abbey;
    And to yond side o' the river lies a wall,
    Piece of a cloister, which in my opinion
    Gives the best echo that you ever heard,
    So hollow and so dismal, and withal
    So plain in the distinction of our words,
    That many have supposed it is a spirit
    That answers.
ANTONIO. I do love these ancient ruins.
    We never tread upon them but we set
    Our foot upon some reverend history:
    And, questionless, here in this open court,
    Which now lies naked to the injuries
    Of stormy weather, some men lie interred
    Loved the church so well, and gave so largely to 't,
    They thought it should have canopied their bones
    Till doomsday; but all things have their end:
    Churches and cities, which have diseases like to men,
    Must have like death that we have.
ECHO. "Like death that we have."
DELIO. Now the echo hath caught you.
ANTONIO. It groaned, methought, and gave
    A very deadly accent,
ECHO. "Deadly accent."
DELIO. I told you 'twas a pretty one: you may make it
    A huntsman, or a falconer, a musician,
    Or a thing of sorrow.
ECHO. "A thing of sorrow."
ANTONIO. Ay, sure, that suits it best.
ECHO. "That suits it best."
ANTONIO. 'Tis very like my wife's voice.
ECHO. "Ay, wife's voice."

DELIO. Come, let us walk further from 't.
  I would not have you go to the cardinal's to-night:
  Do not.
ECHO. "Do not."
DELIO. Wisdom doth not more moderate wasting sorrow
  Than time: take time for't; be mindful of thy safety.
ECHO. "Be mindful of thy safety."
ANTONIO. Necessity compels me:
  Make scrutiny throughout the passages
  Of your own life, you'll find it impossible
  To fly your fate.
ECHO. "O, fly your fate."
DELIO. Hark! the dead stones seem to have pity on you,
  And give you good counsel.
ANTONIO. Echo, I will not talk with thee,
  For thou art a dead thing.
ECHO. "Thou art a dead thing."
ANTONIO. My duchess is asleep now,
  And her little ones, I hope sweetly: O Heaven,
  Shall I never see her more?
ECHO. "Never see her more."
ANTONIO. I marked not one repetition of the echo
  But that; and on the sudden a clear light
  Presented me a face folded in sorrow.
DELIO. Your fancy merely.
ANTONIO. Come, I'll be out of this ague,
  For to live thus is not indeed to live;
  It is a mockery and abuse of life:
  I will not henceforth save myself by halves;
  Lose all, or nothing.
DELIO. Your own virtues save you!
  I'll fetch your eldest son, and second you:
  It may be that the sight of his own blood
  Spread in so sweet a figure may beget
  The more compassion. However, fare you well.
  Though in our miseries Fortune have a part,
  Yet in our noble sufferings she hath none:
  Contempt of pain, that we may call our own.

[*Exeunt*

## SCENE IV

### *An apartment in the* CARDINAL's *palace.*

*Enter* CARDINAL, PESCARA, MALATESTI, RODERIGO,
*and* GRISOLAN.

CARDINAL. YOU shall not watch to-night by the sick prince;
　His grace is very well recovered.
MALATESTI. Good my lord, suffer us.
CARDINAL. O, by no means;
　The noise, and change of object in his eye,
　Doth more distract him: I pray, all to bed;
　And though you hear him in his violent fit,
　Do not rise, I entreat you.
PESCARA. So, sir; we shall not.
CARDINAL. Nay, I must have you promise
　Upon your honors, for I was enjoined to 't
　By himself; and he seemed to urge it sensibly.
PESCARA. Let our honors bind this trifle.
CARDINAL. Nor any of your followers.
MALATESTI. Neither.
CARDINAL. It may be, to make trial of your promise,
　When he's asleep, myself will rise and feign
　Some of his mad tricks, and cry out for help,
　And feign myself in danger.
MALATESTI. If your throat were cutting,
　I'd not come at you, now I have protested against it.
CARDINAL. Why, I thank you.
GRISOLAN. 'Twas a foul storm to-night.
RODERIGO. The Lord Ferdinand's chamber shook like an osier.[57]
MALATESTI. 'Twas nothing but pure kindness in the devil,
　To rock his own child.

*Exeunt all except* CARDINAL.

CARDINAL. The reason why I would not suffer these
　About my brother, is, because at midnight
　I may with better privacy convey

---

[57] A willow.

Julia's body to her own lodging. O, my conscience!
I would pray now; but the devil takes away my heart
For having any confidence in prayer.
About this hour I appointed Bosola
To fetch the body: when he hath served my turn,
He dies.                                                    [*Exit*

*Enter* BOSOLA.

BOSOLA. Ha! 'twas the cardinal's voice; I heard him name
    Bosola and my death. Listen; I hear one's footing.

*Enter* FERDINAND.

FERDINAND. Strangling is a very quiet death.
BOSOLA. [Aside] Nay, then, I see I must stand upon my guard.
FERDINAND. What say you to that? whisper softly; do you agree
    to't? So; it must be done i' the dark: the cardinal would not
    for a thousand pounds the doctor should see it.      [*Exit*
BOSOLA. My death is plotted; here's the consequence of murder.
    We value not desert nor Christian breath,
    When we know black deeds must be cured with death.

*Enter* ANTONIO *and* SERVANT.

SERVANT. Here stay, sir, and be confident, I pray:
    I'll fetch you a dark lantern.                        [*Exit*
ANTONIO. Could I take him at his prayers,
    There were hope of pardon.
BOSOLA. Fall right, my sword!—                           [*Stabs him*
    I'll not give thee so much leisure as to pray.
ANTONIO. O, I am gone! Thou hast ended a long suit
    In a minute.
BOSOLA. What art thou?
ANTONIO. A most wretched thing,
    That only have thy benefit in death,
    To appear myself.

*Re-enter* SERVANT, *with a lantern.*

SERVANT. Where are you, sir?
ANTONIO. Very near my home.—Bosola!
SERVANT. O, misfortune!
BOSOLA. Smother thy pity, thou art dead else.—Antonio!

The man I would have saved 'bove mine own life!
We are merely the stars' tennis-balls, struck and bandied
Which way please them.—O good Antonio,
I'll whisper one thing in thy dying ear
Shall make thy heart break quickly! thy fair duchess and two
    sweet children—

ANTONIO. Their very names
Kindle a little life in me.

BOSOLA. Are murdered.

ANTONIO. Some men have wished to die
At the hearing of sad things; I am glad
That I shall do 't in sadness:[58] I would not now
Wish my wounds balmed nor healed, for I have no use
To put my life to. In all our quest of greatness,
Like wanton boys, whose pastime is their care,
We follow after bubbles blown in the air.
Pleasure of life, what is 't? only the good hours
Of an ague; merely a preparative to rest,
To endure vexation. I do not ask
The process of my death; only commend me
To Delio.

BOSOLA. Break, heart!

ANTONIO. And let my son fly the courts of princes.     [*Dies*

BOSOLA. Thou seem'st to have loved Antonio?

SERVANT. I brought him hither,
To have reconciled him to the cardinal.

BOSOLA. I do not ask thee that.
Take him up, if thou tender thine own life,
And bear him where the lady Julia
Was wont to lodge.—O, my fate moves swift;
I have this cardinal in the forge already;
Now I'll bring him to the hammer. O direful misprision![59]
I will not imitate things glorious,
No more than base; I'll be mine own example.—
On, on, and look thou represent, for silence,
The thing thou bear'st.     [*Exeunt*

---

[58] In earnest.
[59] Mistake.

## SCENE V

### *Another apartment in the palace.*

*Enter* CARDINAL, *with a book.*

CARDINAL. I am puzzled in a question about hell:
    He says, in hell there's one material fire,
    And yet it shall not burn all men alike.
    Lay him by. How tedious is a guilty conscience!
    When I look into the fish-ponds in my garden,
    Methinks I see a thing armed with a rake,
    That seems to strike at me.

*Enter* BOSOLA, *and* SERVANT *bearing* ANTONIO'S *body.*

    Now, art thou come?
    Thou look'st ghastly:
    There sits in thy face some great determination
    Mixed with some fear.
BOSOLA. Thus it lightens into action:
    I am come to kill thee.
CARDINAL. Ha!—Help! our guard!
BOSOLA. Thou art deceived;
    They are out of thy howling.
CARDINAL. Hold; and I will faithfully divide
    Revenues with thee.
BOSOLA. Thy prayers and proffers
    Are both unseasonable.
CARDINAL. Raise the watch! we are betrayed!
BOSOLA. I have confined your flight:
    I'll suffer your retreat to Julia's chamber,
    But no further.
CARDINAL. Help! we are betrayed!

*Enter, above,* PESCARA, MALATESTI, RODERIGO,
*and* GRISOLAN.

MALATESTI. Listen.
CARDINAL. My dukedom for rescue!
RODERIGO. Fie upon his counterfeiting!
MALATESTI. Why, 'tis not the cardinal.

RODERIGO. Yes, yes, 'tis he:
  But I'll see him hanged ere I'll go down to him.
CARDINAL. Here's a plot upon me; I am assaulted! I am lost,
  Unless some rescue.
GRISOLAN. He doth this pretty well;
  But it will not serve to laugh me out of mine honor.
CARDINAL. The sword's at my throat!
RODERIGO. You would not bawl so loud then.
MALATESTI. Come, come, let's go
  To bed: he told us thus much aforehand.
PESCARA. He wished you should not come at him; but, believe 't,
  The accent of the voice sounds not in jest:
  I'll down to him, howsoever, and with engines
  Force ope the doors.                              [*Exit above*
RODERIGO. Let's follow him aloof,
  And note how the cardinal will laugh at him.

      *Exeunt, above,* MALATESTI, RODERIGO, *and* GRISOLAN.

BOSOLA. There's for you first,
  'Cause you shall not unbarricade the door
  To let in rescue.                          [*Kills the* SERVANT
CARDINAL. What cause hast thou to pursue my life?
BOSOLA. Look there.
CARDINAL. Antonio!
BOSOLA. Slain by my hand unwittingly.
  Pray, and be sudden: when thou killed'st thy sister,
  Thou took'st from Justice her most equal balance,
  And left her naught but her sword.
CARDINAL. O, mercy!
BOSOLA. Now it seems thy greatness was only outward;
  For thou fall'st faster of thyself than calamity
  Can drive thee. I'll not waste longer time; there!
                                                    [*Stabs him*
CARDINAL. Thou hast hurt me.
BOSOLA. Again!                                  [*Stabs him again*
CARDINAL. Shall I die like a leveret,[60]
  Without any resistance?—Help, help, help!
  I am slain!

---

[60] A hare in its first year.

*Enter* FERDINAND.

FERDINAND. The alarum! give me a fresh horse;
  Rally the vaunt-guard, or the day is lost.
  Yield, yield! I give you the honor of arms,
  Shake my sword over you; will you yield?
CARDINAL. Help me; I am your brother!
FERDINAND. The devil!
  My brother fight upon the adverse party!

*He wounds the* CARDINAL, *and, in the scuffle, gives* BOSOLA *his
death-wound.*

  There flies your ransom.
CARDINAL. O justice!
  I suffer now for what hath former bin:
  Sorrow is held the eldest child of sin.
FERDINAND. NOW you're brave fellows. Caesar's fortune was
  harder than Pompey's; Caesar died in the arms of prosperity,
  Pompey at the feet of disgrace. You both died in the field.
  The pain's nothing: pain many times is taken away with the
  apprehension of greater, as the toothache with the sight of the
  barber that comes to pull it out: there's philosophy for you.
BOSOLA. Now my revenge is perfect.—Sink thou main cause

  [*Kills* FERDINAND

  Of my undoing!—The last part of my life
  Hath done me best service.
FERDINAND. Give me some wet hay; I am broken-winded.
  I do account this world but a dog kennel:
  I will vault credit and affect high pleasures
  Beyond death.
BOSOLA. He seems to come to himself,
  Now he's so near the bottom.
FERDINAND. My sister, O my sister! there's the cause on 't.
  Whether we fall by ambition, blood, or lust,
  Like diamonds we are cut with our own dust.          [*Dies*
CARDINAL. Thou hast thy payment too.
BOSOLA. Yes, I hold my weary soul in my teeth;
  'Tis ready to part from me. I do glory
  That thou, which stood'st like a huge pyramid
  Begun upon a large and ample base,
  Shalt end in a little point, a kind of nothing.

*Enter below,* PESCARA, MALATESTI, RODERIGO, *and* GRISOLAN.

PESCARA. How now, my lord!

MALATESTI. O sad disaster!

RODERIGO. How comes this?

BOSOLA. Revenge for the Duchess of Malfi murdered
By the Aragonian brethren; for Antonio
Slain by this hand; for lustful Julia
Poisoned by this man; and lastly for myself,
That was an actor in the main of all
Much 'gainst mine own good nature, yet i' the end
Neglected.

PESCARA. How now, my lord!

CARDINAL. Look to my brother:
He gave us these large wounds, as we were struggling
Here i' the rushes. And now, I pray, let me
Be laid by and never thought of.                    [*Dies*

PESCARA. How fatally, it seems, he did withstand
His own rescue!

MALATESTI. Thou wretched thing of blood,
How came Antonio by his death?

BOSOLA. In a mist; I know not how;
Such a mistake as I have often seen
In a play. O, I am gone!
We are only like dead walls or vaulted graves,
That, ruined, yield no echo. Fare you well.
It may be pain, but no harm, to me to die
In so good a quarrel. O, this gloomy world!
In what a shadow, or deep pit of darkness,
Doth womanish and fearful mankind live!
Let worthy minds ne'er stagger in distrust
To suffer death or shame for what is just:
Mine is another voyage.                             [*Dies*

PESCARA. The noble Delio, as I came to the palace,
Told me of Antonio's being here, and showed me
A pretty gentleman, his son and heir.

*Enter* DELIO *and* ANTONIO'S SON.

MALATESTI. O sir, you come too late!

DELIO. I heard so, and
Was armed for't, ere I came. Let us make noble use

Of this great ruin; and join all our force
To establish this young hopeful gentleman
In 's mother's right. These wretched eminent things
Leave no more fame behind 'em, than should one
Fall in a frost, and leave his print in snow;
As soon as the sun shines, it ever melts,
Both form and matter. I have ever thought
Nature doth nothing so great for great men
As when she's pleased to make them lords of truth:
Integrity of life is fame's best friend,
Which nobly, beyond death, shall crown the end.        [*Exeunt*

## POETRY

101 GREAT AMERICAN POEMS, Edited by The American Poetry & Literacy Project. (0-486-40158-8)

100 BEST-LOVED POEMS, Edited by Philip Smith. (0-486-28553-7)

ENGLISH ROMANTIC POETRY: An Anthology, Edited by Stanley Appelbaum. (0-486-29282-7)

THE INFERNO, Dante Alighieri. Translated and with notes by Henry Wadsworth Longfellow. (0-486-44288-8)

PARADISE LOST, John Milton. Introduction and Notes by John A. Himes. (0-486-44287-X)

SPOON RIVER ANTHOLOGY, Edgar Lee Masters. (0-486-27275-3)

SELECTED CANTERBURY TALES, Geoffrey Chaucer. (0-486-28241-4)

SELECTED POEMS, Emily Dickinson. (0-486-26466-1)

LEAVES OF GRASS: The Original 1855 Edition, Walt Whitman. (0-486-45676-5)

COMPLETE SONNETS, William Shakespeare. (0-486-26686-9)

THE RAVEN AND OTHER FAVORITE POEMS, Edgar Allan Poe. (0-486-26685-0)

ENGLISH VICTORIAN POETRY: An Anthology, Edited by Paul Negri. (0-486-40425-0)

SELECTED POEMS, Walt Whitman. (0-486-26878-0)

THE ROAD NOT TAKEN AND OTHER POEMS, Robert Frost. (0-486-27550-7)

AFRICAN-AMERICAN POETRY: An Anthology, 1773-1927, Edited by Joan R. Sherman. (0-486-29604-0)

GREAT SHORT POEMS, Edited by Paul Negri. (0-486-41105-2)

THE RIME OF THE ANCIENT MARINER, Samuel Taylor Coleridge. (0-486-27266-4)

THE WASTE LAND, PRUFROCK AND OTHER POEMS, T. S. Eliot. (0-486-40061-1)

SONG OF MYSELF, Walt Whitman. (0-486-41410-8)

AENEID, Vergil. (0-486-28749-1)

SONGS FOR THE OPEN ROAD: Poems of Travel and Adventure, Edited by The American Poetry & Literacy Project. (0-486-40646-6)

SONGS OF INNOCENCE AND SONGS OF EXPERIENCE, William Blake. (0-486-27051-3)

WORLD WAR ONE BRITISH POETS: Brooke, Owen, Sassoon, Rosenberg and Others, Edited by Candace Ward. (0-486-29568-0)

GREAT SONNETS, Edited by Paul Negri. (0-486-28052-7)

CHRISTMAS CAROLS: Complete Verses, Edited by Shane Weller. (0-486-27397-0)

## POETRY

GREAT POEMS BY AMERICAN WOMEN: An Anthology, Edited by Susan L. Rattiner. (0-486-40164-2)

FAVORITE POEMS, Henry Wadsworth Longfellow. (0-486-27273-7)

BHAGAVADGITA, Translated by Sir Edwin Arnold. (0-486-27782-8)

ESSAY ON MAN AND OTHER POEMS, Alexander Pope. (0-486-28053-5)

GREAT LOVE POEMS, Edited by Shane Weller. (0-486-27284-2)

DOVER BEACH AND OTHER POEMS, Matthew Arnold. (0-486-28037-3)

THE SHOOTING OF DAN MCGREW AND OTHER POEMS, Robert Service. (0-486-27556-6)

THE BALLAD OF READING GAOL AND OTHER POEMS, Oscar Wilde. (0-486-27072-6)

SELECTED POEMS OF RUMI, Jalalu'l-Din Rumi. (0-486-41583-X)

SELECTED POEMS OF GERARD MANLEY HOPKINS, Gerard Manley Hopkins. Edited and with an Introduction by Bob Blaisdell. (0-486-47867-X)

RENASCENCE AND OTHER POEMS, Edna St. Vincent Millay. (0-486-26873-X)

THE RUBÁIYÁT OF OMAR KHAYYÁM: First and Fifth Editions, Edward FitzGerald. (0-486-26467-X)

TO MY HUSBAND AND OTHER POEMS, Anne Bradstreet. (0-486-41408-6)

LITTLE ORPHANT ANNIE AND OTHER POEMS, James Whitcomb Riley. (0-486-28260-0)

IMAGIST POETRY: AN ANTHOLOGY, Edited by Bob Blaisdell. (0-486-40875-2)

FIRST FIG AND OTHER POEMS, Edna St. Vincent Millay. (0-486-41104-4)

GREAT SHORT POEMS FROM ANTIQUITY TO THE TWENTIETH CENTURY, Edited by Dorothy Belle Pollack. (0-486-47876-9)

THE FLOWERS OF EVIL & PARIS SPLEEN: Selected Poems, Charles Baudelaire. Translated by Wallace Fowlie. (0-486-47545-X)

CIVIL WAR SHORT STORIES AND POEMS, Edited by Bob Blaisdell. (0-486-48226-X)

EARLY POEMS, Edna St. Vincent Millay. (0-486-43672-1)

JABBERWOCKY AND OTHER POEMS, Lewis Carroll. (0-486-41582-1)

THE METAMORPHOSES: Selected Stories in Verse, Ovid. (0-486-42758-7)

IDYLLS OF THE KING, Alfred, Lord Tennyson. Edited by W. J. Rolfe. (0-486-43795-7)

A BOY'S WILL AND NORTH OF BOSTON, Robert Frost. (0-486-26866-7)

100 FAVORITE ENGLISH AND IRISH POEMS, Edited by Clarence C. Strowbridge. (0-486-44429-5)

## PLAYS

THE ORESTEIA TRILOGY: Agamemnon, the Libation-Bearers and the Furies, Aeschylus. (0-486-29242-8)

EVERYMAN, Anonymous. (0-486-28726-2)

THE BIRDS, Aristophanes. (0-486-40886-8)

LYSISTRATA, Aristophanes. (0-486-28225-2)

THE CHERRY ORCHARD, Anton Chekhov. (0-486-26682-6)

THE SEA GULL, Anton Chekhov. (0-486-40656-3)

MEDEA, Euripides. (0-486-27548-5)

FAUST, PART ONE, Johann Wolfgang von Goethe. (0-486-28046-2)

THE INSPECTOR GENERAL, Nikolai Gogol. (0-486-28500-6)

SHE STOOPS TO CONQUER, Oliver Goldsmith. (0-486-26867-5)

GHOSTS, Henrik Ibsen. (0-486-29852-3)

A DOLL'S HOUSE, Henrik Ibsen. (0-486-27062-9)

HEDDA GABLER, Henrik Ibsen. (0-486-26469-6)

DR. FAUSTUS, Christopher Marlowe. (0-486-28208-2)

TARTUFFE, Molière. (0-486-41117-6)

BEYOND THE HORIZON, Eugene O'Neill. (0-486-29085-9)

THE EMPEROR JONES, Eugene O'Neill. (0-486-29268-1)

CYRANO DE BERGERAC, Edmond Rostand. (0-486-41119-2)

MEASURE FOR MEASURE: Unabridged, William Shakespeare. (0-486-40889-2)

FOUR GREAT TRAGEDIES: Hamlet, Macbeth, Othello, and Romeo and Juliet, William Shakespeare. (0-486-44083-4)

THE COMEDY OF ERRORS, William Shakespeare. (0-486-42461-8)

HENRY V, William Shakespeare. (0-486-42887-7)

MUCH ADO ABOUT NOTHING, William Shakespeare. (0-486-28272-4)

FIVE GREAT COMEDIES: Much Ado About Nothing, Twelfth Night, A Midsummer Night's Dream, As You Like It and The Merry Wives of Windsor, William Shakespeare. (0-486-44086-9)

OTHELLO, William Shakespeare. (0-486-29097-2)

AS YOU LIKE IT, William Shakespeare. (0-486-40432-3)

ROMEO AND JULIET, William Shakespeare. (0-486-27557-4)

A MIDSUMMER NIGHT'S DREAM, William Shakespeare. (0-486-27067-X)

THE MERCHANT OF VENICE, William Shakespeare. (0-486-28492-1)

HAMLET, William Shakespeare. (0-486-27278-8)

RICHARD III, William Shakespeare. (0-486-28747-5)

# DOVER THRIFT EDITIONS

## PLAYS

## FICTION

FLATLAND: A ROMANCE OF MANY DIMENSIONS, Edwin A. Abbott. (0-486-27263-X)

PRIDE AND PREJUDICE, Jane Austen. (0-486-28473-5)

CIVIL WAR SHORT STORIES AND POEMS, Edited by Bob Blaisdell. (0-486-48226-X)

THE DECAMERON: Selected Tales, Giovanni Boccaccio. Edited by Bob Blaisdell. (0-486-41113-3)

JANE EYRE, Charlotte Brontë. (0-486-42449-9)

WUTHERING HEIGHTS, Emily Brontë. (0-486-29256-8)

THE THIRTY-NINE STEPS, John Buchan. (0-486-28201-5)

ALICE'S ADVENTURES IN WONDERLAND, Lewis Carroll. (0-486-27543-4)

MY ÁNTONIA, Willa Cather. (0-486-28240-6)

THE AWAKENING, Kate Chopin. (0-486-27786-0)

HEART OF DARKNESS, Joseph Conrad. (0-486-26464-5)

LORD JIM, Joseph Conrad. (0-486-40650-4)

THE RED BADGE OF COURAGE, Stephen Crane. (0-486-26465-3)

THE WORLD'S GREATEST SHORT STORIES, Edited by James Daley. (0-486-44716-2)

A CHRISTMAS CAROL, Charles Dickens. (0-486-26865-9)

GREAT EXPECTATIONS, Charles Dickens. (0-486-41586-4)

A TALE OF TWO CITIES, Charles Dickens. (0-486-40651-2)

CRIME AND PUNISHMENT, Fyodor Dostoyevsky. Translated by Constance Garnett. (0-486-41587-2)

THE ADVENTURES OF SHERLOCK HOLMES, Sir Arthur Conan Doyle. (0-486-47491-7)

THE HOUND OF THE BASKERVILLES, Sir Arthur Conan Doyle. (0-486-28214-7)

BLAKE: PROPHET AGAINST EMPIRE, David V. Erdman. (0-486-26719-9)

WHERE ANGELS FEAR TO TREAD, E. M. Forster. (0-486-27791-7)

BEOWULF, Translated by R. K. Gordon. (0-486-27264-8)

THE RETURN OF THE NATIVE, Thomas Hardy. (0-486-43165-7)

THE SCARLET LETTER, Nathaniel Hawthorne. (0-486-28048-9)

SIDDHARTHA, Hermann Hesse. (0-486-40653-9)

THE ODYSSEY, Homer. (0-486-40654-7)

THE TURN OF THE SCREW, Henry James. (0-486-26684-2)

DUBLINERS, James Joyce. (0-486-26870-5)

# DOVER THRIFT EDITIONS

## FICTION

THE METAMORPHOSIS AND OTHER STORIES, Franz Kafka. (0-486-29030-1)

SONS AND LOVERS, D. H. Lawrence. (0-486-42121-X)

THE CALL OF THE WILD, Jack London. (0-486-26472-6)

GREAT AMERICAN SHORT STORIES, Edited by Paul Negri. (0-486-42119-8)

THE GOLD-BUG AND OTHER TALES, Edgar Allan Poe. (0-486-26875-6)

ANTHEM, Ayn Rand. (0-486-49277-X)

FRANKENSTEIN, Mary Shelley. (0-486-28211-2)

THE JUNGLE, Upton Sinclair. (0-486-41923-1)

THREE LIVES, Gertrude Stein. (0-486-28059-4)

THE STRANGE CASE OF DR. JEKYLL AND MR. HYDE, Robert Louis Stevenson. (0-486-26688-5)

DRACULA, Bram Stoker. (0-486-41109-5)

UNCLE TOM'S CABIN, Harriet Beecher Stowe. (0-486-44028-1)

ADVENTURES OF HUCKLEBERRY FINN, Mark Twain. (0-486-28061-6)

THE ADVENTURES OF TOM SAWYER, Mark Twain. (0-486-40077-8)

CANDIDE, Voltaire. Edited by Francois-Marie Arouet. (0-486-26689-3)

THE COUNTRY OF THE BLIND: and Other Science-Fiction Stories, H. G. Wells. Edited by Martin Gardner. (0-486-48289-8)

THE WAR OF THE WORLDS, H. G. Wells. (0-486-29506-0)

ETHAN FROME, Edith Wharton. (0-486-26690-7)

THE PICTURE OF DORIAN GRAY, Oscar Wilde. (0-486-27807-7)

MONDAY OR TUESDAY: Eight Stories, Virginia Woolf. (0-486-29453-6)